Pagodas in Play

The Bucknell Studies in Eighteenth-Century Literature and Culture

The Bucknell Studies in Eighteenth-Century Literature and Culture aims to publish challenging, new eighteenth-century scholarship. Of particular interest is critical, historical, and interdisciplinary work that is interestingly and intelligently theorized, and that broadens and refines the conception of the field. At the same time, the series remains open to all theoretical perspectives and different kinds of scholarship. While the focus of the series is the literature, history, arts, and culture (including art, architecture, music, travel, and history of science, medicine, and law) of the long eighteenth century in Britain and Europe, the series is also interested in scholarship that establishes relationships with other geographies, literature, and cultures for the period 1660–1830.

Recent Titles in This Series

Mark Blackwell, ed., *The Secret Life of Things: Animals, Objects, and It-Narratives in Eighteenth-Century England*

Chris Mounsey and Caroline Gonda, eds., *Queer People: Negotiations and Expressions of Homosexuality, 1700–1800*

Susan Manning and Peter France, *Enlightenment and Emancipation*

Evan Gottlieb, *Feeling British: Sympathy and National Identity in Scottish and English Writing, 1707–1832*

Roland Racevskis, *Tragic Passages: Jean Racine's Art of the Threshold*

Lesley H. Walker, *A Mother's Love: Crafting Feminine Virtue in Enlightenment France*

Ron Broglio, *Technologies of the Picturesque: British Art, Poetry and Instruments, 1750–1830*

Will Pritchard, *Outward Appearances: The Female Exterior in Restoration London*

David Duff and Catherine Jones, eds., *Scotland, Ireland, and the Romantic Aesthetic*

Anne Milne, *"Lactilla Tends her Fav'rite Cow": Ecocritical Readings of Animals and Women in Eighteenth-Century British Laboring-Class Women's Poetry*

Gavin Budge, ed., *Romantic Empiricism: Poetics and the Philosophy of Common Sense, 1780–1830*

Shelley King and Yaël Schlick, eds., *Refiguring the Coquette: Essays on Culture and Coquetry*

Margaret R. Ewalt, *Peripheral Wonders: Nature, Knowledge, and Enlightenment in the Eighteenth-Century Orinoco*

Stephen Bygrave, *Uses of Education: Readings in Enlightenment in England*

Adrienne Ward, *Pagodas in Play: China on the Eighteenth-Century Italian Opera Stage*

http://www.bucknell.edu/universitypress/

Pagodas in Play

China on the Eighteenth-Century Italian Opera Stage

Adrienne Ward

Lewisburg
Bucknell University Press

Associated University Presses
2010 Eastpark Boulevard
Cranbury, NJ 08512

The paper used in this publication meets the requirements of the American National Standard for Permanence of Paper for Printed Library Materials Z39.48-1984.

Library of Congress Cataloging-in-Publication Data

Ward, Adrienne, 1957–
    Pagodas in play : China on the eighteenth-century Italian opera stage / Adrienne Ward.
        p.   cm. — (Bucknell studies in eighteenth-century literature and culture)
    Includes bibliographical references and index.
    ISBN 978-0-8387-5696-6 (alk. paper)
    1. Opera—Italy—18th century.   2. China in opera.   I. Title.
ML1733.3.W37   2010
782.10945—dc22

                                                        2009020539

PRINTED IN THE UNITED STATES OF AMERICA

Roquillard.	What is that figure down there?
Arlequin.	It's a pagod.
Roquillard.	A pagod! What is a pagod?
Arlequin.	A pagod is . . . a pagod. What the devil do you want me to tell you?

Roquillard.	Mais que signifie cette figure, là-bas?
Arlequin.	C'est une pagode.
Roquillard.	Une pagode! Qu'est-ce que c'est qu'une pagode?
Arlequin.	Une pagode, est . . . une pagode. Que diable voulez-vous que je vous dise?

—From *Les chinois,* by Jean Regnard
and Charles Dufresny

Valdimonte. *Garamone.* *Giacinta.* *Carolina.* *Panico.*	As for appearances and such, We'll figure out how to seem Chinese to the Dutch.

Valdimonte. *Garamone.* *Giacinta.* *Carolina.* *Panico.*	E Chinesi—agli Olandesi Comparir si studierà.

—From quintet in act 2 of Carlo Goldoni's
L'isola disabitata

Contents

Acknowledgments

Many people have helped and encouraged me in writing this book, and I thank them most deeply. Stefania Buccini, my dissertation advisor, friend and dear colleague, first suggested the idea of investigating Italian writings on China in the eighteenth century. Colleagues at the University of Virginia have proven unflagging in their support over the years, and have given me valuable insight and direction. I wish to especially thank Enrico Cesaretti, Cristina Della Coletta, David Gies, Ruth Hill, Marita McClymonds, Ricardo Padrón, Deborah Parker, Randolph Pope, Anne Jacobson Schutte, Jenny Tsien, Alison Weber, and Richard Will. Special gratitude goes to Emily Scida and Karen Ryan, both of whose compassionate spirits helped me keep going over the course of a long project.

Friends and colleagues at other institutions also deserve my warmest thanks, for sharing their time, ideas, and general sustenance over the years. A special research summer in Venice with Suzanne Magnanini, Rebecca Messbarger, and Catherine Sama was only a highlight in the ongoing discussions from which this book has benefited. Other scholars who have generously offered their wisdom and helped improve my book include Melania Bucciarelli, Aaron Cohen, Francesco Cotticelli, Clorinda Donato, Michael Eisenberg, Joseph Farrell, Franco Fido, Wendy Heller, Donald Lach, and David Porter. Thanks also go to Susan Bennett, Harry Elam, Ellen Gainor, and Jane Tylus. I wish to also thank the as-yet-unknown readers of my manuscript.

Great appreciation is extended to the Gladys K. Delmas Foundation, whose generous grant facilitated my research in Venice. The librarians and staff at Venice's Casa Goldoni and the Fondazione Cini merit special mention for their kindness and service. I am grateful for the wonderful and prompt attention given to me by my home librarians at Alderman Library and the Special Collections Library at the University of Virginia. Abundant thanks go to the many people who have been involved in the book's production, including Greg Clingham, director of Bucknell University Press, Julien Yoseloff, director of Associated University Presses, Christine Retz, managing editor at AUP, and my excellent copy editor, Mary Cicora. I'd also like to acknowledge technical support and morale boosting received from Laura Downey, Allison Libbey, and Ashley Kerr, all of whom graciously and cheerfully stepped up in the final hours.

My last thanks go to the people who were crucial, not only toward the fruition of this work, but especially in their care of its author over the long, long haul. Sheila and David Daskovsky, Uli Henes, Whitney Morrill and Joe Rinkevich, Kathie and Steve Nitz, and Zoe and Ricardo Padrón have given me the gifts of constant, unconditional friendship, spiked often with laughter and perspective. Dawn Hunt deserves special mention, as she so gently oversaw this journey, coaching the writing and the writer, helping me progress where it often seemed impossible. To my family, for standing by me and interesting themselves in a project far from their daily lives, especially James Ward, and Elizabeth and Tom Ventura; and to John, my husband, friend, and wonderfully buoyant and patient traveling companion, thank you.

Note on Translations

UNLESS OTHERWISE INDICATED, ALL TRANSLATIONS ARE MINE. THE TRANS-lations of libretto verse are provided to convey thematic content and rhetorical flavor, with the full recognition that they do not adequately communicate the prosody of the original Italian lyrics.

Pagodas in Play

Introduction

> If we accept that entertainment is a political category—the "mereness" of the medium doing nothing to diminish the political value of its social place—then it becomes necessary to ask what political or social purpose the materials of entertainment serve.[1]

CHINA MADE ITS MOST SPECTACULAR DEBUT ON the European stage in the eighteenth century. The superlative refers both to number and kind of theatrical performance. Following a handful of productions in the second half of the seventeenth century, in 1706 the Celestial Empire starred for the first time in an opera.[2] *Teuzzone*, a *dramma per musica* written by Apostolo Zeno with music by Paolo Magni and Clemente Monari, was staged at the Royal Ducal Teatro in Milan, for its governor Prince Charles Henry de Lorraine-Vaudemonte. The opera's popularity was such that it enjoyed nine different musical settings in the first three decades of the century, amounting to eighteen runs in sixteen different cities, both in and outside the Italian peninsula.[3] Moreover, Zeno's operatic spectacle was only the first of many subsequent European dramas to treat China. Records document nearly seventy original "Chinese" stage works written and/or performed within the century. The Chinese protagonists in these operas, ballets, intermezzos, tragedies, comedies, harlequinades, and other hybrid theater productions appealed to European theater audiences insofar as they constituted the newest players in a cast of eastern "exotics." As audiences grew ever more familiar with the Tartar, Turkish, and Persian theatrical entertainments performed in the years stretching from the Ottoman Empire's height to its demise—works such as Christopher Marlowe's tragedy *Tamburlaine* (1587), Prospero Bonarelli's tragedy *Solimano* (1620), Moliére-Lully's comedy-ballet *Le Bourgeois gentilhomme* (1670), and Jean Racine's tragedy *Bajazet* (1672)—the charms of a new "exotic," namely, the inhabitants of the Celestial Empire, beckoned.

Of the sixty-six eighteenth-century China dramas for which records exist, those by Italian authors swing the balance.[4] More than half (thirty-six) were written by Italian dramaturgs, next to nineteen of French ori-

gin, and eleven by English playwrights.[5] Moreover, several Italian productions hold important primacies. As mentioned, Zeno's *Teuzzone* was the first full-fledged opera in Europe to focus wholly on China.[6] The first China tragedy in the French classical mode came from Pier Jacopo Martello (*I Taimingi*, 1712). Pietro Metastasio's opera *L'eroe cinese* (1752) constituted the first performance in a European vernacular based on the famous Chinese orphan legend, *The Orphan of the Family Chao*.[7] A number of European adaptations of the orphan story would follow shortly thereafter, among them Voltaire's *L'Orphelin de la Chine* (1755) and Arthur Murphy's *The Orphan of Chao* (1759). Surprisingly, however, nearly all scholarship on this spurt of eighteenth-century adaptations pays lip service—at best—to Metastasio's work.[8]

Generically speaking, the works by Zeno and Metastasio are representative, since about half (seventeen) of the Italian theatrical exemplars fall into the opera category. China figured into either serious (opera seria) or comic (opera buffa) works, the two principal genres of Italian lyric theater. Italian influence asserts itself even in the French specimens. Half of the French China dramas hail from either the Parisian fair theater or the *Théâtre Italien* (the *Comédie-italienne*), both heirs of the commedia dell'arte tradition. The other conspicuous genre for French works is the ballet, or more precisely the *opéra-ballet*, with just over one-quarter of the total in this group.

The difference in the genres in which Chinese subject matter found homes in France and the Italian states supports one of the main propositions of this book: eighteenth-century Italy not only theatricalized China uniquely, but did so more substantively than did other nations. While Basil Guy notes that China theater productions in France evolved "from the rather light and fanciful to the more established forms [ballet, comedy, pantomime]," none of these genres compares to Italian opera, in terms of the breadth and depth of its content and its wide diffusion.[9] Just as scholars note the national and regional specificities of the chinoiserie phenomenon in seventeenth- and eighteenth-century Europe, the same holds for mediations of the Celestial Empire in dramatic texts and performances.[10] Theatrical, and especially operatic, representations of China in eighteenth-century Italy emerged from contingencies dissimilar to those of contemporary France, England, the German states, Holland, Russia, and Spain. The notion of individual contexts applies also to the diverse states within the peninsula. A Neapolitan comic opera mobilized China in different ways and for different purposes than did a Venetian comic opera. A Roman *dramma per musica* would likewise have differed in its treatment of China as compared to its counterpart in Florence. The sheer variety of sociopolitical conditions among the Italian states produced peninsular iterations of the Middle Kingdom diverse from those of countries with more centralized administration.

Since opera ranked—throughout Europe, for the whole of the eighteenth century—above all other theater genres in popularity, its portrayals of China would seem a more significant object of study than those in other theatrical forms.[11] Its ubiquitous appeal in no way compromised its prestige, however. Italian *melodramma* was a genre on the rise, revered and appropriated by courtly publics as it was recognized and celebrated among lower ranks. Its increasing aesthetic and cultural prominence gave greater weight, moreover, to its subject matter. As opposed to the slapstick-vaudeville nature of the French works, many of which were built on the declining Italian commedia mode, opera marshaled the Celestial Empire in more substantive narratives. French ballets could enact stories, but opera included dance, among its many other vehicles of expression. What's more, the Italian dances (*balli*) punctuating the operas were more narrative-oriented than French ballets were.[12] Italian China operas therefore constituted a richly-layered native cultural practice with meanings and operations more resonant than those of China theater works produced by other Europeans.[13]

The spread of Italian opera throughout the continent meant that its images of China migrated far outside the peninsula. Reinhard Strohm points out that the eighteenth-century opera was both "a European art form as well as a major representative of Italian culture, which it helped to disseminate."[14] In its language, its forms, its means of expression, even its subject matter ("the classicizing plots . . . frequently

touched upon peninsular history, particularly that of the Roman republic and empire"), the opera carried a charge of *italianità* clearly recognized and desired by non-Italians.[15] It is beyond the scope of this study to examine the reception of Italian operatic works in extra-peninsular centers. The scale of such a task reminds us, however, of the importance of local context in determining meanings and interpreting interactions between a work and its milieu. With opera especially, given its enormously composite nature and the multiple agents in its production, it is essential to consider the local culture (social, political, economic, religious elements) to understand the significance of a work. As this study analyzes the most well-known (and well-traveled) Italian China operas with respect to their Italian contexts, it might also prompt further work on their reincarnations in the scores of European cities clamoring for musical dramas *all'italiana*.

China's entrance onto the European stage was inevitable. One might only wonder why it took so long, given that the first early modern Europeans to make real inroads into the Chinese nation did so at the turn of the seventeenth century, with the first successful Jesuit mission to Peking.[16] Throughout the 1600s, information about the Chinese empire poured into European centers, initially by missionary, merchant, and other types of travelers, then by innumerable secondary authors eager to comment and expand on the original accounts.[17] Descriptions and illustrations in the literature were concretized by the Chinese wares flowing into European markets.[18] Tea, silks, porcelain, and lacquer figured most prominently in an array of merchandise priced to satisfy inquisitive and fashion-conscious buyers.

Such an omnipresence of artifacts and written reflections on the Middle Kingdom couldn't help but precipitate its appearance in theaters. Indeed, almost every major and minor Italian dramatist wrote a China piece. The Celestial Empire made its way into spoken tragedy in the early decades, and into spoken comedy later in the century.[19] It infiltrated *teatro in musica* first, however, and representations of the Middle Kingdom in this genre held forth for the duration of the Settecento.

One can only fully appreciate the mediation of Chinese culture in eighteenth-century Italian opera by realizing the extensive scope of the genre. Theater itself wielded tremendous power. The following comment about theater in eighteenth-century London holds true for Italian cities as well: "[The] theater world had all of the fundamental, albeit relatively primitive, elements of today's mass cultural production and consumership . . . [It possessed] many of the characteristics of an entertainment industry as we understand the concept today."[20] Martha Feldman goes further, speaking about opera seria in the eighteenth century: "Getting to write the music, or even more prestigiously, the poetry for an opera seria was like getting to write a feature for Dreamworks."[21] Franco Fido contrasts the powerful national or imperial impetus driving theater in sites such as Paris, London, and Vienna, with the relative absence of such interest in certain areas of the peninsula, particularly the "old" dynastic states, like Tuscany and Piemonte. However, his assertion of Italy's "lack of a national market for theater" seems compromised somewhat when he also avers the massive theater-construction enterprise from the seventeenth through the eighteenth century. The buildings intended primarily for opera performances came also to be used for commedia dell'arte spectacles and reform comedies. The popularity of both of these spoken genres, as well as the low entrance cost for a diversity of public theater offerings, leads Fido to call theatergoing in eighteenth-century Italy "an interclass phenomenon," a characterization that certainly implies that theatrical activity in Settecento Italy was anything but languishing.[22]

Despite the charms of other dramatic offerings, however, the *opera per musica* easily attracted the most followers. Its novelty, spectacle, and composite nature proved irresistible. Strohm terms eighteenth-century opera "the most splendid and yet non-ecclesiastical art form in Italy."[23] Every city, "from Palermo to Trieste," had at least one, if not several opera houses, and the craze spread quickly to all the other centers in Europe.[24] Opera was also, moreover, a highly exported phenomenon. Nathaniel Burt states that in the early eighteenth century the Italian *dramma per musica* had the same level of impact and distribution in Europe—by way of traveling Italian composers, singers, and librettists—as the American silent film of the 1920s.[25]

Audiences for the new medium came primarily from the mid-to-upper classes, although members of lower social tiers attended productions perhaps more than might be expected. Tickets to opera seria, which held sway in the first half of the century, were expensive, limiting paying operagoers to those from the privileged ranks. Members of the court, the aristocracy, and the wealthy bourgeois formed the majority of the public that filled the auditoriums. Spectators from the populace were not entirely excluded, however. Those exempt from payment, the so-called *esenti*, included members of the military, visiting dignitaries, and the servants or companions of the patricians. This last group viewed the spectacle from the uppermost balconies, known as the gallery. The fact that most auditoriums were structurally divided into three distinct viewing locations—boxes for the titled families, stalls for younger well-to-do men, accompanied often by courtesans, and the gallery for commoners and persons-in-waiting—evidences a social mixture in the audiences.[26] Records also show that merchants, tourists, "citizenry," and university students were sometimes in attendance.[27]

The galloping popularity of comic opera in the second half of the century corresponds to an increasingly broader social range in the operagoing public, which itself was growing larger. "Its principal component remained the aristocrats, but more and more commoners joined them," notes Franco Piperno.[28] Tickets to opera buffa cost on average about half those of opera seria, which permitted accessibility to greater numbers of people. Though theaters had initially run a composite repertory, combining opera seria, opera buffa, and dance spectacles (*balli*) in their seasonal offerings, as time wore on they began to specialize. The rise of comic opera saw growth in the proportion of "secondary" theaters, that is, those concentrating on buffo dramas, next to the more municipally prestigious opera seria houses. The bigger metropolises typically had one official theater for serious opera, with as many as three, four, five, or more specializing in the comic brand.[29] While opera buffa quickly overtook opera seria in terms of number of performances, the quantity of titles in each category in a given city's annual repertory stayed fairly balanced for the remainder of the century.[30] Piperno takes care to note:

> The expansion and the success of comic opera does not imply a simultaneous and complementary decline of opera seria . . . : although opera buffa outstripped the opera seria in terms of number of productions and popularity with audiences, it never made a dent—nor did it attempt to do so—in the prestige, fashionable cachet, or official character of the latter. The two varieties divided up the field: opera seria was refined, luxury entertainment ruled by protocol and aimed at aristocratic and wealthy city dwellers; opera buffa was a genuinely escapist sort of spectacle, simple, economical, and bourgeois, and aimed at a public that went to the theater for pleasure, not for reasons of form.[31]

Thus, in the Italian states as well as in the rest of Europe, opera galvanized a new culture of entertainment. The stage welcome given to the Middle Kingdom in nearly twenty Italian operas over the course of the century reveals the genre's special capacity to elaborate elements of the "Chinese imaginary" that held Europeans in thrall.

The fact that this body of dramatic and performative works has not been studied corresponds to a general dearth of scholarship on the phenomenon of Sinomania in eighteenth-century Italy. Where China's appeal to French, English, German, Dutch, Russian, and Spanish cultures has been and continues to be seriously researched, few have examined the reception of China in the Italian Settecento.[32] Sergio Zoli's corpus admirably investigates the impact of the Middle Kingdom on Italian intellectuals, and situates their writings within their indispensable European context.[33] Other critics examine the incidence of China in eighteenth-century Italian decorative arts and architecture.[34] No one, however, has undertaken an in-depth exploration of the treatment of the Asian nation in the more encompassing milieu of the theater.[35] Given its literary dimension, inherent in the dramatic text, and its performative dimension, which joined patricians with professionals with plebeians in the public that enthusiastically attended the productions, Italian China opera reveals the cultural dynamics of exoticism much more incisively than scholarly writings or plastic arts alone.

Returning to the extant analyses of China's influence in eighteenth-century Europe, with few exceptions these researches paint a somewhat reductive picture. The phenomenon they often term the Chinese "myth," "dream," "cycle," or "parabola," to describe a craze that tidily rose and fell over the course of the century, is just as frequently characterized in terms of neat dualities.[36] According to these studies, Europeans knew China through missionary or merchant testimony, each of which portrayed the nation amenably (the former) or despicably (the latter); engagement with Chinese culture was either frivolous (chinoiserie) or serious (erudite writings); the Chinese native was good or bad; he was extolled for either his secularism or religiosity (Zoli); Chinese political and social culture illustrated either good despotism (Voltaire) or bad (Montesquieu).[37] Elena Sala di Felice writes: "The myth of China presents itself with two opposed faces in eighteenth century Europe. Some saw in its monarchical government a negative example of personal, and therefore arbitrary, despotism. For others it represented instead a model of the new lawful absolutism, where the sovereign was first among all to be subject to the laws. The king was the guarantor of equality among citizens, itself guaranteed by a justice system articulated in a series of doctrines organized around the ruling concept of equity."[38] When one carefully scrutinizes the texts and conventions involved in the eighteenth-century Italian operatic dramatization of China, however, many more variations surface. A formidable mélange of images and tropes appears, and the uses to which they are put vary enormously as well. While certain dualistic frameworks do hold sway over particular areas, they are joined by a number of other, alternative mobilizations of China. These multiple uses of the Middle Kingdom sometimes occur in a single work, or, where China is valenced similarly in discrete spectacles, the respective representations do not necessarily conform, and may serve entirely different purposes. For example, the negative valuation of the Celestial Empire in Carlo Goldoni's L'isola disabitata is bound up in the image of an isolated, archaic, enfeebled, and hopelessly out-of-touch nation, evoking the decrepit Venetian nobility being forced to give way to an empowered bourgeoisie. Giambattista Lorenzi's nearly contemporaneous L'idolo cinese, on the other hand, shows the very different ends to which a negative depiction of China worked in Settecento Naples. In Lorenzi's comic opera, the Middle Kingdom signifies a bizarre, alien system of governance, one that threatens social stability insofar as it accords political and religious prestige to newcomers without dynastic standing. Chinese culture in L'idolo cinese thus conjures the threatening encroachment of a reform-minded sector onto the sacred territory of the landed class. The larger point here is that representations of China in the works under study manifest striking similarities, inconsistencies, and juxtapositions, all of which point to the highly protean nature of the Chinese signifier and the consequent plurality of meanings it generated.

Excerpts from two eighteenth-century Italian writers easily illustrate not only the range of thinking about the Chinese other, but also the tenacity of particular images, with the result that images sometimes "spoke" to one another across time. Giambattista Vico, emphasizing China's historic isolationism in his Scienza nuova seconda (1725), characterizes the nation this way: "Not having had commerce with other nations for many thousands of years, nations that could have informed them [the Chinese] of the true antiquity of the world, they are akin to a man who, while sleeping, is enclosed in a tiny, lightless room. Upon waking, and because of the horrific dark, he believes the room to be much greater than that which he touches with his hands. The Chinese are like this, in the darkness of their chronology."[39] Forty years later, Pietro Verri averred that China was one of the few nations in the world to have its eyes open, economically speaking: "The nation that first opens its eyes to commerce will profit from the laziness of other nations, and will become rich, populous, and prosperous at their expense . . . When that nation is then great enough to be able to meet its own needs with the fruits of its own lands and its own industry, then it will also be independent . . . In China, in one of the happiest climates, a hundred million inhabitants have been able to eschew all foreign trade and have no need of anything from outsiders."[40] That the Middle Kingdom could be perceived in Naples in the early decades as a sightless intellectual dwarf, and in Lombardy in the latter half of the century as a far-seeing economic giant, substantiates the idea of a spectrum of images, as well as the fact that manifold responses to China emerged from manifold conditions. These comments furthermore challenge the hard-and-fast notion of the parabola to describe European fascination with the Celestial Empire, i.e., that during the first half of the century, Europeans grew increasingly well-disposed toward the Middle Kingdom, only to sour on it in the second half.

In addition to the political, economic, social, religious, and other factors that must be considered when studying the development of any specific impression of Chinese culture, one must also allow for complicated and disparate understandings of individual concepts, especially those that Europeans readily associated with China. On the single issue of despotism, for example, Franco Venturi has amply demonstrated the complexity of the term's significance over the course of the seventeenth and eighteenth centuries.[41] Venturi's parsing of the notion of despotism helps explain how plays and operas might represent China in one of several ways: as a state locked in fear of a rigid tyrant, as a society reduced to passive civil servitude, or as a strong polity enjoying the plentiful fruits of natural monarchical law.

Two broad reasons account for a uniquely Italian theatricalization of China in the Settecento. First, Italy had its own "Chinese legacy," dating from the epoch of Marco Polo in the thirteenth century, and including the first Jesuits to forge a connection with the Chinese in the late sixteenth century. Second, the Italian Enlightenment, while often diminished in scope and status in studies of Enlightenment culture throughout Europe, had its own particular concerns and elaborations.[42] China theater constituted a convenient place for working out these problematics. Opera, above all, with its astonishing capaciousness as a cultural form, provided a potent site for the reception and expression of Enlightenment ideologies.

On the Jesuit front, the famous early Italian missionaries (Alessandro Valignano, Matteo Ricci, Michele Ruggiero) founded the assimilationist and accommodationist policies through which it was hoped the Jesuits would gain acceptance by the Chinese. More to the point, the Italian fathers "accommodated" Confucianism, claiming that it had Christian origins. This theological validation constituted their primary strategy for the hoped-for conversion of the Chinese.[43] Jesuits of Italian descent were prominent in the China mission for most of the seventeenth century. Only in the last decades of the Seicento would French Jesuits take over the accommodationist project. It would soon come under severe fire for conceding too much to putatively heretical Chinese ceremony, and thus blaspheming the Catholic Church. The formative Italian imprint survived, however, in terms of an openness, a curiosity, and toleration with respect to Middle Kingdom differences.

A number of scholars attribute this special tolerance to Renaissance humanism. To a greater degree than other Europeans, Italians had absorbed the liberal, human-centered tradition that recognized as invaluable the contributions of the classical pagan civilizations. The open-mindedness of leaders like Valignano and Ricci owed itself to their strong formation in Italian humanist culture. Zoli states: "The spirit of the Renaissance, together with the Jesuits, was what opened the Orient."[44] Such an attitude suffused not only the missionary credo, but also the outlooks of other Italian travelers to China: merchants like Francesco Carletti, and professional travelers like Giovanni Gemelli-Careri. Both orthodox and heterodox Italians were known over other Europeans for their comprehension and toleration of cultural difference. Henry Kamen underscores this peninsular characteristic when he observes that the greatest leaders of tolerant Protestantism in Europe came out of Italy.[45]

A related advantage which the Italians enjoyed as a result of their grounding in Renaissance humanism, and which facilitated their relationship with the Chinese, was their esteem of antiquity and rhetoric, and their interest in syncretism. Chinese literati responded extremely well to the humanist veneration of the literary precision and elegance in classic texts. The drive to locate, with the help of ancient works, a common theological and/or philosophical underpinning by which all peoples were linked, not only stimulated the Italians' curiosity, but also cemented the respect in which they held the Chinese. According to Donald Lach, Italians in the seventeenth century were better able than other Europeans to appreciate the wealth of history and cultural difference they encountered in China.[46]

An additional aspect of Italy's early modern Chinese legacy resides in the lack of a national impulse behind its enterprises in the Celestial Empire. In contrast to other emerging European powers, Italians never launched state-sponsored embassies to China. Unlike the wide-ranging national ambitions of the Portuguese *padroado*, the Spanish *patronato real*, and the trading conglomerates organized by the Dutch, French, and British, East Asian ventures on the part of Italians were not driven by any sort of expansionist policy. Given the absence of a unified state, Italy's China undertakings were largely private endeavors, when they were not motivated by the transnational aims of the church.[47] The lack of national solidarity or representation influenced the experience the Italians would have in China. Since they had "no colonial axe to grind and were not empire builders," they could sometimes operate free of the complications inherent in the jurisdictional claims and competition among the other Europeans.[48] At least one scholar has suggested that because Italians were not caught in the entanglements of a specific homeland agenda, they were more readily accepted and trusted by the Chinese.[49]

This ideological spaciousness extended beyond the immediate experiences of Italian voyagers to East Asia and into their writings. Italian-authored accounts of China (by both real and armchair travelers, as well as compilers and cultivated commentators, such as Martini, Intorcetta, Bartoli, Magalotti), brought their particular perceptions of the Celestial Kingdom to Italian centers and beyond.[50] The prominent role of the Italian language in the dissemination of information about China emerges when Lach notes that in the seventeenth century "Italian . . . was more current in Catholic Europe than any of the other vernaculars, [therefore] the [Jesuit] letterbooks in Italian were more often than not the means through which news from Asia was transmitted from Iberia to northern Europe or vice versa."[51] "From the Italian materials alone a strangely different view of Asia emerges," continues Lach, referring to the predominance of missionary history in the Italian narratives.[52] Even though the mission focus reduced coverage of other subjects in the Italian writings, and Lach concludes that non-Italian literature more comprehensively addressed aspects of Chinese life, Italian writings nonetheless formed a large, unique, and potent tributary that flowed into the river of European narratives on China into which librettists and playwrights dipped for their material.

The second influence on eighteenth-century Italian dramatizations of the Middle Kingdom is found in the nature and processes of the Italian Enlightenment. Admittedly a too-simplistic expression, the "Italian Enlightenment" embraces a host of diverse intellec-

tual initiatives and cultural phenomena, at once distinct from French, English, and German developments, but also at times highly differentiated among the regions and centers of the peninsula itself. Venturi's hallowed research points out these differences in the realm of intellectual history, and other respected historians of Settecento Italy shine light on the political, economic, and social conditions that distinguished the individual principalities and republics.[53] Here, however, illuminating findings ensue from exploring these differences (or similarities, as the case may be) in the context of a common, virtually "national" cultural institution, that of opera. What might it mean, for example, when one state embraces notions of reform Catholicism (Milan), another stays entrenched in hardline principles—though even then splintering over the defense of the Jesuits (the Papal States)—while yet another's biggest struggles with the church have little to do with theological polemics, and everything to do with issues of legal and financial jurisdiction (Kingdom of Naples)? How does opera mediate the exotic other in a state committed to bolstering its monarchy at the local level (Naples), versus a republic mourning its lost international trade majesty (Venice)? What are the implications for China's role in stage spectacle given that Florence was able to implement modernizing policies originating in the Habsburg capital, while Rome looked to prosper by exploiting its antiquarian and classical legacies? These varying sociopolitical circumstances account for Italy's numerous and diverging "Enlightenment identities," identities that Giuseppe Ricuperati underscores in his entreaty for more nuanced studies of the period.[54]

Yet even as scholars warn against falsely wholistic pictures of eighteenth-century Italian life, some unitary coordinates come into play when juxtaposing peninsular developments with those of other European countries. The most apparent quotient is that of religion. "Enlightened" Italian Catholicism, whatever its contours, diverged at its very source from reform Christianity in other European states. Italy's diversity of approaches to economic reform couldn't begin to compare with the single-minded mercantilist strategy of a nation like England, with its impressive consequences. The majority of Italian states shared with France, Austria, and Spain the political framework of enlightened absolutism, and many common philosophies connected them. But differences figured in as well. One obvious dissimilarity was the lack of a large-scale centralizing monarchy, such as those which rendered Paris and Vienna such catalytic urban forces. One part of the Italian reform spirit sought to keep up with fast-moving, progressive fellow Europeans, while another part tried to recover a bygone status, whether that meant former artistic dignity, power as world merchant, or the familiar comforts and sense of control offered by the feudal mode.

All of these factors affected the creation and enjoyment of operatic entertainment. Surely opera texts and performances constitute one of the not strictly territorial or political "Italian spaces" Ricuperati refers to when he encourages more cultural (vs intellectual) historical study. Within this wider perspective he describes Italy as functioning as an original laboratory rather than simply a reflective prism.[55]

THEORETICAL FOUNDATIONS

In succinct terms, this study concerns itself with the mechanics of exoticism in a particular place at a particular time, and in a particular social art form. The work of Edward Said and his legion of commentators has established the profound degree to which one culture's representation of another is a self-serving construction. At the same time, many of those same scholars and critics have called for greater study of the local contingencies that enable multiple, individualized orientalisms.[56] To that end, this analysis looks at how exoticism works given the discrete conventions of eighteenth-century opera, as produced by Italian practitioners.

The primary tenets of Cultural Materialism and New Historicism guide my thinking with their notions of theater as embedded in surrounding culture. On a very literal level, one cannot evaluate the Chinese characters, settings, and objects inscribed onto the libretto page or the musical stage without also considering the coeval presence of the Middle Kingdom in eighteenth-century Italian "real-life": the flood of Chinese wares into the marketplace, the use of Chinese styles in clothing fashion, interior design, and architecture, and the infiltration of Chinese cultural elements in peninsular political and civic events — Venice's welcome of Augustus of Saxony in 1716 with a Chinese regatta on the Grand Canal, for example — as well as in more domestic activities, such as tea drinking, or Chinese masked balls integrated into private festivities. This is not to mention the massive amount of writing about China that permeated literate spheres, from firsthand accounts by travelers to the Celestial Empire (in circulation since the late sixteenth century), to their elaboration in nearly every textual form imaginable: scholarly works, church writings, reform tracts, journalistic pieces, and moral and escapist fiction, to name only the most prominent. One did not need to be literate, moreover, to take in European ideas about Chinese ways. The plentiful engravings contained in the travel works put in front of "book spectators" a body of intriguing China iconography. Its images, modes, and models soon inspired everything from royal palace tapestries to country villa frescoes, from snuffboxes to "knockoff" teapots to coffeehouse décor. China was thus displayed, in varying quantities, contexts, and evaluative frameworks, to all levels of society.

Moving beyond the most obvious referential sphere, the Chinese operas are also rooted — and much more intensively — in native cultural systems and processes. Here again *Pagodas in Play* draws from New Historicist work which views early modern theater as a nexus of competing local discourses and energies. Italian China operas are works of art that are, as Stephen Greenblatt defines them, "the product[s] of a negotiation between a creator or a class of creators, equipped with a complex, communally shared repertoire of conventions, and the institutions and practices of society."[57] My investigation shows how Italian operatic instrumentalizations of the Celestial Empire served specific movements (or attempted movements) of power and cultural capital in eighteenth-century Italy.

As a site and a practice that engaged with these movements, eighteenth-century opera was especially fecund. It was more "culturally interactive" than other contemporary theatrical forms, given its greater number of constitutive elements, or what André Helbo calls "vehicles of manifestation" for the world that productions put before audiences.[58] Opera was open to artistic and social forms and materialities excluded from other dramatic genres. One thinks immediately of music and singing, of course, in contrast to their absence at least in spoken tragedy and dominant types of spoken bourgeois comedy. In addition to orchestral and vocal augmentation, however, opera also encompassed greater spectacle, larger numbers of bodies on stage, and an enormous range of poetic and performative styles, from the grossly comic to the exquisitely virtuosic to adumbrations of an unprecedented middle range. Despite the number of conventions commonly associated with the genre, Italian opera in the eighteenth century was still an extremely mutable, porous cultural form.[59] To varying degrees, it appropriated all manner of local dramatic and theatrical praxis, including that from commedia dell'arte, pastoral, classical tragedy, and ballet. Its polymorphous iteration on page and stage underscores the often contentious, unresolved nature of its theoretical foundations.[60] All this instability, however, made for multiple nodes in the expression and promotion of ideologies among the myriad subjects—poet-authors, patrons, musicians, performers, theater impresarios, and most importantly, audiences—implicated in operatic entertainment.

The multiplicity of opera's signifiers brings up the question of theater semiotics. A snarly topic (Helbo characterizes "The *Spectacle* [as] a true ordeal for theoreticians"), theater semiology is still far from denoting a definitive critical apparatus.[61] For the purposes of this study, Umberto Eco provides a workable starting point in his discussion of the intense signifying power activated by the staged scene.[62] Most felicitously for this volume, Eco asks: "What is a Chinese pot upon a table in a set design? A natural object? An artificial device? Is it representing something else?"[63] He makes these queries to explicate both the process of sign creation and the fact that meaning is associative. Signs come into being the moment something is ostended, that is, put on display, or is perceived as such. Furthermore, when a person, object, or other entity becomes a sign, then "even those . . . characteristics [of that entity] that are not pertinent to the purposes of representation also acquire a sort of vicarious representative importance . . . The very moment the audience accepts the convention of the mise-en-scène, every element of that portion of the world that has been framed (put on the platform) becomes significant."[64] Quoting the Soviet folklorist Bogatyrev, Eco reasserts the extraordinary "additional connotative power" of objects, behaviors, and words, when they occur on stage.[65] Eco goes on to note that staged persons realize figures of speech (metonymy, antonomasia, irony, for example), and simultaneously are transformed into ideological abstractions.[66] When Eco states "A semiotics of the mise-en-scène is constitutively a semiotics of the production of ideologies," he has arrived more or less at the same conclusion as Greenblatt, simply by way of a different means of transport.[67]

Eco is speaking of the semiology of performance, however, while this study privileges the close examination of dramatic texts, that is, the operatic librettos. For obvious reasons, direct experience of the eighteenth-century productions is impossible. Still, that does not rule out mining the librettos for information about performance. The approaches of theater scholars Patrice Pavis and Jean Alter prove especially fruitful as far as situating and valorizing the libretto in the larger context of theater theory.[68] Both stress the consubstantiality of text and performance, and therefore that theatrical analysis must take both written and acted/staged entities into consideration.[69]

Paradoxically, Pavis's work on the proper ways to conduct performance analysis (wherein he stipulates that one must attend the performance in question), illuminates the importance of the libretto in the study of works whose original stagings—that is, those contemporaneous with the composition of their dramatic texts—cannot be attended. Pavis frames theater as a "textual practice," but not in the customary way, which subordinates performance to text, as a more or less faithful realization of textual or authorial intentions.[70] For Pavis, performance constitutes the text's "scenic enunciation": "Once a text is enunciated on stage, in whatever form, it is treated plastically, musically, gesturally; it has relinquished the abstraction and potentiality of the written text so as to be activated in performance. Colored by voice and gesture . . . , the text becomes texture; it is embodied by the actors, as if they are able to 'physicalize' it, to absorb it, to breathe it in before breathing it out."[71] More importantly, the scenic enunciation gives the text meaning. Performance analysis, then, evaluates the "impact and function of text within performance," and identifies how the performance, as a stage practice involving a text (or a textual practice involving a stage), imparts meaning to the text.

This approach constitutes a compromise, according to Pavis, between the "textocentric" conception of theater, and its opposite, the stage-centered position. The philosophies at either of these poles are known to most, although it bears noting that the latter has come to the fore in recent years. One of the results of modern interest in theater as mise-en-scène and the focus on performance has been "the reduction of the dramatic text to the status of a sort of cumbersome accessory, . . . left, rather contemptuously, at the disposal of philologists. . . . there has been a shift from one extreme to the other: from philology to scenology."[72] Pavis recuperates the text from its castoff standing in his effort to provide a more holistic (and accurate, one assumes) picture of theater: "Perhaps it is time to restore a little more equity and, if possible, subtlety. My aim here is not to return to a purely literary vision of theater, or to engage in an endless discussion as to whether theater constitutes literature or performance. Instead I propose to reconsider the place of text in performance, and to distinguish between text as read off the page of a book and text as perceived in a mise-en-scène."[73] The insights from this type of investigation ultimately issue from analysis of a work's "performance text," which Pavis distinguishes from the dramatic text (the written playscript), and the performance itself (the singular event taking place in a particular context of enunciation).[74] Where these last two are material, and thus empirical, the performance text is not. It is instead "an unwritten text comprising the various choices of a mise-en-scène that the director has consciously or unconsciously made during the rehearsal process, choices . . . apparent in the final product . . . The performance text is the mise-en-scène considered not as an empirical object, but as an abstract system, and organized ensemble of signs . . . an object of knowledge, a theoretical object substituted for the empirical object the performance itself once was."[75] Performance analysis seeks to identify and study the performance text, that which Pavis suggests is the text " 'at the origin' or 'at the heart' of a mise-en-scène."[76]

Given the circumstances of the China operas studied here, the librettos constitute the most substantive empirical evidence from which to get at an idea of performance text. And where Pavis apprehends performance text by mentally moving back, from witnessed performance to dramatic text, here one is constrained to move forward, from libretto to imagined performance. Nonetheless, the librettos still yield plentiful information about the onstage "textual practice" of China operas. More relevant to my purposes, however, they reveal a great deal about the networks of meanings which both activated, and were activated by, the productions. The librettos can serve toward what Pavis terms "historical reconstruction," although not in the usual sense of reproducing a specific performance or set of performances. Rather, they help to reconstruct the structures of signification at play in the period, and how those significations availed or impeded certain kinds of exchange. Which images of China appeared most often on the opera stage, and in which kinds of operas? How was China represented in relation to other nations or peoples portrayed in the opera? Which sorts of ideologies does the opera seem to engage, and how are perceptions of Chinese culture mobilized to mediate those ideologies? Inquiry of this sort is not performance analysis as Pavis conceives it, but nevertheless requires the careful scrutiny of textual and performance contexts, which Pavis finds indispensable for both reconstruction and performance analysis:

> Analysis as [historical] reconstruction is particularly concerned with the study of a performance's contexts; its aim is to understand the nature and extent of these contexts.[77]
> . . . analysis of performance containing text . . . should locate the text historically, at the moment of its production . . . the moment of its inscription in a sociocultural context. . . . one cannot read a dramatic text without imagining a concrete situation, which depends on the ideological conditions of that particular moment, nor without having at one's disposal a minimal amount of preexisting knowledge of the text and the mode of performance.[78]

The particular eighteenth-century contexts this study is most concerned with include 1) the conventions of writing and enacting opera, 2) prevailing images of and discourses about China, and 3) local discourses in social, political, economic, and religious realms, including Enlightenment propositions. This last context naturally focuses on those cultural discourses that, given the operatic evidence, appear to have been most amenable to stage expression in Chinese terms.

Alter's vision of theater lends itself especially well to the appreciation of Italian China operas as eloquent sites for the interactions of the second and third group of contexts mentioned above. He identifies two principal functions operative in any theatrical work.[79] The first is the referential function, that is, a spectacle's "story space," or its narrative dimension inasmuch as a fable is acted out. The second is the performant function, or a work's "stage space," that is, its offering of performative skill. Alter uses the italicized term *performance* to denote this theatrical element, which might include exceptional acting, breathtaking scenery, or musical prowess. Stage business perceived in terms of performative achievement, distinct from story dramatization, constitutes the performant function. Although "story space" and "stage space" compete for attention from an audience, the operations of the two are integrally connected, since spectators constantly shuttle between them, and finally conflate them when responding to the finished Performance.

The intense effect of the interactivity of theater's referential and performant functions derives predominantly, however, from the fact that *performance*, initially presented by Alter as not participating in semiosis, turns out to have a profound referential capacity. That is to say, like traditionally understood theatrical signifiers (actors' bodies, stage props, spoken lines of dialogue), *performance* itself is a signifier, and layers its signified upon that of other more conventional signifiers and their associated signs. In fact, *performance* as signifier is greatly responsible for widening and deepening the referent behind the sign. Alter uses the example of Lawrence Olivier, playing the part of Hamlet. Citing his acting excellence, he states: "Olivier's *performance* may originate in two types of perceived achievement: an extraordinary mastery of style and techniques used to convey general referential notions, such as fear or pride or intelligence or power; or an extraordinary display of style and techniques used to convey a certain image of Hamlet. In either case, ... the *performance* is directly linked to an exceptionally powerful communication of an imaginary referent, simple or complex."[80] He then amends this to say that Olivier's *performance* links to an "almost abstract concept of an ideal referent, a class of possible referents ... Such a class ... corresponds more exactly to ... meaning of a sign, that is, its signified, than to a specific referent. The perceived—and admired—acting Olivier is viewed as the signifier, which, in Olivier as a sign, is associated with a signified defined as a class of fear or a class of Hamlets."[81] *Performance* therefore permits the most richly complex, most meaningful referentiality.

To draw a parallel illustration from eighteenth-century Italian opera, the signified associated with the stage character (sign) of peasant or servant buffoon may include specific qualities such as social inadequacy, fear, or mischievous resourcefulness. It could alternatively involve a precise underdog referent: a ship captain's hireling named Panico, for example, who suffers especially from bad luck in love. To the clown character may even be grafted the attributes of another, similar sign, familiar yet discrete, as in the figure of Arlecchino. These referents theoretically are communicated independent of *performance*. However, when the comic protagonist combines this primary referential capacity with a magnificent buffo stage rendition, when his gestures, singing, movements, speech, and costume are judged impressive by spectators, the range and depth of the signified increases exponentially. According to Alter's theory, the well-performing character (sign) now actuates a class of the downtrodden, or an ideal strain of beguiling ingenuity. The referential world is more satisfyingly concretized, since *performance* trains spectators "for a fuller appreciation of theatre's semiosis, that is, its referential function."[82]

Alter then adds to the mix a third theatrical function, that of cultural *performance*.[83] He differentiates the cultural *performance* from the theatrical *performance* inasmuch as the former derives from areas outside the domain of theater. The cultural *performance* "acknowledge[s] the presence of an outstanding materialization of a value that is highly prized by [a] culture."[84] The cult of celebrity, sexual appeal, wealth, and social prestige are offered as likely culturally oriented values that might be "performed" on stage. A stage feature (animate or not) becomes a cultural *performance*

when it relates to a model located in real life and is perceived to be "a clearly outstanding version" of that model. The qualification of "outstanding" inheres in the feature's actual three-dimensional presence *before* the spectator, since real-life models are usually accessible to spectators only "in the form of flattering [but static] images" or in verbal descriptions. As idealized specimens they are not easily experienced directly. Cultural *performances* in the theater

offer ... physical presence ... that can be directly experienced during the Performance. Even when they do not quite match their media models, they are appreciated because they are perceived to be real, that is, to exist in the same reality as the audience ... [they demonstrate] that media models can have a real existence ... spectators merge the imaginary space of their vision of life with the real space in which they are living during the Performance. Part of the appeal of cultural *performances* stems no doubt from this momentary but reassuring conflation of beliefs and experience.[85]

Like theatrical *performance*, cultural *performances* also raise the spectator's consciousness of the semiotic dynamics of theater and the world. As the theatergoer mentally shifts from apprehending the character Hamlet (referential function) to the actor-performer Olivier (theatrical performant function) to the handsome he-man Olivier (cultural performant function, where virile beauty is among a culture's values and Olivier happens at the time of the production to be extremely muscular and good-looking), she becomes more and more cognizant of semiotic operations everywhere. Her appreciation grows, for the world's as well as her own ability to semiotize, desemiotize, and resemiotize features of reality.[86] Theater, with its "ability to generate more powerful referents than most other figurative arts," prepares its patrons to "receive ... a much enhanced vision of the referential world."[87]

The librettos for the Italian China operas, despite their brevity, communicate much about the performative dramaturgy at work in them. Among other things, stage directions reveal which kinds of cultural *performances* were viable in the period, and how they may have interacted with the other referential and performant operations unfolding before an audience. In some cases onstage cultural *performances* involved China directly, such as when the librettist prescribed an opulent, richly detailed Chinese interior as the backdrop to a set of scenes. *Didascalie* for a *ballo* sequence help toward understanding how spectators might have perceived the "thought-in-action" designed to be communicated by the dance.[88] Alter's theatrical *performance* quotient comes into play when one thinks of an opera principal letting loose her stellar singing voice, or a buffo character excelling at gestural and linguistic antics. These kinds of *performances* are especially relevant in Italian theater, whose practitioners were the first in Europe to formally elucidate the nature of acting, or stage talents, as separate from a theater work's other constitutive elements.[89] Thus, when a prima donna played a Chinese princess, or a buffoon acted the part of a Chinese ambassador, the piling up of signifieds became especially resonant.

METHODOLOGY

Before explaining my rationale for choosing the particular operas under study, I wish to further address the question of the validity of studying the libretto, and more crucially, its value in regard to the aims of this study. The libretto's status in the eyes of opera studies experts naturally varies. Because so many come from the field of musicology, the oppositional relation that has so animated theater studies, that is, dramatic text versus performance, often manifests itself among music scholars as the conflict between words and music. While some scholars refuse to evaluate any opera without examining, indeed, privileging its music, others deem research on the verbal text productive, analyzing librettos with or without their musical settings.[90] Paul Robinson, who leans toward the music side, makes an allowance for the eighteenth-century libretto, given that the smaller theaters, smaller orchestras, even the repetitive nature of the *da capo* aria, made sung lyrics more intelligible than they would be in the following century.[91] Interest in the libretto for its own sake has held fast especially among Italian opera scholars, perhaps allegiant to their eighteenth-century forebears who so strongly defended the prestige of the poetic text.[92] More recently, opera experts of all stripes attribute key significance to the libretto, recognizing its revelatory role in the universe of late early modern musical drama, especially in terms of opera's sociocultural repercussions.[93]

In the case of eighteenth-century works, one might defend libretto analysis based simply on the fact that for many operas, it is the only data available. The number of extant librettos far outstrips that of extant scores. Still, there is yet another reason why the opera text is the best way to understand the mechanics of meaning in China operas. The libretto is of critical importance because eighteenth-century operas were conceived first and foremost as literary works. Not only did operas first come into being as written, poetic compositions, but they continued to be thought of as such, that is, as dramatic literature.

The emphasis on the literariness of opera derives from the reform efforts on the part of Italian intelligentsia at the beginning of the Settecento. Their undertakings to overhaul the atrocious operatic spectacle of the previous century turned on a strictly literary aesthetic—specifically, the rules of classical and French neoclassical tragedy. Chapters 3 and 4 below on opera seria will explicate the details of this reform. What is important to note here, is the extent to which text-based culture inflected on opera, most decidedly in its creation, and, to a significant degree, in its consumption. Despite the lively theater scene in eighteenth-century Italy, dramas were still understood as texts written to be read. The libretto for a heroic *melodramma*, for example, the operatic genre with the most longevity over the course of the eighteenth century, was considered a tragedy to read and evaluate apart from any stage performance. One indication of the intended consumption of librettos away from the theater is the quantity of printed text marked off by quotation marks (*virgolette*). These sections, almost always recitative, were judged by the librettist necessary for an appreciation of the work by a reader. On stage, however, they would have been dispensed with. The redoubtable presence of librettos in private collections is another sign that "*drammi per musica* were widely read at home, like other dramatic literature."[94] For the reform-minded poet as well as for his reader, the proof of an opera's quality lay in its iteration on the page. The printed dramatic poetry could be studied, unlike the music, which, even had it been printed as often as the libretto, did not yet have a mass of connoisseurs able to gauge its excellence.[95] The poet therefore felt much more pressure than did the composer to be correct and aesthetically pleasing. Strohm notes: "The fact that the drama came first determined the artistic demands. Any chance mistakes of the composer's, any rather free use of a colleague's ideas, could not possibly be detected by the general public. In the printed libretto, on the other hand, any educated man could observe any infelicitous expressions or metrical faults and also compare the work of a provincial *littérateur* with that of the famous Zeno, Stampiglia, Metastasio, etc. Everything suggests that the librettist's chief aim was immaculate versification."[96] Other information pertaining to the two creators of early eighteenth-century opera, poet and composer (as yet there was no director or producer), reveals the former's more decisive role. Librettos as well as scores attributed authorship to the poet, such that theater patrons attended a *dramma* by "x" *con mu-*

ùica by "y." Librettos distinguished among dramatic genres (e.g., *dramma per musica, pastorale per musica, tragedia per musica*), but did no such thing with music. The contemporary metaphor designating music as the clothing which dressed the poetry-body says it all.[97] Even when scholars point out the power that singers wielded over the librettist, insofar as poets very often composed their dramas for the voices and personality types of commissioned *castrati* and *cantarine*, the opera's incarnation as poetry still ruled.[98]

Enrico Fubini reminds us of the tight bond in the mind of the eighteenth-century Italian thinker between poetic rhetoric, written or spoken, and Reason. In an age that deified Reason, Italian intellectuals esteemed poetry as a "supremely privileged mode of expression because it clearly and manifestly evinced its relationship to reason, and therefore its moral content, its edifying and pedagogical design."[99] Music, on the other hand, was for many "an inconvenient factor, upsetting and disturbing in many ways because one is hard put to make it coincide with the linear canons of reason."[100] Opera then, at least until mid-century, when new understandings of music began to assert themselves, stood on the firmest of literary-textual foundations. Strohm sums it up succinctly: "The performance of a *dramma per musica* was regarded primarily as the music-dramatic recitation of poetry . . . the stage realisation of a work was not implicit in the theatrical practice of the day and the text of the work."[101]

At the same time, however, a number of realities in the opera world worked against the authority of the text. The sheer demand for spectacles gave libretto production certain machinelike aspects. Poets often had to write very quickly, creating works scheduled for local or distant operatic institutions. Original libretti frequently underwent revision for successive runs in new locales, or by different companies. Under pressure by the demands of singers, composers, theater impresarios, or sponsors of the opera, the poetic text fell victim to serial surgical interventions, executed more often than not by poets other than the original librettist. The infamous "suitcase aria" custom applies here, where singers demanded the insertion into existing texts of a few favorites from their personal song repertoires. Librettos might see adjustments even within individual performance runs. Whether for egoistic reasons or to renew the attention of audience members who frequented the theater every night, singer-actors and their accompanying musicians added performative elements—vocal and orchestral ornamentation, for example—that escaped the bounds of the libretto. "Everything in the theatre of those days was incalculable," writes Strohm, "par-

ticularly anything to do with singers—and this necessitated productions which could be changed easily and at short notice without damaging the effect of the whole; economy of effort and high costs demanded works that could be successfully repeated in later seasons."[102] About the only fixed element in this melee of retoolings was that operas tended to retain their original titles, and texts, for the most part, continued to be ascribed to the original librettists.

One is left with a paradox: how to reconcile opera's textual identity and the aesthetic prestige attached to it, with the effacing realities of its practice? One result of these contradictory energies is that there was little notion of the "individual work."[103] The extremely mutable conditions of opera, especially in the first half of the century, overruled the sense of singularity, of proprietary ownership. Rather, aspirations toward a more generalized artistic integrity prevailed, applicable to text as well as performance. Given this unique situation, Pavis's concept of the "performance text" seems especially apt. Again, his statement: "[The performance text is] . . . an unwritten text comprising the various choices of a mise-en-scène that the director has consciously or unconsciously made during the rehearsal process, choices . . . apparent in the final product . . . [It] is the mise-en-scène considered not as an empirical object, but as an abstract system, an organized ensemble of signs . . . an object of knowledge, a theoretical object substituted for the empirical object." If much of eighteenth-century Italian opera adhered to a standard of collective achievement that transcended individual accomplishment, then the ground is already laid for an investigation of China's role in an opera's "abstract system" and its "organized ensemble of signs." Even better, inasmuch as *drammi per musica* in this period had directors, that job was filled by the librettist. So their poetic product is extremely valuable. They provide the most important data from which to identify the choices made as to China's function in the cultural work of opera. The source stories, the plots, the characters and their associated traits, the range of themes that sustained interest—all of these not only are contained in the libretto, but were of great moment to the literature-minded reform librettist. Moreover, with respect to libretto genealogy, these elements form a basic matrix that generally stayed in place even as varied descendants issued from the parent text.[104] This study therefore works from either the libretto text contained in the authoritative editions of an author's works (this is the case with Metastasio and Goldoni), or the first-printed libretto connected with the opera.[105]

It may be helpful at this juncture to point out what this study does not aim to do. It does not attempt to reconstruct and then analyze the derivative texts and performances for all Italian-authored China operas over the course of the eighteenth century. To do so would amount to a gargantuan enterprise, and more significantly, would serve different goals. Likewise it is not an analysis of reception, nor does it scrutinize a local repertory in a tightly restricted time period, as Mary Hunter does for comic opera in Josephine Vienna.[106] However, some of Hunter's thoughts in her discussion of repertory seem fitting here. Where her assemblage of operas acquires coherence and meaning from the fact that they were all selected for performance in a specific place at a specific time, mine do so from their unified subject matter. Italian China operas constitute a different kind of repertory, but like Hunter's works, they too generate a "repertorial profile." Her profile consists of "the topics and issues iterated and reiterated in opera after opera."[107] In other words, a common thematics emerges from disparate operas, owing to the consistency of local/temporal factors, that is, where/when/to whom the operas played. My profile necessarily comprises more difference. The consistency factor is the subject matter (Chinese people, lands, culture), and the study examines what happens to that common denominator in operas of varying genre (serious and comic), created and performed in diverse moments and places.

Questions of place and time are very interesting where opera is concerned. Hunter is correct when she links repertory choice to local political contingency, saying both 1) that the kinds of operas a city chooses to put on (at a particular moment) might well reveal something about the political function of the choices, and 2) that the same group of operas could function entirely differently in another place/time. On the other hand, a contradiction again arises, given the extensive standardization of eighteenth-century Italian opera. General consensus is that opera's virtually universal appeal in eighteenth-century Europe stemmed directly from a set of core ideologies that engaged multiple sites in similar ways.[108] This study acknowledges the truth of both claims: eighteenth-century Italian opera is and isn't location-specific. My way of addressing this duality coincides moreover with general facts as to the evolution of opera in the period.

Close analysis of the works begins in part 2, "Playing with Dynasty: China in Opera Seria." Interestingly, all Italian China operas in the heroic category premiered in the first half of the century, when opera seria was in the vanguard. Four of the five known works, in fact, were written by 1722, smack in the genre's formative period. Even when one encounters idiosyncracies in these early dramas, most were nonetheless converging on a precise literary-dramatic ideal. My approach is guided by the genre's own emphasis on conformity. For the five opere serie discussed in part 2 I do not consider individual compositional or performance circumstances, but rather examine the broader outlines of the genre's professed goals, and those of the society to which it played. Just as the reforming *dramma per musica* was learning what it was, one might venture that contemporary body politics were likewise educating themselves on how to best embody their enlightened absolutist personas. As I will show, opera seria engaged quite competently—however variously—with conventional ideologies of enlightened monarchy. Since this system and its principles had a hold on so many Italian centers and their European counterparts, my treatment of serious China operas stresses the transmunicipal, transnational aspects of the works. Importance is given to the transcendent, "global" philosophies subtending them. Such aspirations to social and political perfection fed not only the self-image of the reform-minded sovereign, but also that of opera seria itself.

The study of the comic operas, on the other hand (conducted in part 3, chapters 5, 6, and 7), looks more directly at the cultural ambience of each opera's origin. Although these dramas typically heeded a network of habits and prescriptions as dense as those dictating opera seria, several of their constituent elements also made for greater flexibility and openness. The opera buffa put a wider range of social classes on stage, characters who in turn played to a wider range of spectators. The poetics of comic opera rehearsed not only many of the constituent elements of opera seria, but a host of other modalities, pulled from other dramatic and theatrical traditions. Music also had started flexing its semiological muscles, adding another, increasingly intricate language to the mix. The heyday of comic opera coincided with the most ambitious strides (or at least attempts) by social critics, economists, journalists, political theorists, and other thinkers and educators, to modernize a wide swathe of cultural backwaters. The multiplication of variables, and the greater thrust of local reform projects at the time of opera buffa's prime, make it more appropriate to examine the comic dramas in their unique contexts.

As far as which operas are treated, I've chosen to identify and examine the eight most culturally salient China operas of the period. The term "salient" should not be taken to only mean popular with audiences, where popularity is determined by a drama's longevity, in turn deduced from a high number of performance runs and/or an impressive quantity of musical settings and/or performance sites. Generally this is the case, but a few of the operas under review boast only one documented orchestral setting, and according to extant records were performed in only one venue within a single season. These works, such as Antonio Salvi's *Il Tartaro nella Cina*, or Domenico Lalli's *Camaide, l'imperatore della Cina*, have been included owing to the activity and fame of the librettists.[109] Given these poets' prominent place in the sphere of operatic text-writing, their elaborations of the Chinese imaginary should be counted.

As this study privileges the dramatic (literary) text in order to appreciate the cultural work in which the China operas participated, music will not be considered. To reiterate what has been noted above, the China operas were produced in a climate in which practitioners still struggled to define music's meaning and status. The logistical difficulties of studying settings bears on this decision as well, given the unavailability of many scores, and the jungle of (often fragmentary) variants. It should be recalled that authentic Chinese music did not make its way into eighteenth-century opera orchestration; this is discussed in more detail at the end of chapter 2.

CHAPTER OVERVIEWS

Pagodas in Play is structured in three parts. The first, "Setting the Stage," begins with chapter 1, entitled "Eighteenth-Century Exoticism and China." This chapter helps set the stage for analysis of the Chinese operas by giving a brief survey of the encounter between Europe and China in the last centuries of the early modern period. This survey presents the principal ideas about the Middle Kingdom as elaborated in texts ("Texts and Ideas"), the various material forms which manifested European appreciation of China ("Material Culture"), and the special occasions and activities associated with the Celestial Empire ("Events and Practices"). The second half of chapter 1 focuses more intently on notions of exoticism and orientalism, as they apply to the eighteenth century, and to Italian operas incorporating China.

Chapter 2 is called "China's Journey from Page to Stage." It prepares the ground for close reading of the operas by discussing the penetration of Chinese elements in five fundamental areas of eighteenth-century Italian opera: 1) characters, 2) costume, 3) scenery/props, 4) gesture/dance, and 5) music. This historical and technical exposition serves to emphasize the

lively dialogic relationship between China inscribed on the libretto page or operatic stage, and China in Italian life outside the theater. When not occupied with their theater duties, for example, scene painters executed "Chinese" frescoes for the interiors of aristocratic villas; audience members donned Chinese costumes for the parties and dances concluding operatic spectacles; the porcelain, lacquer, fans, lanterns, and other props prominent in stage productions had counterparts in a booming China-wares market. The osmosis between aesthetic practice and the discursive and material forms of daily life underscores the capacity of "Chinese" opera to express concerns originating in that daily life.

Part 2, "Playing with Dynasty: China in Opera Seria" opens with chapter 3, entitled "China in Early Opere Serie (1700–1725)." In this chapter renditions of China in the first reform operas of the Settecento come to the fore. The chapter studies four *drammi per musica* written in the first quarter of the century: Apostolo Zeno's *Teuzzone* (1706), Urbano Ricci's *Taican, rè della Cina* (1707), Antonio Salvi's *Il Tartaro nella Cina* (1715), and Domenico Lalli's *Camaide, l'imperatore della Cina* (1722). The controversial status of opera seria at this time—a relatively fledgling genre, enormously popular with the theatergoing public but intensely contested by critics dubious as to its aesthetic and moral worth—had a parallel in the elaborate and irregular complex of conventions dictating its creation and performance. Thus the generic protocols implicated in these operas' exploitation of China vary widely. *Teuzzone* pivots on the requisite spectacular happy ending, where Zeno conflates Chinese virtues with those of Greco-Roman and Arcadian worlds to promote a return to dignified Italian literary origins. *Il Tartaro nella Cina* mobilizes heroic opera's essentialist characterization to idealize peaceful, orderly polities (China) over violent and tyrannical ones (Tartary). *Camaide* offers an example of an opera that instrumentalizes both received knowledge about the Middle Kingdom—its reputation for paternal solicitude and filial piety—and its aura of escapist fantasy, fundamental to the poetics of chinoiserie. The musical drama often considered the first specimen of Italian China theater, Ricci's *Taican, rè della Cina* (1707), is also treated here to show a more superficial deployment of China onstage—and to illustrate the degree to which the other three operas more seriously engage perceptions of the Asian nation in the interest of homeland issues.

Chapter 4, on Pietro Metastasio's *L'eroe cinese* (1752), demonstrates the mobilization of China in the glorification of the imperial subaltern. *L'eroe cinese* beatified perceptions of Chinese placidity, submissiveness, endurance, and loyalty, to dramatize the ideal behavior of the royal subordinate. Coincidentally, the Metastasian poetics of opera seria were by now fully standardized. The regulated entrances and exits of singers on stage, the carefully monitored progress of themes and sentiments in arias, the set pattern of dramatic deferrals—these and other generic conventions were put to use to maximize impressions of contented Chinese complaisance.

L'eroe cinese predates Voltaire's tragedy *L'Orphelin de la Chine* (1755) in its appropriation of the Chinese orphan legend publicized in the first half of the century. Where the Sage of Ferney would find in Chinese integrity proof of a universal, non-scriptural morality, *L'eroe cinese* mobilized it for more circumscribed ends. Its idealization of the obedient Chinese citizen served the institution of state bureaucracy, crucial to the enlightened absolutist monarchy. The success of the new officialdom would depend on the Chinese-like spirit of willing compliance and cooperation among its workers.

As its title suggests, "Playing with Reform: China in Comic Opera," part 3 deals with the treatment of China in opera buffa. Comic opera did not flourish until the latter half of the eighteenth century, and thus added its own semiological apparatuses to those it inherited from opera seria. Since Italian reformist projects were also most energetically underway at this time, comic operas featuring the Celestial Empire instrumentalize it in discrete, inventive, and unexpected ways. Chapter 5, entitled "Islands of Opportunity: Carlo Goldoni, *L'isola disabitata* (1757)," reveals the appropriation of China to promote a colonialist and mercantile discourse that extends beyond the Venetian sphere to which Goldonian dramas typically confine themselves. Specifically, *L'isola disabitata* contrasts the energetic, productive Dutch with the insular, unenlightened Chinese. The encomium of Dutch trade ambition and corresponding condemnation of Middle Kingdom stagnation serves as a reprimand to backward aristocratic factions, whether in Venice or in Europe in general. The comic opera conventions that most meaningfully abet this campaign include the ensemble finales, and the dances at the act endings.

Chapter 6, "Rejecting False Idols: Giambattista Lorenzi, *L'idolo cinese* (1767)," interrogates the Neapolitan ecclesiastical and political context of Lorenzi's opera buffa. It shows how the opera used prevailing perceptions of Chinese culture—namely, negative judgments of Buddhism, and positive assessments of China's government as based in meritocracy—to address topical questions of jurisdictionalism and class privilege. With respect to the latter, *L'idolo cinese* turns favorable sentiment about the mandarin ruling system on its head. It dramatizes the insanity of such liberal policies, and thus instrumentalizes the Asian nation in support of Naples's conservative grandees. Dramatic practices particular to the Neapolitan clown or buffo opera character—including his exaggerated imbecility, his embrace of the scatological, his pronounced state of abjection in combination with a mercenary opportunism—most effectively assure the send-up of bourgeois ideology.

Chapter 7, "Women Traveling in New Lands: Giovanni Bertati, *L'inimico delle donne* (1771)," shows the deployment of the Celestial Empire in Italian polemics on gender relations and, more precisely, in the eighteenth-century promotion of the bourgeois feminine ideal. This opera casts China consecutively as a utopic space, presumably offering civilized freedoms to both sexes, and as a dystopic site, comprising the difficult social and moral terrain that women in particular must negotiate. The modalities common to eighteenth-century comic operatic treatments of womanly virtue are here integrated with formulations of the Chinese exotic (including scandalous marital practices) to promote a new notion of domestic womanhood.

I
Setting the Stage

1

Eighteenth-Century Exoticism and China

To appreciate the different depths to which China penetrated the cultural interests of Europe in the seventeenth and eighteenth centuries, it is important to distinguish three levels of Europeans who studied and published books on China. The first level consisted of missionaries, mainly Jesuits, . . .

The second level consisted of proto-Sinologists, who had a serious but less focused interest in China than the missionaries . . .

The third level of Europeans with an interest in China consisted of those who were essentially popularizers, and they came to dominate the eighteenth-century view of China . . . Europeans on this third level were interested in finding in China support for European political and intellectual movements, particularly the Enlightenment.[1]

PORTUGUESE LANDINGS ON THE CHINESE COAST in the early sixteenth century marked the beginning of a long, rich encounter between Europeans and the Chinese.[2] The China operas of the eighteenth century were born, at least in part, from two centuries' worth of information, events, and cultural developments comprising early modern Europe's attempt to absorb the Middle Kingdom. This is not to mention the exposure to and elaboration of Chinese phenomena that continued in the Settecento. A detailed treatment of this process, however, would prove too lengthy an undertaking. The first section of this chapter will instead present a summary of those aspects of Europe's response to the Middle Kingdom that seem to have most conditioned the musical dramas. These elements will be discussed within a general framework that aims to give a sense of the overall phenomenon, as it simultaneously focuses on the more salient issues. It is organized into three main categories: texts and ideas, material culture, and events and practices. The second section will discuss China and Italy within the wider context of exoticism in the European eighteenth century.

TEXTS AND IDEAS

European ideas about China expressed in books and other printed texts in the three hundred years from the "rediscovery" of the Asian nation to the dawn of modernity (1500–1800) covered a host of topics, at levels spanning the most erudite to the most mundane. General descriptions of the country and its peoples constituted one of the most frequent kinds of publication, composed by both travelers and home-based authors who compiled, studied, synthesized, and embroidered on the material in voyage accounts to create their narratives. Among the data commonly provided in these proto-ethnographies were descriptions of Chinese history, geography, government and political structure, education system, arts, sciences, laws, religion, social institutions, and economy. The first exemplars date from the late sixteenth century, but the real milestones were written after the mid-seventeenth century, when missionary, merchant, and diplomatic expeditions made deeper inroads into Chinese spheres, making available much more detailed, wide-ranging, and updated information.[3] The Manchu Tartars of the Ch'ing dynasty had also overtaken the Ming Chinese by this time, so these works included treatments of contemporary political events.

General descriptions of the Middle Kingdom written by Jesuit authors dominate the category, given that they were the major disseminators of information on China throughout the seventeenth century and well into the first half of the eighteenth. Martino Martini's monumental geographical and cartographic work, *Novus atlas Sinensis* (1655), was not presented as a general description per se.[4] Yet it included a short general description of China in its *Ad Lectorem Praefatio*, wherein Martini moved quickly through many diverse subjects. One section, for example, jumps from Chinese polygamy to courtesy rites to garments to beverages to highways to ships.[5] This quick sketch was then substantially fleshed out, in the detailed narrative accompanying each of Martini's exquisite maps of China's fifteen provinces. The explanatory text for every province gave its geographic position, name origin, historic evolution, surface contours and boundaries, climate and products, famous mountains and rivers, important cities and towns, population, usages and customs, monuments, and historical figures and their legends.

Dutch embassy secretary Johann Nieuhof was not a Jesuit, yet his account of the 1655 Dutch trade voyage to Peking falls into the group of most-circulated general treatments of China.[6] It covered all the usual topics, and augmented them with over 150 engravings of life in the Middle Kingdom. Illustrations of customary apparel, architecture, household utensils, flora and fauna, sea vessels—these were only some of the plates that graced Nieuhof's work. *Het gezantschap der Neêrlandtsche Oost-Indische Compagnie aan den grooten tartarischen cham, den tegenwoordigen keizer van China* (Amsterdam, 1665) was quickly translated into German, Latin, French, and English (*An Embassy from the East India Company of the United Provinces to the Emperor of China*). It offered European readers their first extensive visual image of China and was extremely successful, to the end of the century and beyond.

The German Jesuit and scholar Athanasius Kircher wrote what has been termed "the encyclopedia of China," his *China Illustrata* (1667).[7] Like Martini's tome, this work provided a gamut of information about the Celestial Empire as it pursued its primary goal, an investigation of Chinese language and writing in light of Egyptian hieroglyphics. Like Nieuhof, Kircher also included a selection of engravings. Those illustrating the religious rituals of the Chinese, and their written language systems, added to the visual offerings in the Dutch work.

The most comprehensive and perceptive general description of China in the last half of the seventeenth century was Jesuit Philippe Couplet's *Nouvelle relation de la Chine* (Paris, 1688).[8] However, it wasn't long before Couplet's text was eclipsed by the extensive treatment entitled *Description géographique, historique, chronologique, politique et physique de l'Empire de la Chine et de la Tartarie chinoise.*[9] Written in Paris by Father Jean-Baptiste Du Halde and published there in 1735, the four-volume opus was the result of Du Halde's consultation of the books and manuscripts of twenty-seven China Jesuits. The *Description . . .* offered the most current information on China to date, and did so using the straightforward style of educated eighteenth-century French, rather than the more scholarly French or Latin of the previous century's treatises. It quickly become the most widely read work on China in the eighteenth century.[10]

Many contemporary works zeroed in on single aspects of the Middle Kingdom. Documented observations of the Chinese were recasting established ways of thinking in a variety of disciplines, especially those of world history, religion, philosophy, geography, and language. European intellectuals therefore plumbed reports on China in the course of conducting their own scholarly inquiries in these areas. The next section will treat the major ideas that emerged, and some of the texts that elaborated those ideas.[11]

Chinese Antiquity

Documentation showing that Chinese civilization had existed long before the first peoples acknowledged by biblical chronology threw seventeenth-century European thinkers into tilt. Martini's political history of the Middle Kingdom, *Sinicae historiae decas prima* (Munich, 1658), was the first text to assert that China had existed several hundreds of years before the Noadic flood.[12] This data coincided with the more theologically based determination by French thinker Isaac de la Peyrère that the Chinese were among a group of world peoples that had existed before Adam.[13] The shocking but riveting information was seized upon by a variety of factions with diverse agendas. Naturally it caught the attention of those interested in epistemological accuracy no matter what the cost. It also appealed to those who saw in this legitimate, "scientific" challenge a means to shake off draconian church authority in this and other arenas of knowledge and behavior.

As one would expect, certain of the clergy reacted hostilely to the claim, and did their best to refute it.[14] Their parries, however, could not hold back the moves of other intellectuals intrigued by the evidence and committed to establishing the truest picture of the world. They integrated the new chronology in investigations not only of the genesis of man, but also of the origins of humankind's various branches (the classical Greeks, Europeans, New World inhabitants), as well as of language, and arts and sciences. For the most part, the Middle Kingdom benefited from these projects, quickly acquiring a commanding historical prestige.[15]

With some tweaking of scriptural dating, scholars were able fairly quickly to reconcile Chinese chronology with biblical chronology, whereupon a new question arose: whether the Chinese had descended from the Egyptians, the civilization in which many scholars placed the origin of humanity and to which they traced their classical Greek heritage.[16] The majority of discussants affirmed China's Egyptian ancestry, thereby putting the Chinese on a cultural par with the ancient Greeks. Confucius was touted by some as the "Socrates" or "Plato" of China, and more than a hundred years later Voltaire and his adherents still revered China as the land of greatest antiquity, older than any in Europe.[17] Antonello Gerbi has observed that identifying the Chinese with heroic Hellenic civilization also worked in reverse. That is, it allowed the newly adjusted biblioclassical system to hold: "serious chronological difficulties could be avoided and the notion of the unity of the human race satisfied."[18] When dissenting thinkers proposed mankind's origins in Babylonia, China still held on to a good portion of its epic status, since in this framework figures like Fénelon compared China to Egypt in their mutual descendance from Babylonia.[19]

China also took center stage in investigations of the origins of language. Many believed there had existed a primitive universal language, and that with close-enough study of the incoming data on non-European peoples it would be possible to identify at least its underlying structures, if not the tongue itself. As early as 1669 John Webb declared that this first language had been Chinese.[20] Others, less interested in origins than in universal principles applicable to the current period, looked to Chinese speech and writing as a viable model for the creation of a new global language.

China maintained its high antiquity in the matter of technological sciences as well. The Chinese were credited with having invented the compass, mirrors, gunpowder, paper money, and the printing press. As time wore on, Europeans qualified their assessments of these developments, and they rarely, if ever, issued accolades for Chinese expertise in the arts. However, during the seventeenth century and for most of the eighteenth, China's multimillennial status held, and contributed to a more penetrating European conception of world history. From the works of Vossius to Voltaire, the Asian nation acquired a patina of authority and respect verging on the sacred.[21]

Recent Chinese History

Equally if not more interesting than China's ancient chronicles, were contemporary events affecting the empire. The Manchu invasion and takeover of the Ming dynasty comprised the most significant recent happening.[22] Certain dramatic moments stood out, such as the capture of the imperial palace in Beijing in 1644, whereupon the Ming emperor sacrificed members of his family and then committed suicide before his adversaries could arrive. Another highlight was the long standoff by rebel warrior Koxinga on the is-

land of Taiwan, finally defeated by the Manchus in 1683. Complete occupation of Chinese lands by the Manchus took most of the seventeenth century, however. Missionaries and other European sojourners in China in this period who wrote of their experiences undoubtedly remarked on some aspect of the conquest. As mentioned, most of the general treatments dedicated text to it.

The most important work by far was Martini's *De bello tartarico historia*, published in both Italian and Latin in 1654.[23] Martini's text comprised the first detailed treatment of the Ming to Ch'ing changeover. Its careful coverage and (in some editions) its engravings, including one of the Ming emperor sacrificing his daughter, made the work hugely popular. *De bello tartarico historia* set the standard for coverage of this event for the rest of the century and beyond.

Martini and the numerous others who wrote about the Chinese-Tartar conflict obviously directed attention to the key incidents in the power transfer, but the topic also engendered reporting on Chinese political affairs, the history of Chinese and Tartar relations, and similarities and differences between the two cultures. The slant of the ethnographic comparisons differed notably. Many writers depicted the two peoples as solid opposites, while others accentuated their compatibility, and the relative ease with which the two societies blended after the takeover. A considerable range arose in qualitative judgment even when the Chinese were opposed to the Manchu Tartars. Lorenzo Magalotti, for example, in a passage of *Relazione della China* (1666) describing the imperial suicide incident, feminizes the Chinese emperor, assigning his downfall to the fact that he is hopelessly lost to love and carnal pursuits.[24] By implication, the Tartar conqueror is painted as the strong, victorious masculine force. In a subsequent section, however, Magalotti appraises the Chinese as civilized and refined, next to the boorish, primitive Tartars.[25] Rousseau and others saw in the Manchu coup d'etat proof of the inevitable failings of highly articulated social organization. In his *Discours* of 1750 Rousseau cited China as clear evidence that a sophisticated culture not only did not triumph morally, but actually resulted in weakness and decay.[26] In any case, the current situation in China proved fascinating to Europeans interested in lessons to be learned from the present.

Religion in China

Of the three belief systems recognized by Europeans as constituting religious practice in China—Confu-

1. **Last Ming Emperor kills his daughter to prevent her ravishment by approaching Manchu armies. Martino Martini,** *De bello tartarico historia* . . . **Amsterdam, 1655. Courtesy United States Library of Congress.**

cianism, Buddhism, and Taoism—only the first gained acceptance among thinkers and scholars to the West. This division resulted primarily from the work of the Jesuit missionaries, who, in their effort to influence the powerful class of Confucianist scholar-officials known as mandarins, elevated Confucianism as an authentic, albeit primitive form of Christianity. The most influential dissemination of Confucian doctrine in Europe began in 1687, with the publication of *Confucius Sinarum Philosophus* (*Confucius, Philosopher of the Chinese*).[27] This collaborative work by Jesuit missionaries contained a biography of Confucius, translations of the famous *Four Books*, and an introduction to the Confucian classics, their Chinese commenta-

tors, and the theism of traditional China. It exposed readers to the critical tenets of Confucian doctrine, emphasizing, of course, those that most seemed to bear a Christian imprint, such as the mandate to honor one's parents, and treat others as one wished to be treated. *Confucius Sinarum Philosophus* generated many additional translations and commentaries, including a good number aimed at a more popular audience. The Parisian *Journal des Savants* immediately published adaptations of the seminal work, and the same year saw the issue of *La morale de Confucius*, a condensed version of the Chinese sage's teachings.[28]

Buddhism and Taoism, on the other hand, received very different press. Though practiced by the great

2. **Chinese rebel Licunguz overtakes Ming emperor during Ming dynasty downfall. Johannes Nieuhoff, *L'ambassade de la compagnie orientale . . .* 1665. Permission of Special Collections, University of Virginia Library.**

majority of Chinese, Buddhism and Taoism were associated with the noneducated masses. For a number of reasons, chief among them the desire to distance the "lower-class" faith systems from the rarefied object of their affections, the Jesuit fathers quickly labeled Buddhists and Taoists as idolatrous. The sections on religious sects in the general treatments of China frequently zero in on Buddhism in particular. Its tenets concerning reincarnation and its complex of rituals were among the problematic aspects not only for the Catholic fathers, but also for commentators of all persuasions. Even the upper-class Chinese perceived the hordes of Buddhist priests, called bonzes, as conniving predators of the common people. Reform Christians as well as papal factions saw fanaticism and heresy in Buddhist believers.

Confucianism had its detractors too, especially among more orthodox Catholics who would not allow for a shred of deviation from their ideas of the principles and proper practices of Christianity.[29] The Rites Controversy and the Debate on Terms, both of which disputed the theological essence of Confucianism, were waged by enemies of the Jesuits quick to castigate the falsehoods espoused by an arrogant, heretical group of literati-philosopher-types.[30] In the main, however, admiration for Confucian philosophy ruled the day. The "cult of Confucianism" in seventeenth- and eighteenth-century Europe furthermore took a number of different paths. The discussion of these trajectories can best be conducted under the next rubric.

Chinese Morality and Politics

When modern scholars point out that the discovery of Chinese (Confucian) morality ironically hurt the Jesuits and aided their enemies, they speak to the enthusiastic welcome of Confucianist philosophy by freethinkers, that is, those who sought a more secular ethics, free of the superstitions, esoterica, and oppression of church orthodoxy (reform Christians, libertines, *philosophes*). To these intellectuals, the commonsense principles of Confucianism seemed based wholly in reason, not in arcane interpretations of mystical scripture or sensational revelation. Embraced as a most viable form of deism, Confucian practice also surpassed Catholicism insofar as it was supremely empirical. Its effectiveness could be gauged, it was thought, in terms of the visible order and harmonious functioning of Chinese society. Leibniz and Voltaire equally praised the private and public utility of Confucianism.[31] Pietro Verri never mentions Confucius, but his satiric dialogue between a mandarin and a European solicitor points up the efficiency and straightforwardness of the former's modes of reasoning, in sharp contrast to the convoluted semantics and avaricious bureaucracy typical of European legal, scientific, and economic realms.[32]

Europeans were especially compelled by the integration of the Confucianist code with China's political system. The Celestial Empire offered a living example of a monarchy guided not by religious dogma, nor by elitist privilege, but by values at once intellectual and pragmatic. The Chinese promoted lettered mandarins to ruling positions in accordance with their erudition and example. Chinese government thus constituted a meritocracy, and assured its people of just, egalitarian, rational treatment. Even the Jesuit mission historiographer Daniello Bartoli, whose essential attitude toward the Celestial Empire was one of suspicion and measured hostility for the trials his fellow missionaries suffered in their conversion attempts, described the scholar-official program in these flattering terms: "the political and moral sciences . . . appear to belong to the Literary Empire, because China has neither princes, nor virtue, nor purity of blood, except through achievement in letters. Knowledge alone, which elsewhere is poorly valued, in China is everything. Thus [from knowledge there follows] the highest dignities, the supreme command, pre-eminence in court, treasures in the home, veneration by the populace, the pride of families and all that is beatified in that reign . . . Each person is worth just what he is, and owes his circumstances to nothing other than his own merits."[33] A great number of authors took up the topic of China's political philosophy based so soundly in pragmatism and social efficacy. William Temple's 1690 essay *Of Heroic Virtue* was but one example.[34] It extolled the civic morality of Confucian statesmanship. For Temple as for many others, the sage Confucius became the indispensable philosopher-prince for the times.

The secular extrapolation of Confucianism did not immediately eradicate its Jesuit version. The impact and longevity of the idea of a "Catholic Confucius" is sometimes forgotten, in the attention paid to the demise of the Jesuit conversion project (not to mention the fall of the Society throughout Europe) and to the transformation of the Order's take on Confucianism to that of libertine thinkers. But just as the Humanists had found Christian value in the writings of Greco-Roman thinkers, so the seventeenth- and eighteenth-century Jesuits and their followers defined Confucius as a virtuous, Christian-oriented pagan. Moreover, this image well served the ideologies of absolutist Catholic monarchies.

Du Halde's 1735 compilation on China reprises the European knowledge of Confucius up to that point. More importantly, however, it shows the missionary spin. His brief biographical section focuses on the Chinese philosopher's simplicity, goodness, humility, and his devotion to living his teachings. Rather than proclaim himself a leader or creator, Confucius holds to his vocation as teacher and transmitter of ancient wisdom. He denounces titles and honors, in order to more assiduously apply himself to his daily work of inculcating self-control and wisdom in others. Even more resounding is the emphasis throughout Du Halde's work on the Confucian tenet of filial piety. Reverence for one's father and one's ancestors comprises the backbone of Chinese social ethics, and Du Halde hastens to note how such respect infuses the body politic as well:

> If the Chinese policy has taken such great care in regulating the Ceremonies that are to accompany publick and private Duties, and if the Ceremonial is so very exact with relation to these Particulars, it is no wonder that filial Piety should not be forgot, on which, as I have said more than once, the Constitution of the Chinese government depends: Young persons being Witnesses of the Veneration that is paid to deceased Relations, by the Continual Honours that are done to them as if they were yet living, learn betimes what Submission and Obedience they owe to their living Parents: Their ancient Sages were convinc'd that the profound Respect, which Youth are inspired with for their Parents, renders them perfectly submissive, that this Submission preserves Peace in Families, that Peace in private Families produces Tranquillity in Cities, that this Tranquillity prevents Insurrection in the Provinces, and consequently preserves Regularity throughout the Empire.[35]

Du Halde was not the first to remark on the integration of proper familial conduct in Chinese social and political structure. Fifty years earlier a popularization of the teachings of Confucius exhorted Europeans not to keep family morals separate from other realms, but to follow the Middle Kingdom in its expectation of filial obedience from its citizens: "Of all the means that can contribute to introducing virtue in a state, the most efficient and singular is to educate children in paternal devotion; that is to say, in love, respect, and total, uncomplaining submission to their father and mother . . . But we are content to voice this merely in passing, in general discussions of moral conduct, in contrast to [the Chinese, accustomed to] making it the mainstay of their political system and the foundation of good government. For them it is the source of virtue and good morals, from which necessarily follows the happiness of the state."[36]

It was only too easy for Catholic monarchies to appropriate the example China provided of a "rational politics whose principle is identified with individual and familial morality."[37] The Jesuits had already assimilated Chinese subservience to parents and forefathers to Christian obedience to the ultimate Father. Per the divine right of kings, the enlightened monarch was God's stand-in on earth, and yet she or he too was beholden to bow before the legacy of honored predecessors and the dictates of dynastic wisdom. The image of Confucius as an extraordinarily wise but humble, compassionate paternal figure, and the Chinese ideology of family, with its strict obligations to elder and deceased members, generated a form of "sentimental Oriental despotism" that worked well for Catholic absolutist princes.[38] Both they and their subjects could aspire to the conciliatory, self-effacing modesty typical of Confucius, in the interests of a Higher Good — God's desire for the state.

An excellent example of the way thinkers coded Chinese traits as Christian is furnished in Scipione Maffei's treatise against dueling, *Della scienza chiamata cavalleresca* (1710).[39] Maffei cites the Chinese as people whose extremely developed sense of civility prevents them from ever engaging in such inane activity. He elevates the Chinese sense of honor above that of the European, because in the Middle Kingdom shame is perceived in and by the person who commits an offense, not the victim of the offense. The Chinese are not drawn toward violent retribution, and Maffei finds the origin of their propensity for pardon and transcendence in the teachings of Confucius, which he likens to the Catholic principles of forgiveness.[40] The Catholicism believed to be at the heart of Confucian practice is evident throughout Du Halde's text, as he stresses the spiritual nature and the devotional quality of Chinese usages. Enlightened Catholic principalities could exploit this line of proto-rationalist thinking, encouraging their administrations and citizenry to emulate the Christianized mandarin—docile, devout, and above all, dutiful.[41]

Social Traits and Mores

The highly involved ceremony required for so many social and institutional transactions among the Chinese had an enormous influence on European perceptions of their native characteristics. As usual, assessments ranged across the board. The Jesuits and their supporters, as has been shown, connected Chinese formalities to a deep-rooted theological integrity. This view was closely related to the opinion that the intricate, methodical rituals signified cultural sophistication and wisdom, in turn thought to derive from the Celestial Empire's impressive antiquity. Basil Guy notes: "If for a time [the Chinese] ideal knew almost universal acceptance, it was because critics of the day, still bound to traditional modes of thought, preferred a civilized past to primitive innocence, sage to savage, reason to feeling, and so China and the Chinese to all others."[42] Others, however, found the Chinese formalities problematic. For some they were excessive and a sign of cultural rigidity. Bartoli appears to be complimenting what he terms the "cultured and polished customs" of the Chinese, but his tone, and his allusions to idolatry, undercut genuine admiration: "The world has not people of such cultured and polished customs. Even the country folk pride themselves on a certain sense of chivalry. They are extremely delicate in their observances, and even though their ceremonies are innumerable, they guard them so possessively! The reverences made to each individual Chinese make him look like half a divinity. Every reception in the home, every meal, has more ceremony, and comings and goings, than a solemn sacrifice."[43] Francesco Algarotti wrote that spoken Chinese was "a shoreless sea" and that in argumentation the Chinese never came to a close. Their daily habits were fossilized just as their intellectual habits and historical annals were.[44]

Some of those skeptical as to whether Chinese social rituals derived from ingrained moral goodness, saw them instead as simply utilitarian—a practical means to safeguard social order, but devoid of any integral belief in human worth or godly respect.[45] The "manners not morals" argument led to the association of Chinese customs with detrimental superficiality, evident in works such as Alessandro Verri's satire on the affectation of upper-class European society.[46] Verri invoked East Asian ceremonials when he disguised his Italian aristocrats as Chinese, engaged in vacuous (when not unwholesome and unsavory), misguided sociability. The manners Montesquieu ascribed to the Chinese were none-too-flattering as well, even as he tried to avoid ethical evaluation. In *De l'esprit des lois* (1748), his attempt to identify and explain the universal laws responsible for differences among cultures, Montesquieu found the Chinese lazy, cowardly, passive, prone to cheat, and sexually overactive, because of climate and physical terrain.[47] Conditions such as these were best served by a despotic form of government, which contributed (again, by necessity) to the nation's fear-based obedience, depleted intellectual capacity, and the confusion of true morality with mere social custom.

Still others subscribed to the notion that Chinese people were primitive, not advanced, and their usages barbarian, not cultured. Some saw the Chinese as stuck in a childlike stage of development, hence their habits were juvenile.[48] Authors wrote about the horrendous tortures and punishments inflicted in the Middle Kingdom, and on the mentality of deception and thievery endemic to all forms of commercial activity. On the topic of commerce, the plethora of complicated restrictions imposed by the Chinese on trade with Europeans spawned denigration of the Chinese by frustrated English and Dutch merchants.[49] Many put the blame for these defects on China's historical voluntary isolation. Vico impugned its isolationism for having kept China from advancing to the next stage of human development.[50] One recalls his simile, whereby the nation was compared to a sleeping man relegated to a dark and tiny room. Vico's thought, however, recalls the citation of Pietro Verri, who, rather than deleterious isolation, saw economic independence, strength, and self-sufficiency in China, one of few nations with its "eyes open."

The perceptual landscape pertaining to sexual and gender relations in China was somewhat less defined than that of other areas. Some authors characterized Chinese women as extremely chaste, although whether due to women's own valuing of sexual virtue or an outcome of timeworn and dubious custom (the binding of women's feet to restrict their mobility, for example, or the elaborate concealment of brides before marriage), is often unclear. One of the first circulated engravings of a Chinese woman shows her beneath a character meaning "beautiful and refined, in the sense of a secluded woman."[51] Gemelli-Careri adamantly defended Chinese women's innate modesty against Dutch claims about Middle Kingdom prostitutes.[52] The Dutch accusations, however, conformed to Europe's overall assessment of Asian sexual mores, whereby lascivious freedoms ruled the day and enervated the culture. Even if they didn't expand on the idea of China's sexual immorality, plenty of commentators noted that men were polygamous, and concubines abounded, ever ready to lure their targets with all man-

3. Chinese woman. Athanasius Kircher, *China illustrata . . . ,* 1677. Permission of Alderman Library, University of Virginia.

ner of dangerously titillating charms. Observe the following remark by Francesco Carletti: "It was said . . . that [a Chinese official] had had nearly all his concubines, and he had many, fried in oil in copper kettles, . . . because it had been discovered that they were pleasuring themselves with certain appropriate fruits."[53]

MATERIAL CULTURE

With the entrance of material emblems of Chinese culture into Europe at the start of the seventeenth century, the cult of chinoiseries began. Interestingly, Italian states had reproduced Chinese styles as early as the fourteenth century, when silk produced in Lucca imitated designs from Yuan dynasty fabrics, obtained through the Silk Route trade during the time of the Pax Tartarica.[54] Serious continental fashion and market activity did not get going until the 1600s, however, when the reestablishment of direct contact between Europeans and Chinese in the previous century bore fruit in multiple channels of exchange. Dawn Jacobson credits England with putting into motion the chinoiserie craze in Europe, with the founding of the East Indies Trading Company in 1600. The Dutch followed suit only two years later. France, although not until the second half of the century, got into the game as well, with its Compagnie des Indes Orientales.

The vogue sparked by the import deluge of Chinese and other East Asian goods throughout the seventeenth and eighteenth centuries took a variety of different sociocultural paths, however. Scholars of the chinoiserie phenomenon distinguish according to geopolitical and chronological factors, and include among their considerations whether European specimens were strongly imitative or not, aesthetically restrained or flamboyant, appropriated more heartily by aristocratic or commoner populations.[55] The latter aspect has significant parallels with national identity, insofar as chinoiserie in the Catholic absolutist monarchies (France, Italian principalities, Catholic German states, Scandinavia, Spain, and Russia) quickly became an instrument of the ruling ranks, whereas in Protestant constitutional polities (Holland, England), it enjoyed a more meaningful province among the bourgeoisie.[56] These divisions furthermore intersect with the diverse purposes that chinoiserie might serve: it could be employed symbolically, or practically; to communicate fashionability, to entertain, or to provide, or enhance privacy. Different uses, in turn, conditioned which of the arts and what kinds of materials were privileged. For example, tapestries, paintings, frescoes, and other large-scale works lent themselves better to the deployment of Chinese iconography in the symbolic representation of grandeur and power. Porcelain, lacquer, and silver came into play more readily for the smaller-scale objects and furnishings for everyday use in a household. This is not to say there was not a great deal of crossover among the various art forms, materials, and end-uses of chinoiserie. Working from the list of purposes offered above, a few examples should give a basic idea of chinoiserie's many faces in late early modern Europe.

Symbolic Chinoiserie

The exploitation of chinoiserie for its symbolic effects was most overt in seventeenth-century France. Hugh Honour writes:

in the early 1670s the court was in a severe fit of Chinamania . . . [the chinoiserie structures and objects at Versailles] had an associative value readily appreciated by a court which revelled in allegory and thrived on symbolism. . . . however strange and unclassical, Chinese art was recognized as being the product of a mighty empire. And at Versailles where every painting and nearly every decorative device celebrated some aspect of Louis XIV's *gloire*, the oriental objects included in this gigantic and carefully contrived stage set may well have been intended to hint at the monarch's universal sway.[57]

In fact, the first Chinese-inspired building in Europe arose per the orders of Louis XIV. The Trianon de Porcelaine at Versailles was a multi-building pleasure pavilion built in 1670–71 for the king's then-favorite mistress, Madame de Montespan. Though the structures rose no higher than one story, they were covered in magnificent would-be porcelain tile (faience), and it is likely they were arranged to imitate the central courtyard at the Imperial palace in Beijing.[58] A short while later, two Siamese ambassadorial visits to the Sun King's court (1684 and 1686), replete with caseloads of lacquerware, porcelain, and silk, let loose another tidal wave of interest in East Asia, and the Celestial Empire especially. Informal "performances" of China contributed to a number of French court celebrations, where courtiers—and on at least one occasion, the king himself—impersonated figures from the Middle Kingdom in the various balls, masquerades, and *collations* that were part of royal festivities.[59]

The Sun King was able to truly indulge his curiosity about China and assimilate its brilliance with his own through the Jesuit mission team he subsidized in 1685.[60] Charged with forging cultural bonds with the Chinese imperial court, the group of highly skilled astronomer-, geographer-, and mathematician-clerics were enthusiastically welcomed by the Dragon Throne. The K'ang hsi emperor entrusted them with some of his prize projects, such as mapping the empire and systematizing celestial phenomena. Over the next several years the royal French Jesuit connection yielded a bounty of Chinese realia for Louis's court, including paintings, books, and still more artifacts. The abundance of material goods and knowledge about the Chinese is reflected in the famous Beauvais tapestries commissioned in the early eighteenth century.[61] Ten "tentures chinoises" depicted the activities of the Chinese emperor and evoked in their resplendent scenes the French crown's own imperial grandeur.[62] In the mid-1700s another set of tapestries was created at the same factory, this time commissioned by Louis XV. Art historians note a marked change in content and style, insofar as these "reveal the charms of an oriental pastoral life rather than the splendours of a court."[63] But the crown's motive of self-promotion remained viable, as the Boucher-designed silk pictures "offered a relief from the mathematical rigidity of classicism, . . . [and] complemented perfectly the rococo of the age of Louis XV."[64]

French court chinoiserie spread to numerous other kingdoms, inspiring Chinese-styled structures and environments. The following are only the most well-known: Elector Max Emanuel of Bavaria's *Pagodenburg* at Nymphenburg (1716–19); Augustus the Strong's Japanese Palace at Dresden (1715–17); Clemens Augustus of Cologne's *chinesisches Haus* at Brühl (ca. 1750); and in Prussia, Frederick the Great's Chinese teahouse at Potsdam (1754–57). In Vienna, Maria Theresa had several Chinese Rooms built at the Schönbrunn palace; Catherine the Great constructed a Chinese pavilion, a Chinese palace, and a complete Chinese village on various of her estates. The trend continued, from Sweden to Spain.[65]

On the Italian peninsula, the most elaborate monarchical chinoiseries were erected in Naples and Sicily. In the late 1750s Charles III and his wife Maria Amalia of Saxony covered the walls of a room—the subsequent "Salottino cinese"—in the palace at Portici, in over three thousand pieces of porcelain. Ferdinand IV made the next most kingly architectural foray, with his villa La Favorita, also known as the *Palazzina Cinese*, built outside Palermo in 1799. The Grand Duke's quarters at the Pitti Palace in Florence flaunted a beautiful room lined with silk chinoiserie tapestries (1764), and farther north, the Palazzo Reale in Turin boasted a breathtaking lacquer room, designed in the 1730s by no less than renowned architect Filippo Juvarra. It included sixty pieces of imported lacquer, enhanced by fine domestic specimens. These manifestations sprung no doubt from various stimuli. Nevertheless, they all seem to concur that imposing displays of ultra-refined Chinese abundance effectively communicated the strength, wealth, and cultivation of the kingdoms behind them.

Practical Chinoiserie

A more utilitarian mobilization of chinoiserie occurred in the Netherlands, where the Dutch were the first to rigorously experiment with the techniques necessary for porcelain and lacquerware manufacture. Dutch merchants had introduced tea to Europe, creating, among their own countrymen first, a demand for suitable vessels with which to partake in the new beverage practice. The Delftware pottery and dishes produced in Holland in the seventeenth cen-

tury sold all over Europe, and fueled the eighteenth-century institution of porcelain makers in most major cities. Many of these companies were also subsidized (when they weren't expressly founded) by the local court, thus offering an example in which chinoiserie's symbolic valence overlapped with its practical function. A royal administration could benefit from both the prestige attached to porcelain—an exquisite, precious, pure substance that when crafted by fine artisans showed off the monarchy's rarefied status—and the economic payoff to be had from the sale of chinaware to householders avid for modern, useful, and pretty products. The Meissen factory in Saxony (founded in 1710), Du Paquier in Vienna (f. 1719), the royal factory at Sèvres, France (f. 1738), Vezzi and Cozzi in Venice, Doccia in Florence, Capodimonte in Naples, and several makers in England—all participated in the enormous market for porcelain commodities.[66] These were not limited to cups and teapots, moreover, but included a great variety of utensils and everyday accessories, among them toiletry articles, snuffboxes, cane handles, and so on.

Chinoiserie in the form of furniture also got its start in Holland. Due to their early importation of lacquer articles and room furnishings, the Dutch learned to excel at the shiny surface varnishing known as "japanning." The diffusion of lacquer chests, mirrors, and other such objects throughout Europe followed a similar pattern as that of porcelain goods.

Fashionable Chinoiserie

Obviously, alongside the patrician's desire to vaunt power and a bourgeois woman's wish for a serviceable teapot, lay an interest in keeping up with trends. Chinese objects, forms, and graphics acquired enormous fashion prestige. In terms of clothing, the pagoda sleeve became the rage for both men and women, joined by other modes of tailoring (the reverse scallop neckline, for example) that mimicked Chinese dress. Apparel made from Chinese silk or other Asian fabrics constituted the ideal, but in their stead, style-conscious patrons sought material printed or embroidered with dragons, birds, and other flora and fauna associated with the Celestial Empire. Chinese-looking designs decorated all things from wigstands to fireplace screens. Especially attractive were items brand new to Europeans, such as fans, wallpaper, and the parasol, which combined novelty, fashion currency, and usefulness. Whether purely decorative or functional, chinoiseries frequently operated as an elite badge, a form of "cultural snobbism," that, thanks to the period's prodigious advancements in fabrication, wide ranges of people could assume.[67] The "Grand Pagoda" and other buildings in the Chinese style erected in the Royal Gardens at Kew, London (1761) offer a good example of the magical appeal of chinoiserie. Jacobson writes that Chambers's numerous structures provided "diversions to suit all tastes" and their images were reproduced in paintings, prints, and chintzes.[68]

Numerous how-to manuals helped spread the craze for Chinese decoration. As early as 1624 a Dutch treatise on embroidering included Chinese figures.[69] Instructional works then appeared to aid craftspeople dedicated to Chinese modes in lacquering, ceramics, dressmaking, architecture, and gardening.[70] The pictorial designs in these works often reprise those in the broader-ranging genre of engravers' manuals, that is, collections of illustrations and motifs for embellishing everything and anything, from fabric to porcelain to wood to metal to paper to canvas to plaster walls.[71] Engravers' books in turn drew from the works of painters who experimented with Chinese scenes, and included Tiepolo, Watteau, Boucher, and Pillement. Their canvases, panels, and frescoes can all eventually be traced back to the first published illustrations of Chinese life, in the travel accounts and general descriptions. The aim of this summary treatment of Chinese iconography is to point out the very dense and active discourse—two- and three-dimensional, visual and textual—pertaining to the Middle Kingdom in eighteenth-century Europe. Images, objects, and verbal references spoke to one another in a complex network, one which implicated most Europeans to one degree or another.

Entertaining Chinoiserie

The entertainment capacity of chinoiseries reveals yet another cultural niche carved out by material sinomania. Deferring for the moment the discussion of stage entertainments, Chinese realia outside the theater provided diversion to spectators and users in a variety of ways. Guy notes the enjoyment derived from the perceived ugliness of Chinese porcelain figurines:

> . . . especially among the wealthy, there was an obsessive desire to acquire imported art objects, purchased at considerable expense without thought of using them in some practical way but merely because of their strangeness. Chinese "magots" were only too well characterized as ugly; but they were also appreciated because of their ugliness, contrasting so cleverly in their enigmatic and absurd attitudes with the harmonious conception and setting of life in the neo-classic period in France. Convenient symbols of the strangeness of a civilization too

recently revealed to be understood completely, they were eagerly sought during most of the eighteenth century for collections both large and small. Frequently offered as gifts because of their small size and delicate colouring, they soon became an indispensable decoration of the salon where they could be admired or mocked by the more spirited members of any fashionable gathering.[72]

The playful, comic potential attributed by Europeans to Chinese culture surfaces in depictions of Chinese figures cavorting with stock characters from the commedia dell'arte. Claude Gillot, for example, in designs for an arabesque, has fiddle-playing harlequins and trapeze artists dangling near cross-legged Chinese idols.[73] An even greater risibile quotient is suggested by paintings of Chinese being waited on by monkeys, who not only wear imperial robes, but also assume positions common to those of Middle Kingdom figures in other standard chinoiseries illustrations. While Jacobson is careful to explain that the origins of eighteenth-century *singeries* far predate the emergence of the China obsession, and that simians may simply have been a novel update on the classical fauns and *putti* of Renaissance ornament, the conflation of mandarin and monkey points to the ludic, recreational charge inherent in certain renderings.[74]

Private Chinoiserie

Chinese icons and styling belonged especially to the realm of the private. The many Chinese kiosks, carousels, *delizie*, follies, gazebos, and teahouses often formed part of what royal and aristocratic patrons termed "solitudes," or places they could repair to to relax, escape their formal duties, and be themselves. The fad of decorating the interiors of villas with frescoes of Chinese life also falls in this category, since the transports of a Chinese panorama would be enjoyed at home, likely within an intimate circle of family and friends. Italian villas all through the peninsula followed this trend, with the Veneto country houses in the lead. Whether inside one's personal pagoda, contemplating the delicate fresco on one's villa wall, at one's toilette, or lounging in a bedchamber, the Chinese-ified atmosphere lent itself to a sense of freedom and lightened strictures.

EVENTS AND PRACTICES

The China craze infiltrated the momentous occasions and ordinary activities of eighteenth-century Europeans as well. Diplomatic and trade embassies to

China come to mind first, although for anyone but participants they had to be experienced secondhand, in reports and sometimes in paintings and engravings made to commemorate them. Visitors from China to Europe, on the other hand, offered onlookers firsthand exposure to citizens and customs of the Celestial Empire. The most common type of Chinese guest was the newly converted Jesuit novitiate, brought to Europe in the entourage of his missionary mentor. As early as 1652 one of these converts arrived in Venice, accompanying Polish Jesuit Michael Boym on one of his return trips to Europe to raise funds and publicize the mission.[75] The two Siamese embassies to Paris in 1684 and 1686 have been noted above. Honour notes that though they spread Chinese fever throughout Paris and its provinces, to make sure that China and not Siam became the rallying cry of his compatriots, Father Couplet, one of the major China Jesuits, "countered" the first Siamese embassy by bringing a young boy from Nanking with him to the capital in 1685. Couplet introduced Mikelh Xin to the French court, where he had an audience with the king. The two then traveled to Rome and England. The *Mercure galante* described the youth's dress, and at least one portrait was done, with prints sold to the public.[76] Numerous other young Chinese men toured Europe with their Jesuit patrons throughout the century.[77] They visited Rome and Paris, principally, and in a short time Naples joined the network.

In 1723, Neapolitan Matteo Ripa returned to Europe from China, bringing with him four Chinese novitiates and one Chinese teacher. Ripa was a Catholic lay priest and painter, who, after having studied the Chinese language at the Rome College of the Society of Jesus, had been sent to the Middle Kingdom in 1710 on behalf of the *Propaganda Fide*. He stayed in China for twelve years, working closely with the imperial functionaries. While in Peking, Ripa established a school there for the training of Chinese clergy. The school was opposed by the Jesuits, who resented the encroachment on their missionary authority. Finally, feeling too beleaguered by the hostility of his Jesuit colleagues, Ripa returned to Naples with plans to continue his conversion work from there. In 1732 he founded the Collegio della Sacra Famiglia, in short order renamed the Collegio de' Cinesi, a school for the training of future Chinese priests.[78] From this point on Naples became the normal point of entry into Europe for Chinese seminarians.

Practices involving China ranged from the private and personal to the public and formal. Tea drinking and lacquering became tremendously popular activities, among both high and middle classes. As mentioned, French court activities incorporated a great deal of Chinese festival, and more significant occasions felt the Chinese influence as well. Louis XIV kicked off the new year of the new century (1700) with Chinese festivities, and subsequently a number of European monarchs reenacted the k'eng-chi ritual, or customary first plowing of the earth each spring by the Chinese emperor. Voltaire praised the rite, and enlightened despots from Louis XV in 1756 to Joseph II of Austria copied the custom.[79]

Italy, because of its penchant for spectacle, took full advantage of the theatrical and celebratory possibilites offered by chinoiserie. Honour puts it best:

> Italians naturally took full advantage of the annual carnival to indulge their fancy for rich oriental costumes, and in the weeks preceding Lent many a bedragonned domino was to be found strutting through the Venetian *ridotti*, sauntering along the Arno in Florence, or stalking around the piazze of Rome. Chinoiserie also played a prominent part in the elaborately contrived spectacles for which Italy was so famous. When Augustus the Strong visited Venice in 1716, for example, he was greeted by a junk bristling with parasols, carrying an exotic cargo of Chinese singers, dancers and musicians, and propelled down the Grand Canal by coolie gondoliers. At Turin *tableaux vivants* of such subjects as the triumph of the Pagod and the Emperor of China were drawn through the straight streets of the city in carnival processions. The *pensionnaires* of the Académie de France in Rome donned oriental attire for the carnival parade along the Corso. And chinoiserie set pieces were frequently used for firework displays, notably those given in Rome on the *Festa della Cinea*.[80]

EIGHTEENTH-CENTURY EXOTICISM, CHINA, AND ITALIAN OPERA

At its most basic, exoticism issues from the notion of difference, and some form of fascination with or desire for difference.[81] It requires the acknowledgment of and value judgments about difference, or otherness, and involves questions such as: What constitutes otherness? Which types of alterity are more and less sought, and why? In what ways does a given society (or sector of a society) satisfy its desire for the other? The answers to these questions, of course, depend on myriad factors.[82] Studies of Western exoticism tend to privilege the chronological quotient, differentiating the substance and workings of exoticism in different time periods. Exoticism in classical times might be exemplified by the Roman emperor Nero's mania for Hellenic culture; in the Middle Ages the demonic other (the Saracens, for example) is desired only to extirpate it. For many, exoticism arose only in the nineteenth century, concomitant with Romanticism. A deeply felt anxiety to escape oneself and one's times motivated the interest in other times and places.[83] According to this line of thinking, exoticism before this moment signified merely the "quiet integration of new things, superfluous and capricious importation, indulgent curiosity or the snobbish obsession with worldly living," and not the wish to "evade the ordinary, confront one's consciousness, and mythicize oneself as a corrupt, restless soul."[84] This is a fairly limiting view of exoticism, however. More telling insights ensue when one considers enthrallment with otherness as shaped by a variety of cultural contingencies.

Scholars of eighteenth-century exoticism, following on the Romanticism-oriented conception above, often assign it a certain innocence. In their study of Enlightenment exoticism, G. S. Rousseau and Roy Porter observe that Europeans in the eighteenth century had attained an unprecedented "cultural maturity," an ephemeral "moment of equilibrium" before the West began its imperial domination over Eastern empires: "Europe . . . was sufficiently self-critical and free from bigotry to be able to confront other cultures, admittedly not as equals, nor even necessarily on their own terms, but at least as alternative versions of living— . . . before the logic of the white man's mission required they be subordinated, eviscerated and destroyed."[85] The assessment of maturity also issues from the idea that the eighteenth century was no longer mired in the monolithic, God-centered cosmography of medieval and earlier early modern epochs. The new science had evolved enough to dispel—or at least lay serious suspicion on—belief in fantastical exotic lands and magical, supernatural beings, be they monsters or men. The period has therefore acquired, in the minds of modern critics, a certain intellectual integrity. Its modern epistemological approach based in observation, experiment, and exacting mathematical or other proto-scientific applications, gave eighteenth-century European exoticism a firmer footing, when compared with that of previous ages.

The innocence, on the other hand, of eighteenth-century exoticism is predicated on later events. Tzvetan Todorov contrasts the morally worthy humanism of Rousseau and Montesquieu with its "deviations" and "distortions" in the nineteenth century.[86] Rana Kabbani finds the narrative voice in eighteenth-century travel literature nowhere as authoritative or ambitious as that of its nineteenth-century counterpart,

"whose scope was imperial."[87] The less-suspect nature of eighteenth-century European exoticism stems from its being untainted with nineteenth-century racism, imperialism, nationalism, colonialism, and the industrial technologies that emerged therein. Even Edward Said appears to let the eighteenth century off the hook, by siting the objects of his criticism of orientalist practices in the nineteenth century.[88] The issue of orientalism shall be addressed shortly.

For the moment, let us return to what Rousseau and Porter have identified as the principal (but not terribly culpable) limitations of eighteenth-century European representations of non-European peoples: they offered only highly stylized and crude stereotypes, they were motivated by a "potent unifying and universalizing drive" based on the "edifying faith that there [was] one single family of mankind," and they were largely self-reflexive and not genuinely or adequately interested in the "other."[89] In one way or another, these alleged flaws proceed from the supposition that truth and accuracy is the attainable goal in representation. Accuracy involves completeness (stereotypes are incomplete representations at best), and the absence of preconceived notions or epistemological structures (one cannot objectively assess an "other" if one seeks to fit it into a certain paradigm, e.g., that there was a single family of man). The third limitation speaks also to objectivity, though in an indirect way. One cannot accurately represent an other unless one focuses on the other sufficiently. The reference to "genuine" interest in the other also brings up the question of motivation and sincerity. In Rousseau and Porter's schema, it is unseemly to represent an alien entity only to refer to oneself. Mobilizations of others must be concerned—adequately, properly— with the other. On the other hand, a multitude of critics absolve eighteenth-century exoticism from any wrongdoing precisely *because* it was not deeply engaged with the other. For these thinkers, the obsession with non-European others was no more than a superficial fashion craze and/or innocuous recreation, and, since innocent recreation intends no harm, it did not result in harm. In fact, the implication seems to be that it did not result in anything. We have arrived squarely at the question of orientalism.

Juxtaposing Saidian orientalism with the China operas opens an interesting pocket of inquiry. Said said he was not interested in representational "truth" per se, but rather in institutional and representational practices that amount to systems which exploit that which is represented.[90] These systems embody and furthermore propagate unjust power relationships, to the great benefit of their originators. This admittedly simplified encapsulation of orientalism can be investigated with respect to the Italian China operas. Are their representations of China involved in systems of this sort? As mentioned, some maintain that the orientalist "machine" as defined by Said was not yet operative in the eighteenth century.[91] Others contend the opposite, exhorting that though the machine may have had different parts and mechanisms, it was as pernicious in the eighteenth century as in successive (and even earlier) ages.[92] My answer falls between these positions. The ambivalence is determined by several factors: chronology, the particular contingencies of the Italian states at that time, and those of opera itself.

Timing and the Explosion of Plurality in Europe

Chronology does play a role in the question of orientalism. Beside the fact that certain developments that would so squarely facilitate racist and colonialist systems had not yet taken root in the eighteenth century, it was also a period of tremendous cultural transformation precisely in terms of othernesses. The Settecento can be characterized as one which witnessed an explosion of categories of difference. Shattering ruptures to traditional knowledge had begun much earlier, with the geographic discoveries of the sixteenth and seventeenth centuries. The realities revealed by these voyages then met with (and in part produced) the embrace of Reason in the seventeenth century. The ideology and practice of rationality reconfigured the world dramatically, organizing known and fresh data into a host of new classifications. It is fair to say that this process peaked in the eighteenth century. The accretion of knowledge and new epistemological methodologies for handling that knowledge produced an unprecedented quantity of othernesses. The criteria for evaluating the new societies now known to Europeans included geographical location, physical traits, religious characteristics, government type, language, and social customs. Genealogy, always an important consideration, plumped up from its conventional determination of blood nobility within European spheres to include biblical ancestry (descended from Adam or not? descended from Noah or not, and which branch?), civilizational age (more or less ancient?), and continental origins (African, Asian, or American?). Internally as well, Europe experienced a surge in kinds of identities. Apart from the proliferation of new religious affiliations, new social classes arose in tandem with new trades and professions, which in turn impinged on the aristocracy, creating new orders and levels of nobility. One could say that

identity politics really came to the fore in the eighteenth century. The period saw an extraordinary increase in the diversity of ways in which to be diverse. It should come as no surprise that so many of the dance spectacles featured multitudes of global peoples (*ballerini* dressed in foreign costume) flitting about the stage. The *ballet des nations* would seem to have been, at least in part, about diversity itself.[93]

The eighteenth century, as a later phase of the early modern period, stands as a window between the less diverse fifteenth and sixteenth centuries, where Catholic faith was all, and the nineteenth century, which largely collapsed the multitude of differences into the positivist scientific apparatus of race, in order to comprehend—or master—a global populace. Such a characterization of the eighteenth century is somewhat different, however, from Rousseau and Porter's above. It pivots less on moral qualification and more on historical accident. That is, the period was not so much "culturally mature" and "free from bigotry" as it was simply coming to first terms with a banquet of difference. Perhaps, as well, the more distinctions there were, the less potent each one was, singly, to threaten hegemonies. By the nineteenth century, the accumulation of so many and such novel human variations had ebbed, and the systems devised to understand and organize them came to be used for agendas more national than universal.

As mentioned above, the other chief factors that conditioned the orientalist element in the eighteenth-century Italian Chinese operas were: the contemporary contingencies of the Italian states, and the nature of Settecento opera. Before probing these areas, however, it will be helpful to point out how the Chinese were perceived in Europe in the context of other Asian peoples. This discussion underscores not only the popularity of and precise knowledge about the Celestial Kingdom that existed in the period (as has been shown above), but also the distinct profile the Chinese enjoyed with respect to other non-European cultures east of the European continent.

The Multidimensional Particularity of China

Within the spectrum of societies living in lands to the east of the European continent, the Chinese stood out more than might be expected. This is despite the fact that scholars of chinoiserie repeatedly remind us of how little the chinaware of the seventeenth and eighteenth centuries had to do with China. The porcelain especially, but in fact, many other objects and decorations that Europeans associated with the Celestial Empire, were more or less ingenious artistic agglomerates of Asian and European elements. The pastiche syndrome extended even to dress, when an eighteenth-century Italian women's journal described one of its featured garments as "a Turkish-style dress made of light blue Pekin."[94] Pagodas depicted or contructed in European venues may well have combined architectural elements from Chinese, Indian, and Siamese traditions.[95] Finally, vaudeville lyrics from the first documented French stage production in which China appears present a fine example of hybridity, this one quite bizarre and apparently born of either glaring ignorance or intentional absurdity. Harlequin, masked as a Chinese doctor, unveils a cabinet in which sits Mezzetino, dressed as a porcelain idol. Mezzetino breaks into a song which begins: "I come straight from Congo, ho, ho, ho."[96] Based on this data, it is easy to imagine that the Chinese on the eighteenth-century opera stage were more or less indistinguishable from other characters marked as Asian. However, this was generally not the case.

The writings on which librettists based their works contained surprisingly accurate information. Guy noted in 1963: "we may say now that Europe's knowledge of China during the seventeenth and eighteenth centuries was as exact as that of any since."[97] As has been remarked, accuracy is not the crucial issue, but the significant fact is that the writings on the Celestial Empire available to eighteenth-century dramaturgs furnished enough discrete information to allow stage Chinese to stand out from other Asian characters. This is not to say that the others—Turks, Persians, Arabians, Indians, and Tartars—all blended into a common Eastern populace. To an extent, each nation or people had a set of traits by which Europeans recognized them. In the spectrum of Asian cultures, however, Chinese protagonists were not only recognizable, but also bore a deeper, "thicker" collection of connotations for readers and audiences. They were more multifaceted, and the facets Europeans associated with China were more relevant to contemporary concerns. As a signifier for eighteenth-century Europeans, the Chinese occupied a unique position compared to other Asian peoples.

A few fundamental similarities united Turks, Persians, Arabians, certain Mongol tribes, Indians, and others (Armenians, Bohemians), and opposed them to the Chinese. On a purely geographical basis, the former occupied regions to the immediate east of Europe, whereas the Chinese, and to a lesser degree the Indians, were much more distant. Spatial proximity translated naturally to the continent's greater familiarity with the near Asian peoples, especially the Ottomans, with whom Europeans had had various

relations for many centuries.[98] Excepting Tartary, the next prominent aspect that separated China from the Levantine territories was the Muslim religion. Turkish, Persian, Arab, and Indian cultures were all viewed as part of the "infidel empire." P. S. Marshall and Glyndwr Williams note that despite fledgling appreciation among scholars of the diversity of Islamic societies, in late seventeenth-century Europe

Muhammad was still portrayed in the terms used by his Christian detractors for centuries as a power-crazed fanatic, or to some as an instrument of the devil, who had carefully manufactured a set of religious beliefs from Jewish and Christian doctines communicated to him by renegades. He was a man of deplorable moral standards, but by cunning, including the forging of miracles and offers to his followers of sensual gratification both on earth and in heaven, he had deluded the Arabs into accepting his divine mission. The Arabs had then exploited the weakness and divisions of their neighbors, including the Eastern Christians, to extend their empire. For his inscrutable purposes God had chosen the Muslims to be the punishment for the sins of Christians. For the same reason he still allowed the great Islamic empires of Turkey, Persia and Mughal India to continue in being.[99]

Geography and faith combined in the case of traditional Christian enmity toward Islam, where since the Middle Ages the term "Turks" could indicate generic Muslims, and the European crusade was both ideological (Christianity) and territorial (Christendom).[100]

Hostility between Europe and its closest and therefore most threatening Islamic power, the Ottoman Turks, had a parallel in the violence perceived to be endemic to the abovementioned cultures. The Ottoman empire's ravages, the Tartar hordes' legendary slaughters, and the history of vicious wars these peoples had waged among themselves through time (the Mongols versus the Turks in the fourteenth century, the Turks versus the Persians), formed yet a third common denominator that divided these cultures from the Chinese in the European mind. Their alleged penchant for aggression, brutality, and bloodshed nourished European tragic genres. The height of Ottoman imperial sway influenced Tasso's tragic epic *Gerusalemme liberata* (1581), but the profane cruelties of the infidel had their most compelling realization on the tragic stage. Major early modern works such as Marlowe's *Tamburlaine* (1587), Bonarelli's *Solimano* (1620), Racine's *Bajazet* (1672), and Voltaire's *Zaïre* (1732) and *Mahomet* (1742), all turned on fearsome, fanatical Tartar, Turkish, or other Muslim characters. These and other works took their place in the long European literary tradition of religious and political conflict between Christianity and Islam, a tradition doubly galvanized by the fires of the Counter-Reformation.

Europeans eventually acquired more discriminating knowledge of the religions of Asian regions. Travelers' reports and scholarly histories unveiled facts about differing sects of Islam, Zoroastrianism in Persia, Hinduism in southern India, and the type of Buddhism native to the Tartars in central and eastern Asia.[101] These differentiations were part and parcel of the growing precision in the period's knowledge about the world. Paolo Preto, writing about eighteenth-century Venetian theatrical representations of the Turk, credits this precision to the willingness to research the "historic truth," and to move from "generic orientalizing exoticism or from the conventional *turcheria* to a more balanced representation of Turkish customs and society."[102]

Looking specifically at Turkey, one must begin with Venice, as Venice was central to the European image of Turkey up to 1800. Its location on the easternmost edge of Europe, its possessions, its long history of commercial and diplomatic relations with the Ottoman Empire, and its role as "the press office of Europe," resulted in its becoming a kind of public relations middleman between its eastern and western neighbors.[103] The astounding territorial achievements of the Ottoman Empire in the fifteenth and sixteenth centuries stimulated a burst of Venetian publications treating Turkish history.[104] In their portrayals of the past and present Turk, authors had to steer a course between recognition of religious heresy and admiration of a culture that had benefited Venetian citizens, namely via well-established economic and political collaborations. The wave of interest in Turkish culture rose in the Venetian republic in the late sixteenth and early seventeenth centuries and swept through parts of Europe, even as stalwart foes, like Rome, remained intransigent. In 1660, a second wave picked up speed when France increased its state-sponsored voyages to the region and initiated colonialist projects in the East. These and the many missionary and diplomatic endeavors undertaken also at this time, generated prodigious written accounts containing richer, more concrete material.[105]

The augmented data together with the decreasing status of the Ottoman Empire on the world stage account for a change in general perceptions of the Turkish figure. His image became less negative, turning from the invincible, terrible Turk into an alternately romanticized, feminized, comical, innocuous Turk.[106] Molière and Lully's comedy-ballet *Le bourgeois gentilhomme* (1670) supports the contention that by 1685

Turkey had passed from the tragic to the comic in French literature and drama, proof of its loss of standing in European eyes.[107]

Persians, like the Turkish, practiced the infidel faith, but Europeans granted them certain concessions. Persia had once been a part of Alexander's empire, so it enjoyed an association with Greek antiquity that mitigated its non-Europeanness. The power that the Hellenic connection wielded for Europeans is revealed in a line from Metastasio's 1751 opera *Il re pastore*, which contrasts the "barren" regions of Asia with those that have known Alexander's civilizing influence. Rueful about the current state of his country, one character says to another: "Asia has not yet seen other Alexanders."[108] Persian despotism was looked upon as milder than that of the Ottomans, insofar as the Persian kings were thought to be kinder to their subjects than the ruthless sultans. Overall the nation was more favorably depicted as more civilized, more learned, and more artistically developed than its Turkish counterpart. Jean Chardin, author of *Voyages de monsieur le chevalier Chardin en Perse et autres lieux de l'orient* (1711) and the greatest eighteenth-century disseminator of information about Persia, called its residents the "most civilized people of the East . . . upon a level with the politest men of Europe."[109] The architectural beauty of the city of Isfahan, and its magnificent artistic and literary works, received special notice.

Indians were less known to eighteenth-century Europeans than the aforementioned peoples, although as of the mid-sixteenth century, the arrival of Portuguese explorers and missionaries to the coastal and inland areas put the Mughal empire into a growing library of works on Asian countries. The northern part of the subcontinent was Muslim, and thus another party to the infidel, while Europeans discovered the practice of Hinduism in the southern regions. Hinduism both intrigued and repulsed Europeans, who initially tried to find Greek ancestral links with the modern Brahmins. The local caste system garnered much attention in European writings, as did the frugal, industrious, and submissive nature of the people. The European authority on the Mughal empire, François Bernier (*Voyage dans les Etats du Grand Mogol*, 1670), judged it a rich land vastly underutilized, and hence wasted, by tyrannical kings.[110]

The lands of Tartary, also known as Mongolia, covered an enormous mass of central Asia. European familiarity with the Mongols extended to those who had impinged directly on territories nearer to the European continent, such as the legendary thirteenth-century invader Genghis Khan, and the fourteenth-century warlord Timur Leng (Tamerlane), as well as to figures farther away, namely Kublai Khan, immortalized in Marco Polo's famous account. Although Polo's stories were soaked in the fantastical, their picture of the fearless, callous Tartar held sway for a long time. The nomadic hordes were considered ruthless warriors, expert archers on horseback, and imbibers of horse's blood when without other recourse. Some Europeans thought they were cannibals.[111] Because the Tartars had such an immediate presence in China's affairs in the seventeenth and eighteenth centuries, they will be treated in greater detail in other sections of this book.[112]

The Asian peoples known to eighteenth-century Europeans were thus fairly well individuated. Among the groups, however, the Chinese had a very clear profile. Paul Hazard puts it succinctly: "even more than the noble savage, the wise Egyptian, the Muslim Arab, than the mocking Turk or Persian, the Chinese philosopher enchanted those who urged the arrival of a new order."[113] China was more than just the land of the reformist philosopher, however. The Middle Kingdom enchanted because it was so many things, to so many different kinds of people. It was thought to have the most functional despotism, "quite unlike the capricious despotism of the Muslim regimes in Turkey, Persia or India."[114] The Chinese appeared less heretical than other non-European peoples, so much so that even a Protestant could write: "Of all the heathen sects which are come into the knowledge of those in Europe, we have not read of any who are fallen into fewer errours than the Chineses, ever since the first ages; for in their books we read that these people have worshipp'd the highest and one God-head."[115] For some, the Chinese appeared in possession of a contemporary wealth, wisdom, and progressive energy that contrasted sharply with the decadence associated with other Asian societies. Marshall and Williams observe that Europeans held Turkish governance responsible for the decline of scholarly dignity in all Arab lands. "Arab astronomy had degenerated into Turkish astrology," and "commentators believed that lands which had once been prosperous and fertile in Biblical and classical times were now wretchedly impoverished by Turkish rule."[116] For others, even if China's Dragon Throne outshone other Asian societies, it posed sorry competition to European achievements. Still others found a host of middle-range traits that could be shepherded in the service of discrete needs.

Facts and perceptions about China, more than those of other non-European cultures, facilitated European cultural work in the eighteenth century. How-

ever, the mobilization of China by Italians was more flexible, and more multifaceted than that of other Europeans, given the unique political constitution of the peninsula.

Diversity among the Italian States

The degree of difference among the states that formed the Italian peninsula is frequently underestimated in studies of eighteenth-century Europe. In 1748, when the Wars of Succession had finally subsided, most of Europe entered what would be nearly half a century of relative peace. The political configuration of each of the major European powers settled in: England's constitutional monarchy, and absolute monarchies in France, Spain, Prussia, and the Habsburg empire. Italian terrain, however, counted more than eleven different states, representing not only diverse governmental forms, but also various ties to dominant European powers. Absolutism on the Spanish model was practiced in the Kingdoms of Naples and Sicily, and on the Habsburg imperial model in the Duchy of Milan and the Grand Duchy of Tuscany. The Papal States bowed to an ecclesiastical sovereignty which exhibited notable variance from other monarchies in its visions and methods. Venice, Genoa, and Lucca each called themselves republics, but actually empowered elite, conservative oligarchies. Authoritarian regalism held sway in the Kingdom of Sardinia, under the regime of the House of Savoy. Due to dynastic intermarriage, the small Duchy of Parma had two major spheres of influence, France and Spain, while the Duchy of Modena carved out yet another unique political and cultural mold. At the same time as it retained many ancient feudal traditions under its long-time Este governance, Modena also implemented new amalgams of state administration. Duke Francesco III of the Este dynasty "took his inspiration from the great monarchies of Europe and at the same time introduced an institutional principle to be found in republics—[for example] in Venice—that of the periodic rotation of the chief political posts." Modena's state organization was "only paralleled by that of France and Great Britain."[117]

Such a multifarious assortment of state structures and ideologies produced (as they were produced by) widely diverging cultural characteristics within each polity. Solidarity or friction among social classes, cooperation between the crown and the various sectors, status of the intellectual, influence of the church and its representatives, development of civil society, of secular government, of trade—these were only a few of the points of divergence one finds among the Italian states in the eighteenth century. Grand Tourists as well noted the heterogeneity of Settecento Italy, singling out for closer examination the states "whose constitution included a republican component," or contrasting the apparent progress in Milan and Tuscany with the stagnancy of the Papal States.[118]

The lack of centralization in the Italian peninsula meant the absence of certain forces that could only emanate from powerful controlling capitals like London and Paris. These ruling metropolises effected not only a certain conformity among their satellite cities, but also a more unilateral elaboration of China across those centers. In England, for example, a strong constitutional government and a galloping national trade enterprise resulted in a double-edged perception of the Middle Kingdom in the eighteenth century. On the one hand, Britons appreciated China's impressive political order, focusing on its commonalities with the strength and effectiveness of the English parliamentary government. Confucianism was appreciated more for its guarantee of civil hierarchies and social harmony than for its moral essence. The constitutional structure of the English monarchy obviously lessened the appeal of Confucianism from the "benevolent patriarch" angle, but the more significant reason for this absence in English spheres came from the nation's fundamental antipathy toward Catholicism and Confucianism's close association with the Jesuits. On the other hand, England's sea trade prowess and its burgeoning domestic economy closed its mind to the beneficial attributes of Chinese culture. Reports from the failed China trade embassies of Captains Weddel (1636), Dampier (1687–88), Anson (1740–44), and finally Lord McCartney (1792), fed an English image of China as arrogant, supremely condescending, and deaf to any sort of meaningful exchange with would-be merchant collaborators.

In France, the megalomania of the absolute monarchy under Louis XIV most conditioned the reception of China. Here too, it had a dual characteristic, although more temporally oriented. The Celestial Kingdom was initially glorified as an eastern double of the magnificence and functionality of Louis's reign. This figuration imbricated a number of French self-images under the aegis of the Sun King. Geographic expanse, political reach, prized erudition, economic riches, Catholic authority, personal charisma of the ruler, and mass obeisance of his subjects—all of these royal attributes were thought to be mirrored in the glories of the Celestial Empire, especially as narrated by the motivated Parisian Jesuits of the late seventeenth and early eighteenth century. Their continued commitment to present Confucianism as orthodox Christian-

ity *in nuce* meshed well with the crown's staunch absolutist ideology relevant to the divine right of kings. Ironically, however, Louis XIV's heavy-handedness contributed to the backfire of the Jesuit strategy of encomium, and thus the second phase of the French elaboration of China. French libertine thinkers instrumentalized Confucianism to counter the autocratic oppression of the royalist administration in the political and nearly every other arena. The desire for liberty from authoritarianism, in potent combination with the rationalist tenor of the times, led to the *philosophes'* China: a living, breathing, enlightened example of deistic morality, political efficacy, economic wisdom, and public happiness—all due to Chinese reverence for *secular* intellectual values.

The idea of China as offering release from constricting ideologies bore itself out in the plastic arts as well. Again, the unitary nature of the dominant European nations inflected this process. In England, Chinese-styled art, architecture, and decorative objects challenged a tired classicist poetics.[119] In France, Chinese elements explicitly deployed in Louis XIV's Baroque classicism morphed, almost in the blink of an eye, into the lighter, brighter, playful exuberance of the Rococo design characteristic of the more lax reigns of Louis's successors.

The Italian states received many of the products of these movements, and faced a number of the same sociocultural realities. However, these realities did not coalesce to bring about a more or less national mediation of China. Because of the diversity among and within the Italian territories, their elaborations of the Middle Kingdom spanned a wider, more variegated arc. By this propensity alone, the China operas are less orientalist. Lastly, opera itself, a uniquely Italian genre, and unique in its capacities to engage both its subject matter and audiences, must be considered in gauging the orientalist component of eighteenth-century representations of the Celestial Empire.

Eighteenth-Century Italian Opera and the Exotic

Assessing the connections between orientalism and eighteenth-century Italian operas focused on China requires traveling in relatively uncharted waters, since most studies of orientalism and opera tend to comment on nineteenth-century manifestations.[120] Furthermore, the work currently being done on early modern opera featuring non-European cultures uses the term "exoticism" rather than "orientalism."[121] This in itself may be indicative of a general belief that orientalist practices are not relevant with respect to seventeenth- and eighteenth-century Italian *melo-*

drammi. In any case, taking all Italian theatrical forms into consideration, scholars agree that the most intensive exploitation of exotic locales and characters took place on the opera stage.

Already in the seventeenth century, *drammi per musica* set in or featuring protagonists from Persian, Egyptian, Turkish, Armenian, North African, and other extra-European spheres played to audiences increasingly enamored of spectacle.[122] Aesthetically speaking, the foregrounding of real individuals from a geographic panorama derived from a shift that occurred initially in the spoken tragedy. Over the course of the seventeenth century, tragedians sought material less and less from mythology and religious subjects, and more and more from histories (ancient and modern), and other accounts of distant but contemporary peoples. These latter texts included sociohistorical tracts, travel narratives, and the mass of baroque novels crammed with extra-European heroics. Seicento *romanzi* and *tragedie* were habitually adapted for the opera stage.

Love of visual and aural marvels continued in the eighteenth century, but now additional reasons nourished opera's growing embrace of the exotic. Desire for commercial gain ranked high, naturally, and critics identify two other significant motivations for Settecento theatrical exoticism: 1) it allowed dramatists to forge innovatory poetics, and 2) it provided a safe haven in which to essay risky subject matter. It must be clarified that these reasons have been cited mainly in regard to Italian spoken theater, and in particular, to the eighteenth-century exotic comedy.[123] However, this thinking is instructive for opera as well. Moreover, it pushes beyond the perspective still held by many scholars of Italian Settecento opera, who see exoticism simply as a reflection of the times (Jean-François Lattarico calls the Settecento "hyper-exoticized"), in combination with a public obsessed with the sensational.[124] Such a view restricts operatic exoticism to superficial exercise, and misses the ways in which it mediated significant social, political, and cultural developments. In this regard, the second point made about exotic spoken plays is especially relevant.[125] The idea that a foreign universe provided a more secure environment in which to treat delicate or dangerous topics infers that the exotic opened a space otherwise unavailable, in which an opera could do its work. Such space wasn't a vacuum, however — depending on which foreign culture occupied the spotlight, particular meaning entered the void. In other words, distinct knowledge of and/or perceptions about exotic peoples furnished discrete entrées into pressing topics. Consider Goldoni's Persian trilogy,

which dramatized the saga of a young man caught between a parentally ordained spouse, and his preferred partner, a slave girl in his harem. Given what was known about Persian familial custom, a drama enacted there could more effectively take up the marriage crisis provoked by the love triangles so endemic to the eighteenth-century Italian upper class. Manlio Stocchi writes:

> In Europe, or at least in Venice, an extra-marital relationship still didn't have the force to impose itself as a viable alternative to the recognized marriage, in a plausible on-stage treatment of such matters. Moral rights and privileges belonged always and indisputably to only one side, while the other party had neither valid arguments nor institutional mandates to cite or renounce, in heroic or insolent acts of self-denial. [Goldoni] understood perfectly that dramatic tension and the uncertainty of outcomes could be brought to their highest pitch only in an environment where wife and concubine were truly able to face each other with equal voice and legitimacy. [Persian culture granted] a sort of parity between the two women [that] was recognized and guaranteed as a matter of course and custom, . . . the potential defeat of the concubine could not be merely and dully presented as obligatory obedience to social rules.[126]

Persia thus gave Goldoni cultural specifics that meaningfully addressed — more than any familiar institution could — social and ideological problematics on the home front.

As effective as the exotic figure may have been in bourgeois prose theater, however, opera's deployment of foreign peoples could far surpass it. The poetics of the spoken comedy mandated not only more restrained visual and aural pomp, but also narrower story boundaries. Even when a play took place on foreign soil, settings could not stray too far from their counterparts in bourgeois drama (household interiors or restricted outdoor spaces, associated with daily routine); their *favole* centered more often than not on questions of social relationship and behavior, on virtue and vice in a more intimate, domestic universe. The exotic opera, on the other hand, could set before its public a much more expansive, extravagant realm, one that might include oceans, battlefields, foreign palaces, pleasure gardens, religious and other cultural spaces, even surreal, imaginary venues. The variety of these spaces allowed not just for a greater number of varying stories, but also for plots treating larger, more "global" matters.

A common formula for exoticism in the Settecento bourgeois spoken comedy was that of the "foreign observer," in which a protagonist in an unfamiliar land comments on its people's customs. This device is most readily associated with the eighteenth-century exotic novel, which typically brought non-Europeans to the continent to remark on their "strange" surroundings. One need only think of Montesquieu's *Lettres persanes* (1721), (inspired, it is commonly held, by the first official foreign-correspondent epistolary novel, Giovanni Paolo Marana's 1684 *L'espion turc*), and its barrage of imitators. The expedient permitted authors to present ample, wide-ranging critiques of their own worlds. Relatively little of the society of the alien came to light in these novels, whose high degree of self-reflexivity is indicated insofar as their protagonists have also been termed the " 'reverse' traveller, or pseudo-traveller."[127] Substantially there is no travel or traveler at all, but rather, a convenient mask through which the domestic voice speaks about itself.[128]

While on the topic of eighteenth-century exotic fiction, it is instructive to cite a second significant category of imaginative prose, the oriental tale.[129] Like the novel, the European book of oriental fables was also restricted with respect to its representation of the Asian other. The tales themselves were infused with magic and fantasy, which served to relegate Eastern life to a less real, less significant space. The crucial factor, however, as Rosalind Ballaster points out, was the framing of the tales. They were typically understood as told by a narrator in order to entrance, defer, or persuade his or her listener, and as such, needed to be told unceasingly. The business of storytelling, then, a strategic activity dependent on incessant, kaleidoscopic powers of invention, overwhelmed the stories' content. Because of its ceaseless movement of narration, the collection of Persian, Indian, or Turkish tales diminished its subjects' power and, ironically, fixed Asian peoples in a static state. Referring to the *Arabian Nights Entertainments*, Ballaster notes that in them "The whole Orient is telescoped into the confined chronotope of the harem, indeed to the sultana's bedchamber. Metamorphosis and endless transformation become a means of keeping things unchanged."[130]

Flimsy masquerade, reductivity, and paralyzing repetition—the alleged sins of eighteenth-century fiction with respect to its foreign others—cannot be leveled at exotic opera, or at least not at its representations of the Middle Kingdom. China is most certainly used as a pivot from which to engage with domestic concerns, but that pivotal space is much more multidimensional than a mask. The simple fact that the operas enacted the exotic, bringing aspects of Chinese culture to visual, aural, and tactile life, allowed spectators a more direct, visceral experience than did fiction. But the operatic exposition of China

drew its greatest substance from the stories, plots, characters, ideas, and ideologies behind the spectacle. Authoritative material on the Celestial Empire was available, and librettists proudly mined these texts to write their works.

Moreover, opera's own history, especially as the seventeenth century gave way to the eighteenth, affected the "weight," as well as the kind of presence China would have on the lyric stage. The polemics surrounding opera's status and legitimacy, and its aspirations to aesthetic eminence, meant that librettists considered more judiciously the subject matter subtending their dramas. They needed to "embod[y] Enlightenment ideals, portraying characters able to overcome selfish human desires in order to achieve greatness in thought and deed in a world where monarch and subject alike must adhere to the highest of moral principles."[131] Eighteenth-century opera's "will to prestige" allowed it to absorb a great deal of contemporary thinking and theorizing about China, and to connect it to relevant issues at home.

This is not to say that the producers of these operas set out to present respectful, conscientious portraits of their Asian object. Speaking of musical works in the early modern and modern age, Jonathan Bellman points out that "exoticism is not about the earnest study of foreign cultures; it is about drama, effect, and evocation."[132] And yet, the picture of China evoked in the operas under study is rich, variegated, and plentiful in detail, enough to forestall quick compartmentalizing of the nation. The lack of a national colonial (or other) enterprise in Italy prevented the fashioning of a precise, politick identity in which to envelop the Chinese. The varied interests of the Italian state and cultural entities producing and consuming the operas further guaranteed the use of a high quantity and quality of data on Chinese society in the works. The drama created when this data channeled local matters clearly exceeded sensation aroused by mere exotic superfice.

To the extent that certain representations in the operas perpetuated stereotypes, and the works made no attempt to focus impartially on the Middle Kingdom, they may be considered orientalist. However, even this last point deserves nuancing. Operas were not in the business of education, at least not the kind solely and consciously aimed at increasing knowledge in the various recognized disciplines. The enormous body of eighteenth-century China-oriented scholarly texts claimed this territory, and many showed sincere effort and estimable results. Opera, on the other hand, sought to edify as it entertained, and in doing so, indeed *to* do so, resolutely took up the most pressing sociocultural-political issues—what Feldman calls "myths"—of its immediate surroundings.[133]

The fact that opera mobilized aspects of China and Chinese culture to engage these myths does not automatically imply orientalism. Rather, insofar as Italian opera considered elements of Chinese society as valuable exemplars of what its own society should aspire to, avoid, or simply look upon and learn from, it facilitated a pregnant contact zone, a place where at least Italian and European audiences could be exposed to alternative views, systems, and histories. This encounter furthermore took place in a productive context, given the cultural work in which opera inevitably participated. Thus, *drammi per musica* such as *Teuzzone*, *Il Tartaro nella Cina*, and *L'eroe cinese* highlighted ancient and modern Chinese history as key foundations on which to treat the underpinnings of absolutist dynastic rule. *Teuzzone* added to the dignity of monarchy that of noble literary tradition, evoked by the intellectual and philosophical achievements of the Celestial Empire.

The blossoming of comic opera coincided with the more sharply delineated reform and enlightenment thought of the second half of the century. Again, discrete knowledge of Chinese culture and society sustains these ideas as they surface in comic musical works. *L'isola disabitata* goes to China to "perform" the business of economic expansion. *L'idolo cinese* pivots on the Chinese political system of meritocracy and on its religious culture, in its bidirectional challenge, to the new middle class, and the old regime, respectively. *L'inimico delle donne* brings several competing perceptions of Chinese social mores to bear on its endorsement of new modes of relating between the sexes.

The stories told in Italian eighteenth-century China operas are not timeless, smoky tales, disempowered by the fabulous. Nor are they merely monologue-ridden reports on the state of the (home)land. They are instead gripping, stirring, beguiling presentations of the drama of social and cultural change. China, more than other foreign others, afforded greater opportunities for these dramatic meditations. Opera, more than other art and entertainment forms, put them in the spotlight, center stage.

2

China's Journey from Page to Stage

Theater life in the eighteenth century was even more lively than in the preceding century. People acted on the stage and in reality . . . This new situation produced a phenomenon of collective imitation that assimilated the actions, gestures, and clothing of daily life to their counterparts seen on stage.[1]

ONE OF THE MOST ELOQUENT INDICATORS OF THE polyvalence of the Chinese signifier for eighteenth-century Europeans is the term "pagoda." For modern-day English speakers its primary meaning is that of a Chinese or Asian temple, often in the shape of "a pyramidal tower with an upward curving roof."[2] In eighteenth-century French, however, the word had several meanings, in addition to its architectural denotation. Guy observes:

> Among the multifarious definitions of the word "pagode" current in the seventeenth and eighteenth centuries, let us note, in addition to that which usually calls to mind a decorative garden temple in the form of a tower . . . , the following two meanings:
> 1) a small decorative figure of china [porcelain] with a mobile, grotesque head; a nodding toy or porcelain mandarin . . .
> 2) a sleeve which is loose and flared at the wrist; a pagoda or bell sleeve.[3]

In his gloss to one of the last productions by the *Théâtre Italien* in Paris, a comedy sketch which featured singers costumed as East Asian idols, Charles Mazouer states:

> The Siamese embassy [to Paris] in 1686 started the fashion of their temples, or *pagodas*, in which they placed metal statues, i.e., the idols they worshipped. The same word designated moreover the temple and the idol adored. The *Dictionnaire de l'Académie* (1694) distinguishes *un pagode* (for the temple) and *une pagode* (for the idol). According to A. Furetière's *Dictionnaire universel* (1690), the term *pagodes* was used in a generic way by the curious to indicate the small porcelain idols that came from China.[4]

Finally, authors of a study on Asian influences on Euro-American apparel assert that "almost anything that flared in eighteenth-century dress, whether hat or sleeve or collar, was called *en pagode* [in the pagoda style]."[5] Thus the term "pagode," in French, depending on its gender, and indeed, its grammatical function (nominal or adjectival) could mean: a religious edifice, a religious deity, an image or statue considered as the deity, an ornamental figurine used for indoor or outdoor furnishing, and a clothing style. When Mazouer gives as a frequent usage "small porcelain Chinese idols," and Guy notes these sometimes were toys, another set of possible conceptions blooms. For the European owner or viewer of the *pagode* (fem.), it could have constituted a souvenir, a plaything, a collectible, a mere household embellishment, or some combination thereof.

In Italian, "pagoda" did not have quite the same semantic slipperiness. It indicated only the temple structure and the garment cut ("alla pagoda").[6] For all the other meanings, however, the term "idolo" took over. "Idolo" could refer to the divinity, its iteration as sculpture or statue housed in the pagoda, and the decorative porcelain figurines gracing Italian ledges and tabletops. "Idolo" moreover was a common endearment used by lovers ("mio idolo"), so that the title of Lorenzi's opera *L'idolo cinese* spoke to both of its ostensible subject matters: Chinese idolatry and enamored youth. The juxtaposition of these referents points clearly to a third layer of meaning as well, one loaded with irony: the follies (and dangers?) of certain kinds of infatuation.

Lastly, the fact that the porcelain figurines might be shaped as idols or as mandarins, opens a new Pandora's box of meaning. Technically, the idol and the mandarin belonged to opposing camps. As discussed above, Jesuit writings drew a hard line between China's false religions (Buddhism and Taoism), and the philosophical system they allied so warmly with Christianity (Confucianism). Chinese idols would have belonged to the world of the former faiths, with their numerous bizarre divinities and mysterious rituals. The mandarin, on the other hand, was a member of the revered Confucian scholar-official class with whom the missionaries bonded to advance their cause. The camaraderie the Jesuits sought with the Chinese literary elite was reflected in iconography depicting certain famous clerics dressed as mandarins. Thus the notion of "mandarin" in European minds could well evoke one of their Jesuit brethren, for better or worse. The diminution of either the learned Chinese scholar or the erudite Jesuit ecclesiastic to the world of ceramic knickknacks resonates with the shaky, debased status of the Society of Jesus as the century drew on. It furthermore underscores the fluid

4. **Father Von Schall at Chinese imperial court. Athanasius Kircher, _China illustrata . . .,_ 1677. Permission of Alderman Library, University of Virginia.**

interrelationship of these terms and their material referents. "La pagoda," "l'idolo cinese," and "il mandarino," whether inscribed on the libretto page or blocked on the opera stage, kept a mass of cultural baggage in play for eighteenth-century audiences. This chapter will outline the appearance of Chinese elements in five fundamental areas of eighteenth-century Italian opera: 1) characters, 2) costume, 3) scenery/props, 4) gesture/dance, and 5) music.

CHARACTERS

Eighteenth-century dramatic aesthetics conditioned the China operas with respect to their protagonists. Opera seria, modeling itself on French neoclassical tragedy, staged only personages of regal or heroic historical standing: Chinese kings, princes, queens, counselors, military captains, and other members of imperial retinues. Most of the characters in opere buffe came from lower classes, and included merchants, traveler-adventurers, and the ubiquitous servant(s). Typically, however, the bourgeois and plebeian protagonists of the comic works also had one or more members of the ruling ranks in their midst. _L'isola disabitata_ featured a Chinese princess, _L'idolo cinese_ starred a provincial governor-mandarin, and _L'inimico delle donne_ included a Chinese prince, a pair of royal advisors, and a trio of court damsels in its character roster. These higher-ranking figures might perform in accordance with the conventions attached to them in opera seria. Goldoni's Princess Gianghira from _L'isola disabitata_, for example, maintained her dramatic gravity amid the antics and middle culture of the other characters. More often than not, however, the noble protagonists of comic opera parodied these conventions. Specifics about the performative parameters of the various character types will be discussed in the chapters dedicated to the individual operas.

While literary convention as to the social station of characters impinged on the operas, additional factors affected the character types. Certain protagonists derived precisely from circulating information about Chinese culture. The two most singularly "Chinese" of the operas' characters were the mandarin and the Chinese idol, or pagod. No other society known to Europeans in the Settecento had members with the particular identity and function of these two. Before discussing their phenomenology as operatic heroes, however, three other types will be discussed: the Chinese traveler, the Chinese woman, and the Chinese emperor.

The Chinese Traveler

As mentioned in chapter 1, the foreign observer/ cultural critic, standard fixture in eighteenth-century exotic novels, had his day upon the China stage as well. Several theater productions utilized the device, although the dynamic differed substantially. Typically, the Chinese voyager in the dramas was a young man who had already completed his journey to Europe and, once back among his own, he recounted his discoveries to them. The earliest documented incidence of the Chinese traveler on the opera boards is in the comic intermezzo *Il cinese rimpatriato,* written by an unknown Italian librettist, sometime before 1748.[7] A Chinese nobleman just back from a European trip courts a damsel sitting at her toilette by regaling her with European customs among lovers. He presents the open flirtation and gallantry of Western *innamorati* as an exciting, attractive cultural trait, hoping to win over the chaste young lady before him. A similar use of the traveler from the Middle Kingdom occurs in Louis Anseaume's French *intermède, Le Chinois poli en France* (1754). In this piece also, a Chinese youth who has visited Paris returns converted to its lively manners.[8] These pieces demonstrate a fairly shallow use of the foreign-observer, insofar as they establish two poles: France and anywhere that isn't France. The Chinese travelers merely represent those Europeans who come to realize Parisian primacy in all things. The dynamic is a variation on the ballet plots of the previous century, where the world's nations arrived one at a time to pay tribute to the French court (see "Gesture/Dance" section below). There is hardly a cautionary element in these dramas, such as the one abounding in the foreign-observer novels. At most they must have prompted chuckles, as members of high society poked some good-natured fun at themselves and their obsessions with the latest (French) modes.

The Chinese Woman

The portrayal of Chinese women in the operas does not meaningfully deviate from that of other female operatic characters in contemporary works. For the most part, the significant Chinese feminine characters have imperial or noble standing. The malevolent Queen Zidiana in *Teuzzone* is roughly equivalent in character to Roxane of *Bajazet,* on whom she is modeled. When she deviates, it does not point to any inherent "Chineseness" in her.[9] The three Chinese maidens within the imperial entourage in *L'inimico delle donne* give off a whiff of entertaining licentiousness,

and this trait will be exploited in ethnographic terms. However, much of their character composition also assimilates them to the archetypal rivals of the traditional *ingénue* at the center of comic works. As gossipy coquettes, these types vie among themselves and with the heroine for the attentions of the privileged male, and serve to highlight the virtuous qualities of the naïve, but morally pure woman who rightly wins him. When the *ingénue* is Chinese, as occurs with Princess Gianghira in *L'isola disabitata,* she is no different in personality and comportment from the hundreds of other sweet, innocent, well-bred *donzelle* gracing the eighteenth-century Italian stage.

5. **Chinese woman convert. Jean-Baptiste Du Halde. *The General History of China.* Trans. John Watts. London, 1736. Permission of Special Collections, University of Virginia Library.**

In the intermezzi turning on the repatriated male voyager, particular gender issues come into play. The young Chinese woman that the newly converted gallant tries to convince represents (however tongue-in-cheek) the modest, timid, virtuous maiden, reluctant to stray into a potentially dangerous world of sexual excess and indecent freedoms. Though they don't seem to press a point, other than to jokingly condone the libertine practices of the nobility, these colloquies between "educated" young squires and their sheltered, hesitant female initiates do evoke contemporary polemics on feminine beauty, women's fashions, and courtship and marriage propriety. Where the Frenchified Chinese suitor presses for liberality, his chaste Chinese interlocutor holds back, citing the restraint and decency supposedly proper to her gender. Witness this exchange between the two Chinese youths from *Il cinese rimpatriato*:

Vessore. Why the blushing? Though this is perhaps
Not the fashion among us Chinese,
It is among European countries.
At the first meeting
Every lover can declare his or her love
Without being accused of boldness.

. . . .

Slaves, seraglios, eunuchs,
Are unknown things and unknown names
On those remote shores.

Argese. Women. . .

Vessore. Have free recourse
To little bitty sighs, faintings, and tears,
and to a crowd of upstanding lovers.

Argese. Heavens! What are you saying!
Is European custom so perverse?
I turn to ice at the sight of a man
Like a little lamb at the sight of the wolf.

I am a young maiden
The only one in this court
Who goes about looking at no one.
With eyes downcast
If someone comes near me
I move away ever so quietly
And if someone touches me
I turn a bit red.
Then I say modestly
Sir I'm unmarried
Please move over there a little.
If any Mandarin
Should come close to me
So virtuous am I
I don't know how to be outraged;

But in a dreamy fashion,
I say to such a one:
Sir, leave me in peace,
I beg of you, please.

[*Vessore.* Perchè rossor? La moda
Forse questa non è fra noi Cinesi,
Quell'è però degl'Europei paesi.
Al primo incontro
Senza taccia d'ardire
Può l'amor suo colà ciascun scoprire

. . . .

Schiave, Serragli, Eunucchi
In quei lidi remoti
Sono incognite cose, e nomi ignoti.

Argese. Le donne . . .

Vessore. Arbitre sono
Di sospiretti, svenimenti, e pianti,
E d'uno stuol di rispettosi amanti.

Argese. Ciel! Che mi narri! Ed è perverso tanto
D'Europa il costume? Io per me gelo
Degl'uomini all'aspetto
Come a vista del lupo, d'Agnelletto.

Io sono una Donzella
Che sola in questa corte
Nessun mirando vò:
Colle pupille à terra
Se alcun mi vien vicino
Mi scosto pian pianino,
E se talun mi tocca
Mi faccio rossa un po'.
Poi dico con Modestia
Signore son Zitella
Si facci un po' più in là.
Se un qualche Mandarino
A me sen vien vicino,
Io che son buona tanto
Sdegnarmi già non so;
Ma languidetta alquanto
Così dico a quel tale:
Signor mi lasci andare
La prego in carità.]10

Vessore goes on to say that the bold European lovers make fun of Chinese respect and lovers' modesty. The piece then turns back on itself, jovially mocking European ardor, unchecked flirtation between the sexes, and women's games. China becomes an entertaining foil for libertine ways, as it also points to the tension between, on the one hand, women's greater emancipation, license, mobility, and participation in polite society, and, on the other, ideals of feminine containment.

6. **Chinese-Tartar emperor, mid-1600s.** Athanasius Kircher, *China illustrata . . .,* 1677. Permission of Alderman Library, University of Virginia.

The Chinese Emperor

The imperial Chinese ruler also deviates little from his European counterpart in coeval operas. He anchors each of the five opere serie studied here, although a more accurate statement is that the *institution* of sovereign rule dominates, for the works clearly focus on the young up-and-coming heirs to the throne. In fact, in four of the five heroic *melodrammi* studied here, the imperial patriarch never appears onstage and is only referred to by other characters. Three such emperors have died in the opera backstory (*Teuzzone, Taican, L'eroe cinese*), and one kills himself offstage by the end of the first act (*Il Tartaro nella Cina*). Only Lalli's *Camaide, l'imperatore della Cina* puts the Chinese emperor on stage. Like kings in other serious operas of the day, Camaide is an intelligent, well-intentioned patriarch, but he is also susceptible to errors born of passion and to the challenges of recalcitrant children.

In the comic operas the supreme Chinese ruler plays a very negligible role. Furthermore, as one would expect, where he occurs he is not afforded the dignity granted him in the serious works. In *L'isola disabitata* the Chinese king is an offstage presence, depicted as a calcified *paterfamilias*, restricting both his daughter and his nation. Neither *L'idolo cinese* nor *L'inimico delle donne* have a grand monarch among their protagonists. Rather, provincial rulers star in these operas—a regional governor (*Idolo*) and a local prince (*Inimico*). While these protagonists constitute important catalysts for instrumentalizations of precise aspects of Chinese culture, the attributes of stateliness commonly associated with the Chinese emperor don't figure in the picture.

The motley authority of kings is in keeping with the aesthetic of comic dramas. However, the lower profile of the Chinese emperor in the serious works is slightly surprising, given the pomp and glory accrued to him at the turn of the century. The French crown especially had exploited the star quality of the Chinese emperor, helped by works like Father Joachim Bouvet's *Portrait historique de l'Empereur de la Chine* (1697), which had drawn similarities between Louis XIV and the K'ang hsi emperor. Bouvet portrayed each as leading world monarchs, who through their enlightened policies and social structures would advance the cause of Christianity throughout the globe. By the early decades of the new century, however, the aura around the Sun King's absolutist ideal had waned. The Settecento marked a time of resizing the idea of divine monarch, of identifying strategies to make the institution as rational and enlightened as it was sacred. In this atmosphere, perhaps, the person of the Chinese emperor lost some of his earlier standing, as interest fell more on the organizational policies and praxes that had brought about such an amazingly efficient, productive empire.[11]

The Chinese Mandarin

The Chinese scholar-official, with social status and bearing so similar to that of the most respected European clergy, blended in a single individual the powerful cachet of several elite European sectors. The mandarin was at once an intellectual, a ruler, and a high priest, if one considers Confucianism a theologically oriented philosophical doctrine, as the Jesuits and many Europeans did. In China there were actually two mandarinates, those of letters and those of arms. The former, with their vast knowledge of Confucian doctrine, Chinese history and sciences, were privileged. Among the heroic operas considered here they usually appeared as either a high-ranking imperial minister, or a local and well-respected sage. The character of Colao in *Il Tartaro nella Cina*, and to a lesser extent Mitrane in *Taican*, embody the wisdom and status associated with the literary mandarin. The mandarin protagonist is most developed in Leango, patriarchal figure in Metastasio's *L'eroe cinese*. This drama fastens on perceptions of the mandarin as Confucian disciple, that is, utterly beholden to an ideology of humility and obedience.

On the comic stage, the great erudition ascribed to the Chinese dignitary facilitated his portrayal as a scholarly fool. Whether one views it as the sinicizing of the commedia mask of the Dottore, or the "commedia-fication" of the mandarin figure, much popular theater exploited this role. As noted, the Chinese mandarin could also blur identities with the Jesuit priest. The musical-comedy *Le chinois* by Regnard and Dufresny (1692) suggests this synthesis. Harlequin, playing a Chinese doctor (*docteur*), is one of three suitors for the hand of a wealthy man's daughter. His expansive knowledge presumably sets him apart from his less educated rivals, a huntsman and a military captain. He enters the scene carrying a Chinese cabinet, but before he opens it, his soliloquy establishes his arrogance and stupidity. He boasts of his knowledge of doctrine, letters, and sciences, contrasting the latter with others' meaningless experience, and he spouts nonsense latin and absurd logic ("the moon is a common star, women depend on the moon, ergo women are common").[12] At every turn he interrupts, insults, and overpowers the father and daughter, and finally asks how many daughters he shall be given, since he is worth so many men. The harlequinade's verbal

7. **Chinese colao. Jean-Baptiste Du Halde. *The General History of China*. Trans. John Watts. London, 1736. Permission of Special Collections, University of Virginia Library.**

pagod. What the devil do you want me to tell you?"[15] Thus the Chinese mandarin turns out to be a charlatan, ignorant of his own culture, suggesting that the Jesuit-mandarin has no real purchase on the culture he so pompously claims to understand. The commedia theatrical tradition appropriates an integral Chinese personage not only to play with the oddities of an exotic culture, but also, to denude a religious celebrity on his own home ground.[16]

The Chinese Idol

The second distinctly Chinese entity, the idol, acquired its iconic status not only because its effigies were so distinct in appearance—characteristically squat, seated, placid, adipose, sometimes quite grotesque, rendered in porcelain or other sculptural material—but also because of the high-pitched debates waged in Europe over China and religion. Even

8. **Father Matteo Ricci and Chinese convert. Athanasius Kircher, *China illustrata . . .*, 1677. Permission of Alderman Library, University of Virginia.**

pièce de resistance and surely the zinger in the Jesuit roast was this line: "So, [all of] you don't know then, that I am a philosopher, orator, medical doctor, astrologer, jurisprudence expert, geographer, logician, barber, shoemaker, apothecary, in a word, I am every man, that is to say, I am universal man."[13] At this moment the cabinet opens, "filled with grotesque Chinese figures who make up a music academy, a melee of violins, and figures representing rhetoric, logic, music, astrology, etc. In the middle of these figures one sees a fat pagod."[14] The pagod, of course, is Mezzetino, smugly introduced ("C'est une pagode") by Harlequin. When asked what a pagod is, however, the Chinese doctor cannot answer: "A pagod is . . . a

9. Frontispiece engraving, *Les chinois*. Regnard and Dufresny, in *Théâtre italien*. Amsterdam, 1701. Courtesy United States Library of Congress.

an immensely popular format for the beloved mask.[19] The sketch entitled *Arlequin Barbet, pagode et médecin* (1723), a "Chinese piece in monologues," apparently sees the jester in both the role of pagod and doctor-mandarin.[20]

The creative potential inherent in the Chinese idol did not escape the makers of eighteenth-century opera. At the most basic level, a corpulent, avuncular deity wearing an inscrutable expression was easily absorbed into the Italian *zanni* tradition. As this legacy evolved in the opera, the idol—and sometimes the mandarin, bloated with self-importance—moved smoothly into the buffo roles. Harlequin's declaration above hints at the versatility of the Chinese idol/mandarin masquerade. It could be used to declaim the falsehoods or vanity of a number of institutional identities in eighteenth-century Italy, including, but not limited to, "philosopher, orator, medical doctor, astrologer, jurisprudence expert, geographer, logician," et cetera. The buffo parts in *L'idolo cinese* and *L'inimico delle donne* made productive use of the Chinese pagod and mandarin guises.

COSTUME

The appearance of Chinese-style apparel on the Settecento opera stage was of a piece with the increasing shift toward authenticity in theater costume that began in the eighteenth century.[21] The term "Chinese-style" is used, however, because the embrace of realia in dramatic dress was slow and circuitous. James Laver maintains that throughout most of the eighteenth century theatrical costume reflected very little historical accuracy, moving from imperial Roman battle attire to the fantasy and ebullience of Rococo, and only to authenticity when interest in geographically and historically correct costume rose in the very late part of the century, with the advent of Romanticism.[22] Still, along this route, garments and accoutrements recognizable by European audiences as "Chinese" appeared, both on stage and off.

One of the obstacles to ethnographically appropriate costume was the persistence of the seventeenth-century French classical dramatic aesthetic, which, for a good part of the Settecento, outfitted all heroic protagonists in Roman military dress tunic and helmet regardless of their geographical or chronological provenance. Another significant force was the dominance of French court fashion. France dictated clothing styles in nearly all of Europe in the eighteenth century. The power and extent of its influence meant that not only in Paris, but in all other important the-

if one professed no interest in the polemic, the sight or possession of a meditative Chinese pagod was a reminder of the challenge to monotheistic Christian faith.[17]

As the idol in the abovementioned comedy sketch, Mezzetino sang a nonsense ditty, underscoring his untenable foundations. In a collection of script outlines (*canovacci*) for Neapolitan commedia spectacles put on in the early 1700s, Pulcinella undergoes a series of transformations, alternately becoming a Chinese astrologer, a Chinese pagod, and an Egyptian mummy.[18] Another Parisian fair theater piece dated 1712 shows Harlequin impersonating the Tartar idol Kam, again as part of a chain of metamorphoses, itself atrical centers, stage costuming had to accommodate actors, sponsors, and impresarios who desired to show off the latest and most prestigious fashions.[23]

For exotic theater, the obsession with French court *couture* resulted in bizarre amalgams and extravagant enhancements of customary aristocratic apparel. Jean Bérain, *dessinateur du Cabinet du Roi* and the most influential *costumista* of the early eighteenth century, put before spectators a native American tribal chief clothed in a Roman tunic with Louis XIV decoration, and dancers wearing Turkish turbans festooned with billowing feathers.[24] Tassels, stripes, and other details common to turqueries might be grafted onto an essentially European silhouette, or Chinese textiles used in a French-tailored costume.[25] Gradually the Rococo taste gained stride, and in its long heyday from 1730 to 1780, produced even more eccentric concoctions. The performers representing Peruvians, Turks, and Persians in the famous opéra-ballet *Les Indes galantes* (1735) looked more like elegantly coiffed courtly youth in their corsets and flounces, than like inhabitants of distant continents.[26]

"Chinese" stage costume evolved in this environment, one of competing and sometimes contradictory practices. Critics urged veracity and certain practitioners attempted it, but audiences didn't necessarily welcome the more genuine clothing. When the well-loved Parisian singer and dancer Marie Favart broke with tradition in 1747 by matching her costume to her actual role in Nivelle de la Chaussée's *Amour castillan* —she dressed plainly and severely as a Spanish woman, abandoning the customary panniers—audiences greeted the change most coolly. The reaction was worse when just a few years later she donned simple peasant attire for the pastoral *Amours de Bastian et de Bastienne* (1753), written by her husband Charles Simon Favart. Only in 1761, playing Turkish princess Roxane in *Soliman the second*, did her showy oriental sultana gown (allegedly made in Constantinople) meet with surprised approval. But engravings of Mlle. Favart in this role actually reveal little deviation from current Parisian fashion.

In the same decades, the actors Mlle. Clairon and Alain Louis Le Kain also attempted greater accuracy in dramatic costume. At the Versailles theater, in a production of *Bajazet* ca. 1750, Clairon wore what Jean-François Marmontel called "a true oriental costume."[27] Le Kain followed suit in his roles. When in 1755 both actors starred at the *Comédie-Française* in Voltaire's tragedy *L'Orphelin de la Chine*—Le Kain as Genghis Khan, Clairon as Idamé—their Chinese-Tartar garb (in combination with the scenery) demonstrated a "much closer approach to realism than any-

thing that had been seen before."[28] Yet even as Voltaire himself preached authenticity in drama, prevailing taste conditioned anything that might have been construed as too alien. Reverence for *bienseance*, or decorum, both aesthetic and moral, led Voltaire to order his costume designer to create outfits "Chinese enough and French enough not to arouse the spectators to laughter."[29]

The following remark by Metastasio in regard to his heroic opera *L'eroe cinese*, produced three years before Voltaire's *L'Orphelin*, suggests not only that Chinese theatrical costume was well known by Italian theater audiences, but also that it was less susceptible to audience ridicule. Writing to the Countess of Sangro in Naples about prospective performances of his opera, Metastasio assures her: "*L'eroe cinese* is perfect for summer performance; its Tartar and Chinese costumes are more recognized among us than sack gowns or *palatine*. And I can't imagine that there isn't someone in Naples, city of such artistic talents, who can design these costumes so that they don't offend the European eye; if at any time you want the costume designs which we used, Signor Abate Grossatesta knows how to get them to you."[30] In Turin, Chinese-style costumes designed by the artist Leonardo Marini, *costumista* for the Royal Theater, mixed the fantastical elegance of the Rococo with elements evoking native styles of the Celestial Empire. The Chinese emperor depicted in Marini's design for the ballet *L'orfano della Cina* (see book cover) wears imperial robes with the wide sleeves and the dragon insignia common to the Ming governing orders.[31] His headdress is shaped *alla pagoda*, and his long, skinny moustaches, beard, and bound pigtail indicate some awareness of Chinese reverence for proper hair care.[32] The predominantly yellow color of his costume also reflects knowledge that yellow was the most preferred of colors for Chinese ceremonial. The birds and flowers pattern of the fabric no doubt mimicked a Chinese textile. At the same time, the bright flurry of plumes atop the hat, the tassels, cuffs, sash, and scimitar suggest a rustle-y layering of delicate silks and what Marialuisa Angiolillo refers to as "courtly, mannered exoticism."[33] Marini had a sincere interest in the authentic, however, conveyed by his volume of plates entitled *Abiti antichi di diverse nazioni d'Europa e d'Asia, inventati e disegnati da Leonardo Marini, torinese ed eseguiti al Real Teatro di Torino* (1771).[34]

Other Italian opera practitioners and critics who urged greater realism in costume included Benedetto Marcello and Francesco Algarotti.[35] The latter wrote in his 1762 *Saggio sopra l'opera in musica* that the costumes and activities of both dancers and singers "must match as well as possible the time periods and nations they are representing on stage." It must not be allowed, he continued, to portray "Aeneas' companions smoking pipes and wearing trousers in the Dutch style."[36] Ten years later, however, Francesco Milizia complained about overdone, anachronistic, inappropriate costuming, so progress was not seamless.[37]

Due to the tremendous permeability among different artistic spheres in eighteenth-century Italy, *costumisti* almost always worked in multiple capacities. The same painters who drew costume sketches for the theater also designed clothing for daily life and for public and private celebrations. Even more customary was their crossover labor as set designers, festival decorators, and ceremony directors. The Mauro family in Venice counts as only one among several clans dedicated to spectacle in various forms and city quarters. Over the years they designed not only apparel, but also boats, floats, and décor for use in both China theater and the Chinese-style ceremonies, dances, and outdoor public galas adored by resident and visiting spectators.[38]

Italian costume and dress designers undoubtedly took cues from French artists, many of whom raised decorative chinoiserie to rarefied heights. The Bérains, Claude Gillot, Jean-Antoine Watteau, François Boucher, Jean-Baptiste Martin, Louis René Boquet, and Jean Pillement were among the most prominent visual interpreters of the Chinese craze. Gillot made Chinese figures cavort with commedia dell'arte characters in his painted panels. The paintings of Watteau, Boucher, and Pillement inspired a Rococo exuberance in stage costume.[39] Both Boucher and Martin, his successor as *dessinateur des habillements de l'Opéra*, wrote or published works treating stage costume. Boquet followed Martin as *costumista* at the *Académie Royale de Musique*, and his fantastical style dominated French costume design for the second half of the century.

The extent to which the costume designers consulted travel reports and other "ethnographic" compilations for information on Chinese garments will never be known. Nevertheless, the data existed. Nieuhof, Kircher, and Du Halde provided engravings of the customary dress of diverse subjects in Chinese lands. Some even featured front and back angles, so as not to miss a detail! Theater professionals with access to higher echelons might have been able to consult stunning depictions of imperial uniforms and robes in the paintings sent back to Europe by Jesuit missionary artist Giuseppe Castiglione, court painter in Beijing for a good part of the eighteenth century.[40] Other ideas may have come from narrative descriptions in the China treatises.

Many of the illustrated texts that provided models for costumes also contained visuals helpful in the creation of operatic scenery. The general descriptions especially showed Chinese landscapes, architecture, and interiors. In the case of opera seria, the China productions featured the same environments standard in all heroic dramas: resplendent royal pavilions, reception halls, throne rooms, prison chambers, courtyards, gardens, and other grandiose locales common to princely palaces and grounds. Thanks to the iconography from the publications, however, these spaces could be rendered stylistically àla chinese.[41] Designs by Fabrizio Galliari (1709–90) for the opera *Arsinoe*, performed at the Teatro Regio in Turin in 1758 and again in 1777 (as *Gengis-Kan*), show the effervescent flora, pagoda-style cupolas and rooflines, slender towers, delicate statuary, fretwork, and other Chinese embellishments incorporated in the architecturally imposing stage sets typical of opera seria.[42] For a scene from the ballet *L'orfano della Cina*, performed at the same theater in 1790, a drawing by Giovannino Galliari (1746–1818) depicts a Chinese city scape with sepulchers in the foreground.[43] Unfortunately, few designs for eighteenth-century operatic theater sets exist. Maria Ida Biggi notes that on rare occasion a libretto contains an engraving that hints at actual staging.[44] The frontispiece to *Taican, rè della Cina* exemplifies the austerity of such illustrations, although it showcases one of the most reproduced images of China, the Nanking tower. For the most part one must mentally extrapolate from the lists of sets and the stage directions in the librettos, as well as from data offered by text and pictures in contemporary treatments of the Middle Kingdom, to envision intended scenery.

Besides the Nanking tower, the buildings and atmospheres most often replicated in the China operas included other types of pagodas, Chinese gardens, the Great Wall, and indigenous structures for funeral rites. Six of the eight operas under consideration situated either a series of scenes or an entire act in the pagoda, the principal site of idol worship. The same number of works also specify a Chinese garden or nature-scape, sometimes indicated in the libretto as a "paesaggio delizioso" or "artifizioso" ("exquisite" or "imaginary landscape"). Such terms underscore the deliberate stylization sought in the re-creation of Chinese scenarios on stage.

One of the more tantalizing examples is Antonio Salvi's *Il Tartaro nella Cina*, produced in Reggio Emilia in 1715. Among the twelve different stage sets he pre-

10. Chinese masquerade costume, "King of China," attributed to Jean Bérain. Permission Bibliotèque Nationale de France.

11. Chinese costume design by Louis Boquet. Permission Bibliotèque Nationale de France.

12. Tartar women. Athanasius Kircher, *China illustrata . . .*, 1677. Permission of Alderman Library, University of Virginia.

13. Tartar men. Johannes Nieuhoff, *L'ambassade de la compagnie orientale . . .*, 1665. Permission of Special Collections, University of Virginia Library.

14. Chinese women. Johannes Nieuhoff, *L'ambassade de la compagnie orientale . . .*, 1665. Permission of Special Collections, University of Virginia Library.

15. Tartar women. Johannes Nieuhoff, *L'ambassade de la compagnie orientale . . .*, 1665. Permission of Special Collections, University of Virginia Library.

16. Chinese priests. Johannes Nieuhoff, *L'ambassade de la compagnie orientale . . .*, 1665. Permission of Special Collections, University of Virginia Library.

17. Tartars and their domiciles. Athanasius Kircher, *China illustrata . . .*, 1677. Permission of Alderman Library, University of Virginia.

18. Chinese dress according to province. Athanasius Kircher, *China illustrata . . .*, 1677. Permission of Alderman Library, University of Virginia.

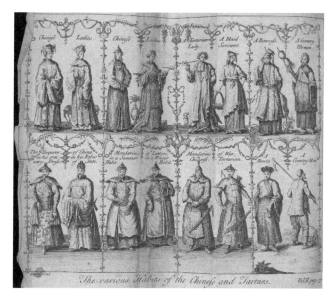

19. Chinese and Tartar dress. Jean-Baptiste Du Halde. *The General History of China*. Trans. John Watts. London, 1736. Permission of Special Collections, University of Virginia Library.

scribes in his libretto, Salvi includes nearly all of the most popular "native" Middle Kingdom milieux.[45] He calls for a:

> Pagoda, or circular temple with altar and deity; pedestal, where the torch burns, Bonzes and Ministers (1, 5);
> Countryside, in which the city walls are seen with a view of the bulwark, on which Vanlio advances (2, 5);
> Delightful walkway shaded with palms, with awnings spread from tree to tree (3, 8);
> Piazza covered by a great funeral tent, nighttime illumination from a raised pyre, decorated with gold and silver vases, typically in use at the Chinese king's table; the pyre is surrounded by veiled victims, with ministers, bonzes, mandarins, holding various musical instruments; populace and guards. Throne, where Assuana and Timurta sit. (3, 17)[46]

The dazzling quality of these stagings is virtually guaranteed by the fact that all of the opera's sets were designed by Francesco Galli-Bibiena (1659–1739), member of another family even more famous for scenographic invention than the Galliari clan.[47] Juxtaposing a couple of engravings of Chinese sites from the general treatises with one of Bibiena's extant drawings for a coterminous opera allows a sense of the spatial exotica presented in the China operas. For example, one can imagine the Nanking tower popularized by Nieuhof and Kircher, or the Great Wall, rendered with the extravagant dimensions and decoration of Bibiena's stage designs for a 1716 production of *Alcina*.

Texts that dealt strictly with Chinese architecture, furnishings, and garden design must also have provided inspiration to the artists who conceived of the scenic Celestial Empire for the opera stage. Jesuit father Jean-Denis Attiret's approving review of the imperial gardens in Beijing was famous all over Europe.[48] English writers published many works on varied topics of interest, such as William and John Halfpenny's *New Designs for Chinese Temples, Triumphal Arches, Garden Seats, Palings, &c.* (1750–52), *Chinese and Gothic Architecture properly ornamented* (1752), and William Chambers's *Designs of Chinese Buildings, Furniture, Dresses, Machines, and Utensils* (1756).

Almost all the major Italian stage designers show up in the China opera libretti sooner or later. Domenico Mauro of the renowned line of Venetian scenery painters and stage architects designed the sets for the Venice performance of Zeno's *Teuzzone*. One of the Quaglio family produced stunning scenery for a 1754 Viennese performance of Metastasio's *Le cinesi*.[49] Productions of his *L'eroe cinese* utilized the talents of the Bibienas and the Galliari brothers. Like the sets for *Il Tartaro nella Cina*, these must have been breathtaking, as Metastasio was so exacting in his specifications. Giuseppe Baldo and Domenico Fossati, renowned scenographers, invented the scenes for the Naples and Venice performances of *L'idolo cinese*, respectively. Francesco Costa, and again the Galliaris, had their hand in devising scenography for various performances of *L'inimico delle donne*.

As already noted, the eighteenth century did not differentiate among the theater arts in any measure approximating today's practice. Thus the above professionals were at once stage designers, scene painters, and theater architects, to name only their most prominent roles. In addition to their theater work, moreover, they often applied their abilities to promotional projects on behalf of the ruling powers, and related civic events. The *bissone* (ceremonial boat) mentioned in the previous chapter, outfitted *alla cinese* to celebrate the arrival of the German Elector Augustus to Venice, was designed by another Mauro family member, Alessandro. These artists were additionally employed by individuals from the patriciate who wanted to add a spectacular touch to their elegant domiciles. Andrea Urbani, highly prized Venetian painter, composed not only the scenes for Goldoni's *L'isola disabitata*, but also created the chinoiserie frescoes for at least three major villas in the Veneto.[50] Gian Domenico Tiepolo painted opulent frescoes for the Villa Valmarana in Vicenza, and likely was responsible for those commissioned by Charles III at the Spanish Bourbon palace at Aranjuez.

20. Chinese city, stage design by Fabrizio Galliari for 1758 opera *Arsinoe*, Teatro Regio, Torino. Pinoteca Nazionale di Bologna. Permission of the Ministero per i Beni e le Attività Culturali.

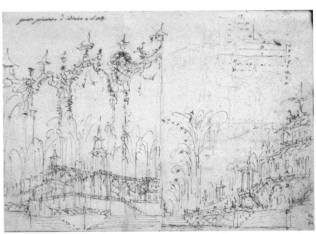

21. A Chinese fantasy, stage design by Fabrizio Galliari for 1758 opera *Arsinoe*, Teatro Regio, Torino. Pinoteca Nazionale de Bologna. Permission of the Ministero per i Beni e le Attività Culturali.

22. Frontispiece facing page, *Taican rè della Cina*. Permission Casa Goldoni, Venice.

TAICAN
RE' DELLA
CINA.

Tragedia per Musica

Da rappresentarsi nel Teatro Tron di S. Cassano l'Anno 1707.

IN VENEZIA, M. DCCVII.

Appresso Marino Rossetti.

In Merceria , all' Insegna della Pace.

Con Licenza de' Superiori, e Privilegio.

23. Frontispiece facing page, *Taican rè della Cina*. Permission Casa Goldoni, Venice.

24. Nanking Tower, Johannes Nieuhoff, *L'ambassade de la compagnie orientale . . .*, 1665. Permission of Special Collections, University of Virginia Library.

25. Nanking Tower, Johannes Nieuhoff, *L'ambassade de la compagnie orientale . . .*, 1665. Permission of Special Collections, University of Virginia Library.

27. Gate in the Great Wall of China. Athanasius Kircher, *China illustrata . . .*, 1677. Permission of Alderman Library, University of Virginia.

26. Nanking Tower, Athanasius Kircher, *China illustrata. . .*, 1677. Permission of Alderman Library, University of Virginia.

The osmosis between the stage and public and private life continued in the case of porcelain, which effected a true merging of stage setting and stage property. The elaborate porcelain rooms constructed by royals in their palaces, mirrored in the cabinets of fine chinaware proudly possessed by the nobility, and aped in turn by the smaller, cheaper collections owned by less wealthy patrons of the China craze—operas put all of it on display. Librettists wrote scenes in both heroic and comic operas in which a suitor unveils the beautiful porcelain chamber, or cabinet, that he intends as a gift to his future bride.[51]

Normally the comic operas set forth less regal settings than those of opera seria. However, in their Chinese banquet scenes (L'idolo, L'inimico), and ritual ceremonies in honor of Middle Kingdom divinities (L'idolo), they too spectacularized Chinese fashion and merchandise. Even more intently focused on chinoiserie commodities, the China intermezzi may have functioned almost like television commercials. So frequently set in the private apartments of the nobility, they directly spotlighted the exotic accoutrements (bibelots, toiletries, accessories, trinkets) beloved by style-conscious men and women. The opera stage trumpeted the prestige of local princes or aristocracy, at the same time as it promoted a mass market many of whose prime constituents—the growing bourgeoisie—ranged outside of the ruling classes. The degree to which these parties agreed in their goals for society inflected on the underlying dynamics of the operas.

Gesture and Dance

Gestures and other physical movement constituted quite effective means to express alterity on stage. In the case of the Chinese, travel accounts and related writings had remarked especially on their complex social decorum. The reported behaviors ranged from precise seating arrangements at both formal and domestic gatherings, to protracted bowing when two parties encountered one another, to elaborate acts of deference when worshipping ancestors or the local deities. The kowtow, a ritual Chinese gesture of homage required in audiences with the emperor, was discussed widely, as were meals, which involved intricate ceremonial and the pacing of eating and drinking in accordance with formal rules.

Physical shows of Chinese protocol probably first entered the Italian theatrical repertoire in commedia dell'arte performances. Records of these spectacles are few, but librettos from French fair theater offer some evidence of the kind of postures adopted by commedia-style characters pretending to be Chinese. The frontispiece of Regnard and Dufresny's musical comedy Les chinois shows Mezzetin sitting cross-legged on a raised platform, in the exaggeratedly placid mode of a Chinese pagod, while Arlecchino as a Chinese doctor gestures in professorial ostentation (see figure 9). Clearly, physical performance was crucial to the humor of these pieces. The eccentric, hyperbolic deportment characteristic of commedia dell'arte easily entered eighteenth-century comic opera. A prime example is Goldoni's L'isola disabitata, where he prescribes excessive ceremony on the part of the actors playing Chinese ambassadors.

It is impossible to know exactly how the actors moved on stage as they impersonated Chinese protagonists. Studies on eighteenth-century dance, however, comprise a vital source of information on how European performers may have represented Chinese movement. Certainly one of the most arresting forms of exotic performance, in terms of creating an expansive visual impression, occurred by means of dance.

One of the first instances of exoticism in Italian choreography occurred with the moresca, one of the most popular of pantomimed dances in court performance of the late fifteenth century.[52] The moresca comprised a dance version of a mock battle between Christians and Moors. Chinese appear to have first tripped onto the European stage around the turn of the seventeenth century, according to a French ballet libretto dated 1600–1601, entitled Stanzas written hastily for the Ballet of the Princes of China.[53] This ballet presented the topos of Oriental rulers leaving their prison-like home domains and flocking to France for its beauty, and in particular, the grace and elegance of the French court. "In court ballets for years to come, figures from the far reaches of the world—Turks, Persians, Ethiopians, Moors, (South) Americans, or 'masques assez hideux et sauvages'—drawn by the fame of the beauties of the French court, would arrive to recite verses in their praise."[54]

Whether for an in-house entertainment or a theatrical performance open to the public, dance historians and critics generally agree that the exotic figure often performed at the level of burlesque. His dance style belonged to the grotesque, or low comic manner, the last of four modes Edmund Fairfax identifies for eighteenth-century stage ballet, but which apparently operated fairly regularly in the seventeenth.[55] The famous French carnival ballet Le Grand bal de la douairière de Billebahaut (1626) was a case in point. Louis XIII took part in the production, which "carried this topos [of non-Europeans bowing before the French] to a level of grotesquerie that could never be surpassed."[56] Together with her fiancé, the "Dowager of Disorder" received extravagant amorous homage from Turks, Persians, Africans, Tartars, and "People of the North," who included Greenlanders and Frisians. The exotics spoke a vague Spanish-Catalan gibberish not meant to be intelligible. The dancer playing Mahommet was instructed in the libretto to enter "with a grave but silly step . . . one can hardly believe . . . he has learned to dance in Paris."[57] According to Mark Franko, antinomies between the Catholic French monarchy and the heretical Turkish empire accounted for the programmatic clumsiness of the prophet and his countrymen.[58] The inferior other had to be differentiated from the normative, privileged European. Thus the awkward, comical movements of the alien (however much physical skill they may have required) contrasted sharply with the refined, courtly movements executed by representatives of the European sector.

The above dances partook in the formation of a genre that became extremely popular over the course of the century, the *ballet des nations*. Consisting of a succession of dance vignettes each based on a different nationality, the *ballet des nations* paraded multitudes of wildly costumed dancers before rapt audiences.[59] On Italian terrain, choreographer Filippo d'Aglié wrote and directed several of these productions for the Savoy court, including *Il Tabacco* (1650) and *La Primavera trionfante dell'inverno* (1657). The latter featured indigenous peoples from "Groelandia" (Greenland), "Nuova Zembla" (Siberia), "Estorilandi" (Lapland? Finland?), pygmies, two Lapps, women from "Guaiana," two savages from Tierra del Fuego, two Floridian islanders, inhabitants of Iceland, Abyssinians, and others.[60] In the eighteenth century, the *ballo delle nazioni* became integrated into the overarching aesthetic of comparativism and universalism. Ballet was deployed to demonstrate a totalizing, comparatist, idealized "picture of society."[61] The most famous of this variation was Louis Fuzelier-Jean Philippe Rameau's *opéra-ballet Les Indes galantes* (1735), in which Love journeys around the globe—to Turkey, Persia, Peru, and North America—in search of followers.[62]

Choreographers and composers also created *balli* dedicated to single nations, designed to convey to spectators a true idea of their peoples. Giovanni-Andrea Gallini dedicated a good portion of his *A Treatise on the Art of Dancing* (1762) to "various Kinds of Dances in different Parts of the World," wherein he included dance customs of diverse European nations, as well as those in Asia, Africa, and America.[63] The

Italian choreographer recommended the integration of authentic processions into these mono-culture ballets, and cited "a dance in Chinese characters" as an example.[64] A Chinese ceremonial march performed as a preamble to such a *ballo*, would, according to Gallini, enhance the meaning of the dance for its audience. Thanks to its rich ethnographic content, and the fact that its spatial arrangements and pacing avail good visual apprehension, the introductory procession would help more clearly communicate the nature of the Chinese people to be represented by the main dance spectacle:

> where a dance in Chinese characters is intended, a procession might be previously brought in, of personages, of whom the habits, charactures, and manners might be faithfully copied from nature, and from the truth of things, and convey to the spectator a juster notion of the people from which the representation was taken, of their dress and public processions, than any verbal description, or even prints or pictures. After which, the dance might naturally take place, in celebration of the festival, of which the procession might be supposed the occasion.[65]

To support his point, Gallini included an engraving of "the procession of a Chinese mandarin of the first order." He also described each section of the pageant, so as to indicate "what scope or range a composer may have for the exhibition of processions and pageantry of other nations, as well as of the Chinese."[66] Interestingly, apart from one plate of a European-looking dancer at the front of Gallini's book, he includes no other engraving except that of the Chinese parade.

The rise of China's popularity resulted in the century's most famous exotic ballet, Jean Georges Noverre's *Ballet chinois*, or *Les Fêtes chinoises* (*Chinese Festivals*) (1754).[67] Dedicated solely to the Chinese, Noverre's work was a lavish, opulent production, with music by Rameau, set décor after Boucher, costumes by Boquet, and sixty dancers to show them off: "as many as eight rows of bedragonned mandarins and attendants were to be seen dancing at a time; pagods in palanquins carried by teams of black and white slaves traversed the stage."[68] At its finale "thirty-two vases rose up and hid thirty-two dancers so that the stage seemed transformed into a china cabinet."[69] *Les Fêtes chinoises* roused the applause of all Paris.

Fairfax writes that Noverre's ballet featured "both sitting positions and bobbing movements, the latter evidently parodying the Chinese custom of multiple bows." He also notes the pointed-finger gesture, "wherein the forearms were held upwards with one finger of each hand pointing aloft."[70] These kinds of

28. **Chinese procession.** Giovanni Andrea Gallini, *A Treatise on the Art of Dancing,* London, 1772. Courtesy of Madison U. Sowell and Debra H. Sowell, Brigham Young University, Provo, Utah.

actions and gestures maintained the tradition wherein the exotic performer moved in less-than-graceful ways. In fact, continues Fairfax: "Chinese characters were particularly apt to employ bizarre movements. The iconography suggests that squatting or sitting positions were traditional . . . with the performer standing in a bend in a forced second position of the feet, . . . or sitting on his heels, or alternately sitting with his legs crossed."[71] Descriptions of ballets also reveal a complicated *pas chinois,* performed from a cross-legged position on the floor.[72]

In Italy these sorts of choreographies were likely even more exaggerated. The dance styles of France and Italy had always differed. Where the French preferred pure form and refined movement, the Italians incorporated more referentiality and storytelling, in performances sometimes classified as pantomime-ballets.[73] Italian *ballerini* also performed more athletically, with virtuosic jumps and other spectacular bodily feats. The reasons for these traits are several.

Italians opened public theaters sooner than the French, so were playing to both smaller, private court groups and larger, less elite audiences. This greater number of theaters also had deeper stages than their French counterparts, necessitating higher leaps and broader physicality for performers to be seen. The larger explanation for the heightened narrative action in Italian ballet, however, was the long commedia dell'arte tradition, where physical expertise and dance-like agility not only abounded but also were inextricably fused with expressiveness.

The popular dance manual written in 1716 by Gregorio Lambranzi, Venetian ballet master who choreographed and danced in performances in France, Germany, and Italy, reveals the Italian penchant for dramatic content.[74] It completely emphasizes character dance, a mainly Italian legacy documented back to the fifteenth century, where dancers patterned their movements on those of a person or a thing (a shoemaker, or a Turk, or Music, for example). In this

29. Costume design for Chinese dancer, ca. 1755, by Louis Boquet. Permission Bibliotèque Nationale de France.

30. Design for Chinese male dancer by J. B. Martin, ca. 1750, for ballet *Les Indes galantes*. Permission Bibliotèque Nationale de France.

32. Dwarf dancer in role of Chinese emperor. Anonymous. The dancing dwarf. *Theatralische Zwergen Tantz-Schul,* 1720. Courtesy Jerome Robbins Dance Division, The New York Public Library for the Performing Arts, Astor, Lenox and Tilden Foundations.

31. Design for Chinese female dancer by J. B. Martin, ca. 1750, for ballet *Les Indes galantes*. Permission Bibiotèque Nationale de France.

choice Lambranzi departed from the Feuillet system
of stenochoreography, which developed in 1700 and
stressed the French concern with refinement in form.
Lambranzi instead offers, for each of his nearly one
hundred dances, a short musical air, a paragraph containing suggestions for the steps, and an engraving of
the imagined dancer on stage, replete with costume
and setting. There are dances for particular trades,
sports, and nationalities, such as the Swiss piker, and
the Dutch sailor. His stable does not include any Chinese *ballerini*, however, there is a quartet of Turkish
steppers. Interestingly, an engraving from another
work shows a dancing Chinese figure within the same
framing device as that used in the Lambranzi plates.
That is, the dancer is clearly in action, on stage, with
the perspective scenery in the background. His broad
Chinese-style hat, long moustaches, and definitive
Asian eye-shape mark him as associated with the Celestial Kingdom, while his harlequinesque costume
and effusive props—both the balls he holds in each
hand and the large matching pom-pons piled at the

34. Turkish dance. Gregorio Lambranzi, *New and Curious
School of Theatrical Dancing,* Nuremburg, 1716. Permission of
Princeton Book Company.

33. **Dutch sailor dance. Gregorio Lambranzi,** *New and Curious
School of Theatrical Dancing,* **Nuremburg, 1716. Permission of
Princeton Book Company.**

peak of his cap—suggest a comical and acrobatic
elaboration of the exotic.[75]

Many of Lambranzi's dancer-figures are traditional
masks from the commedia dell'arte, each with individual characteristics. The preoccupation with thematic specificity for individual characters is conveyed
in this passage from the "Author's Foreword":

the lively and burlesque types represented in Nos. 23
to 49, such as Scaramouch, Harlequin and the like, must
be expressed in the eccentric style of dancing; and with,
of course, ridiculous and comic positions suited to the pe-
culiar characteristics of each. Hence it would be quite out
of place for a Scaramouch, Harlequin or Purricinella to
dance a *Menuet, Courante, Sarabande* or *Entrée,* since each
has his own droll and quaint *pas.* Thus Scaramouch
dances his long, unformed and heavy imitations such as
the *pas de scaramouche;* the same applies to Harlequin,
Mezzetino, Scapino, Matto, the Bolognese Doctor, Nar-
cisino, Fenocchio, Orbo, Zotto, Strupiato, Pantalone and
so on. For these, no *pas,* figure or costume can be used
other than that usually employed on the Italian stage.[76]

The music provided was just as precise, and was titled to correspond with its dance and dancer: "Scaramouche air No. 26," for example.

In the absence of other documentation, the care with which Lambranzi communicated his dances should give an idea of the attention to detail likely spent on Italian renditions of dancing Chinese. The following *balli* show that physical performance was very much a part of the representation of the Celestial Empire on the Italian Settecento boards: *Fiera di mercanti cinesi* (1757), *L'orfano della Cina* (1762), *Feste Persiane e Chinesi* (1772), and *Lo sposalizio dell'imperatore della China* (1785).

MUSIC

General consensus with respect to the presence of authentic Chinese music in the scores of eighteenth-century European opera (or in any musical pieces for that matter) is that it did not appear.[77] The most immediate sense of the exotic was conveyed by nonmusical means, primarily by settings, costumes, plot, characters, and language. Though scanty, information about Chinese music-making and native melodies did exist, however. In a brief section of *Description geographique...*, Du Halde wrote about Chinese music, describing particular instruments and providing musical notation for five different indigenous melodies. Rousseau included one of these "Chinese airs" in his *Dictionnaire de musique* (1768), together with an assortment of other non-European tunes.[78] A decade later, China Jesuit Joseph-Marie Amiot published *Mémoire sur la musique des Chinois* (1779), "one of the earliest and most detailed studies of non-Western music by a Westerner."[79] Amiot claimed to have played music for the imperial court in Beijing. At the very least he must have had access to the Chinese music world, for his text comprised an in-depth treatment of Middle Kingdom instruments and ancient Chinese musical systems. Among the music he transcribed was that used in the famous Confucian ancestor rites. Amiot provided European musical notation for the traditional sung hymn, its lyrics, and even illustrations of the disposition of musicians and dancers as the ritual unfolded. A short while later he published *De la musique moderne des Chinois* (ca. 1780), another treatise on ancient and current Chinese music.

Despite the circulating data, however, no real Chinese music crept into the operas. Miriam Whaples notes that whatever nondomestic music was known to Europeans in the seventeenth and eighteenth centuries, was generally degraded.[80] The one foreign music type most familiar to continental ears was the janissary music native to the Turkish military. Europeans would have heard these marching arrangements with strong percussion and horns from the Turks themselves, and from European composers who on occasion imitated the style for appropriate moments in their works. Turkish musical elements show up in Mozart's *Die Entführung aus dem Serail*, for example.

In part because of the Turkish connection, and because passages on Chinese ceremonial in the Jesuit and other writings frequently mentioned the use of cymbals, bells, drums, and gongs, percussion and percussive instruments came to code a certain Chinese essence in music.[81] Heidi Lee observes that "instruments that were not part of the ordinary symphonic orchestration were associated with 'magical' qualities, . . . for example, the glockenspiel in Mozart's *Die Zauberflöte*."[82] The instruments would have been played both in the orchestra, and sometimes on stage by the actors. Stage directions in Goldoni's *L'isola disabitata* specifically call for an exaggerated instrumental beat to accompany the entrance of four Chinese ambassadors. Concertmaster Karl Ditters von Dittersdorf, attending the 1754 Schlosshof performance of Metastasio's *Le cinesi*, recounted its musical brilliance in his diary: "Gluck's god-like music! It was not only the delicious playfulness of the sparkling symphony, accompanied now and again by little bells, triangles, small hand-drums, etc., sometimes singly, sometimes all together, which at the very outset, and before the raising of the curtain, transported the audience: the music was from first to last an enchantment."[83] Gluck's setting for *Le cinesi* also evidences another strategy for evoking an exotic feel. The use of polonaise or hongrois-style sounds and dance rhythms was thought to lace conventional music with foreign flavor. Gerhard Croll notes that the addition of polonaise rhythm to *Le cinesi*'s final dance ensemble created "something strange that was felt to be, even if most attractive, 'foreign,' perhaps even 'exotic.' "[84]

In fact, theater composers regularly used music associated with dances they considered foreign to convey exoticism and exploit its semantic power. The music associated with a Spanish *zarabanda*, a French *minuette*, even a Sicilian *tarantella* may or may not have been danced to—it was enough just to play it to characterize a personage or scene as nonnative.[85] Thus, even the musical gestures of peoples within or close to one's own society—and yet perceived to be alien—could furnish an exotic expressiveness.[86]

By far the most utilized method for communicating otherness musically was to deviate from conventional idioms. This might include inserting nonmusical ef-

35. Chinese airs. Jean-Baptiste Du Halde. *The General History of China.* Trans. John Watts. London, 1736. Permission of Special Collections, University of Virginia Library.

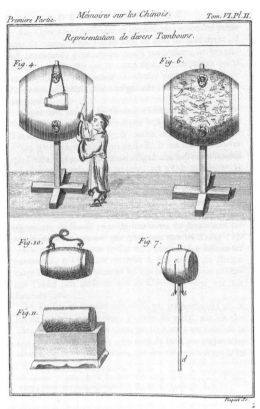

36. Chinese instruments. Amiot, Joseph-Marie. *Mémoire sur la musique del Chinois,* Paris, 1779. Courtesy of the University of Texas.

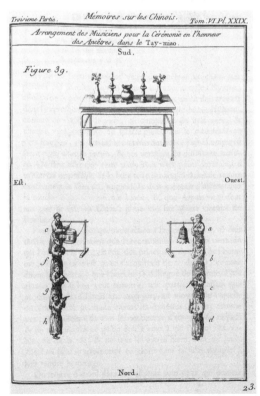

37. Chinese arrangement of musicians. Amiot, Joseph-Marie. *Mémoire sur la musique del Chinois,* Paris, 1779. Courtesy of the University of Texas.

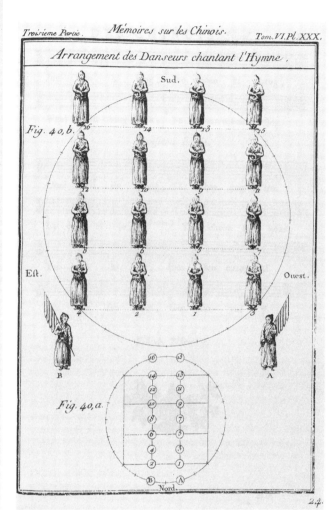

38. Chinese hymn to ancestors and arrangement of dancers, facing page. Amiot, Joseph-Marie. *Mémoire sur la musique del Chinois*, Paris, 1779. Courtesy of the University of Texas.

39. Chinese hymn to ancestors and arrangement of dancers, facing page. Amiot, Joseph-Marie. *Mémoire sur la musique del Chinois*, Paris, 1779. Courtesy of the University of Texas.

fects, but it especially meant altering expected instrumentalization. Jarring key changes, tonal ambiguity, unbalanced phrase structure, asymmetrical phrase length, and/or creating a sense of monotony numbered among the ways to make a "deficient or messy version of European music," tantamount to exoticizing in the eighteenth century.[87] In the case of music specifically created for a staged *ballo*, the more straightforward referentiality of theater dance (as opposed to a dance intended only as an activity for the participants at an occasion) increased the likelihood that a composer would customize music to correspond with the dance's subject. Thus, a dance by and about

non-European peoples would likely be accompanied by distinctive orchestration. Still, this did not mean using authentic music from the particular culture, but rather, mixing elements of familiar musical language in untraditional ways.[88] Even purely instrumental pieces whose titles implied a definite foreign musical stamp—Dutch composer Simoni dall Croubelis's *Simphonie chinoise* and *Dans Le Gout asiatique*, for example, substantiate their alleged exoticism with no more than their titles and nonstandard musical arrangements.[89] Not until the nineteenth century would European composers assimilate authentically Chinese melodies into their compositions.[90]

II
Playing with Dynasty: China in Opera Seria

3

China in Early Opere Serie (1700–1725)

Most Serene Highness
    Today, following the Greek, Roman, and Persian characters that in the last years have played on these stages, we present before you a sort that is almost unknown in our climes. These are the dominant Tartars, and the Chinese. The first find themselves occupied in assaulting, the second in defending, the city of Peking. To the bellicose clash, we now join Actions which have some greatness in them . . .[1]

CHINA MADE ITS GRAND ENTRANCE ONTO THE European opera stage in four different works by Italian dramatists in the first quarter of the eighteenth century. The earliest of these, Apostolo Zeno's *Teuzzone* (1706), was the first Western opera to feature a Chinese setting and characters. *Teuzzone* presented a story of the Chinese imperial heir, challenged in his rise to the throne by evildoers from within the royal entourage.[2] The three operas soon to follow, *Taican, rè della Cina*, by Urbano Ricci (1707), *Il Tartaro nella Cina*, by Antonio Salvi (1715), and *Camaide, l'imperatore della Cina*, by Domenico Lalli (1722), evidence the continuing interest in seeing Chinese rulers stride across the boards. The travails of noble personages of the Middle Kingdom, just like those of the highborn protagonists of all *drammi per musica* at this time, provided readers and audiences abundant entertainment. Even knowing that the political and sentimental dilemmas would work out happily, in accordance with the conventions of the genre, spectators of opera seria fell under its spell. Before starting to analyze how and to what ends the early China operas mobilized received knowledge about the Middle Kingdom, a brief discussion of opera seria will be useful.

Opera seria, known alternatively as Arcadian opera, and a bit later as Metastasian reform opera, first emerged in the late seventeenth and early eighteenth centuries.[3] It developed from the desire by Italian *literati* to purge the "monstrosities" that had accumulated in the *opera per musica* over the course of the Seicento.[4] These aesthetic and moral defects included but were not limited to: the mixing of tragic, comic, and pastoral elements, unintelligible compound plots, excessive spectacle, and interminable numbers of arias whose frivolous, poorly wrought po-

etry was rendered incomprehensible by music run riot. The wish to repair these abominations was symptomatic of a larger need, however. The operatic product of the Seicento was thought to mirror the deplorable *cattivo gusto* (bad taste) of Italian Baroque literature in all its forms. The most programmatic response to the perceived decline in Italian literary arts came from the Arcadian Academy, whose members vowed to restore grandeur, clarity, and above all, Reason, to poetic production.[5]

The achievements of the French neoclassical theater especially motivated the Arcadians. In the hopes of offering a native dramatic exemplar equal in excellence to works by Corneille, Racine, and their peers, the academicians focused their energies on the purification of the Italian spoken tragedy, which also, over the course of the seventeenth century, had suffered from the "shock and awe" strategies of Baroque taste.[6] Naturally, Italian reverence for French and classical dramatic tenets also entered into discussions on how best to revise the *dramma per musica*.

French influence on Italian opera of the eighteenth century was formidable.[7] Not only did the Arcadian librettists frequently turn to Gallic tragedies as source texts, but they also dutifully followed neoclassical poetics in composing their works.[8] Their efforts resulted in *melodrammi* with fewer characters—usually six to eight—and simpler, clearer plotlines. They eliminated all undignified, indecorous, or immoral elements, including comicity, dance, magic, and other forms of the supernatural, and any type of staged violence or bloodshed. The reformers toned down the overblown spectacular effects, and honed the dramaturgy, taking special care with the story action between the aria performances—the recitative sections—so as to create a believable, organic, motivated whole. As for the arias, their number was greatly reduced, and the Arcadian poet-librettist paid exacting attention to their rhetorical substance.

Additionally, the supporters of the new *melodramma* theorized a more intellectually satisfying explanation for sung speech, the improbability of which had been a major complaint leveled against opera by its detractors. The arias, where song was most prominent, became the domain of the passions, a sort of emotive stopping place in the drama, whereas action and dramatic movement took place in the recitative sections. Strohm, however, claims the "aria=emotion, recitative=action" formula did not suffice to justify singing heroic-historical figures. He stresses the fact that conscientious reform librettists made their musical works compatible with classical dramatic theory by making their arias function just like the standard building blocks of "regular," that is, literary, drama. Arias became the song equivalents of "deliberative monologue, part of dialogue, oration, sermon or reproach, sentence, and so on." They were charged with carrying "whatever communication was required by the drama at this point, within the boundaries of necessity and verisimilitude. . . . Julius Caesar and Alexander were just as welcome to sing as was Orpheus and Apollo, as long as their words in the aria conformed to their characters, thoughts, feelings and the dramatic situation."[9] In any case, whether the aria expressed rarefied emotions, profound reflection, or motive sentiment, its new status required precise, carefully calibrated language. Librettists took greater care with the tone, diction, and linguistic harmony of the aria stanzas. No longer did operas regale audiences with a profusion of mostly trite songs scattered throughout. They now presented an organized network of fewer but longer and more highly crafted verse compositions for the voice. With the new dramaturgical and poetic integrity of the aria came the pattern of "staging" it exclusively at the end of a scene. Thus was born the exit-aria convention, whereby a singer-actor would close a scene with the import-laden aria, after which he or she would leave the stage. While the standard nomenclature *dramma per musica* had been in use since the seventeenth century, given all the changes prompted by the new dedication to literary-dramatic dignity, its meaning must surely have been rejuvenated.

Preoccupation with poetic worthiness led to music's marginalization. In fact, one of the more noteworthy features of opera seria in the first decades of the eighteenth century is the lesser role that music plays in terms of dramatization. It had had a more im-

pactful presence in seventeenth-century opera, and would assume an increasingly prominent position with the advent of Metastasian *melodramma* in the 1730s, and especially with the mid-century sophistication of comic opera. In the intervening years, however, from the end of the Seicento through the first decades of the Settecento, music functioned more imagistically than as dramatic expression, and was generally subordinate to the poetry, considered both in its content and vocal and gestural rendering. Strohm observes:

> Until about c. 1730 . . . the decisive factor was the rhetorical significance of the poetic and musical *concetti* (conceits, images) and the theatrical-allegorical language incorporating them . . . what counted was not only the convincing identification of the character with her or his role, and thus with the contents of the words, nor only the beauty of the voice, but just as much the unique, convincing recitation (*pronuntiatio*) according to the precepts of rhetoric, vitally supported by the appropriate action, gesture and mimicry. These precepts were by no means restricted to aria-singing, but were equally valid for recitative.[10]

The overarching principle uniting the revisions that led to opera seria was verisimilitude. The Aristotelian origin of the concept referred to art's accurate imitation of nature so as to make clear the necessary courses of things—especially the essence and inevitable outcomes of human actions. The French neoclassical tragedians' turn to historical subjects was motivated in part by the thought that history, as opposed to myth, romance, and the pastoral, provided real, human experience, and thus better fodder for the exposition of man's actions. History contained figures and episodes which, if rendered properly on the tragic page or stage, would serve to teach the laws of human nature at the same time as they purified the emotions.

Seventeenth-century opera had abounded in flagrant infractions of this classical poetics. Its implausible plots, absurdly contrived endings, and what to many was its biggest sin—outlandish interventions by all manner of supernatural forces—assaulted the notion of the verisimilar and drove the reforming efforts of the Arcadian Academy. To this aesthetically oriented concept of versimilitude, eighteenth-century Italian thinkers also added a socio-philosophical layer. They used the *verosimile* to highlight the power of human reason and virtue. In other words, man's capacity to achieve personal happiness and social harmony through the exercise of his rational mind became a new law of nature that theater could inculcate. Dramas still presented the trying vicissisitudes of heroes, but their stories hinged on the triumph of the virtues of prudence, honor, loyalty, moderation, self-sacrifice, clemency—virtues emblematic of an enlightened society and attainable by reasoning people.

The universal truth of humankind's ability to rise above primitive impulses and destructive passions was most powerfully demonstrated by the happy ending. *Drammi per musica* had traditionally concluded on a joyful note, but now the *lieto fine* had a more doctrinal raison d'etre.[11] The happy ending became an integral part of the didactic goals of theater, insofar as it proved the consubstantiality of reason and virtue, and their superior strength against moral nemeses. Antonio Planelli stated it thus in his treatise *Dell'opera in musica* (1772): "Tragedy's passage from the sad to the happy ending is real verification of the progress made by humankind in terms of its peace, its urbanity, its clemency . . . atrocity had to be eliminated from the modern tragedy; over and above the question of moving its spectators, it did not wish to disgust them, as happens even today simply from reading the Greek tragedies."[12] When the Arcadian reformers altered the endings of the French tragedies they adapted, they did so to show the necessity of the triumph of moral nobility. Thanks then to their adherence to sound neoclassical dramaturgy, the happy endings were much better integrated, far from "the rather implausible and sudden way in which the *lieto fine* [was] sometimes reached" in Baroque musical theater.[13]

The ideals cited above dovetailed with the political picture in early eighteenth-century Italy, as well as in other major European centers, insofar as the absolute monarchy ascribed to itself an ethos founded in Virtue and Reason. Rulers claimed the attributes of nobility, honor, magnanimity, and clear-sighted wisdom, and a good number of opere serie zero in on these aspects of sovereign celebrity. Metastasio's *Alessandro nelle Indie* (1729) and *La clemenza di Tito* (1734) plainly glorify the strengths of the reigning emperor-protagonist. Other serious operas focused on the qualities of a worthy ruler by allegorizing his governance with pastoral nobility. *Il re pastore,* for example, exploits a pastoral setting and characters, and the encounter between Alexander the Great and a lowly shepherd, whose innate goodness and nobly born status (unknown to him, however) destines the *pastorello* for future rule. The opera dramatizes how good kings guide their subjects with the same gentle, diligent care with which the responsible shepherd tends his flock.

Since these were also the years of the wars of the Spanish, Polish, and Austrian successions, a great quantity of *drammi per musica* wove their encomiums to kingly virtue around stories of contested ascendancy.[14] Pretenders, usurpers, betrayals by family members or presumed friends, and all other manner of adversity conspired against a deserving heir to block him from his proper place. As in the dramas mentioned above, the monarch's right to govern was understood to stem from not only blood lineage, but also his or her innate moral excellence. Obstacles in the operatic plot served to demonstrate the inevitable triumph of this royal goodness, signs of which were always discernible even if a character's highborn status was initially hidden. The words and actions of the operatic hero—like those of the supreme ruler—ineluctably revealed the most sublime virtues. These, in turn, validated and effectuated his rise to power. Zeno's *Ormisda* (1721), for example, showcases the duty-bound temperament of the firstborn son and rightful claimant, who triumphs over the mistakes of his father and scheming of other family members. As a topos of serious opera, the trials besetting dynastic continuance ranked mightily. When the noble hero or heroine rose inevitably to his or her rightful spot on the throne, all was well with the world.

The repeated dramatizations of triumphant sovereignty have prompted many scholars of opera seria to identify its primary cultural function as that of celebrating and promulgating hereditary monarchy.[15] While the political angle certainly commands a great deal of operatic space, the spectacles actually affirm a bigger system. They promote a larger universe of moral propaganda which contained, but was not limited to, the absolutist government. Don Neville puts it nicely when he states the following in regard to Metastasian operas: "Although Metastasio was aware of his court responsibilities, it is difficult to ascertain the extent to which calculated propaganda ruled his thinking. The dramas advocate universal moral conditions rather than the principles of a specific regime, yet political conduct had much to gain by association with the moral principles extolled."[16] The new system banked on decorum and cooperation, not the resistance and abandon that had animated the operas of the previous age.[17] Heroic operas modeled for their audiences how to reconcile passions with duty, how to rule and be ruled, how to marry, how to be a friend, a lover, a child, a parent. They celebrated the victory of princely virtues, even when they were not practiced by the prince. This occurs for example in one of the very first reform operas, Domenico David's *La forza di virtù* (1693), where the honorable conduct of a mistreated bride finally overcomes her tyrant-king husband.

The thematic focus on rational virtue was matched in opere serie by their aesthetic virtue. Arcadian poets sought to propagate Virtue and Reason in dramatic works whose very form embodied those qualities. Stripping the Baroque opera of its excesses and immorality, Arcadian librettists wrote simpler, streamlined, "purer" dramas, centered on mellifluous poetry that rejoiced in its upstanding object.

The discussion of opera seria must also include its ideology of entertainment. It may seem strange to speak of entertainment as ideology, but the reference is to Mary Hunter's work on the "poetics of entertainment" in eighteenth-century comic opera.[18] Hunter defines entertainment simply as "the general function of supplying pleasure and diversion," negating distinctions between "low" and "high" art.[19] While she lays out the various ways in which opera buffa provided pleasure to its audiences, her more important point is that pleasure is part of the *meaning* of the dramas. The texts themselves thematize pleasure and enjoyment. Joyful, celebratory story endings, scores of recognizable archetypes that allow for a sense of game mastery in the spectator, and the inscription of performance within performance—that is, moments deliberately designed to jar viewers from the dramatic illusion and remind them that (and how much) they are enjoying the talent displayed before them, are the principal modes in which the buffo work communicated the high value of pleasure.

The affirmation of pleasure in serious opera worked in similar and dissimilar ways. Its familiar sources, plots, characters, and musico-dramatic devices allowed for the same feeling of consumer competence evoked by its comic counterpart. However, Hunter observes that the delights of meta-performance were much more typical of comedy (spoken and musical) than of heroic opera, given that the former has more "opportunities for characters explicitly to enact a performance on stage, often, but not always, for the benefit of an onstage audience as well as for the auditorium spectators."[20] As the "performed performances" of opera buffa temporarily distanced the spectator from the dramatic narrative, they focused attention on the "pleasures of the moment." These sorts of pleasures were not so readily induced by opera seria, which more tightly inhabited its story space.

On the other hand, opera seria's deeper and more prolonged immersion in story space compensated for its lesser offering of overt performativity. The intrigue and suspense in the plots of serious operas made for a kind of pleasure not possible in opera buffa. Opere serie were chock-full of false reports, misunderstandings, treachery, star-crossed love, pride, jealousy, youthful impulse, imprisonments, surprise military routs, imminent uprisings, death sentences, shifting alliances, fraught friendships, and last-minute rescues. They also drew spectators in with greater depth in characters and their passions, compared to those of the previous century. Strohm remarks: "the growing tendency towards heroic-historical subjects (as opposed to mythological ones) helped to make characters appear more human, more 'psychologically' motivated, even more sentimental. The spectator was now encouraged to identify with the heroes in their humanity."[21]

The pleasure that Hunter locates in the consistency between comic opera's poetics and society's conventions must have been intensified for readers and spectators of serious opera, since the conformity was so much more overt.[22] In its content and its form, the reform libretto openly privileges hierarchy, structure, rules and their abiding. With its ritualistic character and "its apparent freedom and spontaneity of personal artistic expression [the *dramma per musica* came] to symbolize aristocratic norms of morality and rulership."[23] Gratifying happy endings only reinforced the legitimacy of ruling-class ethics.

Serious opera's engrossing protagonists, the gripping nature of its story dramas, and the satisfying complexity of their denouements, should not be underestimated. These attributes counter modern criticism that too frequently has narrowed in on the formulaic constraints of opera seria, or reduces the genre to spotlight moments of virtuoso singing linked by the thin connective tissue of recitative.[24] Arias were certainly an enormous attraction, but the narrative schemes supporting them captivated attention perhaps in the same way as do the intrigues of a politically oriented Harrison Ford movie, or the popular television series *West Wing*.[25] The fact is, until comic opera began to hit its stride in the second half of the century, heroic opera dominated the scene. Of the ten operas per year staged in Venice from 1701 to 1745, approximately nine were of the serious type. Even when opera buffa joined the offerings, opera seria held its ground, matching it in number—five to six operas in both categories annually—until the last decade of the eighteenth century, when bourgeois theatrical tastes tipped the scale definitively on the side of the comic.[26] With the exception of France, which excluded Italian opera, the kingdoms outside the peninsula also privileged opera seria for the greater part of the century.[27]

⁂

The four operas to be treated below engage the Middle Kingdom in different ways. As early manifestations of China's operatic debut in Europe, they reveal not only which aspects of Chinese civilization were found most fascinating in the first part of the century, but also how those aspects served the interests of the genre. Two of the works, *Teuzzone* and *Il Tartaro nella Cina*, take up contemporary perceptions of China at a deeper level, that is, in support of discrete political, moral, or aesthetic principles. The mobilization of the Celestial Empire in *Camaide, l'imperatore della Cina* is less focused and less embedded in doctrinal concerns. *Taican, rè della Cina* exploits China in a still more superficial manner. Its representation of China appears to be principally geared to satisfying theater patrons hungry for titillating sensation, variety, and spectacle.

APOSTOLO ZENO, *TEUZZONE* (1706)

Set in vaguely contemporary times, *Teuzzone* concerned the struggles and eventual victory of a rightful Chinese heir over devious in-house contenders.[28] It would appear then to advocate for dynastic continuance, one of the customary themes of serious opera. Zeno, however, was a major proponent of the reform of Italian literature in the early eighteenth century. His *melodramma*, therefore, has much to do with Arcadian poetics. In *Teuzzone*, he uses China to address the problem of a lapsed literary aesthetic in Italy.

Zeno profits from ideas first expressed in the encomiastic Jesuit writings to capitalize on China's special access to Virtue and Reason. Italian *literati* quickly took up these missionary portrayals, producing glowing, harmonious portraits of the nation, or what Zoli calls an "Arcadian image" of the Celestial Kingdom.[29] Disseminating this image, however, required sidestepping certain polemics surrounding the European understanding of China, especially those provoked by the Jesuit missionary intervention there. It is beyond the scope of this study to detail the issues involved in the Rites Controversy, but suffice it to say that arguments among European religious and intellectual figures over whether Chinese philosophical doctrine constituted heresy reached a vehement pitch at just the time of *Teuzzone*'s creation.[30] Associated with the religious question were debates on Chinese history and language, since assertions of their antiquity jolted traditional European conceptual frameworks with respect to the age of the world and origins of language.[31] *Teuzzone* nevertheless barely references these potentially provocative topics. No mention is made of Confucianism or ancestor worship, nor does Zeno cite aspects of the Middle Kingdom that would have

evoked religious issues, such as the mandarin class and the bonzes, lower-grade priests ministering to the Chinese populace. Despite the Tartar takeover of Chinese territory just decades earlier, the conflictual elements of which proved desirable dramatic material for a number of his contemporaries, Zeno steers clear of the Chinese-Tartar tension. Instead, he projects a version of the Celestial Empire that stresses its mythic potency. Taking advantage of the cultural authority accrued to China, thanks primarily to the Jesuits, *Teuzzone* exploits a tidbit of Chinese lore to promote the classical principles retained essential to Arcadian ideology.

Zeno prepares readers and audiences for the onstage representation of this lore—specifically, a Chinese legend explaining the beginning of the world, and its annual commemoration ritual—by including it in a list of customs contained in the *Argomento* section of the libretto: "On a certain day of the year, that here is indicated to be the first of May, the Ritual of the Mare takes place; the Hall, or the Royal Courtyard, is adorned with pastoral decoration; this is done in memory of the birth of the world, which the Chinese believe happened on this day, by way of a cow that kicked an egg; they say that this universe came forth thereof."[32] The dramatization of the Chinese world birth day takes place in the opera's final scenes (3, 12–14). Stage directions indicate a "Pastoral Hall, which represents the Reign of Spring, completely adorned with flowers" ("Sala pastorale, che rappresenta la Reggia della Primavera, tutta di fiori adornata"). Crowns of flowers decorate the chorus members, who sing a song of joy and thanks for new beginnings. At the same time, Zeno achieves dramatic chiaroscuro as first Teuzzone, then Zelinda, the wrongly condemned protagonists, are brought on stage to hear their death sentences. In the midst of this suspense, a mobile platform from which rises a gigantic golden horse is wheeled upon the stage, symbol of "the Ritual of the Mare."[33] The *colpo di scena* occurs when, instead of proclaiming the victims' sentences, Cino reads the authentic will naming Teuzzone the imperial successor. At just this moment the huge horse comes apart, emitting a phalanx of soldiers who rush to avenge the rightful heir. As the crowd cries out for retribution ("Vendetta, vendetta!"), the surprise army overcomes Zidiana and her followers, permitting Teuzzone to take the throne with Zelinda as his queen.

The use of an allegedly authentic Chinese tradition to support the drama's culminating peripety served several purposes. First, it allowed for the spectacle so pleasing to audiences, but also justified it. In an age overcome with gratuitous mechanical effects, often in

IL
TEUZZONE
DRAMA PER MUSICA

Da rappresentarsi nel Regio Ducal
Teatro di Milano l'anno 1706.

CONSECRATO

Al Serenissimo

PRENCIPE

DI

VAUDEMONT, &c.

IN MILANO,

Nella Reg. Duc. Corte, per Marc' Antonio
Pandolfo Malatesta Stampatore Reg. Cam.
Con licenza de' Superiori.

the form of gargantuan structures erupting in crowds of actors or dancers, the Chinese festival permitted such a showstopper, but from within the bounds of the verisimilar.[34] Second, quoting the documented Chinese ceremony availed dramatic verisimilitude. The happy ending comes about not only because the jilted Cino decides to expose Zidiana's fraud, but also because the palace celebration with its customary colossal horse gives Teuzzone's supporters a convenient, effective way in which to retaliate on his behalf. The outcome is thus doubly plausible.[35] Third, couching the issue of China's version of world history in an innocuous myth blunted possible thorny points regarding the true age of the universe.

In addition to all this, however, these scenes accomplish still more. China as figured in the "Ritual of the Mare" confers visual, gestural, and allegorical significance to Virtue and Reason, the touchstones of Arcadian poetics. Obviously, the golden mare disgorging its army of just defenders blatantly evokes the Trojan horse episode of European classical history.[36] The "sala pastorale," with its springtime floral embellishments, also suggests an Arcadian setting, reinforced by the rusticity conjured in the *Argomento*'s reference to a legendary Chinese cow knocking open an egg with its hoof. What might appear a mere exploitation of an exotic Asian festivity for its visual theatrics, is in fact a conflation of three potent meditations on origins and original virtue. Zeno merges China, Troy/Greece, and Arcadia in a single stroke, fusing his concept of virtue with the notion of civilizational authority, of which the Celestial Empire now plays a part. Gliding over the troublesome issues of Chinese chronology, Chinese linguistic ancestry, and Chinese religious integrity, *Teuzzone* seamlessly aligns Chinese with Greco-Roman antiquity. In perhaps the same spirit of syncretism or osmosis that allowed the biblical and Roman myths of origin to be assimilated for so long, *Teuzzone* represents Middle Kingdom antiquity not as a competitor with that of Europe, but as a complement, even a virtual equivalent —China as the incarnation of the same originary virtues elsewhere.[37]

The specification of a pastoral ambience in the Chinese palace hall ("sala pastorale, che rappresenta la Reggia della Primavera, tutta di fiori adornata") suggests cultural convergence, since it visually combines disparate elements: outside and inside, country and court, naïveté and sophistication. The blossoms, the focus on nature, and the rebirth of spring point up the innocence and untainted beginnings typically associated with the outdoors and seasonal change. But here the bucolic environment flourishes indoors, inside the

royal chambers. The courtly interior, emblematic of refinement, of man's civilized domestication of nature's wild impulses, embraces the simplicity and purity of rural spring.

Of course, serious operas commonly celebrated the conformity between court and pastoral spheres. Ruling administrations ascribed to themselves the "healthy" values associated with nature's innocence, beauty, and cyclical generativity. However, on stage, the two milieus were generally kept distinct. Dramas took place in their entirety in *either* pastoral *or* palace environs. A temporal distance also separated the two, inasmuch as operas typically presented the able ruler as having benefited from a pastoral apprenticeship, a crucial preparation phase experienced in youth, before undertaking the more complex duties and responsibilities of the throne.[38] *Teuzzone* erases this difference, merging one world with the other. The towering war machine in the midst of the pastoral roomscape infers the same felicitous coexistence of guileless naïveté with prudent military cunning. Moreover, the scene presents China as the place in which these worlds blend: sophistication with virtue, the currency of the present with integrity of the past.

Again, the notion of origins proves meaningful. As members of the Arcadian Academy decried the bad taste of the poetry of the Seicento, they not only extolled the formal and musical excellence of ancient Greek lyric, but also urged contemporary *literati* to recall (and recreate) the infallible eloquence of the first great masters in the Italian literary canon. Scipione Maffei, founder of the Arcadian colony in Verona (1705), laments in his inaugural speech how the previous century has forgotten the origins of Italian poetry, embodied in the peninsula's first and magisterial writers, including, of course, the Dolce Stil Novo poets, Dante, and Petrarch.[39] Maffei, together with all *arcadi* of the early eighteenth century, envisioned the Trecento and Cinquecento as dual apogees of Italian literary production, containing the illustrious examples of writing upon whose originary beauty and purity contemporary poets should model their own work.[40] In this perspective whereby past excellence generates fresh, present excellence, origins beget new origins. By observing the perfection of their national authorial sources, Arcadian poets and critics could create new poetic beginnings. Maffei writes: "putting before ourselves so many sublime exemplars does not infer, however, that one is bound to imitate these works; doing so would prohibit the mind from forming new worlds, if such are to be had; these should be formed in our language, since, from what we know about living languages, it is the only one fitting true

Poetry, if such can be said, and it is always capable of new things."[41] The Arcadians thus welcomed the formation of "a new world," of poetic as well as moral virtue. China, as paragon of a past and present cultural authority, could buttress these poetics. As the Trojan horse evocation naturalized China, China likewise legitimized the Arcadian effort. Dignity could be restored to Italian letters and artistic culture by redressing them in a new, contemporary iteration (Chinese) of the old, the revered, the authentic (Greek).

On yet another level, the Chinese pastoral stage set may have had further resonance for Arcadian Academy members, whose regular gatherings took on theatrical overtones when they dressed as shepherds and called one another by bucolic names fashioned on Greek figures.[42] Zeno's "pastoralizing" of the Middle Kingdom in the last scenes of *Teuzzone* does not limit itself to languid evasion, however. Rather, the courtly Chinese Arcadia spawns the sudden anagnorisis that reinstates Teuzzone on the Chinese throne. This outcome in turn evokes the starkly directive message and method of the Arcadian aesthetic: "the poet's meditation should not be unique nor highly individual, but generic and thus all the more universal . . . Skill is no longer signaled by originality or by the complexity of an image or poem, but in de-personalizing and in generalizing; the more expertly one does this the more one makes known the human and existential validity of certain absolute truths."[43] China's depersonalization in *Teuzzone*, and the merging of its wisdom and antiquity with that of classical Greece, postulates that the opera's happy ending derives not merely from the deserving ruler's ultimate ascension to power. Rather, in this instance, the *lieto fine*, one of opera seria's most significant dramaturgical moments, *is* the China-Greece synthesis. That moral and political rightness emerge victorious in China, a nation that, like Italy, can make claims to ancient, unassailable ethical foundations, drives home the universality of the virtues promulgated in *Teuzzone*.

Antonio Salvi, *Il Tartaro nella Cina* (1715)

Unlike Zeno, Antonio Salvi turned to recent Chinese history and to proto-anthropological data for his 1715 *dramma per musica, Il Tartaro nella Cina*. The opera is based on events in the seventeenth-century takeover of Ming China by the Ch'ing dynasty, or Manchu Tartars. Specifically, it exploits perceived contrasts in the natures of the Chinese and Tartar people, using this opposition to sustain the essentialist characterization endemic to early opera seria.

The differing traits of the Tartars and Chinese had been noted by nearly every European author on China since Marco Polo. Their historically conflictual relationship accounted for much of the interest, moving European historians to faithfully narrate the repeated incursions of the Tartars into the Celestial Empire, starting with the earliest known dynasty (Ch'in, ca. 200 BC), the period in which the Great Wall was erected against the Tartars, to the time of Genghis-Khan (thirteenth century).[44] These accounts generally depict China as a peaceful, civilized, and educated nation, repeatedly forced to submit to a ruthless, belligerent Tartar oppressor. Common appellations applied to the Tartars included "the enemy" and "the barbarian." Their nomadic life explained their battle readiness and savage nature:

> it is no wonder they are so quick, for they never carrie with them any Baggage, nor do they take care for Provision: for they feed themselves with what they finde, yet commonly they eat Flesh, though half rosted, or half boyled; if they find none, then they devour their Horses, or Camels: but ever when they have leasure, they go a hunting all manner of wild Beasts, either by some excellent Dogs and Vultures, which they bring up for that end, or else by incompassing a whole Mountain, or large Field, they beat up all the wild Beasts into a circle, and drive them into so narrow a compasse, as that they can take as many as they please, and dismisse the rest. The earth covered with their Horse-cloath is their Bed, for they care not for Houses, and Chambers; . . . but yet their Tents are most beautiful, which they fix and remove with such Art and dexterity, as they never retard the speedy march of an Army. Thus the Tartars train their souldiers to hardnesse for War.[45]

Martini wrote further that "like a Torrent," the Tartar overran many small cities, and "struck such a terrour into the hearts of all the Countries he had passed, as both Souldier and Citizen quitting their Houses left the empty walls to the Tartarians' possession, knowing the Tartar to have that custom and practice, to destroy and put all to fire and sword that did resist, and only pillage the Cities that submitted."[46] Nieuhof labeled Tartars "a Nation of Plunderers and Robbers, being naturally inclin'd to those Vices. And no wonder, for they live . . . without . . . any Religion."[47] His words below neatly sum up the perceived difference between the Chinese and their northern neighbors:

> how much the Tartars and Chineses differ in their Customs and Manners, will easily be made appear by the daily Employments and Actions each of them affects from the Cradle. The Chinese is of an affable and peaceable Disposition, addicted to Husbandry, and loving all

IL
TARTARO
NELLA CINA.
DRAMA PER MUSICA
Da rappresentarsi nel Teatro dell' Illustriffimo
Pubblico di Reggio in occasione della
Fiera l' Anno MDCCXV.

Dedicato all' Altezza Sereniffima
D I
RINALDO I.
DUCA di Reggio, Modona,
Mirandola, &c.

In Reggio, per Ippolito Vedrotti. 1715.
CON LIC. DE' SUPERIORI.

41. Frontispiece, *Tartaro nella Cina.* Permission Fondazione Giorgio Cini, Raccolta Rolandi, Venezia.

good Arts and Sciences. But the Tartar, on the other Hand, delights in nothing so much as Hunting, being very cunning and deceitful, lusting after War, and of a very loose and uncivil Comportment. It is true, both endeavor to shun Idleness, but with Intentions very incoherent; the one to live temperately and honestly; but the other only to range abroad in a wild and beastial Barbarism.[48]

On occasion, however, the terms sustaining the polarization changed. The placid Chinese disposition appeared as weakness and timid effeminacy, in contrast to Tartar virility. In parts of his text Martini describes the Chinese as "a flock of silly sheep," killed by Tartars whose very image "was grown so terrible to them, as they fled at the very sight of their Horses."[49] Nieuhof credits the rise of the Ming in 1368 to the degeneration of Tartar might: they became like "effeminate Chineses."[50]

Mitigation of the mostly black-and-white characterization of Tartar and Chinese ensued in coverage of the most recent Manchu conquest of Chinese territory. Given its currency, and the fact that a number of European chroniclers were actually present to witness its episodes, the seventeenth-century Manchu rise to power received greater textual attention than earlier Tartar-Chinese conflicts, and the narratives offered a less divisive picture. Writers cited bloody individual instances, but many observers recognized the relatively peaceful transition from Ming to Ch'ing. As noted above, they disseminated an assessment of the conquest that noted Chinese weaknesses as well as Tartar strengths. A frequent comment concerned the positive transformation of the Tartar rulers, once possessed of Chinese lands. Their improvement results in part from their contact with the Chinese, but also from their own perspicacity. Martini writes that Zungteus, Tartar king and new emperor of China as of 1636, surpassed

> all the Kings of Tartary in Humanity, and obliging courtesie: For when he was young, he was sent by his Father into China, where he lived secretly, and learned the China's Manners, Doctrine and Language, and now coming to the Kingdom, he changed, and far surpassed all the Examples of his Predecessors. For having observed, that their too hard and cruel usage of the Chineses, had been the principal obstacle of their advancement, to the end he might conquer that empire he so much thirsted after, as well by Love as by Arms, he courteously entertained and cherished all those of China which came unto him, using all Prisoners with great sweetness, and inviting them either to submit freely to his government, or take their course with full freedom.[51]

Nieuhof notes: "The Tartars, having clear'd the Kingdom of the two great Robbers, Licungzus and Chan-

glianchus, . . . immediately endeavor'd by all fair means to settle the Kingdom in Peace and Quietness; which they shortly to their great satisfaction and content brought to pass, and enjoy the same at this time without any further disturbance."[52] The good Tartar rulers knew to conquer China "more by Civility and Humanitie, than by force of Armes," and their newfound humanity even surpassed that of the Chinese.[53] In the seventeenth-century reports the Tartars were merciful governors, unlike the harsh Chinese, whose laws allowed for the beheading of the simply misfortunate. In certain respects the Tartars were also more like Europeans than were the Chinese, for example, in their sensitivity to a marriageable woman's social extraction. Nieuhof points out that the Chinese ignore the station of a prospective wife and consider only her outward beauty. This results at times in unions between a royal and a woman of mean extraction, a person not of quality.[54] According to Martini, the Tartars "in no way like the grimness and sourness of the Chinese gravity, and therefore in the first abords they appear more humane."[55]

Returning to *Il Tartaro nella Cina,* Salvi's libretto exhibits none of this evenhandedness. Instead, in keeping with the moral absolutism required in opera seria, *Il Tartaro nella Cina* dramatizes the magnanimity, order, and innate virtue of incumbent dynasty—represented unequivocally by the Chinese—by juxtaposing it against the violence, brutality, and tyranny of invaders—emblematized by the Tartars. With the exception of Ermanda, who plays a minor role, the emperor Licungo is the only Tartar figure among the protagonists. Vanlio describes Licungo with these words after having discovered that the Tartar ruler has imprisoned his father, Colao:

> For Licungo
> every right, every law, every rationale
> resides in the sword.
>
> (1, 7)

> [Licungo
> Nella spada ripone
> Ogni dritto, ogni legge, ogni ragione.]

Licungo himself revels in his penchant for torture and bloodshed as he tells Vanlio to cede Peking or he'll murder Colao in front of him. He then details exactly how Colao will be killed:

> With tight shackles
> Have him tied to that tree. The target
> Of a hundred arrows, his soul
> Shall leave him through all the wounds: then let

The cadaver hang from the branch; so it dangles
A spectacle for the people,
Food for the vultures, mocked by the winds.
And you, arrogant son,
So that your cruelty is all the more recompensed,
With your now dry eyes count the wounds
In your father's breast;
    Count the wounds; and then
    Say to yourself
    You're equal to my heart, cold eyes.
    Yes, my barbarian heart
    Opened those wounds
    And worse, you look upon them.

                             (2, 7)

[Con tenaci ritorte
A' quel tronco s'annodi. A' cento strali
Fatto bersaglio, esali
L'alma da più ferite: indi s'appenda
Il cadavere al tronco; e quindi penda
Spettacolo alle genti,
Pascolo agli Avoltoi, ludibrio a' venti.
E tù, superbo figlio,
Perche tua crudeltà vie più s'appaghe,
Or con asciutto ciglio
Nel petto al Genitor conta le piaghe.
    Conta le piaghe; e poi
    Dì pure agli occhi tuoi:
    Al pari del mio cor, luci spietate.
    Sì, barbaro il cor mio
    Quelle ferite aprio,
    E più barbare ancor voi le mirate.]

The Chinese characters (six of the opera's total eight), on the other hand, variously dramatize positive, noble qualities. Colao and Arturo/Zunteo figure most prominently in this aspect. Their recitative sections and arias explicitly delineate the heroism that the drama attaches to the persevering, inherently worthy Chinese and their counterpart, a meritorious European dynasty.

Arturo, no matter his circumstances, epitomizes goodness and valor. He is respectful of his elders, merciful to Colao, and unfailingly honorable in his dealings with every faction. Amidst the Chinese imperial forces, Arturo cooperates with potential enemies, and his alliance with Vanlio, son of Colao, is especially noteworthy in this regard. He and Vanlio work together as if they were loving brothers. He fully recognizes his father's failings, such as in the following exchange with Assuana, daughter of the deceased Chinese emperor:

My fate is the only thing to blame,
Queen; that I was born
Son of your enemy, and an enemy

Who cruelly offends
Every law, every right
Of the people, and the Heavens.

                             (3, 2)

[Colpa è sol del mio Fato,
Regina, ch'io sia nato
Figlio d'un tuo Nemico, e d'un Nemico,
Ch'ogni legge, ogni dritto
Delle genti, e del Ciel crudele offende.]

Nonetheless, he later petitions Vanlio for mercy toward Licungo should he be captured by the Chinese. The blunt evaluation of his father (clearly echoing Vanlio's of act 1) by such a loving, loyal son exacerbates Licungo's depravity. In turn, it elevates Arturo. He is ever the faithful, dutiful son/friend/lover, and when he acts as a subject or minister of an elder or ruler's commands, he embodies a sense of justice based in clemency and moderation.

Arturo's compassionate forbearance is so pervasive not even he fully comprehends it. When he finds himself suspending the sentence he was to carry out against Colao, he expresses puzzlement over his apparent disobedience. His powerlessness over his will to leniency only emphasizes the inevitability of virtue in certain individuals, and the necessity of their eventual ascendancy. As mentioned, opera seria ideology ties the idea of predetermined goodness to heredity. Colao underscores this concept of excellence preordained by nature, in a simile aria wherein he compares Arturo's incomprehensible genetic relation to the villain Licungo to nature's miracles: that clear waters spring from unlikely sources, that beautiful flowers bloom sometimes from rank, malodorous plants:

Oh God, can such a pious son
Be born from such an impious parent?
    As from the dark, ignoble mountain,
    From the vile, muddy spring
    The clearest stream is born as son;
    As the vile, fetid, stinking plant
    Can boast the birth
    Of the white lily, king of flowers.

                          (2, 10)

[E nascer puote, oh Dio!
Da un'empio Genitor Figlio sì pio?
    Sì da oscura ignobil Monte,
    E da vil torbida Fonte,
    Nasce il Rio più chiaro figlio;
    Sì da vil fetida pianta
    Tutto odor nascer si vanta
    Rè de' fiori il bianco giglio.]

The revelation of Arturo's princely lineage at the end of the opera, and his ultimate triumph as Chinese monarch over the Tartar interlopers, proves the truth of imperial destiny. Inherited virtue supersedes all impediments, and always belies contrary appearances. A single declaration by Arturo, made before he realizes his Chinese ancestry, not only implies this ideology, but also shows the precise terms that Salvi chose to bring it to life:

> I am Tartar, it is true; but in my nature,
> My genius, and my affection I am Chinese.
>
> (3, 3)

> [Tartaro, è ver, son'io; mà per natura,
> Per genio, e per affetto io son Cinese.]

China constitutes natural virtue, Tartary its opposite.

Stage directions for the sets of *Tartaro nella Cina* reinforce the Chinese-Tartar difference. Salvi is careful to distinguish between the two cultures, with respect to landscape, architecture, furnishings, and other visual details. He prescribes a pavilion "in Tartar style" ("all'uso Tartaro"), and a battlefield strewn with tents "alla Tartara." For scenes that take place in Chinese environs, on the other hand, he calls for all the familiar accoutrements of the Celestial Empire:

Act 1
Pagoda, or circular temple with altar and deity; pedestal, where the torch burns, Bonzes and Ministers.
(1, 5)
Royal Cabinet decorated with porcelain.
(1, 16)

Act 2
Countryside, in which the city walls are seen with a view of the bulwark, on which Vanlio advances.
(2, 5)
Hall with throne. Assuana dressed in mourning with her entire entourage, all dressed in white; she ascends the throne waited on by Taicungo and Mandarins.
(2, 13)

Act 3
Hallway with statues of Chinese kings, and porcelain urns.
(3, 1)
Delightful walkway shaded with palms, awnings spread from tree to tree.
(3, 8)
Piazza covered by a great funeral tent, nighttime illumination from a raised pyre, decorated with gold and silver vases, typically in use at the Chinese king's table; the pyre is surrounded by veiled victims, with ministers, bonzes, mandarins, holding various musical instruments; populace and guards. Throne, where Assuana and Timurta sit. . . .
(3, 17)

The "delizioso" (exquisite, delightful) quality that Salvi specifies for the Chinese tableaux must have diverged strikingly from the Tartar military panoramas. Stage sets for the only known performance of *Tartaro nella Cina* were furthermore designed by Francesco Bibiena, of the famous Bibiena family, suggesting an especially spectacular visual representation of the two peoples.[56]

DOMENICO LALLI, *CAMAIDE, L'IMPERATORE DELLA CINA* (1722)

Domenico Lalli's *Camaide, l'imperatore della Cina* (1722) reprises the oppositional characterization of *Tartaro*, except that it does not involve two contrary cultures. Here the antithesis between virtue and vice is played out between two Chinese brothers. Even though each eventually teams up with Chinese and Tartar forces respectively, their individual correspondences with the ethnographic difference doesn't obtain. Rather, the measure which determines the integrity of Tico (the good Chinese brother) and Cambice (the bad Chinese brother) is filial piety. *Camaide* is about loyalty to one's father, paternal authority and filial duty, reverence for familial, ancestral (and hence imperial) hierarchy. Indeed, the following recitative and aria in which Tico rallies the Chinese army quite neatly packages *Camaide*'s foundational ideology:

> Friends, the mighty defense
> Of the fatherlands
> Depends on you. Hear the prayers
> Of your trembling wives,
> Of your tender children,
> That you render them safe
> From hostile fury.
> *May you be spurred to the task*
> *Not by honor, nor by faith. I point only*
> *To your betrayed king, my father,*
> *oppressed by a disloyal son.* All hope
> lies in your strength. From you awaits
> Either the court's salvation, or vendetta.
>
> Rise up! Take on every challenge;
> *A father deserves such;*
> *You owe it to your King.*
> Death, bloodshed, fierce terror,
> Be they the rally cries of your honor;
> The glory of your faith.
>
> (3, 6) (italics mine)

CAMAIDE
IMPERATORE
DELLA CHINA.

O VERO

LI FIGLIUOLI RIVALI DEL PADRE.

DRAMMA PER MUSICA,

DA RAPPRESENTARSI

NEL TEATRO DI CORTE.

PER

ORDINE DI S. A. R.

MONSIGNOR

FRANCESCO
ANTONIO,

ARCIVESCOVO, E PRENCIPE

DI SALISBURGO,

Prencipe del S. R. I. Legato Nato, della
S. Sed. Apoſt. Primate della Germania,
E PRENCIPE D'HARRACH, &c. &c.

POESIA

Del Sig. Domenico Lalli.

MUSICA

Del Sig. Antonio Caldara, Vice-Maeſtro
di Cappella di S. M. C. e C.

SALISBURGO, Appreſſo Giovanni Gioſeppe Mayr,
Stampatore di Corte di Sua Altezza Reverendiſſima.

42. Frontispiece, *Camaide, l'imperatore della Cina.* Courtesy Schatz Collection of Opera Librettos, United States Library of Congress, Music Division.

[Amici, à voi si deve
Dè le patrie contrade
La possente difesa. Udite i voti
Dè le spose tremanti,
E de i teneri figli, acciò che salvi
Da l'ostile furor voi li rendiate:
Non l'onor, non la fede io vi rammento
Per sprone à l'opra. Io sol vi addito il vostro
Tradito Rè, mio genitor, che oppresso
È da un figlio sleal. Tutta la spene
Post'è nel vostro braccio. A voi si aspetta
O la regia salvezza, ò la vendetta.

    Sù s'incontri ogni cimento;
      Tanto merta un genitore;
      Lo dovete al vostro Rè.
    Morte, stragi, fier spavento
      Vanti sien del vostro onore;
      Gloria sien di vostra fè.]

The stimulus to patriarchal fealty suggests a different way in which the opera mobilized the Middle Kingdom. Perceptions of Chinese respect for ancestors, and the intricate protocols of deference practiced by Chinese children toward their parents, reinforced the dramatic summons to honor one's father at all costs. In a more general fashion, the larger system of Chinese social relationship and ceremonial served the work's constant stress on roles and hierarchical position. Over and over again characters invoke the designations of son, father, parent, husband, vassal, lord, king, emperor, and judge, qualifying the nature of each as well as the ideal interaction between the roles. As the opera's antagonist, however, Cambice defies the sanctioned relationships, in both action and word. Speaking of his father Camaide and his claim on young Lovamia, who Cambice himself desires, he says:

    The father
    Is son to the successor;
    He will soon see he must give her up.

                             (2, 6)

    [Il padre
    Al successore è figlio;
    Cederla ben saprà.]

He challenges his father directly with these words:

    You hope in vain.
    Attribute it my failing
    That I am your king, and you my vassal.

                            (3, 8)[57]

    [In van tu speri.
    Scusa sia del mio fallo
    L'esser io tuo Sovran, tu mio Vassallo.]

The defection of Cambice—the villain—from China at the opera's end, points to the figuring of the Celestial Empire as a model for social order.

Lalli's exploitation of received ideas about China is nowhere as direct or extensive as that in *Teuzzone* and *Tartaro*, however. Unlike the self-conscious cultural characterizations in Salvi's libretto, Lalli's text makes no reference to filial deference as a Chinese trait. Nor is the Middle Kingdom very integral to any of the opera's chief conventions. China even figures minimally in the stage sets, at least judging from the libretto. The settings described there confirm Lalli's overall reliance on generic underpinnings for his opera. With one exception, the elaborate, explicit descriptions seen in Salvi's text have been reduced to concise, boiled-down labels.

Act 1
    Royal courtyard.
    Royal Piazza of the Nankin palace.

Act 2
    Temple, where one sees a statue of Camaide, adorned in imperial fashion; in front of the statue dances are performed in the Chinese style, to augur the health of the Emperor; around the dancers swirl various Parasols and Banners, upon which are painted the signs of the Zodiac.
    Imperial rooms.
    Chamber in remote place.

Act 3
    Delightful garden.
    Royal fortress wall.
    Loggias leading to various royal apartments.[58]

For only one set of scenes (beginning with 2, 1) does Lalli elaborate on the constituent elements of the backdrop. This portion of the opera offers a key to understanding *Camaide*'s dependence on China. The sequence (2, 1–5) appears to contain the preponderance of Chinese "paraphernalia" represented over the course of the opera. Moreover, it presents a slightly haphazard mix of Chinese elements—religious (temple, idol), political (rituals in honor of emperor), and sociocultural (Chinese-style dances, parasols, banners, zodiac symbols). The five scenes that unfold in this setting concern Lovamia's great consternation in love. She recounts how her passion for Tico revived on hearing that his father, her betrothed, was dead; now that the patriarch turns out to be alive and she is still beholden to marry him, she is filled with torment; Camaide mistakes her diffidence toward him as love for Cambice; Tico and Lovamia admit their love for each other, but bemoan the conflict between love and duty.

The combination of the miscellaneous Chinese properties with the dramatic action centered on love hints at the phenomenon of chinoiserie, together with its sociocultural repercussions. David Porter identifies the aesthetic of chinoiserie as a "celebration of superfice," an elevation of illegible, and therefore illegitimate forms, that destabilized classicist preeminence.[59] Openly deflating the cultural authority (philosophical, theological, linguistic, historical) associated with China, chinoiserie reveled in fantastical insubstantiality, "transforming symbols of awe-inspiring cultural achievement into a motley collection of exotic ornamental motifs."[60] Its patrons sought only pleasure and delight in the emblems and articles of Chinese or pseudo-Chinese provenance crowding the European marketplace and thence their homes.

Such self-indulgence does not surprise, given that chinoiserie was also connected almost exclusively with private areas and personal entertainments. Typical of secluded, informal spaces, Chinese import items and their facsimiles initially comprised decorative elements, furnishings, and objects for interiors, usually the more intimate sections thereof. From bedrooms, dressing rooms, cabinets, closets, and private apartments, chinoiserie expanded to include whimsical structures in gardens, and architectural elements of secondary residences, such as chateaus. Rarely, however, was chinoiserie employed in large-scale artistic works or buildings.

With its elemental intimacy and playfulness, so similar to the Rococo style with which it was frequently blended, the chinoiserie aesthetic also evoked notions of sensual and hedonistic love. The culture of gallantry had developed in France, and among its sybaritic pleasures, it ennobled the purely voluptuous, physical aspect of love. Many criticized such hedonism as corrupt and antithetical to proper love sentiments, ideally based in moral decency. In place of this, *galanteria* substituted a gay, carefree, blithe mode of affection, oblivious to virtue and bordering (dangerously? tantalizingly?) on the libertine.[61]

This chinoiserie aesthetic emerges clearly in the opera's two intermezzos, also authored by Lalli.[62] In the first of these comic sketches, the "Marchesina di Nanchin, Dama affettata," sits at her toilette preparing herself for a party she will be attending later that evening. Despite the appellation, the *dama* is clearly Italian, given her European setting and dialogue with the "Conte de Pelusio, Cavaliere di Moda." Count Pelusio is in fact her *cavalier servente*, and when he hears her demand that her servant bring her "That Chinese Fan, / The Turinese Scarf, / That Japanese Wrap, / Those French Hoops, / Those Dutch Ribbons," he chides the Marchessa for her obsession with the latest fashions.[63] The craze for such accoutrements, he claims, has eroded behavior and values once revered in good society. But the chevalier hardly heeds his own moralizing. The second intermezzo shows the two having returned home from the *festino*. Again foreign imports take the stage, as the couple turns to tea, coffee, and Cuban, Spanish, and Brazilian tobacco varieties to remedy their post-party headaches. After each experiences the "restorative" effects of tobacco (dramatized in exaggeratedly absurd sneezes), they sing its praises. The count excitedly attributes its invention to Bacchus, while the signora claims "this is the antidote / To all my chronic illnesses," and calls for snuffboxes of every size to be made handy at all times.[64]

Interestingly, Lalli's theatricalized "morning after" corresponds markedly to a William Hogarth painting of 1743 (more than twenty years later!), in which Porter finds patent warnings of "the dangers of foreign—and in particular Eastern—luxury."[65] The second plate in Hogarth's *Marriage à la mode* series shows a sitting room in which a disheveled couple collect themselves after a wild night they have apparently hosted. The parlor is filled with Eastern wares, among them a bevy of porcelain figurines crowding the mantel, a Chinese fire screen against the wall, and on the table, the proverbial Chinese tea set. As Porter states, "these ornaments reflect the moral tone of the scene, . . . one of generalized debauchery."[66]

While the intermezzos in *Camaide* may not have admonished this severely, they certainly problematized the aristocratic fixation with exotic novelty. At the most sober end of the moralizing arc, they frame it as a compulsive desire for shallow luxury, a pernicious indulgence harmful to time-honored social scruples. At the very least they fuse the exotic with the comic. Either equation subverts the gravity of the Chinese signifier, however, and thus has repercussions for the opera. For even though the noblewoman's Chinese fan and handkerchief exist amidst a number of items imported from other locales, the interludes nonetheless label her "Marchesina di Nanchin," aiming their joke on the aristocratic fantasy of playing at being Chinese.

When, back in the *dramma* proper, the Chinese maiden and prima donna Lovamia laments her love predicament, it can't help but be tinged by the ludic chinoiserie ambience of the intermezzo just preceding it. This is not to say that the *entr'actes* overpower or negate her expressions of feminine passion. Yet the meanings cannot not migrate somewhat, contributing to a slight trivialization, or at least a sensationalizing, of Lovamia's emotional palette. The juxtaposition of her operatic dilemma as a lover with the couple's sit-

43. **William Hogarth (British, 1697–1764.)** *Marriage à-la-Mode, Plate II,* 1745. Etching and engraving, 38 x 46.6 cm. (c) The Cleveland Museum of Art, Gift of Mr. and Mrs. Milton Curtiss Rose, 1959.312.

uation in the intermezzi links Lovamia's *affetti* with the more coquettish, frolicsome sorts of devotions between paramours, exactly the kind depicted in Antoine Watteau's contemporary painting *Idole de la Déesse Ki Mao Sao,* which decorated Louis XIV's private chambers in the Château de la Muette.[67] The extant engraving shows a young, elegantly gowned woman seated centrally above two adoring men. She holds a parasol in one hand, a decorative staff crowned with feathers in the other. Two men kneel before her with heads bowed, in positions of absolute deference. Their robes, the traditional iconographic composition of idol-worship, and the painting's title, indicate that she is a deity and they are devout priest-figures (mandarins or bonzes?), paying their religious respects. But as several have pointed out, the woman is entirely European in her facial features, perhaps a "beautiful Paris *salonière* transplanted from one of the artist's *fêtes galantes* paintings."[68] The men kowtowing before her suggest also the adulations of competitive suitors, at once flattering and wooing their common object of affection. One of the men appears older, as he is bald, the other younger. Could they be *galante* versions of Camaide, the aging would-be husband to Lovamia, and Tico, the dashing, youthful swain, model specimen of the next generation and the man opera seria typically rewards with both throne and belle of the ball? The woman in the print is a goddess, yes, but conceivably she reigns over a male congregation more carnal than clerical.

The visual medley of Middle Kingdom effects that surrounds Lovamia's scenes of tormented love corre-

44. Antoine Watteau, *Idole de la Déesse Ki Mao Sao,* ca. 1740. Permission of the Metropolitan Museum of Art, Gift of Mr. and Mrs. Herbert N. Straus, 1928 [28.113(2)] Image (c) The Metropolitan Museum of Art.

sponds to the hybridity symptomatic of the chinois-erie aesthetic. Not only does chinoiserie mix tradi-tionally unrelated elements, but also, its amalgams transform traditional valences. A Watteau-school drawing depicting idol worship inscribed in highly decorative rococo surroundings "both mocks and dis-places the . . . pious reverence represented . . . , trans-forming an emblem of Chinese religious authority into a fetish of rococo taste."[69] Likewise, in the *Camaïde* scene set, the Chinese parasols and pennants, the cos-tumes on the dancers (who, it should be noted, Lo-vamia refers to in her aria as "pastorelle," inferring that the ballerinas are got up as Chinese shep-herdesses), and the temple, with its ornate statue of the emperor, present a jumble of competing connota-tions. Not only are Lovamia's meditations on love ex-pressed in a temple, but the atmosphere itself is adulterated with fanciful, lighthearted components. The sum total infuses her anguish (as well as Ca-maide's, and Tico's) with a sense of vanity and escapist fantasy.

Given the lack of other substantive deployments of the Chinese imaginary anywhere else in the work, one can further propose that the essence of these love scenes underlies its whole—that the implementation of China throughout *Camaïde* is of a more recreational, less ideological nature. To borrow a term from Porter, *Camaïde* "flattens" China, just as he says chinoiserie flattens cultural values.[70] This thinner version of the Celestial Empire, simultaneously gutted and glamor-ized, appealed no less to audiences, however. The chi-noiserie aesthetic attracted powerfully, and in this sense *Camaïde* used China precisely to augment the purely diversionary capacity of opera.

Urbano Ricci, *Taican, rè della Cina* (1707)

Taican, rè della Cina, written by Venetian librettist Urbano Ricci in 1707, works similarly to *Camaide*. Ricci
also instrumentalizes China mainly for its entertainment utility, concentrating on visual marvels and
heightened spectacle. Far surpassing *Camaide*, however, *Taican* takes chinoiserie hybridity to the extreme.
Here the idea of hybridity derives from Oliver Impey,
who defines chinoiserie as embracing all "oriental"
cultures, and characterizes the European appetite for
eastern fashions and products as consistently indiscriminate:

> the innumerable eastern objects . . . were in a very
> wide range of styles from different eastern countries
> whose native arts (and export arts) were markedly dis-
> similar. . . . not only were there . . . different styles to im-
> itate, but the European craftsman was perfectly happy
> to mix together quite dissimilar ideas from quite distinct
> regions.
> . . . it is not possible always to sort out the exact ori-
> gins of chinoiserie things—they may be descended from
> a mixture of Chinese, Japanese, Indian or Persian styles,
> they may even be more than second or third hand in de-
> scent . . .[71]

Taican's highly convoluted plot shows just this type of
culture collage: Chinese, Japanese, and Indian characters cavort in a relentless series of *romanzesco*
episodes. The three nations are also represented in the
processions (funereal, ambassadorial, matrimonial)
that march throughout the opera. Though sparse,
geo-ethnographic touches crop up, such as the mention of the Japanese city *Osacca*, and the reference to
the Indian custom of burning widows.[72]

The culture medley continues in the intermezzos,
where the usual flirtations ensue between "Lisetta
cinese" and "Astrobaldo indiano." In addition to these
generic interludes, the operatic acts are bracketed by
dance intermezzos, where again the emphasis on eastern diversity for diversity's sake emerges. To mark the
Indian princess Elmirena's entrance at the opening of
act 2, the first *ballo* calls for Indian men and women,
dark- and light-skinned. Act 4 ends with a *ballo* by
male and female bonzes, and *Taican* concludes with
Chinese nobility of both sexes performing the choreography. The aggregate of these dances by inhabitants of different Asian areas recalls the *ballet des
nations* so popular on French stages in the last part of
the seventeenth century. As evidenced by these wordless performances of the exotic, emphasis lay not as
much on distinctions as on unifying attributes, on pre-

senting a composite population of "others" to convey
universalism and harmony among societies.

Stress on the totality of peoples notwithstanding,
Taican's libretto does contain more extensive and precise information about China than about India and
Japan. For example, Ricci cites a specific Chinese
river, and notes that the Chinese wear white for
mourning and that golden dragons embellish royal
wall hangings. His most explicit exposition of Middle
Kingdom ways emerges in a list of customs placed in
the *Argomento*. Here he explains imperial marital practices, native concerns about origins and class status;
the Chinese privileging of reason, the struggle between
lettered and military mandarins, and internecine
struggles for power. Despite this small harvest of information, however, none of the data appears mobilized specifically in the service of ideological interests.
It would appear to function more as an ethnographic
curiosity, a textual enticement to lure readers, but one
that goes no further once the drama commences.

More than anything else, *Taican* rehearses the seventeenth-century opera deemed "monstrous" by early
eighteenth-century critics. Ricci essentially overlays
Asian decoration and folkloric particulars onto the
outdated "Baroque love maze" that constituted the
dramma per musica before its Arcadian reform.[73]
Taican's political complications are sublimated to its
love pathos, which takes the fore via the skirmishes of
three different pairs of lovers.

Just to give an idea of the opera's exaggerated *romanzesco* element, the dominant love story concerns
the reuniting of an Indian princess with a Japanese
king. Their tragic affair had hinged on false accusations of adultery and the king's violent retaliation—
he plunged his sword into the princess's side—after
which he ordered that she be put to death at sea. The
unsnarling of their misfortune involves her transport
by dolphin to the China coast and her chance recovery by a royal mandarin. The rescued damsel's astonishing beauty and gentility entrances the Chinese
emperor, whereupon he makes her his empress. When
he dies, the widow of still-unknown origins is only
able to rejoin her original lover, the King of Japan, by
offering as proof of her travails her physical wounds
and her breathtaking regal garments and jewels. The
ascendancy of her son Taican, legal heir to the Chinese throne, is but a secondary outcome of this fairy-
tale resolution.

Much of the Chinese data contained in Ricci's stage
directions serves this fantastical element. For example,
Gemira's apartments border the imperial park, through
whose gates can be spied "the most extravagant fruit

trees produced in China."[74] Another atmosphere of magic and wonder materializes when 3, 8 calls for an "Artificial forest made by that Chinese king who, annoyed by the bare trees in winter, created this perpetually green one. The trees are adorned with fruits made of gold, with fake birds on their branches, and the earth is covered with silver flowers. In the distance stretch two great avenues, which terminate in a grotto made of conch shells and coral, with falling water." In yet another scene, the Temple of Fo, the legendary first Chinese god, is surrounded by trees with heart-shaped, ruby-colored leaves and snowy-white fruit.

All of the opera's China lore can be verified in the plurality of sources Ricci states he consulted (Kircher, Le Comte, Bartoli, Semedo). Even the engraving on the frontispiece to his libretto features the Nanking tower, the famous Chinese architectural icon of the time (see earlier illustration of frontispiece). Nevertheless, *Taican* does not exploit a single component of the European Chinese imaginary in the way that *Teuzzone* profits from the Chinese world-birth commemoration, or *Tartaro nella Cina* applies the Chinese-Tartar ethnic contrast. The accumulation of Chinese details in Ricci's opera does not amount to anything beyond the immediate entertainment aims of old-style opera. Variety and spectacular display rule the day, as *Taican* parades a brilliant pageant of cultures before readers and viewers. Despite its title, *Taican, rè della Cina* sublimates the Middle Kingdom in a highly improbable Asian culture cocktail — full of inverosimilar exhibition, exactly the sort of undisciplined dramatic endeavor that Zeno and other Arcadians were attempting to reform.

4

The Enlightened Imperial Subject:
Pietro Metastasio, *L'eroe cinese* (1752)

"In China, Obedience Isn't a Virtue Anymore."
  A growing number of bishops, priests, and faithful of the official Church are refusing to submit to the communist authorities.[1]

I N 1752 PIETRO METASTASIO WROTE THE *DRAMMA per musica* titled *L'eroe cinese*, at the express wishes of Habsburg ruler Maria Teresa, following the success of *Il re pastore* one year earlier. Both were occasional pieces, written for performance in the Garden Theater at the Schönbrunn palace by the daughters of the empress and their friends, the "distinguished young damsels and gentlemen" ("giovani distinte dame e cavalieri") belonging to the Habsburg court.[2] Despite the court's enthusiasm for Metastasio's poetic and dramaturgical gifts, however, the royal commission imposed several restrictions on his new production, one of which prohibited costumes that might expose the legs of the princesses playing male characters. Prevented thus from staging Greek and Roman episodes, Metastasio writes to a friend that he wracked his brain trying to come up with a dramatic subject "that doesn't require the noble actresses to bare their legs to the public. Hence I'm heading out toward Asia."[3] However, even if Metastasio ostensibly conceived of staging a Chinese story because classical Greek and Roman attire proved too risqué for the young female royals acting in the opera, his decision to "head out for Asia," and specifically the Middle Kingdom, must be examined in a context wider than that of theatrical dress propriety.

The mid-century date of *L'eroe cinese* (1752) puts it exactly at the time in which opera seria had consolidated its standard form. Although scholars of serious opera point out the often-neglected degree of deviation from this form,[4] by 1750 the Arcadian reform opera—also referred to as the Metastasian opera—turned around a set of commandments regarding composition and practice that generally dominated the genre. These paradigms will be discussed below in relation to *L'eroe cinese*, but first a word on the political and social situation that inflected opera seria's ideology at this time. Like the textual and performative properties of the genre, opera seria's philosophical underpinnings had also consolidated at mid-century, in relation to the conditions of the period.

The halfway point of the eighteenth century marked the end of the last of three grueling wars of succession in Europe (Spanish 1700–1713; Polish 1733–38; Austrian 1740–48). Desire was greater than ever to consolidate the peace, and to validate the restorations by touting the capacities of the newly ascended to maintain social stability. The promise of a durable peace injected new vigor into the ethos of the enlightened monarchy. The absolutist sovereigns who now reigned per the terms of the various treaties sought to improve past methods and create "modern" governments that would realize prosperous, powerful states. Their aims to this end included: curbing, if not eliminating outright, the abuses of the feudal society; steering the concept of nobility away from lineage and toward individual ability; and better managing state wealth. The last imperative required more often than not the redistribution of assets, both to improve the nation's productivity as well as to remedy the severe economic imbalances between groups. Social inequality of such great proportions threatened the stability of the state. Equally threatening, it was believed, was the idea of liberal systems based in notions of democracy, separation of powers, or parliamentary bodies. The English model did not suit enlightened absolute rulers who desired above all a strong, resistant *patria*.

Circumstances in the Habsburg empire reflected the situation indicated above. Maria Teresa's fight to

L'EROE CINESE

Del Sig. Abate

PIETRO METASTASIO

DRAMMA PER MUSICA

DA RAPPRESENTARSI

Nel Teatro GIUSTINIAN
di SAN MOISE'.

Nella Proſſima Fiera dell' Aſcenſione.
L'ANNO MDCCLIII.

IN VENEZIA,

Per Modeſto Fenzo.

Con Licenza de' Superiori.

009278

45. Frontispiece, *L'eroe cinese*. Permission Casa Goldoni, Venice.

a commanding, centralized government, which Maria Teresa duly formed. The carefully structured Austrian bureaucracy employed multitudes of royal officials and officers, most of whom needed only a minimum of education, but could look to their jobs for secure social advancement.[6]

Religion played an important role in the enlightened Catholic monarchy, even as it allowed for some modifications, in order to remain viable in cultures increasingly exposed to "progressive" thinking. Rulers invoked the divine right of kings, and confidently ascribed to divine will the implementation of whatever institutional reforms they attempted. In Austria, Maria Teresa benignly permitted the activities of the Jansenists and others connected to Reform Catholicism (*Reformkatholizismus*), the growing movement against exaggerated forms of piety judged to be baroque in nature, based in superstition or excessive scholasticism, and worst of all, associated with the Jesuits.[7] Despite the growing antagonism toward the Society, Maria Teresa remained very devout and generally faithful to the Jesuits. The Viennese populace followed suit, continuing to revere a religious order that had "made deep and lasting impressions" on their sensibilities.[8]

In the Italian kingdoms, enlightened Catholicism took the shape of a moderate reformism that managed to keep religion in all political, economic, educational, and intellectual considerations. One of the pinnacle products of this conciliatory approach was Muratori's *Della pubblica felicità*, published not coincidentally in 1749. A great many of Muratori's works throughout the first half of the eighteenth century had promoted the commingling of morality and reform, and encouraged a rational form of religion, making him one of Italy's most prominent exponents of enlightened Catholicism.[9] *Della pubblica felicità* summed up his preceding arguments in a single work. In Ricuperati's words, Muratori addressed "a prince enlightened by Christian virtues and a philosophy of good taste and reason, who could not fail to try to carry out a programme of reform."[10] Interestingly, Ricuperati also notes that *Della pubblica felicità* earned its greatest fame in the Habsburg empire, "where it was probably read by Maria Teresa."[11]

The enthusiastic reception offered to Muratori's writings in Austrian lands was no accident. Jean Bérenger observes that Vienna had a long-standing penchant for Italian (Latin) Catholic culture over all others, and that Enlightenment initiatives in Habsburg territories resembled those in centers such as Naples and Milan more than they did the projects emanating from France.[12] The sociopolitical tenor par-

defend her father's decree granting her authority over the realm had been exhausting. Following her victory, she set out to repair the defects that had developed in the Habsburg state apparatus before her, and to build a robust Austria worthy of her more illustrious predecessors. As part of the settlement of the Peace of Aix-la-Chapelle (1748), she mandated certain reforms. These entailed reducing the financial authority of the orders, splitting the judiciary powers from those of administrative offices, removing financial burdens for the military from subjects and placing them onto the state, and assuring education to ever greater numbers of imperial subjects.[5] All of these efforts necessitated

ticular to these enlightened absolutist Catholic states was one that opera seria readily reflected and responded to.

Heroic opera engaged with its surrounding culture by stressing more than ever the attitudes, behaviors, and qualities necessary to the successful functioning of the enlightened Catholic state. The motifs of early opera seria—the celebration of civilized peoples and the virtues of proper hereditary monarchies—still obtained. But the contests for the crowns had been decided. Now it was time to recognize the merits of the victors and their policies for peaceful governing. The wish to entrench the newly acquired tranquility led to a heightened emphasis on the values of clemency, loyalty, and personal sacrifice for the greater good.

How did *L'eroe cinese* in particular serve these needs of the rational, "modern" Catholic sovereignty? Generally speaking, it turns on the ideals of constancy in the face of obstacles, submission to one's superiors, and self-abnegation. These were all components of the overall ethos of duty and public-mindedness of eighteenth-century high culture, however. What sets *L'eroe cinese* apart is its use of a culture whose unique connotations for Catholic administrations permitted a felicitous expedient for their goals and policies. Metastasio's opera exploits the Jesuit glorification of Chinese obedience understood as originating in religious, indeed, Catholic foundations. That deference is then exalted, to commemorate the subject, not necessarily the ruler, of the enlightened absolutist kingdom.

As mentioned in the previous chapter, many scholars of opera seria identify its primary purpose as that of glorifying the local sovereign. The intent seems apparent in dramas that spectacularize the outstanding virtues of a ruling figure, such as *Alessandro nelle Indie* (1729), and *Clemenza di Tito* (1734), two of Metastasio's most popular operas. *L'eroe cinese* is different from these works in certain key aspects, however. The most obvious of these lies in the office of the opera's hero, Leango. While he is a patriarchal figure, he is not ruler. He cannot boast of conquest nor of clemency toward the vanquished. Rather, Leango's heroism lies in his refusal of the canonical totems of greatness. In addition to his supreme act of sacrifice giving up his son to save the imperial child, he continually renounces glory. Asked by the people to accede to the throne, he forswears it, stepping aside for the proper successor. Leango embraces only his provisional status—he is regent, advisor, behind-the-scenes facilitator—and at all times humble subordinate to the greater entity of the monarchy. A character of this type could speak compellingly to a program dedicated to public over personal happiness. More specifically, he could evoke

a particular protagonist of the absolutist Catholic admininistration, the new bureaucrat. A deferential Chinese perfectly embodied the proper state official, a subjectivity requiring equal parts humility, efficacy, and devotion to a higher authority.

The virtues of the dutiful monarchical servant assume a special valence when infused in the figure of a subservient Chinese. As mentioned, the Jesuit encomium of Chinese civilization arose around the conviction that the Confucianist system had derived from ancient Christianity. The Chinese people, at least the educated mandarins, were thus not only theologically aware, but lived in accordance with an authority the Catholic fathers could acknowledge as more or less doctrinally worthy. One might say that for the Jesuit missionaries, and their hopeful supporters back in Europe, the Chinese constituted "virtual Christians." The supposed docile, pacifist mentality of the Chinese also recommended them, especially when the Jesuits ascribed it to their latent religiosity. The missionary fathers attributed the remarkable social order they perceived in China directly to Confucianism.

A passage from Du Halde's massively popular compilation on the Chinese (and the text from which Metastasio culled his libretto plot) emblematizes the work's unstinting celebration of the trait of submissiveness in the Chinese. Again and again Du Halde emphasizes the cultural tradition of filial piety, which the author calls the "Grand Principle. . . the Basis of their Political Government, . . . the Veneration and Submission of Children to their Parents, which continues even after their Death."[13] Encompassed in the idea of filial piety was a larger habit of respect for and obedience toward authority, as evidenced in this portion of a previously quoted passage:

> Young persons being Witnesses of the Veneration that is paid to deceased Relations, by the Continual Honours that are done to them as if they were yet living, learn betimes what Submission and Obedience they owe to their living Parents: Their ancient Sages were convinc'd that the profound Respect, which Youth are inspired with for their Parents, renders them perfectly submissive, that this Submission preserves Peace in Families, that Peace in private Families produces Tranquillity in Cities, that this Tranquillity prevents Insurrection in the Provinces, and consequently preserves Regularity throughout the Empire.[14]

The Chinese citizen thus blended a Catholic spirit with clear submission to authority, an ideal combination for the programs of enlightened absolutism.

Precisely because of the Jesuit project in the Celestial Empire, then, the Chinese were especially suited for an encomium to imperial duty and sacrifice inspired by the Divine. Certainly they could evoke religious integrity more so than could the Turks, who, despite European dramatizations of the magnificence and noble bearing of certain of their leaders, were associated on the theological plane with the infidel. The Ottomans, furthermore, together with the Persians, had formidable reputations as world conquerors. The Chinese lack in this realm worked to their advantage in this respect. The violence and crude savagery attached to Tartars rendered them less-than-appropriate representatives of respectful servitude as well. The Chinese in Metastasio's opera thus effect an ideal that other others were unable to offer. More compellingly than any other non-European, the Chinese epitomized a reverential nation, compliant with a reputable higher law. With their Jesuit-forged links to Catholicism, and the impressive civil harmony thought to derive from it, the Chinese offered the enlightened Catholic kingdom a convenient mix of old and new values. They integrated traditional devotional substance with the efficiency and modernization the monarchy desired to implement.

One of the first indications of the opera's adulatory position toward China surfaces in its prescriptions for its stage sets. Metastasio calls for the following:

Act 1: Apartments in the imperial palace housing the Tartar women prisoners. The chambers are decorated with strange paintings, transparent vases, rich fabrics, brightly patterned carpets and everything else necessary to Chinese exquisiteness and luxury.

(1, 1)

Act 2: Ground-level loggias, which reveal a large part of the royal city of Singana and the river that runs past it. The towers, the rooftops, the pagodas, the ships, the trees themselves, and all that can be seen, shows off the diversity produced no less by nature than by art, in such a unique climate.

(2, 1)

Act 3: A solitary and shady spot in the imperial gardens.

(3, 1)

The illuminated interior of the largest imperial pagoda. The structure of the magnificent building and its ornamentation equally express the nation's genius and culture.

(3, 7)

No other China opera studied here, serious or comic, specifies in as scrupulous a manner the desired Chinese ambience. Nor do any other of Metastasio's *drammi per musica* set in "exotic" places exhibit the same level of detail.[15] The directions for the scenery are, moreover, plainly interpretative, giving a clear indication of the high esteem in which the Chinese nation is held. Several scholars have noted the patent

parallels between Metastasio's scenery and descriptive passages in Du Halde's compilation, where Jesuit accolades of the Middle Kingdom reach their apex.[16] The specifications for the settings also bear out the Middle Kingdom's instrumental role in the propagation of Habsburg dynastic mythologies, especially those related to geographical expanse, cultural brilliance, and historical longevity.[17]

Clearly, the portrayal of the Chinese in *L'eroe cinese* does not reflect Montesquieu's treatment in his monumental *Esprit des lois*, written only four years prior. As Sala di Felice notes, Metastasio openly takes a position diverging from Montesquieu, whose climatological theories led to the evaluation of China's political system and social structure as inferior to European models.[18] In brief, this view held that the extreme heat of eastern and southern Asian regions necessitated rule by tyranny, and created peoples who acted justly only when motivated by fear.[19] Metastasio challenges the notion of Chinese citizens as oppressed and tyrannized, and reformulates the image as one of dignified and welcome subordination.

At the same time, the protagonists in *L'eroe cinese* refute Voltaire's representation of Chinese as heroically godless. Voltaire praised the Chinese in a great number of works over his lifetime, focusing on their extraordinary moral grounding, possessed without a shred of scriptural revelation or other theological or ritualistic baggage.[20] He wrote his own China drama at more or less the same time as *L'eroe cinese*, based on the same imperial orphan story. Like his other writings, *L'Orphelin de la Chine* (1755) presents the Chinese as proof of deism, Voltaire's professed theology. The mobilization of the Chinese in *L'Orphelin de la Chine* will be discussed in relation to Metastasio's opera further on in this chapter. For now, let us begin a more in-depth investigation of the unique ways in which *L'eroe cinese* exploits the Jesuit panegyric of China to celebrate the dynastic subject.

L'EROE CINESE AND ITS SOURCE MATERIAL

As Metastasio states in the *Argomento* section of the libretto, *L'eroe cinese* is based on a chapter of ancient Chinese dynastic history ("La storia Tchao-kong") contained in Du Halde's *Description....*[21] The episode in the Du Halde compilation is quite succinct, however, and as such provides the librettist with only the barest skeleton. It describes the events befalling Chinese emperor Li vang, and his loyal minister Tchao kong, in the ninth century BC. Li vang is a tyrant whose family is massacred when his subjects revolt.

He escapes and goes into exile; Tchao kong manages to save Li vang's infant son and heir to the throne by giving up his own child to the raging masses. Thinking Tchao kong's infant is the imperial heir, the crowds slit his throat in front of the faithful minister. The story ends in the spare style of its entirety:

> Li vang henceforward lived in Obscurity, a Wanderer and Fugitive: Tchao kong tried the utmost of his Power to appease the people, and to re-establish him on the Throne, but he could not succeed in it, so that the Throne was vacant for some Years. . . .
> Li Vang died in his Exile, the Tenth Year of the Cycle, and the Throne was filled by the young Prince Suen vang, whom Tchao kong had saved from the fury of a revolted People. This Minister by degrees brought the People to obedience, and to acknowledge Suen vang Emperor after the Death of his Father.[22]

As one can see, the Du Halde passage does not explain how the people came to be appeased and allow the tyrant's progeny to take the throne. It does go on to say that the heir, Suen vang, turned out to be a good ruler, effectively forcing rebellious provinces to submit to the laws and customs of the empire.[23]

Metastasio situates his drama at the moment just following the exiled emperor's death, when the crowning of a successor is finally permissible.[24] *L'eroe cinese* thus fills a silence in the annals, imagining the events that led to the legitimate ascendancy of the orphaned imperial heir. Metastasio retained the name of the royal scion from the historical account, Svenvango (Suen vang), as well as that of his father, Livanio (Li vang), but changed the minister's name from Tchao kong to Leango. Until the opera's end, when Svenvango's true identity is revealed, Leango passes him off as his own son, Siveno. Because the opera begins at the time of Livanio's death, Leango and Siveno/Svenvango are the only historical personages to figure on the stage. To these key protagonists, Metastasio added three others: two Tartar princesses and sisters, Lisinga and Ulania, and the enterprising Chinese youth Minteo, a foundling taken in by Leango and raised together with Siveno. Naturally, the four young people form two couples: Lisinga and Siveno love each other, as do Ulania and Minteo. This then is the bare-bones opera seria character roster, the patriarch with the dual love pairings.

The core of the dramatic tension derives from whether or not Leango will succeed in convincing the masses that Siveno/Svenvango is the legitimate heir, and to accept him on the throne. The people are increasingly impatient without a ruler, and many, pleased with Leango's regency in the interim since the routing of the emperor, want him to take the crown. In the event he will have to quell protestors to his plan to install Siveno, Leango seeks aid from the Tartar army, with whom the Chinese have just established a peace. The introduction of the Tartars in the episode (they do not appear whatsoever in the Du Halde account, nor in the Chinese sources on which it is based) serves Metastasio in several ways. Beside nodding to popular episodes in more recent Chinese history, their presence permits the essential plot suspense: will Leango receive Tartar support in time to reveal his secret and put Siveno peacefully on the throne? What's more, Lisinga, the elder of the Tartar sister-princesses, both of whom have been held captive in China to this point, has been promised by her father in marriage to the heir to the Chinese throne, to signal the reconciliation of the two states. The operatic love strife thus constitutes itself on two fronts: 1) will Lisinga be forced to marry the as-yet unknown heir and give up her beloved Siveno?, and 2) can either of the royal maidens licitly unite with consorts of unknown (and possibly nonroyal, nonprivileged) origins? All ends programmatically happily, of course. Metastasio manages to respect the trajectory of the historical legend, while at the same time using it to propagate the precise social values of his time.

The discussion of Metastasio's sources must include mention of the Chinese musical drama based on the imperial orphan story, Ji Junxiang's *Tchao chi cou ell* (*Orphan of the Family Tchao: A Chinese Tragedy*). This thirteenth-century Chinese opera was translated into French by the Jesuit father Joseph Prémare and included in Du Halde's compilation.[25] Junxiang's work reveals the details that had accumulated in the various narrative versions of the orphan legend since its first appearance in Chinese records.[26] The core story animating *Tchao chi cou ell* no longer figured the royal infant as the emperor's son, but rather his grandson. The child had been born to the emperor's daughter and her husband Zhao Suo, a member of the Tchao (Zhao) family, cherished by the emperor for its long years of faithful service to the dynasty. The Tchaos have enemies, however, in the rival Tu clan. The ruthless Tu'angu, head of the rival clan, slyly manages to have all Tchao members assassinated. To make sure that he also rids the realm of the infant heir, he orders the killing of all newborn children. A retainer loyal to the Tchao family saves the baby by substituting his own son. Later, when the emperor is apprised of the wrongs done to the Tchao family by Tu'angu, he executes the entire Tu clan and reinstates the orphan.

In keeping with Chinese theatrical tradition, which prescribed epic length (i.e., dramatizations of extensive spans of time articulated in correspondingly long texts), *Tchao chi cou ell* covers seventy-five years in a prologue and five acts.[27] Naturally, Junxiang fleshed out the story with his own creative interpretations. He accentuates the viciousness of Tu'angu toward the Tchao, and the legendary virtues of the latter. He includes the violence and gore of several Tchao deaths before the Tu clan begins to search for the orphan. When they find him (in actuality the child of the faithful retainer), the scene of his slaughter is quite horrific. Tu'angu stabs the baby to death in front of his father, and the retainer must repress his tears. At the sight of such a tragedy, an accomplice to the retainer kills himself. Tu'angu sees a baby he takes for the retainer's child (actually the royal orphan) and decides on the spot to adopt him as his own heir, since he has no offspring. The greater part of Junxiang's drama—the prologue through part 3—covers these events. The remaining parts 4 and 5 treat of Tu'angu's continued treachery over the years, and its ultimate failure. Tu'angu tells his adopted and now-grown son of his plans to assassinate the current emperor and eventually put the son there. Before this plan can unfold, however, the elderly retainer tells the orphan the truth of his adoptive father's former evil deeds. The Tchao orphan informs the emperor, who authorizes him to slay the traitor Tu'angu, whereupon the adopted son immediately and gladly murders his so-called father. The orphan successor is then raised up, and the honor of the Tchao house restored, with the granting of memorials, titles, and official tombs. The dutiful retainer is duly rewarded.

Scholars characterize Junxiang's opera as a popular work whose main attribute was its essence as a revenge drama.[28] Most of its antecedent historical narratives had come to explain the orphan's restoration by way of an eventual act of retaliation by the Tchao family against the rival Tu clan. *Tchao chi cou ell* thus capitalized on the power—in Chinese culture—of a story of obligatory, honorable revenge on behalf of one's ancestors.

Despite the fact that the Chinese drama has been regularly cited as a source for *L'eroe cinese*, it should be noted that nothing in Metastasio's work suggests a direct reference to Junxiang's text. It is certainly reasonable to assume that Metastasio read *Tchao chi cou ell* as he was reading the dynastic history section of Du Halde's work. However, one can also conclude that the librettist chose deliberately not to follow the path of the Chinese playtext. This is plausible for not only did Du Halde harshly criticize Chinese dramatic principles in a preface to Prémare's translation, but also, much of Junxiang's drama turns on the brutality of

the Tu clan, not to mention the strident reactions by the avenging Tchaos. Such moral and physical savagery would have had little place in a Metastasian reform opera. On the other hand, it makes sense that Metastasio turned the story of exposed treachery, righted wrongs, and family vendettas, into a story of the slow, peaceable, and inevitable triumph of the devoted supporter of the ruling administration.[29]

One can also explain the sanitized version in light of the imperatives that Metastasio had received from the empress. Since her children would be performing the opera, it could have no eroticism, nor traces of violence.[30] The imperial poet had to eliminate vice from the traditional vice-and-virtue formula, so as not to offend the young princesses, and the opera on the whole is reduced from the regular size—five characters rather than the usual six to eight, a lesser number of scenes per act, and no set changes except for one in the last act.

The focus on goodness and Leango's forbearance is not motivated wholly by these factors, however. *L'eroe cinese* also exploits the potent Jesuit party line that idealized the Chinese. Looking back on the previous serious operas, it is interesting to note that Zeno left the Tartars completely out of his drama, while Salvi pitched his squarely on the Tartar-Chinese conflict. Metastasio chooses yet another approach: total reconciliation, indeed, well-meaning cooperation between the two. *L'eroe cinese*'s conciliatory atmosphere, supported by a representation of the Chinese as fusing civil competence with moral worth, made for a wholesome *and* politically effective entertainment.

LEANGO AND THE DRAMATURGY OF *L'EROE CINESE*

The particular appropriation of China in *L'eroe cinese* emerges most clearly when one examines the work as a patriarch opera, that is, as a drama that showcases the beneficent character and actions of an elder male protagonist. Most *drammi per musica* in the Metastasian oeuvre featured a significant patriarchal figure —father, king, royal counselor, decorated army captain—whose interactions with younger interlocutors, be they princely sons, royal daughters, foreign sovereigns, rising officials, or up-and-coming military stars, constituted a key plot strand and abetted the resounding triumph of virtue over vice. Examining the nature of the character Leango, patriarch in *L'eroe cinese*, will reveal just how Metastasio instrumentalized the model of Chinese subjecthood.

First, however, it is essential to recall the integral connection between opera seria roles and the compositions of singing troupes and talents of their members. Typically a company included a principal male/female couple, and a secondary one, their respective status determined by their vocal skills. These singer-actors were joined by other individual performers, and the constellations of singing stars then helped determine operatic plots and characters. The story line of a usual *dramma per musica* featured a pair of young lovers who formed the primary couple. In line with their prominence in the drama, they each were given the greatest number of lyrical items (mainly arias, and on occasion duets and ensembles) by the librettist. Obviously, these lovers were played by the first-ranked singing duo, each of whom sang soprano or soprano castrato, the most prized voice type.[31] The second set of *innamorati*, with a somewhat less momentous love story than that of the principals, were played by the second-ranked vocalists.[32] They sang soprano and/or alto, and were allocated one or two fewer arias than the headliners.

In clear contrast to the soprano voices of the lovers, the patriarch sang tenor. This role was also slightly more flexible than theirs, since the patriarch could perform either as a principal, that is, with the *primi* as a first-ranking singer, or at the level of the *secondi*. Metastasio's *Attilio Regolo* (1740) provides an example of the former, where the elder ex-Roman consul shares singing prominence with the first-level *cantanti*.[33] Alexander the Great, on the other hand, in *Alessandro nelle Indie* (1730), is clearly second-ranked, below the rank of the lovers Cleofide and Poro. So too is the emperor Titus, in *Clemenza di Tito* (1734), probably Metastasio's most well-known celebration of the ruler-patriarch. Titus receives four arias to the five apiece assigned to the *primi* Vitellia, Servilia, and Sesto. Third-ranked singers, performing in alto, baritone, and sometimes bass, took the parts of the least crucial characters, such as the confidants and helpers. Naturally, librettos reveal that they had the fewest lyrical pieces.[34]

By now the performance hierarchy in opera seria should be clear. The principal couple not only sang the majority of the arias (with the addition of a lovers' duet in most cases), but also, they sang them at the most pivotal moments in the work. With the exception of the third act, which normally ended in chorus with all characters on stage, the conclusion of acts 1 and 2 were privileged spots for the exit aria and thus reserved for the first-ranking singers. Marking a major transition both in terms of opera form and content (the act end signaled the culmination of each progressive layer of story drama), the act-end position garnered the most attention for the diva or divo, who would never leave the stage without stunning an audience with a display of his or her talents. Other ways in which the principals secured applause included singing an aria at the beginning or midway through a scene (known as a cavatina), and with monologues, which might or might not precede an aria. In the context of recitative performance, the monologue was similar in prestige to the aria, inasmuch as it concentrated attention on the experience of the single character. Finally, the performative heroics of the leading couple usually conformed with their story heroism. They overlaid their pleasures and agonies as embattled lovers with the armor of moral virtue, modeling exemplary ethics for their spectators.

As for the patriarch's moral standing, he has quite a bit of room in which to move. Here the Metastasian opera demonstrates its superiority over its predecessors earlier in the century, which used characterization in a much more black-and-white way to present virtue and vice. Notwithstanding the usual virtuous countenance of his principal lovers, Metastasio did not typically distill in single protagonists purely noble or ignoble behaviors. True, one can identify an opera's main hero and villain in individual characters, but rarely are they solely good or bad. Likewise, a variety of good and bad comportments and sentiments are spread among the secondary and tertiary roles. In the case of the patriarch, Marita McClymonds points out their lack of uniform integrity across Metastasio's *drammi*, a finding which flies in the face of the conventional belief that his operas glorify rulers by unfailingly presenting them as irreproachable.[35] The father figure Artabano, in *Artaserse* (1730), the blockbuster of all Metastasian *melodrammi*, is the clear villain of the drama, conniving throughout and confessing his sins at the opera's redemptive end. *Siroe, re di Persia* (1726) shows the first-ranking patriarch Cosroe to be well-meaning, but disappointingly blind to the deceptions of one son and the virtues of the other. Some operatic elders approach the ideal at the center of Metastasian drama, embodied in those moral heroes who "must not only triumph over [their] own spontaneous desires but also uphold a moral vision against the onslaughts of the morally weak who fall victim to their personal desires"—but many do not.[36] The patriarch's elevated social position in the story universe, and even his high performance status in the stage space, did not always translate to the moral superiority associated with an enlightened paternal figure.

Here is where the Chinese minister Leango stands out in sharp relief. He is a moral paragon and first-ranked as a singer. The quantity of his arias not only indicate his status as a top-tier vocalist, together with the principal lovers Lisinga and Siveno, but he actually has more lyrical items than Siveno, putting Leango just after the *prima donna* Lisinga in performative significance and suggesting that they are the most prominent of the opera's players (see diagram below).

	Act 1	Act 2	Act 3	Total lyrical items
Lisinga	aria + monologue/aria	aria + duet	cavatina + aria	4 arias (3 + ma) + duet + cav
Leango	monologue + aria	aria	aria + aria	4 arias + monologue
Siveno	aria	aria + duet	aria	3 arias + duet
Ulania	aria	aria	monologue/ aria	3 arias (2 + ma)
Minteo	aria	aria	aria	3 arias

Leango's importance is borne out further in the structural dramaturgy of *L'eroe cinese*. The discussion above explained how act endings functioned as formal and referential focal points for the drama, and that principals customarily commanded the set pieces at these junctures. Metastasio's China opera keeps to this convention, insofar as Lisinga concludes the first act with a monologue and aria, and she and Siveno sing a lovers' duet to complete act 2. After the act endings, the next most eminent position for (aria) performance was at the end of a scene grouping. A scene group, or cluster, was formed by the presence of characters on stage. Typically, before one character exited another entered, making a sort of "chain" of characters so that the stage was never empty.[37] Once the last remaining character exited, the scene cluster was considered over. Another way to identify scene series in opera seria is by stage set: a new set marks the start of a new scene cluster. In the canonical Metastasian *melodramma*, acts 1 and 2 normally had two stage sets/scene groupings, and act 3 was divided by three sets/scene groups. Since acts 1 and 2 typically had about fifteen scenes apiece, grouped into two scene clusters per act, and act 3 divided its ten total scenes into three scene clusters, one gets a sense of the accelerating energy of an opera seria. Like the act ending, then, the final moment of a scene grouping marked a climactic point in the drama. The stage would have been emptied to just one protagonist, and he or she closed with a meaning-laden aria or monologue plus aria.

The business of scene groupings may seem largely irrelevant to *L'eroe cinese*, since, as mentioned earlier, there are no set changes in the first acts, and only one in the third. But even without the overt marker of a fresh backdrop, other libretto data from within the acts signal the presence of scene groups. These indicators include the progression of plot drama (that is, the organization and rhythm of complications and resolutions), the rise and fall in the number of characters on stage, and the type of lyrical items assigned to particular characters. Investigation of these elements shows that despite its smaller dimensions, *L'eroe cinese* has the same structural patterns of a canonical Metastasian drama. More significantly, the character consistently entrusted with the dramatic weight of the scene group endings is Leango.

Act 1 is effectively partitioned into the scene groups (1, 1–6) and (1, 7–9). In terms of plot advancement in this act, the four young lovers are confounded to hear of a living Chinese imperial heir, and all wonder who he is. Lisinga, in particular, feels distress, as she is to marry this unknown, and worries about her future with Siveno (1, 1–3). Her sister, Ulania, and the young Chinese military hero Minteo, also wonder if they will be able to remain together given this news (1, 4). In 1, 5 Leango assures himself of Minteo's constancy as he readies to set his plan in motion; in 1, 6 he lays it out. Alone on the stage, in a full-scene recitative monologue Leango tells of the hardships leading up to this day, as well as the relief he feels now that the hoped-for reward is so near:

> Here is the day that even now
> Costs me so much sweat, sighing and care.
> Today I will make known
> the well-kept heir to the Chinese empire.
> Today I will return him
> To the widowed paternal throne.
> I see myself finally
> Near the port, and there are
> No more rocky shores to fear.
> Time has snuffed out the unworthy instigators
> of the rebel takeover,
> My worry has dissipated; the army generals
> Are loyal to me; in a short while
> I will have the foreign help
> of the best Tartar military ranks
> At my command; it's time, it's time
> To complete the good deed. Ah you,
> Supreme minds
> who order human affairs,
> Grant me this fervent desire! You know
> That it cost me a son. Ah! This is all
> I ask, in exchange for my constancy:
> You can then end my days;
> I've lived enough.
> But . . . what is that tumult?. . .

(1, 6)

[Ecco il dì che fin ora
Tanto sudor, tanti sospiri e tante
Cure mi costa. Il conservato erede
Dell'impero cinese
Oggi farò palese; oggi al paterno
Vedovo trono il renderò. Mi veggo
Al fin vicino al porto, e non mi resta
Scoglio più da temer. Gli autori indegni
Del ribelle attentato il tempo estinse,
Dissipò la mia cura: a me fedeli
Sono i duci dell'armi; avrò d'elette
Tartare schiere al cenno mio fra poco
Lo straniero soccorso; è tempo, è tempo
Di compir la bell'opra. Ah voi, supreme
Menti regolatrici
Delle vicende umane,
Secondate il mio zel! Mi costa un figlio,
Voi lo sapete. Ah! Questa sola imploro
Sospirata mercé di mia costanza:
Poi troncate i miei dì; vissi abbastanza.
Ma . . . qual tumulto . . .]

Leango expresses both satisfaction and anxiety as he rhapsodizes about the imminent dynastic renewal ("la bell'opra") and prays to higher beings for assistance in this last stage. The final step of his strategy involves securing foreign aid from the Tartars, with which to buttress his maneuver. Their help is imminent, he states, auguring his success, but at the same time his words remind spectators that their support is still pending. Scene 1, 6 functions as the dramatic capstone to the preceding scenes insofar as Leango's nearly completed strategy resolves the dilemmas expressed by his co-characters in the preceding scenes. It simultaneously introduces the next strata of suspense ("Will he have Tartar backing in time to deal with the restive populace?").

The conclusive nature of his monologue results also from characteristics of the successive scene. Leango ends his discourse on a note of uncertainty, as he hears sounds of chaos: "But . . .what is that tumult? . . ." At this point Siveno bursts in with a group of mandarins, to apprise his regent-father that the restless Chinese masses want him to take the crown. The entrance of a new character(s) on stage always marks a new scene, and, even though Leango did not exit, leaving an empty stage for a new scene grouping, the commotion of Siveno's arrival with a band of extras distinguishes 1, 7 as the first bookend to another set of scenes. This grouping will present a new set of plot sub-issues ("Will Leango give in to the crowds?"; "If he does, can Siveno, as Leango's son, be considered the new heir and therefore betrothed to Lisinga?"). The prospect of affirmative answers to these questions leads to Lisinga's monologue-cum-aria at act-end, in which

she abandons herself to nearly unbearable joy at the prospect of union with Siveno.

In act 2, Leango again takes the spotlight at the end of what shapes itself as the first scene series. Scene 2, 6 between Siveno and Leango is rich in action and revelation, inasmuch as a page delivers to the minister a letter confirming Tartar support, galvanizing Leango to tell his alleged son the truth about his origins. This is clearly a climactic moment, given the buildup of obstacles from the opening of the act. Act 2 had begun with great anguish for the primary lovers, thanks to Leango's refusal to take the throne.[38] The disconsolate Siveno made plans to leave the kingdom, imagining that he would never merit Lisinga (2, 1–2); Lisinga despaired and angrily told Leango she would not marry the still-to-be-announced heir (2, 4–5); Minteo had got word of an uprising among the people impatient for a ruler, and left to address them (2, 3). All of these problems dissolve with Leango's account to Siveno of his royal heritage. Siveno can hardly believe the good news, and wants to rush to tell Lisinga, while Leango admonishes him to slow down and consider first the grave responsibilities he now bears as sovereign. Aside from its general position halfway through the opera, 2, 6 constitutes a pivotal moment as it marks the transformation in Leango, from elder-father-ruler to younger-son-subordinate. This shift will be treated in greater detail in the discussion of Leango's arias below. For the moment, suffice it to say that the faithful minister once more dominates at a crucial turning point. His exit aria in 2, 6 communicates the flood of emotion that overcomes him as his dream of service to the dynasty comes true.

The second and final scene cluster in act 2 presents yet another set of complications that prepares for the intense pressure—and inevitable happy denouement—of the last act. Minteo has heard from a trustworthy source that *he* is the imperial heir, and he happily relates this news to Siveno (2, 7). Thrown into doubt once again, Siveno and Lisinga conclude the act with an impassioned but fretful duet (2, 8).

As stated above, the heating up of action in act 3 results in shorter and more numerous scene groups. The divisions in the final act of *L'eroe cinese* are (3, 1–4), (3, 5–6), and (3, 7–9). In 3, 4 Minteo appears before Leango and declares his continued constancy (after Leango had been told Minteo was advancing upon the palace at the head of the angry populace, with designs to topple the state). The scene ends with an aria by Leango praising Minteo's fealty. The only scene grouping not capped by Leango is the last before the opera's end. In 3, 6 Ulania takes center stage, rapturing in her love for Minteo.

The diagram below identifies the scene groups for all three acts of the opera. With the exception of the act endings, at which the principal lovers sang, the chart shows Leango's placement at three of the four scene group endings.

Leango's stature within the structural dramaturgy of the opera corresponds to his ethical stature in the drama's moral problematics. The happy outcome in *L'eroe cinese* is largely attributed to Leango's tranquil wisdom, patience, and selflessness. His composure routinely prevails over the impetuous emotions of the younger characters. Behind the travails and flirtations of the lovers on stage, he quietly choreographs his master plan with the Tartars. In the face of unexpected reversals, he does not suffer outbursts of impatience or anger, as do patriarchs in other of Metastasio's operas. The only time Leango's calm demeanor wrinkles is when his protégé Siveno is (wrongly) reported dead and the minister fears his efforts to preserve the rightful heir have been for naught.

The fact that Leango's only instance of crisis comes about when he thinks his nation has been deprived of its just leader focuses attention on the subjectivity of the subject. That is, Leango is exploited in the *favola* most intensively in the role of a person who derives identity in relation to a superior: supporter not supported, subaltern not superior. As others have noted,

in his capacity as mentor to the young Siveno, Leango does pronounce on the necessary qualities of a good ruler. However, he expresses these thoughts in recitative. His arias, on the other hand, concern subjecthood. Since arias function as the most important carriers of meaning in serious opera, that which Leango explores in his set pieces takes precedence over what he treats in recitative.[39]

Peter Kivy refers to opera seria's characters as "obsessed personages" whose "emotional fanaticism" is perfectly dramatized in their *da capo* arias, "the most obsessive, fanatical of musical forms."[40] The poetry of Leango's arias in *L'eroe cinese* is equally obsessive, returning repeatedly to the mandate of submission to a superior order, and progressively intensifying the message. Leango performs his first aria following a somewhat tense exchange with Siveno, where the latter, a little imperiously, pleads with the former to please the Chinese people and take the crown. Leango cannot yet tell his "son" that *he* in fact is destined to rule, so he puts him off by reminding him, a bit harshly, about the difficulties a good sovereign must endure. After dismissing the mandarins who accompanied Siveno, Leango tells his son to follow him to the temple, to pray for an auspicious outcome as regards China's new emperor. With Siveno still on stage, Leango sings:

Structural dramaturgy of *L'eroe cinese*

	1	2	3	4	5	6	7	8	9	Total items
ACT ONE										
Lisinga			a						ma	a + ma
Leango						m	a			m + a
Siveno		a								a
Ulania				a						a
Minteo					a					a
ACT TWO										
Lisinga					a			d		a + d
Leango						a				a
Siveno		a						d		a + d
Ulania				a						a
Minteo			a							a
ACT THREE										
Lisinga	c	a								c + a
Leango				a			a			a + a
Siveno	a								CORO	a
Ulania						ma				ma
Minteo					a					a

a = exit aria   m = monologue
c = cavatina   ma = monologue followed by exit aria
d = duet

On the road of our life,
Without the rays of the kindly heavens
Every earnest soul gets lost,
The heart trembles, the foot hesitates.
  Art helps, wisdom plays a part
In accomplishing great acts;
But art and wisdom prove empty
If the heavens are not friendly.

              (1, 7)

[Nel cammin di nostra vita,
Senza i rai del Ciel cortese
Si smarrisce ogni alma ardita,
Trema il cor, vacilla il piè.
  A compir le belle imprese
L'arte giova, il senno ha parte;
Ma vaneggia il senno e l'arte
Quando amico il Ciel non è.]

The blatant Dantean reference in the first line of lyric and continued elements from the Dantean lexicon throughout the first quatrain ("rai," "smarrisce," "piè"), alert one immediately to the religious charge of these verses. Here Leango stresses the importance of abiding by the divine in the execution of one's actions.

He furthermore addresses Siveno, imparting to him this crucial rule. Interestingly, several terms in Leango's poetry rehearse identical words from Siveno's aria at the end of 1, 2. Here the youth turned to the heavens for help fearing separation from his beloved Lisinga. Siveno's first strophe reads:

Ah, kind stars, if in the *heavens*
Pity is not *lost*,
Either take my *life*,
Or leave me my beloved!

       (1, 2) (italics mine)

[Ah se in *ciel*, benigne stelle,
La pietà non è *smarrita*,
O toglietemi la *vita*,
O lasciate il mio ben!]

When these same words issue from the minister four scenes later, they are raised up from the temporal context of lovers' strife, and given a more profound meaning. For Leango, the heavens are not simply a canvas on which stars spell out lovers' destinies, nor is life a commodity one trades depending on amorous vicissitudes. Leango's "Heaven" ("Cielo") is capitalized, an indication of the more solemn import of his words. What's more, Heaven is conflated with the court ("Ciel cortese"), the rays of which are essential to one's well-being. It is perhaps a stretch, but the word "ciel" had enormous prominence in the part of the Chinese Rites

Controversy known as the "Debate on Terms." The Jesuits tried to postulate that the Chinese word for "sky" (T'ien) also meant something akin to "Heaven," with its connotations of the divine. One would have to study the incidence of "cielo" across reform opera aria poetry to see if it has any unusual presence here, but it is possible that the word in the mouth of a revered Chinese mandarin may have conjured further Jesuitical associations of the Chinese with citizens of a devout nation.[41]

Juxtaposing Siveno's song text next to Leango's serves also to highlight the nature of the latter's lyric as a sentence aria. That is, Leango's aria encapsulates a more expository, aphoristic sentiment, as opposed to expressing an emotional state. Even though Metastasio used the same double quatrain composition in each aria, and the quatrains have the same line-length pattern (eight syllables in the first three lines, seven in the last), the punctuation of each aria suggests very different poetic affects. Siveno's quatrain is broken in the middle of its first line, and again at the end of each line, betokening more breathy, urgent movement. A more ethereal sensation is created also from the unadorned vowel sounds with which three of the four lines commence: "Ah . . ." and the repeated "O"s. Leango's text, on the other hand, concedes nothing to wordless sound. The three instances of enjambment ground the poetry in a more sententious realm. The message he pronounces is one of Catholic subjecthood for all, including rulers.

Leango's second aria, at the end of 2, 6, heightens the imperative to recognize rank and offer due homage. The analysis above noted the critical import of this scene, both in terms of its central position in the opera, and its climactic plot substance. In this scene Siveno learns from Leango of his imperial origins and impending advancement to the Chinese throne. Just preceding his minister-father's aria, the astonished heir expresses this impassioned recitative:

Siveno: You call me Lord!
     Ah no, call me son. Ah, this name
     Is my greatest gift! I, what would I be
     Without you? . . . You alone
     Father, benefactor, teacher, friend,
     You have been everything to me; to you
     I owe all my gratitude, my respect,
     My love, my faith . . .

             (2, 6)

[*Siveno:* Signor mi chiami!
     Ah no, chiamami figlio. Ah, questo nome
     È il mio pregio più grande! Io, che sarei

Senza di te? . . . Tu solo
Padre, benefattor, maestro, amico,
Tutto fosti per me; tutta io ti deggio
La mia riconoscenza, il mio rispetto,
L'amore mio, la mia fede . . .]

Leango responds to this outpouring of deference by emphasizing the reverence he now owes to Siveno, his king:

Leango: Son, ah! no more: tenderness overcomes
    me.
(he embraces him tenderly, then retreats with respect)
      Pardon the love
    That surges from my soul,
    My glory, my hope,
    My son, my king.
      May the blood, the tears
    That I shed for you
    Give me the right
    To clasp you to my breast.

                        (2, 6)

    [Perdona l'affetto
    Che l'alma mi preme,
    Mia gloria, mia speme,
    Mio figlio, mio re.
      Di stringerti al petto
    Mi ottengano il vanto
    Quel sangue, quel pianto
    Ch'io sparsi per te.]

Leango's few words before his aria are important, because they signal a key transformation. Just as Leango claims to no longer recognize Siveno as his son ("Son, ah! no more"), he also will no longer assume the role of father. The hierarchy in their relationship to this point reverses, as Leango moves from an elder-superior role to that of younger-subordinate. And, as Leango's aria and the rest of the opera will show, *L'eroe cinese* is much more interested in this part of the continuum. That is, Leango's welcome demotion and the glories of his deferential position, rather than those of Siveno's rise, carry the lion's share of the opera's dramatic and emotional force.

The shorter, six-syllable lines of the aria text (compared to the eight-syllable ones of Leango's preceding sentence aria) indicate a more intense emotive charge. Punctuation breaks within several lines increase that charge. Leango employs a language and tone of obsequiousness, both in his heaping up of epithets to praise Siveno ("My glory," "My hope," etc.), and especially as he asks pardon for what may have been indecorous behavior toward the young successor (his spontaneous embrace). Even more than the minister's

subservient register, however, certain elements of the lyric constitute clues to the powerful emotional experience that overcomes him in this moment. In asking for forgiveness for his unchecked intimacy toward Siveno, Leango reveals a degree of confusion in the midst of the sudden change. His fatherly affection for his son up to now collides with the respectful attitude a subject should demonstrate toward majesty. Leango's sentimental turmoil is also conveyed because the stream of endearments he directs toward Siveno are also those invoked by parents toward their progeny ("My glory, my hope, / My son . . .")—but he caps the list with the sharply contrastive "my king."

The second quatrain veers away somewhat from Leango's relationship with Siveno to speak of his *other* fatherly experience. Leango justifies his rushed gesture toward the new heir by recalling the paternal anguish he experienced sacrificing his own child to spare the dynasty. As the minister cites "That blood"—his real son's—and "those cries"—his own, perhaps blended with the infant's wails—he vividly summons the parental grief attending his earlier heroic action. The aria thus conjoins these two divergent psychological states, or, two sides of paternal love: affection and agony. More than simply link them, however, the lyric blends the two emotional experiences, and from the blend creates the sensation of overwhelm and surrender proper to a dutiful subject. When, per the requirements of the *da capo* aria, Leango returns to the phrase "My son, my king," the term "son" has been enriched. It has a double valence, inasmuch as it refers both to Siveno, his acquired son, and to his real son, relinquished to the interests of the dynasty. The verbal pairing "Mio figlio, mio re" communicates in the most condensed way that everything Leango has done as a parent, adoptive or otherwise, has been in the service of his final and most important role, that of subject to his monarch.

It bears mentioning that the "my son, my king" motto does not speak to dynastic continuance in the traditional way. Certainly, this bulwark of opera seria ideology is supported by the return of Siveno's imperial line to rule China. But the young prince's father is long absent. More than a contested handover of the scepter from actual father to son, the conflict in *L'eroe cinese* hinges on the outcomes of a subaltern's strategies. Leango is not Siveno's true father, nor is he the emperor. As provisional regent to the Chinese nation he is greatly respected, but when the people present him with the opportunity to ascend to the throne, he renounces it. Leango chooses at all times to remain in a ministerial role, and with the succession of Siveno-Svenvango, he will simply serve a different master.

The subject identity thus requires fluidity, that is, the willingness to adjust and be ready to serve in a variety of contexts. *L'eroe cinese* is about the imperial servants whose flexibility makes possible the long healthy life of the kingdom.

Leango sings his third aria just after learning that the report of Minteo's hostile advance upon the kingdom was false. Minteo himself appears before Leango to declare his continued loyalty and subservience to the regent, to which Leango responds:

> You are not a king, but even without a kingdom
> You are as great as any king.
> When a soul is this beautiful,
> It finds everything it needs in itself. (*exits*)
>
> (3, 4)

> [Re non sei, ma senza regno
> Già sei grande al par d'un re.
> Quando è bella a questo segno,
> Tutto trova un'alma in sé. (*parte*)]

Here the poetic encomium to the faithful subject reaches its height. Monarchical servants who behave as Minteo does are king-like, avers Leango, the opera's highest authority. The longer line-length suggests again an air of didacticism, while the brevity of the composition might mean greater repetition of the "rule," i.e., that devoted subalterns are duly compensated.

The fourth and final lyrical item given to Leango falls at the end of 3, 7, the onset of the last and most crucial scene group. Lisinga has entered hurriedly to announce that Siveno/Svenvango has been murdered by an angry populace. Leango, who up until now has remained unruffled by the course of events, finally breaks. Thinking that his protégé and China's new emperor has been been killed, his emotional reaction clarifies the major crisis of the opera: the subject's loss of his ruler. Leango furthermore is not just any subject, but one who has worked hard and long for the good of the state, and now sees no reward for his years of willing selflessness. The recitative leading to his aria is as follows:

> We have lost,
> You, Chinese, have lost your king,
> I the many years of fear, of sweat . . .
> . . . Have my honor and my faith
> thus merited from the Heavens
> the sacrifice of such a long life?
> Ah, what good did it do you, Svenvango,
> To have the tender pity of such a faithful vassal?
> I refuse a kingdom,

> I buy your days
> With those, oh God, of my own son, and now?
>
> (3, 7)

> [Abbiam perduto,
> Voi, Cinesi, il re vostro, io di tant'anni
> I palpiti, i sudori . . .
> . . . Han meritato in Cielo
> Dunque il martir di così lunga vita
> L'onor mio, la mia fede? Ah, d'un vassallo
> Così fedel, che ti giovò, Svenvango,
> La tenera pietà? Ricuso un regno,
> Ricompro i giorni tuoi
> Con quelli, oh Dio, d'un proprio figlio; e poi?]

Leango's anguish translates into a series of questions, addressed to a somewhat ambiguous interlocutor. Sala di Felice points out an expedient she terms "the world as spectator ("il mondo spettatore"), that is, any technique by which an actor not only calls attention to the notion of audience to his circumstances, but also invokes the empathy of said audience for those circumstances.[42] Leango calls this expansive world of witnesses into being when he directs his grief to the Chinese populace: "We have lost / You, Chinese, have lost your king." With these words he conflates the stage Chinese with the auditorium's masses, all of whom are invited to imagine the disaster of being without a (their) sovereign. Leango's use of the first-person plural is significant here as well, as with it he includes himself in the body of kingless subjects. He emphasizes his position of servitude by referring to himself as vassal, when he cries "Ah, what good did it do you, Svenvango, / To have the tender pity of such a faithful vassal?" By the time he sings his final aria, he has completely elided himself with the identity of the child-subject, who despairs the loss of the father-king:

> Ah! May this be
> the last of my days.
> For whom, for whom would I live
> If my Lord were to die?
>
> (3, 7)

> [Ah! Sia de' giorni miei
> Questo l'estremo dì.
> Per chi, per chi vivrei,
> Se il mio signor morì?]

The simple, straighforward lexicon and syntax make this song more visceral than any of Leango's previous items. Here there is none of the moralizing or the peaceful satisfaction expressed in his first and third arias. Poetically speaking, this final piece is closest to Leango's third aria, in which he grappled with a flood of mixed passions (joy, pain, confusion) upon telling Siveno of his royal origins. This aria is even more emotionally charged, however. Its one-stanza length suggests much more repetition than that in the already repetitive two-strophe *da capo* aria. Leango wishes for an end to his life in short, six-syllable lines, verses that emphasize his angst by their *tronco* endings. This aria brings the operatic catastrophe to its highest pitch. It is the last individual number in the drama, before the plot resolves. And the plot resolution is about Leango —the subaltern's—triumph. Although it involves the king (Svenvango), insofar as he—his line—is successfully restored, *L'eroe cinese*'s celebratory conclusion is really about the recompense coming to the royal servant, for proper services rendered.

The importance of the Chinese to this rendering of an ideal state official can be grasped by comparing *L'eroe cinese* to *Demetrio* (1731), a Metastasian opera of twenty years prior. Zoli has stated that *L'eroe cinese* is merely *Demetrio* set in China.[43] On a first reading it might appear thus, since the earlier *dramma per musica* is constructed on a similar business of reversals and revelations resulting in the legitimate heir's ascendancy. However, the Syrian court elder Fenicio is not nearly as calm, nor as sanguine as Leango. *Demetrio* also spotlights the new monarchs much more than it does the facilitator of their rise. In fact, the true star of *Demetrio* is the incumbent Queen Cleonice, who spends most of the drama vacillating over whether to force her subjects to accept her marriage to her beloved, the commoner Alceste (Siveno's counterpart, unknown to all as the noble and authentic heir). Fenicio's lower status in this context is indicated by the fact that, unlike Leango, he is not one of the opera's principals. The point is, *Demetrio* stresses an altogether different aspect of enlightened absolutist ethics. It offers an operatic meditation on proper marriage custom, and on the nature of true rulers. If, on the other hand, one wished to mount a drama of the ideal dynastic functionary, one could not do better than to travel to China.

METASTASIO VS VOLTAIRE

The unique framing of the Chinese in *L'eroe cinese* becomes further clarified when considered next to that of Voltaire's nearly contemporaneous tragedy, *L'Orphelin de la Chine* (1755). Voltaire states in the preface to his drama that he and Metastasio worked from the same Chinese historical subject. He then notes, however, that the Metastasian work diverges markedly from the Chinese tragedy on the subject, and that his own drama constitutes yet a third variant:

> The celebrated Metastasio has made choice of pretty nearly the same subject as myself for one of his dramatic poems, an orphan escaped from the destruction of his family, and has drawn his plot from a dynasty nine hundred years before our era.
> The Chinese tragedy of the "Orphan of Tchao" differs in many respects; and I have chosen one that is not much like either of them, except in the name, as I have confined my plan to the grand epoch of Genghis Khan.[44]

Voltaire's comment that Metastasio drew his plot "from a dynasty nine hundred years before our era" lends credence to the idea that the Italian depended primarily on the historical account (and not the Chinese drama) as his source. The French *letterato* then notes that he too has diverged from the Chinese opera. Our interest here is to gauge how far Voltaire strayed from *Tchao chi cou ell*, and how differently—compared to *L'eroe cinese*—the resulting French tragedy instrumentalized perceptions of Chinese culture. Just like Metastasio, Voltaire in *L'Orphelin de la Chine* drew an ultra-benevolent picture of Chinese society, but there the similarities fade.

As Voltaire states, he resituated the temporal setting from the mid-ninth century BC to the early thirteenth century, the age of Genghis Khan and his marauding hordes. The timing choice evolved from a prior consideration, however. Voltaire notes in the preface that he wished to demonstrate the "natural superiority which reason and genius have over blind force and barbarism."[45] The thirteenth-century invasion of Chinese lands by the Tartars furnished Voltaire with the perfect example of the supremacy of reason and genius. The roving Mongol warriors were reputed among Europeans as one of the most barbarous world peoples. Nonetheless, Voltaire writes: "The Tartar conquerers did not change the manners of the conquered nation; on the other hand, they protected and encouraged all the arts established in China, and adopted their laws."[46] The fact that the Chinese-authored *Tchao chi cou ell* was written in the subsequent period of tranquil Mongol rule further evidenced the moral and artistic heights of the nation. According to Voltaire, the drama was "a masterpiece, when placed in competition with the pieces written by our authors in the fourteenth century."[47] The French *philosophe* reinforces the power of Chinese cultural influence by observing that the most recent instance of

Tartar subjugation of China offers yet another proof of the latter civilization's superiority: "when they [the Tartars] had once more subdued this great empire, the beginning of last century, they submitted a second time to the wisdom of the conquered, and the two nations formed but one people, governed by the most ancient laws in the world; a most remarkable event."[48] Thus Voltaire diverges from the Chinese opera in terms of both its time period and its protagonists. He transforms the opposition from one between rival families into one between rival civilizations. He converts internecine struggles between clans over the mandate to avenge ancestral wrongs, to a contest between cultures and their respective virtues. *L'Orphelin de la Chine* sets one society against another, to demonstrate that when they mix, they effect a reaction as natural and universal as that of oil and water.

As regards the plot of the tragedy, Voltaire retained the central event of a minister's effort to spare his nation's heir by offering his own son to hostile forces. Briefly, the five-act tragedy proceeds as follows: Genghis Khan, having conquered China, seeks to exterminate the last traces of the Chinese royal family. The Chinese mandarin Zamti and his wife Idamé have been entrusted by the dying emperor with his infant heir. Their unwavering loyalty to his wishes provokes from each different but equally stolid resistance to the orders of the invader, Genghis Khan, that the surviving heir be killed. Zamti proposes that they offer instead their own son, disguised in royal clothing. Idamé cannot bear such an act and says she would rather sacrifice her own life than submit either her son or the infant king to the executioners. Genghis Khan admits surprise at their fealty, a virtuous resolve with which he is not familiar. Shortly thereafter, he confesses his love for Idamé. It is revealed that as a young soldier he had loved her, but she had refused him. The old love stirs anew in his heart, and he asks once more for her affections. Again, Idamé holds her ground. Genghis Khan threatens that if she does not leave Zamti and join him on the throne, he will order the death of her husband. To this new turn of events Zamti shows his mettle by telling Idamé to accept the offer. She does not, of course, and the final scene shows Genghis Khan totally won over by the astonishing example of the Chinese couple. He returns their son (despite being in his custody, the child had not yet been killed), and he restores Zamti to his previous position as justice official. Converted by their heroism, the Mongol ruler renounces his former ways, and becomes a sovereign in the style of Confucius.

The Chinese-Tartar admixture was not merely an arbitrary choice on Voltaire's part to prove the inex-

orable triumph of enlightened reason over primitivism. As eighteenth-century Europe's most vocal sinophile, Voltaire was convinced that of all global societies, the Chinese had most properly developed this kind of reason. For him, Chinese culture offered a nearly flawless model of the tolerance, common sense, civil action, and nonreligious morality that comprised the foundation of his religious, political, and philosophical agenda. In *The Philosophy of History* (1765) he wrote: "superstition seems to have been established in all nations and among all people, except the men of letters in China."[49] He especially revered Confucianism, seeing in its practical, rational values and lack of dogma a brilliant example of the spiritual deism he staunchly supported. *L'Orphelin de la Chine* also served to refute China's detractors among Voltaire's fellow *philosophes*. When Rousseau in the first *Discours* (1750) stated that the inherent failings of China's allegedly civilized society were proven by its defeat at the hands of the crude Tartars, Voltaire reacted strongly. Many critics maintain that the tragedian wrote *L'Orphelin de la Chine* expressly to counter these remarks, and that it formed merely one part of an ongoing debate between the two thinkers.

One way to further appreciate the treatment of the Celestial Empire in the French work is to consider it in the context of Voltaire's body of tragic productions. He wrote twenty-eight tragedies over his lifetime, and for the most part continued to embrace seventeenth-century neoclassical poetics. The five-act structure, the three unities, Aristotelian arousal of both terror and pity, decorum in speech, stage movement, and the actions represented—for the Sage of Ferney as well as for his predecessors, adherence to these principles assured the literary integrity of a drama. Once these prescriptions were satisfied, Voltaire's principal concern was with freshening and enlivening the stage offerings. He advocated greater variety with respect to subject matter, which meant that he put more recent and local history on stage. He recommended increased action and spectacle, authenticity in costuming, and simpler, clearer dialogue over stage language often written for rhetorical effect. Critics have remarked on the "operatic" quality of his tragedies, thanks to his interest in the heightened picturesque element and in emotionalism, achieved through arresting *coups de théâtre*.[50]

Voltaire's commitment to revitalizing the tragic genre led him to compose a good number of "exotic tragedies," some of which (*Zaïre* and *Mahomet*, for example) count among the most well-known and beloved works in his time. Scholarly consensus is that Voltaire generally used the non-European other to address questions of religious tolerance.[51] Dramas like *Zaïre* (1732) and *Alzire* (1736), for example, set fanatical exotics against reasonable Christians, and by this contrast Voltaire sought to rebuke fanatical elements in Christianity and promote its more humane, dispassionate qualities. In *Mahomet* (1742), the author took a different tack to condemn religious bigotry. This time all of the protagonists were Muslim, and Voltaire claimed to illustrate the danger of intolerant theological factions (especially the papacy) via the atrocious barbarity of the Islamic prophet.

In *L'Orphelin de la Chine* he presented still more variations on the exploitation of the exotic culture to advance his *lumiéres*. Like *Mahomet*, it did not feature any Christian heroes, but clearly, Voltaire's virtuous Chinese and their positive effect on the violence-prone Genghis Khan embodied the author's conception of a heroic, deistic Christianity. Where *Mahomet* presented an example to be avoided, *Orphelin* dramatized that which should be emulated. One need never wait long for an enactment of or meditation on the steadfast goodness of the Chinese. Genghis Khan especially remarks on their nature, as is keeping with his gradual conversion to their ways over the course of the play:

Genghis.   'Tis strange,
That sentiments like these, to us unknown,
Should rise in mortal breasts: without a groan,
A murmur, or complaint, a father breaks
The ties of nature, and would sacrifice
His child to please the manes of his sovereign.
And the fond wife would die to save her lord.
The more I see, the more I must admire
This wondrous people, great in arts and arms,
In learning and in manners great; their kings
On wisdom's basis founded all their power;
They gave the nations law, by virtue reigned,
And governed without conquest . . .
                                    (4, 2)[52]

Claudia Marie Kovach identifies in the three principal characters three types of law: Genghis Khan represents the law of brute force, Zamti the patriarchal law decreeing loyalty to fatherland, and Idamé the law of nature, which includes all-powerful love.[53] Such associations seem well borne out in the text. When Genghis Khan declares that he will spare the infant heir only if Idamé leaves Zamti and joins him on the throne, and that if she does not obey, Zamti will be killed, the faithful Chinese mandarin and husband entreats his wife to accept the terms:

Zamti.   Forget me, live
But for thy country, give up all to that,

And that alone; heaven points out the fair path
Of glory to thee, and a husband's death,
For Zamti soon must die, shall leave thee free
To act as best may serve the common cause:
Enslave the Tartar, make him all thy own;
And yet to leave thee to that proud usurper
Will make the pangs of death more bitter to me:
It is a dreadful sacrifice, but duty
Spreads sweet content o'er all that she inspires:
Idame, be a mother to thy king,
And reign; remember, 'tis my last command,
Preserve thy sovereign, and be happy.
                                    (4, 6)[54]

Idamé, for her part, nearly always invokes her inborn drive to love, and grounds it in nature's immutable principles. When Zamti pleads with her to give up their son in the name of duty to the state, she responds:

Idamé.   What is your country, what your king to me?
The name of subject is not half so sacred
As husband or father. Love and nature
Are heaven's first great unalterable laws,
And cannot be reversed; the rest are all
From mortal man, and may be changed at
    pleasure.
                                    (2, 3)[55]

Idamé's passionate scenes would appear to steal the show fairly frequently, and whether Voltaire intended to distinguish nature's law from Zamti's unflagging code of patriotism and privilege the former, is open to debate.[56] One could conclude that it is the combination of these impulses, so inborn and "natural" to each of the spouses, that ultimately mitigated Genghis Khan's barbarity. For Voltaire then, the Chinese ideal resides in the successful, functional blend of Idamé's imperative to love and her husband's stoic dedication to country. Together they formed the natural, scripture-less morality that he was so enthusiastic to ascribe to the Chinese people. Certainly this reading corresponds with the reformed Mongol ruler's last words as the tragedy ends:

Genghis.   I admire you both;
You have subdued me, and I blush to sit
On Cathay's throne; whilst there are souls
    like yours
So much above me; vainly I have tried
By glorious deeds to build myself a name
Among the nations; you have humbled me,
And I would equal you: I did not know
That mortals could be masters of themselves;
That greatest glory I have learned from you:
                          . . . once
I was a conqueror, now I am a king.

(*to Zamti*)
Let wisdom reign, and still direct our valor;
Let prudence triumph over strength; her king
Will set the example, and your conqueror
Henceforth shall be obedient to your law.

. . . .

Idamé.   What could inspire
            This great design, and work this change?
Genghis.   Thy virtues.

(5, 6)[57]

The above analysis of *L'Orphelin de la Chine* is admittedly summary. However, one of the goals of including Voltaire's work in a study of Metastasio's opera is to show the range of mobilizations of the Chinese, even when portrayals tend equally toward idealization. Metastasio's use of the Jesuit encomium supported the enlightened absolutist monarchy by effecting a paean to its increasingly important bureaucratic subject. At virtually the same time, Voltaire manipulated the flattering Jesuit treatment to prove the efficacy of a socio-philosophical doctrine that, at least at times, conflicted gravely with the religious ideology of enlightened despotism.

A second aim of this examination is to dispel the idea that either drama more meaningfully or more deeply deployed perceptions of Chinese culture than the other. Studies of Voltaire's tragedy (not to mention the simple *fact* of the scholarship on *Orphelin*, in contrast with its near absence on *L'eroe cinese*) imply that his—and France's—engagements with Chinese society were more expansive, more thoughtful, more ideologically oriented, than those of other eighteenth-century states and cultures. These value judgments arise from thinking that automatically equates subversion with progress, or links overt intellectualism with greater consequence.[58] Such a bias only aggravates the assumption that other—in this case, Italian—instrumentalizations of China were narrower, more pragmatic, and therefore somehow more shallow, than their counterparts across the Alps. None of these suppositions are necessarily true. Both dramas were embedded in the contingencies of particular European social cultures, and as such reflect and generate unique, complex networks of meaning.

For example, despite the fact that Voltaire's tragedy seems to marshal China in the promulgation of "big" ideas, it also contains contradictions to that liberal progressivism. A surprising comment in the preface to *Orphelin* gives the sense that Voltaire's claims about contemporary China were much more about mythmaking, that is, bound in an invented nation he imagined had existed many centuries earlier. How convinced could he have been of the inherent functionality of contemporary Chinese ethics when, alongside the prefatory compliments, he also wrote: "These people, whom we take so much pains and go so far to visit; from whom, with the utmost difficulty, we have obtained permission to carry the riches of Europe, and to instruct them, do not to this day know how much we are their superiors; they are not even far enough advanced in knowledge to venture to imitate us, and don't so much as know whether we have any history or not."[59] Again in the preface, Voltaire's statement that *Tchao chi cou ell* exhibits the high level which Chinese dramatic arts had reached takes on new significance when at least one scholar has suggested that Junxiang's revenge drama constituted mainly a masked protest by Chinese "against the Tartar's bloody rule" in the fourteenth century.[60] Kovach has advanced the most cogent argument for wrinkles in *Orphelin*'s unequivocal affirmation of China's ideal combination of reason and genius. She provides several convincing examples of problematics surrounding the alleged Chinese perfection in the tragedy, and her larger point is that these problematics derive from Voltaire's own developing identity.[61]

Findings such as these matter because Voltaire's "depth" with respect to China is often attributed to his progressive appreciation of it, concomitant with an admirable proto-secular humanism. This depth is not without local idiosyncrasy, however, and his embrace of China is not without qualifications. Likewise, Metastasio's *L'eroe cinese* does not mount as superficial or as gratuitous a representation of its Asian heroes as some might hold.

CONCLUSION

The mobilization of Leango's qualities as a devoted minister to the state takes full advantage of the Jesuit encomium to China. What's more, China's propensity to serve as a model for the enlightened Catholic sovereignty derives specifically from the Jesuit interpretation of Confucianism. In some ways, Leango might be construed as an Italianized Confucius—not, however, in the direction of natural morality and deistic ethics that so attracted philosophically minded French and English sinophiles. Rather, Leango epitomized the traits of modesty and self-effacement connected with Confucius. Du Halde's brief treatment of Confucius's life in fact emphasizes his constant renunciation of titles and privilege. The Middle Kingdom

masses wish that he would assume leadership in a
more traditional mode, but the gentle philosopher
continually refuses such pomp and espouses a life
dedicated to less ostentatious example. Likewise, in
his role as wise but humble vassal, by way of his strategic and gracious demurrals, Leango demonstrates that
heroism equals servitude.

The Confucian mandarin, together with the throngs
of would-be Christian converts believed to be waiting
in the wings behind him, constituted the Jesuit idea
of a "Chinese hero." For the absolutist Catholic
monarchy, the hero next in line after the king would
be his or her devoted court official, entrusted with realizing new policies of prosperous state functionality.
L'eroe cinese appealed to its spectators to identify the intellectual and material wealth of the Middle Kingdom
with the local court. More crucially, however, it invited them to admire and imitate the actions and attitude of the court advocate Leango. As the chorus
points out at the opera's end:

> The entire world will hear of it,
> Every age will know,
> The unheard-of loyalty
> Of the hero of this empire.
>
> (3, 9)

> [Sarà nota al mondo intero,
> Sarà chiara in ogni età,
> Dell'eroe di questo impero
> L'inudita fedeltà.]

The original Chinese legend, which told of the sur-
vival of the orphaned dynastic heir, spawned several
variants, each with its own compelling protagonist.
The hero of the Chinese musical drama *Tchao chi cou
ell* was the orphan himself, who exacted rightful revenge on the enemies of his family. The hero of
Voltaire's tragedy was the potent combination of respect for state and the reaches of a tender heart—together these secular virtues could transform the
brutishness of a people. Only Metastasio reprises the
same hero from the first saga. Like the faithful minister Tchao kong in Du Halde's presentation of "La storia Tchao-kong," the triumphant figure in *L'eroe cinese*
is the patient facilitator, the one who puts aside all personal interests for the benefit of the public good. The
concept of "public good" had become the new virtue
of the enlightened Catholic state. In these states the
influence of the Jesuit panegyric of China lingered,
longer than it did in other European centers. These
monarchies could easily welcome the "Chinese hero,"
stalwart custodian of their imperial ambitions.

III
Playing with Reform: China in Comic Opera

5

Islands of Opportunity:
Carlo Goldoni, *L'isola disabitata* (1757)

Prato has the highest proportion of Chinese immigrants of any Italian province, with most (95%) originating from just two provinces in the south of China: Zhejiang and Fujian. Typically these immigrants come seeking to establish their own business, and take advantage of an often illegal migratory chain that exploits networks of existing relationships. In turn, the development of these networks may also be laying the foundation for a new model of immigration, with implications for levels of integration within the host country as well as future patterns of economic activity.

In general, local government, business and civil society in Prato have tended to be pro-active in their dealings with these immigrants, recognizing not just the problems associated with high levels of immigration, but also the potential benefits. Attitudes to, and relations with, the Chinese community have varied, however, since the early 1990s, with much of the debate centering on the degree to which the Chinese have formed a closed community, and the implications of this for the second generation.[1]

IN 1757, CARLO GOLDONI, FOREMOST COMIC LIBrettist in eighteenth-century Europe, ventured into Chinese territory with the *dramma giocoso* titled *L'isola disabitata*.[2] Its festive portrayal of the adventures of Dutch sea traders in the China seas took advantage of the mid-century European rage for things oriental. More importantly, however, *L'isola disabitata* deployed China in specific ways to articulate Goldoni's social reform project. The Goldonian campaign to both promote bourgeois economic activity and morals and denounce the values of a declining Venetian aristocracy is most familiar to connoisseurs of Italian theater in the dramaturg's enormous repertoire of spoken comedies. Plays such as *La famiglia dell'antiquario* (1748), *La locandiera* (1752), and *I rusteghi* (1760) derive their force from the brilliantly dramatized and humorized tension between merchant and noble classes. While the generic nature of musical comedy mandates different tactics for its exploitation, the same class polarity nonetheless animates Goldoni's comic operas. Furthermore, the conventions of musical comic theater in eighteenth-century Italy permitted Goldoni to extend his ideological program advancing the middle class beyond his usual reach. *L'isola disabitata* shows Goldoni breaking out from his normative Venetian milieu and applying his philosophy of ethical and economic revision in a much wider context. While it is generally accepted that Goldoni was not an overtly political figure and rarely, if ever, openly allied himself with the programs of Enlightenment reformers and *philosophes*, *L'isola disabitata* belies such reticence.[3] Its emphasis on concepts of liberty, happiness, peace, and productivity promotes moral and mercantilist values espoused by Enlightenment thinkers both in and outside the Italian peninsula. Behind the veil of eighteenth-century exoticism, *L'isola disabitata* is plainly grounded in contemporary cultural developments, and engages in social criticism on a global scale.[4]

Before analyzing the particulars of *L'isola disabitata*'s instrumentalization of the Middle Kingdom, it will be instructive to discuss Goldoni's relation to the comic opera and its Venetian context. Goldoni not only wrote the largest number of comic librettos over the course of the eighteenth century, but he profoundly influenced the genre's development. Originating in the Neapolitan opera buffa, the eighteenth-century Italian comic opera came into its own only when the popular Naples entertainment made its way to Venice, where Goldoni, together with innovative composers from both the north and south of Italy, made highly creative and enduring adjustments.[5] Goldoni called his version of the opera buffa the *dramma giocoso*, and its innovations made their first significant impact at mid-century, with *Arcadia in Brenta* (1749).[6] Set to music by Venetian composer Baldassare Galuppi ("il Buranello"), *Arcadia in Brenta* introduced textual-musical elements that established the model for the most successful comic operas of the century. The two most im-

L' ISOLA
DISABITATA

DRAMMA GIOCOSO PER MUSICA

DI POLISSENO FEGEJO

PASTOR ARCADE

DA RAPPRESENTARSI

NEL TEATRO GRIMANI

DI S. SAMUEL

L'AUTUNNO DELL'ANNO 1757.

IN VENEZIA , MDCCLVII.
Appreſſo Modeſto Fenzo,
CON LICENZA DE' SUPERIORI.

46. Frontispiece, *L'isola disabitata.* Courtesy Schatz Collection of Opera Librettos, United States Library of Congress, Music Division.

portant of these were the multi-section ensemble finale placed at the conclusions of acts, and the introduction of a new singing role, that of the *mezzo carattere.*

Goldoni's formulation of the first element, sometimes called the "chain" or "action finale," involved heightening plot complications at the ends of the first two acts, and setting their events to continuous orchestration. These more complex vocal and instrumental sequences, altering in tempo and key according to stage activity, opened up enormous expressive possibilities for dramatists and composers. For the first time music was charged with translating character action, and not merely emotional sentiment. Daniel

Heartz states that "Goldoni was responsible for the new dramaturgy in the full-length comic opera."[7]

The second of Goldoni's innovations, the *mezzo carattere* role, came into being as he made changes to the usual composition of singer-actors in the Neapolitan opera buffa. Originally, these works featured primarily peasant-level characters played by performers whose comic acting abilities often outshone their singing talents, especially if one compares their vocal performances to the virtuosity of the stars of opera seria. This is not to say that the singer-actors of opera buffa were not gifted lyrically. But the social station they portrayed dictated certain conditions, which in turn cultivated a different category of singing skill and style. In contrast with the highborn protagonists of opera seria, lowborn heroes of opera buffa utilized a more colloquial Italian, often dialect. The informal character of their language made it appear as if they improvised much of their speech or song. The talents of the operatic buffoon were therefore exploited in different sorts of vocal compositions. Comic heroes excelled in the artful expression of straightforward melodies, frequently employing exaggeration, repetition, and sudden shifts in tempo. Known for their "simple song-like ditties and rapid dialogue exchanges," they typically sang in the bass or baritone range, again in contrast to the normative voices for opera seria singers (soprano, alto, tenor).[8]

On occasion the Neapolitan productions would include noble characters together with the clowns. Goldoni's crucial adjustment, however, involved mixing in aristocratic types regularly, and allowing them to more fully participate, musically and dramatically, in the comic scenes. These were nobles who "got silly," so to speak, interacting with the lower-ranking protagonists in the less lofty twists of plot and sentiment. Their involvement in goofier spheres led to the creation of the *mezzo carattere* singing part, that is, between (*di mezzo*) the stratospheric stylistic reaches of the opera seria idol, and the less-pretentious yet still agile acrobatics of the opera buffa simpleton. Singer-actors in *mezzo carattere* roles declaimed in standard Italian, or Tuscan prose, versus the elevated poetic verse characteristic of the *divi* and the dialect slang of the *buffi.* Like opera seria singers, they could sing soprano, alto, or tenor (the bass voice was still strictly relegated to the lower-rank figures). In time Goldoni introduced purely serious roles (*parti serie*) into his *dramma giocoso,* resulting in three fairly distinct tiers of performance. Again, the *mezzo carattere* parts can be distinguished from those of the *parti serie,* since the latter never express or partake in the comical. Furthermore, the nobles playing the serious roles never appear in the ensemble finales, which is where one will find both *mezzo* and *buffo* characters thoroughly engrossed in an escalation of action and singing.

The median position of the *mezzo carattere* allowed him or her tremendous flexibility in terms of vocal and dramatic range. At home with both the low-ranking and the elite, the *mezzo carattere* role could partake in humorous and serious modes, as well as in styles belonging to a new expressive space, the sentimental. In Da Ponte-Mozart's 1787 masterpiece, Don Giovanni and Elvira—in contrast with Ottavio, the Commendatore, and Donna Anna, on the one hand, and Masetto, Zerlina, and Leporello on the other—exemplify the full development of this type, instituted by Goldoni decades earlier.

The versatility of the *mezzo carattere* corresponded moreover with composers' growing use of a "middle" style of music. McClymonds notes that the musical middle style was widely utilized, in fact it dominated both opera seria and comic opera in the eighteenth century.[9] To complicate matters, middle style music could form the basis of a lyrical item for any rank of character. In other words, if written as an *aria di mezzo carattere*, the love song crooned by a maid in a comic intermezzo would be as stylistically light, pleasing, and genteel as the same aria type sung by a queen in a heroic opera. Of course, juxtaposition of each woman's lyrical piece with the other elements of the respective works would alter the songs' import in each. Whether viewed as neutral or richly ambiguous territory, the middle style of music indicates the complexity of factors in opera that work together to convey meaning. In *L'isola disabitata*, the presence of middle style music must surely have abetted the opera's articulation of the balanced, but extremely fertile potential offered by bourgeois commercial activity.

The characters of *L'isola disabitata* exemplify the tripartite division of dramatic and singing roles. As the iconic lovers, Roberto and Gianghira play the *parti serie*, and Panico clearly acts the pure buffo role. The four remaining characters, Valdimonte, Garamone, Carolina, and Giacinta, perform as *mezzo caratteri*.[10] They are subordinate to Roberto, as members of his crew, although the men occupy the highest-ranking leadership positions under their commander. Valdimonte and Garamone, together with their respective lovers, Carolina and Giacinta, comprise the key constituents of the settlement project. As *mezzo caratteri*, their contribution to the progressive ideology of *L'isola disabitata* comes from their relation to their superior, Roberto, as well as from their comic execution in the "finti cinesi" ("the pretend Chinese") scene, both of which shall be discussed below.

Heartz points to several motivations behind Goldoni's decision to mingle social and vocal-dramaturgical factions on the stage. The first of these may be considered material, insofar as showing a broad spectrum of social classes would ideally attract a wider paying public.[11] The choice stemmed also from aesthetic concerns, whereby Goldoni sought to improve artistically upon the opera buffa as it emigrated to Venice from Naples. Elevating the comic operatic genre required introducing more variety and sophistication: dramatically, musically, and textually. Goldoni certainly achieved these goals by means of the more complex and multifaceted act-ending finales. He also did so by establishing the protocol of regular *mezzo* and *seria* roles, both of whose level of singing raised the aesthetic bar, so to speak, in the opera buffa. In this light Goldoni's nomenclature is significant, for with the classification *dramma giocoso* he seems to want to raise the opera buffa from a level of pure buffoonery to a more respectable (*dramma*) gradation.[12]

The third and most meaningful reason for diversifying the ranks of protagonists in his comic productions evolved from the author's didactic goals. Portraying a multitude of types and social classes more accurately evoked the "World," which Goldoni famously figured as one of the two books (together with "Theater") that most provided him inspiration for creating realistic and edifying dramas.[13] With the addition of *mezzo* and *seria* roles, humbler members of the audience could experience, and thus be edified by, the nobler entertainments. Both served also as models of comportment and attitude for lower-class spectators. They could furthermore help to reshape those less-than-ideal sectors of the patriciate by providing a benchmark toward which to strive. *Mezzo caratteri* were crucial to this revisionist exercise, inasmuch as they could appropriate the desirable qualities of an exemplary upper class and mesh them with those of a pragmatic, productive, morally grounded intermediary sector. The corrupt, feeble, or prepossessing aristocrat was refigured in the *mezzo carattere* protagonist as a socially viable hero, one whose values, activities, and emotional range embraced the purposeful moderation Goldoni wished to teach. The existence of a true Venetian middle class at this time is debatable, but the dramatization of so-called middle-class values by commending, indeed, canonizing the growing ranks of merchants, professionals, and other non-noble bourgeois citizenry, speaks to the dramaturg's faith in a new social order.[14]

Goldoni's preoccupation with modeling a distinct class, rooted in sound economic and moral systems, conforms with the political and cultural situation in

Venice at the time. Historians of the Enlightenment in Italy cast the Venetian Republic in that group of Italian states in which serious, effective reform thinking never got off the ground.[15] This they attribute to rigid rule by a long-standing oligarchic aristocracy, whose heritage of entitlement rendered it unwilling to update ancient policies and institutions.[16] What's more, this oligarchy, governing from Venice, often conflicted with other pedigreed sectors in the Republic. These included blood nobles from non-merchant families residing in the capital, and patrician landowners in the mainland provinces, both of whom possessed formidable wealth and local authority, but were routinely reined in by the powers in Venice. The Venetian state thus suffered from an aristocracy fragmented into contentious groups of various levels of wealth and political influence.

The most pernicious result of the impasses among these factions concerned economic policy. Where Venice progressed in matters of jurisdictionalism, its Enlightenment failings can largely be traced to its paralysis with respect to economic progress.[17] Carpanetto locates the problem in the crippling tension between the "call of trade," i.e., the sea, wherein lay the Republic's former magnificence and superiority, and "the call of the land," i.e., the economic potential to be derived by applying new cultivation methods on the mainland.[18] While both alternatives proved ultimately inachievable, the 1740s and '50s marked the period of the most strident attempts at economic reform in Venice.[19]

The timing of *L'isola disabitata* and its ideology supportive of a global free market speak directly to these local circumstances. In the figure of the Dutch colonial merchant traversing Asian oceans, adept at harvesting gains from land *and* sea, the opera envisions a new breed of citizen. As the *mezzo carattere* suggests, this enlightened figure blends the honorable moral refinements attached to an ideal nobility with the admirable qualities of those beneath the gentry—sincerity, simplicity, the capacity for honest labor. Most importantly, the modern man possesses industry, enterprise, and business aptitude.

Here it is important to note the negligible ideological distance between Roberto, who plays a *parte seria* role, and his *mezzo carattere* crew members. Admiral Roberto has the highest social rank, but as a sea captain he is active and assiduous in his mission to establish a fertile island community. He commands his crew, but works alongside them, contracting the social distinctions that separate him from his band of settlers. As has been mentioned, Valdimonte, Garamone, and their women partners are the principal ex-

ecutors of the colonial endeavor. As his next-in-command, the men are would-be Robertos; as all four *mezzo* protagonists voice their hoped-for gains from the island settlement—greater wealth, less backbreaking work, a dowry, and marriage—they simultaneously voice middle-class advantages. With the exception of Panico, the buffo servant in their company, Goldoni's Dutch characters evoke a middle class inasmuch as they point to a refashioned nobility: persons who enjoy the comforts of the well-off, earned honestly.

The relative conflation of Roberto with the *mezzo caratteri* makes a strong case for middle-class economic and ethical doctrines. It also means that the counter doctrines, that is, the values of the old, degraded Venetian families, must be located in another of the opera's factions. Using the Chinese for this purpose, Goldoni provides an opposition with which to inspire change in Venice. More significantly, by casting his inimical parties as Dutch sea traders and their Chinese opponents, Goldoni suggests a grander universe than that of the lagoon republic. In relation to other progressive peninsular powers and the burgeoning European nations, the Serenissima was a slow study. Thus *L'isola*'s antithesis between the Chinese and the Dutch serves as a microcosm of another, perhaps more troubling disparity: that between the Venetian Republic and its other, i.e., the enlightened European states.

An initial examination of the opera's libretto focusing on plot, rhetoric, and characterization yields valuable findings in terms of how *L'isola disabitata* does its cultural work. Specifically, these aspects show the opera dipping into cultural production belonging to other European nations—namely, colonialist discourse. By basing his *dramma giocoso* on the conflict between Dutch sea merchants and their Chinese interlocutors, Goldoni appropriates real trade endeavors in East Asia. It should be remembered that 1756 marks the start of the Seven Years' War, among whose outcomes was the establishment of British colonial domination in Asia, if not in the world. At this time no Italian state had an international colonial project, in contrast to the aggressive campaigns of Holland, England, and, to an extent, France. Eighteenth-century Italy was essentially a spectator in relation to the commercial expansion of the other European powers. Goldoni therefore goes outside the immediate experience of the Italian peninsula and effectively corrals transalpine imperialist discourse in the service of his own discrete philosophies.

One of *L'isola*'s singularities among other "Chinese" theater works of the time was its presentation of a literal imperialist encounter, that is, the meeting in East Asia between a Western power seeking expansion and its interlocutor. This focus on an overseas commercial expedition felicitously portrays aspects of eighteenth-century European imperialism, since the protagonists of the global economy at this time were not bankers or industrialists, as they would be in the nineteenth century, but rather the seafaring merchants themselves.[20] While the actual staged contact between the Dutch and the Chinese is rather meager, the conflictual relationship between the two nations wholly subtends the opera's plot. *L'isola disabitata* is framed in terms of the contest between a vital, peace-seeking West and a repressive, belligerent East. The Dutch meet Gianghira because of her father's cruel punishment and are portrayed as beneficent "righters" of his wrong insofar as Roberto intends to "save" the princess as he simultaneously settles the newly acquired territory. Although Gianghira does not intend it, her presence in the midst of the Europeans provokes discord among the lovers. Her plight and the fascination she holds for the young men generate the series of tricks and plots the youths play on one another. Finally, the opposition between Chinese and Dutch is heightened, when the Holland crew trounces their Asian adversaries in the sea battle scene at *L'isola*'s conclusion.

Colonialist discourse is rendered in explicit language choices as well. Some of the more traditional rhetoric surfaces in Gianghira's recitative at her first stage appearance, where she has just sighted the recently arrived Dutch:

Gianghira.   What fear, what hope
            awakens in my breast
            This first sighting of the unknown foreigners?
            They are not from my country. By their
                equipment
            it seems they are from Europe, and not
                Chinese.
            The heavens have sent them
            to deliver an unhappy woman from death.
                                                    (1, 5)

            [Qual timor, qual speranza
            Risvegliami nel petto
            Degl'ignoti stranieri il nuovo aspetto?
            Di mia patria non sono. Ai loro arnesi
            Par che siano d'Europa, e non Chinesi.
            Il ciel li ha mandati
            Per sottrar dalla morte un'infelice.]

To this ideology of religious salvation brought by colonizers may be added demonization of the Chinese, in

the form of the tyrannical cruelty, intolerance, and impenetrability attached to Gianghira's father, who so coldly banished her from her home. Gianghira describes herself as the daughter "Of a parent so cruel / I don't believe there exists a monster like him" (1, 7).

The perpetrator-rescuer formulation continues throughout the opera. Goldoni ennobles the Dutch as courageous, aggressive, and ethical merchant-adventurers, in contrast to the despotic, repressive, anachronistic Chinese. In his portrayal of the former, he reflects prevailing Italian admiration for the Dutch. Ortolani writes, "Goldoni, like so very many of his contemporaries, had formed an ideal image of England and Holland. They were considered to be more selectively educated, countries that had given birth to 'philosophy,' as it was understood in the eighteenth century, countries where morality ran deeper."[21] Such veneration had moved Goldoni to write the play *Il medico olandese* in 1756, where he drew a very flattering picture of both Dutch men and women, emphasizing their qualities of pragmatism, industry, honesty, and intellectual freedom.[22] When Goldoni relocates the Dutch to Southeast Asia and figures them in relation to the Chinese, he continues to paint them in awe-filled and enthusiastic tones. Roberto and his shipmates are continually confident, enterprising, and victorious over the Chinese.

Such idolizing is somewhat misleading, however, for it plainly ignores some of the gruesome, problematic realities of the actual Sino-Dutch encounter. One example lies in the Dutch massacre of the entire Chinese community at Batavia in 1740, only seventeen years before *Isola*'s debut.[23] Still more revelatory is the fact that the Dutch in Chinese territory were rarely as successful nor heroic as they appear in Goldoni's portrayal. Despite their best efforts, they had never had success trading directly with China, since European merchants were always beholden unto Chinese authorities for permission to land, to remain, and to engage in commercial dealings. Those traders who did obtain concessions were forced to negotiate in outlying areas, or relegated to the coast and forbidden to penetrate the mainland.[24] It is interesting to note that Gianghira's father's act of isolating his daughter from home and society parallels what the Dutch underwent at the hands of the Chinese authorities, who used restrictive measures to harness them to coastal and island regions. In the opera's final act, as Chinese ships under Gianghira's father advance upon the island and the Dutch go to meet them, Roberto's last aria expresses the venom the traders must have felt in the face of such exclusion:

A. *Chinese Barks.* B. *A kind of Gally.* C. *A Bark in ye shape of a Dragon, used on a famous annual Festival.* D. *Small Boats.* E. *A Raft of Timber with Booths built on it.*

The Manner of Catching Wild Ducks. p. 237.   *An uncommon Method of Fishing described page 244*   *Vol. II pag. 277.*

47. **Chinese watercraft. Jean-Baptiste Du Halde.** *The General History of China.* **Trans. John Watts. London, 1736. Permission of Special Collections, University of Virginia Library.**

Roberto. Let us go to meet the Chinese army.
Let us defend our freedom.
Do you see that ship
that so boldly disdains the storms?
But as soon as the wind roars,
With its terrifying might,
courage flees its breast.
That's just how the arrogant Chinese,
so bold in their threats,
will be seen to tremble.

(3, 3)

[L'oste chinese ad incontrare andiamo.
La nostra libertà noi difendiamo.
Quel passeggier vedeste
Che sprezza le tempeste,

E baldanzoso sta?
Qualor poi freme il vento,
Ripieno di spavento,
Più ardire in sen non ha.
Così il Chinese altero
Che è in minacciar severo,
Tremar poi si vedrà.]

The anger this fictional Dutch admiral aims at his rigid, intractable, arrogant Asian foe is but an emblem for the hostile, antagonistic relationship between Western merchants and the Chinese, documented in many contemporary texts. The 1748 account of the Englishman Lord Anson's embassy to China (*A Voyage Round the World*), and Montesquieu's *Esprit des lois*

48. Chinese vessels. Richard Walter, *Anson's Voyage Round the World*, London, 1748. Permission of Special Collections, University of Virginia Library.

(1748) both describe a China trapped in an outdated tradition, victim of its own convoluted social and political restrictions. Most critics agree that these negative depictions by British and French writers were due primarily to the failure of their ambitious trade ventures. What's more, the resentment the merchants felt about the rigid barriers and control surfaced in accusations of stagnancy and blockage that spilled out onto cultural aspects not even related to commerce.[25]

In Italy, these sorts of disparaging perspectives were absorbed by intellectuals like Antonio Genovesi and Giuseppe Baretti. In *Lezioni di commercio* (1765) Genovesi explains China's rigid isolationism as a clear liability: "[To the idea that] it would be useful, because expedient, to achieve a state of total independence, I say no. First, it goes against nature. Should it be put into law, one would lose rather than gain. Furthermore, the nation would deprive itself of the bright ideas of other nations. Over time it would become the most dependent of all countries. We saw this happen to the Hebrews, before the time of Solomon, and it will doubtless come to pass with the Chinese, if they do not change their political method."[26] Worse, Genovesi translates the nation's reluctance to engage with others as a sign of civilizational immaturity: "China . . .

seems to me still very far from being a learned nation, and one of mature men. They still possess a great deal of childishness."[27] Baretti's evaluation of Chinese society was noticeably more unforgiving. His admiration for the account of Lord Anson's voyage to China reflected Baretti's greater anglophilia, no doubt at the root of his vindictive remarks. The following comment suggests patent correspondences between the British fleet's misadventures in the Middle Kingdom and Goldoni's imaginary encounter between the Dutch and Chinese at sea: "Are you trying to tell me that a Chinese warship, if those half-women even have one, could cross our seas like ours cross theirs? They should only hope as much! And even if one were to sail across, do you think that its captain would take charge in one of our ports like Captain Anson did when his ship arrived in Canton?"[28] Reflections such as these that characterized the Chinese as juvenile, effeminate, and impotent were easily appropriated for the comic opera stage. Inscribed within Goldoni's reform concept, however, the typology accrues additional meaning. Not merely impossible trade partners to the English and Dutch, Goldoni's Chinese represent the difficult Venetian nobility, posing obstacles to the benefits of a liberal economic system.

The best illustrations of *L'isola*'s mobilization of
China to dramatize the impediments to free trade occur at the act endings. As mentioned above, the ensemble finales figure among the most semiotically
charged sections of the opera. The act finales also lead
to the dance intermezzos, and these three *balli*, for
which Goldoni provides stage directions, also constitute distinct and eloquent "colonial moments." The
following section will analyze the ensemble at the end
of act 2, and the staged dance spectacles at the end of
each act. It will show how they function to devalue the
problematic old economic guard and idealize its aggressive challenger.

The Comic Quintet Ensemble following Act 2

The second-act ensemble ending occurs over three
scenes (2, 14–16). The first of these involves the arrival of the two male lovers disguised as Chinese envoys, wearing false moustaches and dressed in Chinese
fashions ("con finti baffi, vestiti alla chinese"). Stage
directions further note that their entrance is marked
by instrumentation ("a suono di strumenti"), and that
they move in tune to its rhythm, affecting exaggerated
steps and gestures ("facendo i passi e le cerimonie con
caricatura, a tempo di suono"). Garamone and
Valdimonte address Roberto in a duet, explaining
that they have come on behalf of Kakira, Gianghira's
father, from the land of "Kamenitzkatà." They are
charged with bringing her back, as her repentant father has found a husband for her, a certain "Kakiro
Karaká." The scene ends as the servant Marinella announces the arrival of another set of ambassadors.
Scene 15 opens identically, with orchestral sounds
and farcical rhythmic movements enacted now by Giacinta, Carolina, and Panico, all in Chinese garb. The
women parallel the men as they approach Roberto,
asking for Gianghira on the part of her lover "Kankai
/ Signor di Kalankai," who desires that she return to
his country, "Karamanakira." Roberto says that he
must think the matter over and exits. Scene 16 constitutes the official episode of the "finti cinesi" ("the
pretend Chinese"), centered on the interactions among
the five would-be Chinese ambassadors. Stage directions call for the reprise of the melodic instrumental
from the previous two scenes ("gli stromenti tornano
a ripigliare l'aria di prima") and indicate that the actors perform the same steps and gestural formalities
("i finti Chinesi fanno fra di loro i soliti passi, colle so-
lite cerimonie").

With respect to the singing, however, the actor-
singers now switch from Italian to a form of nonsense
verse, spitting out jumbles of syllables that alternate
between pure invention and thinly-veiled Italian. Significantly, the libretto states that these expressions are
Chinese compliments (". . . mostrano che queste parole siano complimenti chinesi"). Both pairs of ambassadors exchange these civilities, with Panico joining
in at the end:[29]

Valdimonte.		Timbuktù-cuckoo.
Garamone.	*(together)*	Cheng-feng-shui-to-you.
		I bust-a-you-butt—watcha-you-gut,
		Tung-hu yu-a-foo'.

(they indicate to the others that these words are Chinese compliments)

Giacinta.	(Listen!) *(to Carolina and Panico)*
Carolina.	(What did they say?) *(to Panico)*
Panico.	(Who the hell knows?) *(softly to Carolina)*

Carolina.		Belly nakka-pu.
Giacinta.	*(together)*	Bing-ho sooka-doo.
		Bong-a-drum-one, bong-a-drum-two.

(they correspond with similar compliments)

Panico.	Scribble-dibble bally-hoo.
	Willy-nilly cock-a-doodle-doo,
	Ming-ho yu-go poo-poo-poo.
	(2, 16)

[Valdimonte.		Karamenitzkatà.
Garamone.	*a due*	Macaccorebeccà.
		Ti menaccà—paraticà,
		Baracca papagà.

(verso degli altri mostrano che queste parole siano complimenti chinesi)

Giacinta.	(Sentite!) *(a Carolina e Panico)*
Carolina.	(Che han detto?) *(a Panico)*
Panico.	(Chi diavolo il sa?) *(piano a Carolina)*

Carolina.	*a due*	Panciri nascattà.
Giacinta.		Penaci caraccà.
		Timpana là, timpanaccà.

(corrispondono con simili complimenti)

Panico.	Scarbocci mascabà.
	Chichirichi caccaraccà,
	Quaiotta squaquarà.]

Following this sequence the libretto once again specifies that the actors resume the Chinese bowing and
scraping ("Tornano a fare alcune cerimonie"), and
that each of the women individually approach her
consort. With greater proximity the four begin to de-
tect the others' true identities, and their compliments

turn to insults. Simultaneously, their language shifts from silliness to comprehensible Italian:

Car.		Stinky-poo blowhard. (*to Valдimonte*)
Giac.		Stinky-poo blackguard. (*a Garamone*)
Pan.		Garamone's a poop.
		Valmonte's a poop.
Val. *Gar.*	(*together*)	Ah, ah, damn you! Poopy Panico's a poop!
Car.		Blowhard! (*a Valдimonte*)
Giac.		Blackguard! (*a Garamone*)
Val. *Gar.*	(*together*)	Everybody poopin' shut up.

(2, 16)

[*Car.*		Baronacaccà. (*a Valдimonte*)
Giac.		Bricconacaccà. (*a Garamone*)
Pan.		Garamon caccà.
		Valmonta caccà.
Val. *Gar.*	(*a дue*)	Ah, ah, maledetta! Panicaccaccà.
Car.		Barone! (*a Valдimonte*)
Giac.		Briccone! (*a Garamone*)
Val. *Gar.*	(*a дue*)	Tacete caccà.]

The scene ends as all five protagonists register, in Italian this time, the danger they risk should Roberto discover their sham. Together they sing a quintet in which they vow to keep their secret:

Quiet, quiet, let's get going,
Who's who let's not be knowing.
(*softly among themselves*)
As for appearances and such,
We'll figure out how to seem Chinese to the Dutch.

(2, 16)

[Zitti, zitti, andiamo via,
Non lo sappia chi si sia.
(*piano fra дi loro*)
E Chinesi—agli Olandesi
Comparir si studierà.]

The piece finishes loudly, however, with what one can only guess might be a paean to their conspiratorial solidarity, since they return to singing nonsense, and exit the stage mimicking Chinese gesticulations:

Kara mella karacà
Caccomiri napatà
(*all loudly*)
Gnascatà—papagà
Carobella caraccà.

(*They exit singing and enacting the usual ceremonials*)

(2, 16)

This laughable performance of Chinese diplomatic formalities probably accounted more than anything else for *L'isola*'s success. Goldoni's careful specifications for Chinese apparel and moustaches, but especially the libretto's frequent prompting of physical performances of Chinese decorum, had precedents in the renditions of Chinese characters in popular theatrical institutions, such as ballets, commedia dell'arte, and fair theater.[30] But contained in the entertainment quotient of the comic parody of purported Chinese ambassadorial behavior is a denaturalization of Chinese culture. Since the Chinese in *L'isola disabitata* stand in for Venice's unyielding, inflexible old social and economic ranks, the alienation effected in the "finti cinesi" scene serves to reinforce the latter's outsider status, and their incompatibility with supposed mainstream values. Linguistic aspects of the quintet make this most clear.

Verbal technique in the emissary scene derives primarily from the commedia dell'arte. Allardyce Nicoll points out the crucial role language played in the commedia dell'arte theatrical form.[31] Excellence in performance hinged not only on ready wit and adroit verbal sparring, but also on the use of diverse dialects and tongues, to provide variety and richness. The distinguishing qualities of different languages both enlivened the aural component and buttressed characterization.[32] A key feature of the commedia's poetics of improvisation involved the virtuoso linguistic performance, in which a character would spew forth exaggerated and comical but authentic-sounding streams of foreign language, sometimes switching deftly among different tongues. Initially Italian dialects composed the array, but soon it included various European tongues, and eventually extra-European speech. One of the most famous of these verbal stunts, "La pazzia d'Isabella," dates to the first half-century of known commedia practice:

Finding herself the victim of Flavio's deceit and with no remedy for her sad case, Isabella abandoned herself to grief. Defeated by passion and yielding to rage and fury, like a mad creature she roamed the city scene, stopping one passer-by, then another, speaking now in Spanish, now in Greek, now in Italian, and in many other languages, but always irrationally; and among other things she began to speak French and to sing French songs . . . Then Isabella fell to imitating the manner of speech of all her fellow actors, Pantalone, Gratiano, Zanni, Pedrolino, Francatrippa, Burattino, Capitan Cardone, and Franceschina, all so naturally and with such hilarious absurdities that it is impossible for tongue to tell the matchless worth and powers of this Woman.[33]

As impressed as audiences may have been, it is important to note that a magisterial performance by a commedia mask often had the paradoxical effect of eclipsing that character and the content of his or her act, in favor of the actor playing the role. The skills of the actor or in the case of opera, the singer, took center stage, relegating performance content to the wings, so to speak. Thus the content of Isabella the desperate lover's speech—expressed in the French, Spanish, Italian, et cetera that she reeled off so dexterously— was subordinated to the aggrandizement of professional actress Isabella Andreini and her amazing feats.

Another commedia dell'arte approach to language that distanced its semantic substance was the practice of *grammelot*. Antonio Scuderi defines *grammelot* as "a fake language which consists of nonsensical sounds that imitate the inflection and cadence of real speech."[34] He also notes that "The insertion of a limited number of key words that are identifiable to the audience conveys a sense of semantic value and thus a sense of real speech to the otherwise nonsensical sounds."[35] The early mode of replicating a foreign language particularly suited eighteenth-century exotic theater, as more and more linguistic others came into consciousness. The scene of the "finti cinesi" clearly exhibits its traits.

Of course it was extremely unlikely that audience members would have been able to understand any variant of spoken Chinese. *Grammelot*'s purpose lay in comic performance, not as a translational strategy to facilitate cultural encounter. It was used not only for eminently unfamiliar languages, like Chinese, but also to parody languages that at least some audience members would have known (for example, the French and Spanish of Andreini's act). Indeed, *grammelot*'s sporadic use of recognizable terms suggests a degree of linguistic knowledge on the part of spectators. For cognoscenti, the *grammelot* technique diluted the host language, rendering it a caricature. For languages virtually unknown to audiences (and playwrights as well), vocal aping had to confine itself only to sounds and rhythm. In the case of *L'isola disabitata*, where authentic Chinese words were apparently not known or practical, sung *grammelot* imitating an absurd notion of the cadence and sonority of Chinese speech devalued the Asian idiom even further by reducing it to cartoon status.[36]

One of the most recognizable instances of this sort of linguistic play occurs in the famous Turkish ennoblement ceremony in act 4 of Molière's *Bourgeois gentilhomme*.[37] Here the *grammelot* spouted by Cléonte, disguised as the son of the Grand Turk, and his alleged servant, played by Covielle, has the ultimate aim of mocking the misplaced class aspirations of Monsieur Jourdain. But wedding such foundational commedia vocal slapstick with the Turkish culture also served to discount the heritage of its native speakers. Certainly it is relevant that Louis XIV commissioned the *comédie-ballet* in order to make fun of the then Turkish ambassador to France who had not adequately acknowledged the king's elevated station when granted an audience.

Denaturalized perceptions of a nation's language transferred to perceptions of the nation itself. The *scenetta* of the imaginary Chinese debased their homeland in its framing of Chinese language as gibberish. In his work on linguistic colonialism, Stephen Greenblatt points out the tendency of early New World colonizers to equate the unfamiliarity of indigenous speech to a complete *lack* of speech, and thence, to a lack of civilization.[38] Although to European eyes the Chinese were ostensibly more civilized than the New World inhabitants, showcasing the unintelligibility of spoken Chinese evokes on a larger scale an incomprehensible culture. And in fact, at just this time the Middle Kingdom was being denigrated by certain European commentators as incomprehensible for its ridiculously "over civilized" practices—in some cases considered more nonsensical than the customs and ritual of the American "savages."[39] Exotic effects aside, the spectacle of spoken language in the scene of the "finti cinesi" elucidates the concept of language as instrument of empire, in which the strangeness of the other's speech amounts to its lesser status and reinforces Western correctness. The fact that the "finti cinesi" scene terminates with a forceful reprise of nonsense verse once more contrasts Chinese talk (opaque, meaningless, risible) with European vernacular (transparent, sensible, functional).

A final note remains on the scene's linguistic methods of communicating China's impotence. The two sets of lovers have been identified as *mezzo caratteri*, but in this scene they clearly perform at the more colloquial, comic end of their dramatic and vocal range. The clownish atmosphere, abetted by their disguises and eccentric gestures, is matched by language at a lower register. For example, Giacinta expresses her wariness with the common expression "Oibò" (2, 16). The recitative asides between the ambassadors are rushed and conversational:

> *Giac.* (Listen!)
> *Car.* (What did they say?!)
> *Pan.* (Who the hell knows?)
>
> (2, 16)

and lead to a barrage of name-calling once they penetrate each others' ruses. The scatological also wafts throughout their verse, with repeated use of the occlusive syllable "ka" (the Chinese emperor "Kakira," who resides in "Kamenitzkatà," has arranged his daughter's marriage with "Kakiro Karakà"; Gianghira's alleged lover is "Kakai, Signore di Kalankai"). Panico, the opera's true buffo character, concretizes the hint, as his language sinks to the vulgar corporeal level typical of his buffoon role: "Garamon caccà. / Valmonta caccà." His scurrilous phrasing in the lines "Chichirichi caccaracchà, / Quaiotta squaquarà," is equally overt, as "squaquarà" evokes the colloquial expression for diarrhea, "la squaquerella."[40]

The scene of the "finti cinesi" embodied the opera's most colorful and detailed exposition of Chinese society. It is revealing that the exposition was rendered visually, and linguistically, at the base level of the comic opera actor. Technically, the episode of the ambassadorial missions was entirely gratuitous with respect to the opera's plot. The very next scene reveals that Roberto had seen through the sham immediately, and he brushes it aside in the course of more important events: professing his love to Gianghira, which she accepts, and readying his forces to face the approaching armed Chinese ship that seeks to recapture both Gianghira and the island. While not crucial to the plot, however, the scene was likely necessary in the sense that comic opera audiences expected at least one "over the top" bit of funny business. Given the Dutch-Chinese opposition on which L'isola turns, it is not surprising that China serves as the butt of this joke fixture.

THE DANCES AT ENDS OF ACTS

The concluding piece of act 2, the comic quintet of the "finti cinesi," used all the semiological resources of the multi-section finale to establish the burlesque status of the Chinese within the universe of the opera. The entr'acte balli, on the other hand, move away from characterizing the Chinese subject, and instead reinforce the opera's ideological position by glorifying the project of colonization. Portraying the Dutch settlement in the Middle Kingdom as productive, meritorious, and culturally valid, the dances offer yet another instance of colonialist discourse on stage.

Before investigating the dances as outlined in the libretto, an exploration of the larger ideology underpinning them is in order. The dramma giocoso's very title, L'isola disabitata (uninhabited or deserted island), reveals Goldoni's debt to an established literary tradition of island symbolism, or what Michael Seidel calls "island fictions," and their particular notions of "self"

and "other."[41] The remote "island" not only reifies alterity in physical terms but is also rich in figurative connotations: separation, strangeness, the suspension of prevailing norms, punishment, rescue, salvation, utopia, innocence, freedom, individual sovereignty. The trope of the uninhabited, or empty island further recalls the tabula rasa mentality of the colonizer, by which the absence of knownness in the other is equated with nothingness, and somehow mandates the colonizer's task of inscribing the "correct" culture onto the blank field.[42] Focusing on emptiness allows one to entertain re-creation and utopistic visions, insofar as the void is valued for its great potential—whether that be land to be cultivated, commodities to be traded, or beings to be civilized.

Act 3 opens, in fact, with a rousing choral piece in which, under Roberto's leadership, the Dutch group performs the ritual of cultural inscription par excellence, naming the new territory:

> All of you gathered here together,
> All of you united in a single society,
> Now that we possess this land,
> Let's give our city a name.
>
> (3, 1)

> [Tutti insieme ragunati,
> Tutti uniti in società,
> Del paese impossessati,
> Diamo il nome alla città.]

The proposed appellations emphasize the aura of utopia stimulated by the island (and express again the high esteem in which Goldoni held the enlightened United Provinces): City of Good Fortune, Land of Love and Mercy, New Holland, Dutch China, New City, Beautiful Island (Città della Fortuna, Terra di buon amore e di pietà, Nuova Olanda, China Olandese, Città novella, Isola bella). The naming procedure also recalls the language business of the "finti cinesi" scene. Here, however, the strangeness of the foreign land is not stressed but eliminated, by recasting the island according to the terms of a European signification system. The colonizers decide finally to call the island New Island (L'isola nuova), and its capital city Land of Love (Terra d'amore).

The diffusion of island stories at this time was prolific and had a substantial heritage. Fido points out Cervantes's Don Quixote (1605) and Shakespeare's The Tempest (1611), in addition to the contemporary Robinson Crusoe (1719) by Defoe.[43] Certainly the wildly popular Robinson Crusoe must have been circulating among Goldoni's audiences, especially since its many Italian translations up to this point had all issued from Venice, including an edition published in the same year as *L'isola disabitata*.[44] To these works can be added a host of coeval operas featuring or based on islands: *L'isola d'Alcina, L'isola beata, L'isola capricciosa, L'isola d'amore,* and *L'isola della luna* are just a few of the titles.

L'isola disabitata clearly evidences the idealistic hopes of the newcomer to virgin terrain. Upon landing the chorus sings:

What sublime pleasure to joyfully land
from the threatening sea onto the precious beach,
to enjoy peace, liberty!

The wind that blows in this pretty place
promises us a happy sojourn,
inspires hope for a happy life.

Our grand enterprise was guided by the heavens,
we will be able to enjoy happiness
on this beautiful uninhabited island.

Sweet sweat, sweet fatigue,
May our friend the land
produce its treasures for us over time!

(1, 1)

[Che bel piacere dal mare infido
Scender contenti sul caro lido!
Goder la pace, la libertà!

L'aria che spira nel bel contorno,
Qua ci promette lieto soggiorno,
Vita felice sperar ci fa.

La grand'impresa dal ciel scortata;
Nella bell'Isola disabitata
Goder potremo felicità.

Dolci sudori, dolce fatica,
Se con il tempo la terra amica
I suoi tesori ci produrrà!]

Soon afterward the main characters also state their expectations that the island will bring them their just rewards—riches for Garamone and Valdimonte, noble status for the servant Panico, a respite from hard labors for Carolina, and a dowry and marriage for Giacinta.

The island has saved them from the treacherous sea, and it promises peace, freedom, happiness, and treasures. Mary Louise Pratt notes that colonial discourse reveals a gaze particular to the European exploiter, in which there figures "a landscape imbued with social fantasies—of harmony, industry, liberty, unalienated *joie de vivre*."[45] Such joyful fantasies come at a price, but, as the chorus stresses, the costs are

sweet: "dolci sudori, dolce fatica." Thus even the labor required to cultivate the island is imbued with a jubilant discipline. Admiral Roberto expresses this happy, democratic industry as he directs the island's settlement, conjoining honors and tasks, and taking care not to exclude himself from the necessary work:

Roberto. The rewards and labors
Must be distributed among us.
Everybody get to work now.

. . . .

You, Valdimonte,
You're in charge of our economy,
Garamone is head of the craftsmen,
and poor Panico,
who until now has had menial jobs,
will take over the kitchen.
You women are assigned
to the usual tasks
of your sex.
I too will arrive to toil with everyone.

(1, 1)

[Distribuiti
Esser denno fra noi gli onori e i pesi,
Tutti per ora ad operare intesi.

. . . .

Voi avete, Valmonte,
Di nostra economia la direzione,
Degli artefici capo è Garamone,
E il povero Panico,
Il qual ebbe finor sorte meschina,
Abbia la direzion della cucina.
Voi, donne, destinate
Alle incombenze usate
Siete del vostro sesso.
Verrò cogli altri a faticare io stesso.]

This first scene ends with a choral reprise of the optimistic opening verses. With scene 2 the opera's intrigue commences. Garamone discovers Gianghira and tries to sequester her from the other men, most notably his superior, Roberto; Roberto meets her nonetheless, and feels the beginnings of love; Giacinta and Carolina, having discovered from Panico that their men have taken up with a strange beautiful woman, erupt in jealous tirades against them. Act 1 ends with a boisterous quintet, where the women feign attraction to Panico, inciting irate astonishment in their consorts.

The dance following this chaotic ensemble, however, transforms its atmosphere entirely. The squabbling, spiteful lovers are replaced by a crowd of settlers, animated by a spirit of utopian cooperation and productivity. Stage directions show how this first dance interlude revives the settlement fantasy of the opera's opening epithets: "Countryside consisting of plains and hills, crowded everywhere with cooking tools and utensils, tables, cooking fires and everything else needed to prepare victuals for the company that has landed on the island. Dotted here and there, on meadows and mountains, one sees all the dancers, dressed in various styles, representing men and women of various nations who have disembarked with the Admiral and are intent on distributing the provisions." The dance specified for the end of act 2—just after the nonsense scene of the "finti cinesi"—also effects a passage from comic confusion to earnest, uplifting order. Here the settlers start to build their homes:

The scene shows a kind of *Arsenale* [italics mine] chock-full of supplies necessary for the establishment of housing on the island, with some workshops in the background, foregrounded by bricklayers with ladders and equipment, etc. The men dancers enter, dressed according to the various tasks with which they are employed, each one practicing his particular craft. The women dancers arrive, carrying baskets of food for the laborers, and they wait for the work recess. At the stroke of the hour, everyone leaves his labor; they go to eat and have fun dancing with the women. Then at the signal to return to work, each goes back to his job.

Multiple elements of these dance spectacles reify the rapturous colonialist aspirations of the opera's incipit. The emphasis on the abundance and preparation of food recall what Julia Douthwaite terms the "archetypal Thanksgiving story," found repeatedly in the discourse comprising the master narrative of encounters between Europeans and their non-European interlocutors.[46] The use of the term *Arsenale*, left here in its Italian form, shows Goldoni conflating a Venetian myth of power and dominance with the Dutch conquest in China. More than simply a well-stocked warehouse or arsenal, *Arsenale* with a capital *A* refers to the renowned shipyard of Venice, on which the Republic's fame as a maritime power rested for several centuries just preceding Goldoni's time. In addition to its role as shipbuilding site, the symbolic *Arsenale* now serves the construction of domiciles, necessary to the founding of colonies and nations.

The most redolent of Goldoni's dictates is that the dancers of the first *ballo* represent "men and women of various nations." By the mid-eighteenth century the *ballo delle nazioni* was a familiar production, originating from the seventeenth-century French dance genre known as the *ballet des nations*, or international suite, and consisting of a series of dance vignettes depicting various nationalities.[47] Traditionally it formed the final performance (whether in a standard three-

part court ballet, or the later multi-part *ballet à entrées*), since its large number of *ballerini* satisfied the requirement that the last dance episode be the most spectacular.[48] *L'isola*'s version of this choreographic spectacle typifies the eighteenth-century dance aesthetic which sought to stage idealized, wholistic panoramas of human society. Some of the events choreographers judged most suited to representing "virtuoso displays of dancing skill as well as . . . dramatic tableaus of social life . . . included festivals, ceremonies, games, duels, or even social dance scenes."[49] Colonial settlement now joined the roster of cultural activities capacious enough to represent the full spectrum of humankind engaged in model behavior. Physical dramatization (the dancers' choreography, the richness and symmetry of Goldoni's specified set design) combined with aural dramatization (the music's arrangement, rhythms, volume, etc.) to express the tenets of colonial enterprise: order, efficiency, progress, and prosperity.

A last aspect concerning dance performance within the dramatic stagework merits consideration. As mentioned, the *balli* in *L'isola* repeatedly shift attention from the affair of the Chinese maiden and her Dutch interlocutors to the larger ideal of global harmony, represented by the settlement of promising land. This consistent return to the universal from the personal, to stasis from crisis, corresponds to the theorizing of Charles Delmas, who characterizes the relationship between dramas proper and their intermittent dance sequences as one of alternating disharmony and harmony. Delmas observes that dance intervals in the Renaissance usually celebrated some notion of the Golden Age, and as such contained or annulled the transgressive elements in the drama surrounding them.[50] Franko discovers the same pattern in his study of seventeenth-century burlesque French court ballets, where he concludes that the customary performance of the *ballet des nations* at the end of these transgressive ballets served "to pay lip service to order, stable values."[51] Similarly, the colonization dances in *L'isola disabitata*, in which peoples of all nations partake in the worthy, productive industry of developing foreign territory, can be seen as eighteenth-century interpretations of the Golden Age, the Enlightenment ideation of a perfect world that ultimately absorbs all tumult. Like a steady pulse in the body of the performance, or a compass needle, the dance segments indicated the direction in which the whole work was proceeding. Movement toward resolution occurred thus on two planes: within the acts, as plot discord eventually untangled and happiness was achieved, and within the production's whole, as the dances reiterated the inevitable triumph of the values they illustrated.

49. Stage design for Dutch settlement dance interlude, *L'isola disabitata*. "Arsenale di arti meccaniche con qualche fabbrica principiata," Andrea Urbani. Permission of Casa Goldoni, Venice, Italy.

The parallel progression of the dramatic acts and the dance interludes in *L'isola disabitata* converge in the opera's final scenes, the most grandiose part of the spectacle. The last scene depicts a coastal battle camp, with Chinese warships approaching. Upon landing, of course, they are promptly routed by the Dutch. The final *ballo* choreographs the battle, which then transforms into the danced celebration of the marriage between Roberto, Dutch admiral, and Gianghira, Chinese maiden. The choral accompaniment to the nuptial dance reprises all of the bulwarks of colonial/Enlightenment aspiration: peace, love, freedom, and happiness.

The staged clash between Chinese and Dutch at the opera's end acquires even more potency as it borrows from some of the ideological strategies belonging to the Goldonian spoken comedy and thought unavailable to musical comic works. The typical reform comedy closed on a serious moral note, based on a formulaic mix of repentance and conversion which reaffirmed the superiority of bourgeois ethics to those of the dissipated nobility. As Ted Emery has noted, the celebratory atmosphere required in comic opera's ensemble dance finales generally prohibited even a trace of this sort of *gravitas*.[52] But the festive ending in *L'isola disabitata* derives precisely from the unequivocal victory of the merchant class over the established gentry. The ancient noble class is shown to be entirely at the mercy of a brash and powerful new citizen, and must perforce concede to a new age. Deploying the colonial fantasy for his opera, Goldoni mounts an ideologically compelling production that fully respects its generic commandments to provide audiences their expected entertainment.

CONCLUSION

Michael Hays writes that at times theater operates not only to justify the subjugation of the colonial "other" outside of the state, but also to resolve conflicts within a state, or as he puts it, to effect a kind of "cultural colonization" inside a nation. In his essay on imperialism in nineteenth-century British popular theater, he writes "the political and cultural imagination of the lower classes had to be captured and made to work for the empire as well."[53] The play he analyzes, Charles Reade's *It's Never Too Late to Mend*, constituted "the occasion for the production of willing participants in middle class economy at home and the imperialist adventure abroad."[54] For the Italian states, no such adventure abroad existed for which to unite popular consciousness. However, as the Republic of Venice suffered the last tenacious grip of an increasingly decrepit social structure, there was no better strategy to point up its obsolescence than to find its analogue in images of a rigid, isolationist, retrograde China. Likewise, the freedoms, progress, and vigor which Goldoni celebrated in his ennobled merchant class found felicitous parallels in the legends of the enterprising Dutch. The colonial adventurers' paeans to "freedom!" and "peace!" are not simply overused commonplaces or precise calculations to support the opera's musical economy.[55] Rather, they are the same "freedom" and "peace" that underpin a morally grounded bourgeois community, as Don Marzio so ruefully notes at the end of *La bottega del caffè*, one of Goldoni's most strident reform comedies of the 1750–51 season. The ridiculously tactless and troublemaking aristocratic busybody is finally rejected by all of the other upstanding or rehabilitated characters. He regretfully departs from Venice: "I've lost my good name and I'll never get it back again. I'll leave this city. I'll leave in spite of myself, and because of this awful tongue of mine, I'll give up a city *where all live well, all have freedom, peace, and joy* as long as they know how to be cautious, careful and honorable" (italics mine) [177].[56] The settling and cultivating of a colonial island outpost thus echo the establishment of a smooth-functioning, productive "colony" at home, one that enriches the state and raises the moral character of a people.

By going outside his Venetian environs and piggybacking on the exploits of some of the period's most zealous empire-builders, Goldoni gives the nod to the mercantilist notions and liberal economic theory propagated by Enlightenment thinkers operating far afield of Venice. These include reformers not only in other Italian states, such as Pompeo Neri in Milan, Gian Francesco Pagnini in Florence, Girolamo Belloni in Rome, and Ferdinando Galiani and Antonio Genovesi in Naples, but also those across the Alps, namely French economic theorists François Quesnay and Anne-Robert-Jacques Turgot, and Adam Smith in Great Britain.[57] Thus, in *L'isola disabitata* Goldoni addresses not only an inter-polity dilemma, championing one sector against another within the Venetian state, but he also looks outward, pitting Venice (should it not reform itself) against other more modern-minded European states.

Carpanetto notes that the history of the Italian republican states in the Settecento was "marked by a . . . prevailing stagnation which showed itself in neutrality and isolation vis-à-vis other European powers . . ."[58] As for Venice, it "proudly and unbendingly defended a system whose splendid façade of republicanism concealed adminstrative inefficiency, an inability to make decisions and political confusion . . . the ruling patrician class turned more and more inwards to its past history and the certainty, as tenacious as it was unfounded, of the invincibility of the republic."[59] Goldoni's paean to the enterprising Dutch and belittling of the Chinese in *L'isola* functions as an entreaty to fellow Venetians to put an end to isolationism, self-absorption, hostile and stagnant "Chineseness." Taking full advantage of the performative conventions of the *dramma giocoso*, Goldoni invites audiences to participate in a program of Enlightenment liberalism that has cosmopolitan scope. If his spectators will embrace the progressive principles embodied by the Dutch, and reject the repressive attitudes represented by the Chinese, they will exercise agency in an international sphere that promises happiness and prosperity to all. A very different picture emerges in a Neapolitan comic opera staged only ten years later.

6

Rejecting False Idols:
Giambattista Lorenzi, *L'idolo cinese* (1767)

The Deities, Gods, the Idol, Fate and similar beings [mentioned herein] are poetic inventions, and do not reflect the sentiments of those [such as the present author] who claim to be true Christians.[1]

THE 1767 PREMIERE OF GIAMBATTISTA LORENZI'S *operetta giocosa* entitled *L'idolo cinese* at Naples's Teatro Nuovo comprised a number of firsts. It marked the librettist's initial collaboration with Giovanni Paisiello, a pair that soon would be recognized as two of the most skilled Neapolitan lyric theater artists of the century.[2] *L'idolo cinese* was also Paisiello's first notable success in Naples. The year 1767 furthermore was when Ferdinand IV came of age as ruler of the Kingdom of Naples. The most significant of *L'idolo*'s inaugural moments, however, lies in the fact that it induced the Bourbon regime to break a forty-year ban on opera buffa performances at court.

Owing to its perceived scurrilous content and appeal to the general populace, opera buffa had been held in low esteem by Austrian viceregal authorities. Its disfavor continued with the ascendancy of Charles III and the Bourbon monarchy in 1734. Like their Habsburg predecessors, the Bourbon royals considered opera buffa beneath the dignity of the titled ranks. The new administration's negative assessment meant not only that opera buffa was excluded from regal theatrical venues, but also that its performances in the public theaters were kept under careful surveillance, should the content or productions in any way menace royal authority.[3] However, when *L'idolo cinese* premiered in spring of 1767 at the Teatro Nuovo, its resoundingly positive reception by audiences impelled Chief Minister Bernardo Tanucci to attend the production. Luciano Maggi writes that Tanucci actually attended the premiere after having been ordered to do so by church authorities, to determine whether a banner featured in the opera was too similar (and thus immoral) to one used in solemn papal liturgical ceremonies. Maggi continues:

Tanucci not only judged the banner not irreverent, but enjoyed himself so much that he convinced King Ferdinand IV to have the opera performed in the Grand Salon of the Royal Palace.

Its success was overwhelming and following this performance the King decided to transform the salon into the present Court Theater.[4]

The arrangements to have *L'idolo cinese* played at the Teatrino di Corte (Real Teatrino) at Caserta in 1768 marked Ferdinand's official change of mind about native comic opera. The Bourbons not only loved *L'idolo cinese,* but also clamored for more. According to Martorana, "they enjoyed it so much, both for the poetry as for the music, that they ordered Lorenzi to write some other comedies in the same genre."[5] Ferdinand began ordering command performances by public companies in the palace, and appointed Lorenzi "Direttore and Concertatore" of all productions (Director of Improvised Comedies) for the King of Naples.[6] Thus began a period of royal familiarization with musical comedy that would culminate eight years later in yet another first: Ferdinand's attendance at a comic opera in the public theater, Zini-Paisiello's *Dal finto il vero* at the Teatro Nuovo (1776). From then on, Ferdinand regularly frequented both the Teatro Nuovo and Teatro Fiorentini, boosting social acceptance of opera buffa as well as the prestige of its theaters.

The contagious appeal of *L'idolo cinese* had certainly to do with the comic performance backgrounding the traditional lovers' plights: the absurd impersonation of a Chinese deity—the "idolo cinese"—by a European menial, coupled with the Chinese ruler's obsessive and idiotic belief in the false idol. Both Pilottola's bumbling rendition of the Chinese god Kam and

L'IDOLO CINESE

OPERETTA GIOCOSA

PER MUSICA,

DA RAPPRESENTARSI NEL REAL TEATRINO
DI CASERTA,

PER DIVERTIMENTO

DELLE

MAESTÀ LORO

NEL FELICISSIMO ARRIVO

DI

S. M. LA REGINA.

IN NAPOLI MDCCLXVIII.

PER VINCENZO FLAUTO

IMPRESSORE DI SUA MAESTÀ.

Tuberone's hilarious fanaticism as local governor and Kam's high priest drew from a long tradition of Neapolitan clownery, one of the chief impetuses for the birth of opera buffa.[7] As far as the infiltration of East Asians into the buffoon universe, *L'idolo cinese* looks like a consummate example of eighteenth-century cultural production that commandeered the "bizarre" religious beliefs and practices of an exotic culture to deride the church. In an age where even Catholic monarchs were convinced that the pope and his clerical legions needed serious enlightening, novels like Claude Crébillon's popular *Le Sopha* (1742) and theater works like Voltaire's *Mahomet* (1742) profited from representing the strange and strangely amusing worship customs of non-European peoples to critique problematic aspects of Christian holy men and their influential domains. If one concentrates on *L'idolo cinese*'s raucous depictions of Middle Kingdom gods, devotional protocols, and theological propositions, one is easily convinced that the opera is but another hilarious send-up of an institution nearly everyone could find reason to snicker at. It might therefore seem emblematic of works, such as *L'isola disabitata*, that urged reform across key, if not all, societal spheres.

Substantive reform, however, of the kinds taking place in Lombardy, Tuscany, and even the Veneto, had a steep, if not impassable road to climb in the Kingdom of the Two Sicilies. While the established nobility could tolerate an entertaining roast of ecclesiastical types, they would not stand by while a new capitalist class appropriated their authority, whether on stage or in "real life." This disposition against a bourgeois culture surfaces plainly in *L'idolo cinese*. Imbricated in its satire of the church is a more subtle but no less caustic stab at the claims of a new generation of non-noble professionals, merchants, and intellectuals. In addition to the attractions of its native comic legacy then, *L'idolo cinese* must have galvanized attention because of the ambiguity it posed with respect to contemporary political currents and social class relations. In terms of peninsular Enlightenment, it reveals the particular landscape facing eighteenth-century Neapolitan reformism and the forces thwarting its endeavors.

On the one hand, *L'idolo cinese* reflects the specific desire of the Bourbon monarchy to rein in the church. King Charles III's 1736 appointment of Bernardo Tanucci as prime minister aimed to curb abuses of power rampant among Neapolitan papal authorities, and Tanucci's multitudinous provisions in this regard had some success. Over the forty-year period of Tanucci's office (1736–76), his legislation curtailed

ecclesiastical profiteering to an admirable, even if finally insufficient, degree. On the other hand, the administration's second nemesis, the old baronial families, proved much more difficult to discipline. Deeply entrenched both at court and in the countryside, the ancient Naples nobility clung to its inherited power. Charles's court was hamstrung with respect to advancing anti-feudalism laws among them, as many had influential posts at court and naturally did not want to see their privileges diminish. What's more, the monarchy needed their financial support for the wars that still aggrieved the dynasty. Consolidation of the Bourbon regime was therefore forestalled in large part by its vexatious relationship with the ruling elite.[8]

For its part, the elites saw their power threatened in the name of allegedly "enlightened" monarchical policy. Tanuccian reforms seemed bent not only on paring their aristocratic domain, but also on granting favorable status to a relatively small but worrisome *borghesia*. Thanks to the baronial sector, intent on "preserving its traditional freedom in the face of the rise of modern despotism," Tanucci's initiatives to promote certain members of the bourgeoisie never got very far.[9] For Neapolitan avatars, "modern despots" assumed the shape of ambitious merchants, tradesmen, and civil professionals, just as readily as enlightened royals and their revisionist proposals. Given the permeation of the Bourbon regime by the old guard, it is no surprise that Venturi describes its reform policy as "a phenomenon which was already out of date and out of time, forced to operate in a situation of crisis, economic difficulties and growing political unrest . . . an eleventh hour chance thrown away and lost forever."[10] *L'idolo cinese* clearly enacts this foundering.

The two most contentious players for power in eighteenth-century Naples then, the Bourbon monarchy and the nobility, had, in addition to each other, other discrete opponents: the church, and a growing bourgeois class, respectively. Both are ridiculed and disempowered within the universe of *L'idolo cinese*. By invoking particular religious conventions of the Chinese and inscribing them onto the devalued world of the buffo characters, *L'idolo cinese* instrumentalizes the Celestial Kingdom to discredit ecclesiastical authority. Similarly, the association of apparently liberal Chinese sociopolitical practices with the same fool-figures serves to undermine encroaching middle-class sway. Unlike *L'isola disabitata*, which exploited China uni-directionally, as emblematic of the old aristocratic guard hindering the beneficial progress of a new economic and moral program, *L'idolo cinese* mobilizes China in two directions. It stigmatizes an antagonist of the monarchy—arrogant clerics—as well as a nemesis of the patrician aggregate—upwardly mobile *borghesi*. Of the two, despite the persistent scourge of the theological satire, the negative identification of the Celestial Empire with "modern" methods disposed to an emerging Neapolitan parvenu carries the day. Thus, in contrast to *L'isola disabitata*, *L'idolo cinese* exploits China to *bolster* the traditional guard. Lorenzi puts China on the losing side of the opera's economy, as does Goldoni, but here what is acutely defeated are the liberal programs and policies that involve renovation and change. In this sense *L'idolo cinese* clearly bears out Hunter's assertion of the conservative tendency of the opera buffa genre.[11]

TAKING AIM AT THE CHURCH

As mentioned, the two buffo roles, Pilottola and Tuberone, respectively play the parts of the Chinese idol Kam, and his dutiful and reverent priest. Pivotal scenes include Tuberone's extravagant preparation for and welcome of the deity, who is believed to descend from the moon once a year to grant an oracle on earth; the idol's tirades against Tuberone's failings; and the grand banquet offered in the temple in honor of the idol. However, *L'idolo cinese* does not target the church simply by assigning buffo actors to the theological roles, and exploiting their comic enactment of hieratic custom. Nor does it suggest a blanket association between East Asian other and false religion. Details of the buffo performances, including lexical terms and the specific rituals chosen for comic interpretation, indicate that the opera exploited Chinese Buddhist practices in particular.

The idol's name "Kam" constitutes the most obvious correspondence. An orthographic version of Ch'an, it refers to a popular sect of Buddhism in China.[12] In addition, the proper noun "Kam" designates a kingdom of eastern Tibet neighboring the kingdom of Tangut, a Buddhist region about which Kircher wrote extensively in the section on Chinese idolatry (*De idolatria*) in his famous seventeenth-century treatment of China, *China illustrata* (1667). For his part, Lorenzi does not specify anything beyond the general "Chinese histories" when referring to sources in his *Argomento*. However, engravings in the chapters of Kircher's book on image worship suggest compellingly that *China illustrata* numbered among the popular sinological works Lorenzi consulted.

The choice to dramatize Buddhist practice is significant, since by the mid-eighteenth century, many *philosophes* had fixed on the parallel between its superstitions, corruptions, and heresy, and those of the Catholic Church. The Buddhism-Catholicism conflation had evolved over a relatively long period, however, taking shape in three distinct phases.[13] The first of these comprises the initial period of the Jesuit missionary project in China (1600–1680 ca.). Of the three principal religious systems practiced in the Middle Kingdom—Confucianism, Buddhism, and Taoism—the wealthy, powerful, and educated mandarins, the class on which the Jesuits fixed their sights, practiced the first, whereas the latter two comprised the faiths of the rest of the teeming populace, from shopkeeper to peasant.[14] The inferiority attached to Buddhism and Taoism arose initially from their association with the poorer Chinese masses. In order to persuade European supporters of the Christian-Confucian synthesis, Jesuit fathers had not only to extol the virtues of Confucianism, but also to distance it from Buddhism and Taoism. The task of promoting the former was not so difficult, initially at least, given that Confucianism appeared to be a philosophical system, rather than a competing theological creed. Buddhism, on the other hand, with its idols, its frequent rituals and incantations, its "charms, amulets, medicines, prognostications, and consolations," quickly and easily lent itself to being branded a form of idolatry.[15]

To complicate matters, however, Buddhist institutions, ceremony, and paraphernalia bore unsettling resemblances to those of Catholicism. More than the other two systems, Buddhism was quite detailed on spiritual matters and procedure. Like Catholic priests, the class of Buddhist monks known as bonzes performed intricate rituals—surrounding births and deaths, for example—on a daily basis. These similarities posed a second obstacle to the Jesuits, resulting in their vehement rejection of the cult. Mungello notes that the missionaries denigrated Buddhist leaders and devotees "for their intellectual superstitions, immoral practices, and social coarseness, while the [Confucian] literati were praised for their refinement and emphasis on learning."[16]

Luckily for the Jesuits, they could count on support for their anti-Buddhist stance even from certain Chinese. The mandarinate disdained the bonzes as lower-class priests of the common people, and saw the promulgation of Christian principles as an opportunity to rid Confucian teaching of Buddhist and Taoist contamination.[17] One of the more famous Chinese converts to Catholicism popularized the phrase exhorting that Christianity "supplement Confucianism and displace Buddhism."[18]

These sentiments quickly made their way into popular works in the Italian vernacular. An example of the antipathy for bonzes in this first phase of distaste for Buddhism occurs in the brief but highly circulated *Relazione della China* (Florence, 1666), written by Lorenzo Magalotti.[19] On bonzes, Magalotti wrote the following: "today in all of China there is no group more abominable and ignominious. An upstanding man should take care not to speak to or deal with them, unless he is both constrained and justified in doing so by superstition, which this rabble then lords over and lives off of. At every wedding, birth, and burial, they [the Chinese] run immediately to the bonzes, to discuss and arrange the required procedures."[20]

The immensely popular travel narrative of Neapolitan Giovanni Francesco Gemelli-Careri also reflects the contempt for Buddhism that evolved during the seventeenth-century Jesuit effort in China. Originally a functionary in the Habsburg court in Naples, Gemelli-Careri turned his sights to travel and became a sort of aristocratic "professional voyager," spurred by scholarly, humanist intentions. In 1693, after traversing continental Europe and England, he set out on a circumnavigation of the globe.[21] The volume on China from his six-volume opus *Giro del mondo* (Naples, 1699–1700) freely mixed his own observations with those from others' published works, including accounts by China Jesuits Magalhães and Le Comte.[22] Gemelli-Careri writes of both Tibetan Buddhism, practiced by the Tartars, and the more common type of Buddhism (originally from India), embraced by the Chinese rank and file.[23] Each sort is denigrated in the author's remarks on the hundreds of idols and "baby idols" ("idoletti") found everywhere, the stunning proliferation of temples, and the lies, hypocrisy, licentiousness, and greed of the countless bonzes, all of whom prey on the population, especially the poor.

One of the most suggestive of Gemelli-Careri's passages allows one to imagine what Lorenzi might have envisioned for his two buffo characters, Pilottola acting as a Chinese idol, and Tuberone as a high priest. First Gemelli-Careri derides the popular practice of rubbing idols' lips with grease from cooked meat in the belief that in this manner the deities eat. He then continues:

> Even more impious, and laughable is the adoration these same Tartars render unto a living man, who they call Lama, that is, Great Priest, or Priest of Priests. He is called thus because from him, as the source, comes the whole foundation of their religion and idolatry. . . . He is adored as a God, not only by the inhabitants of the place, but by all the kings of Tartary, who consider themselves his subject in accordance with the religion. For this reason not only the kings, but even their peoples make pilgrimages to him with great quantities of gifts, in order to

worship him as true and living God. In a secluded part of the palace he lets himself be seen, adorned with gold and silver and illuminated by many hanging lamps. He is seated on a pillow made of gold drapery, upon a wooden dais raised high above the ground and covered with the most elegant carpets. In this way everyone prostrates themselves in front of him, with their faces to the ground (no different from what we do with His Pontifical Highness). With incredible humility they kiss his feet, and "Father of Fathers," and "Great Priest," and "Priest of Priests," and "Eternal Father" are spoken . . . Those priests that merely attend to him convince the unwitting foreigners of the prodigies owing to his divinity.[24]

Enmity toward the idolatry of Buddhism intensified in a second phase, marked by the intensification of the Chinese Rites Controversy (roughly 1680–1750).[25] By the end of the seventeenth century, skepticism toward the Jesuit accommodationist methods (now carried out by Parisian missionaries, the descendants of Matteo Ricci's generation) had turned to entrenched abhorrence. Those opposed to the Jesuit approach now labeled all Chinese religions blasphemous, further stigmatizing Buddhism. Catholic investigatory delegations such as the *Congregazione di Propaganda Fide* and the *Missions étrangères* traveled to China in the last decades of the seventeenth century to enforce papal prohibitions of Chinese ceremony among Jesuits and their alleged converts.

Interestingly, Neapolitans held several key posts in these organizations. Catholic lay priest Matteo Ripa was sent to China in 1710 as an independent missionary on behalf of the *Propaganda Fide*. Despite ongoing antagonistic relations with the Jesuits there, he stayed in Peking for twelve years training Catholic clergy. He continued that work on his return to Naples, where in 1732 he opened the Collegio della Sacra Famiglia (later the Collegio de' Cinesi), a school for the education of future Chinese priests.[26] Ripa recorded his experiences in *Storia della fondazione della Congregazione e del Collegio de' Cinesi*, written sometime between 1732 and 1746.[27] Characterized as the "antithesis of the panegyric of the Jesuits," its detractions of Chinese culture are scathing.[28] Ripa appears obsessed with not contaminating himself by inadvertently engaging in heretical Chinese religious customs. One effect of his preoccupation, nonetheless, is to draw attention to those same usages. Witness his narration of the ceremonial upon the death of the K'ang hsi emperor in 1722:

> We entered the palace with the other missionaries, all clothed in mourning . . . Some of the missionaries, after speaking aside with the mandarins, followed them to the

51. **Buddhist idols and ceremonial. Athanasius Kircher, *China illustrata . . .*, 1677. Permission of Alderman Library, University of Virginia.**

entrance of the inner palace, where the corpse lay, and the funeral rites were performed . . . I did not know what ceremonies they intended to perform . . . Father Rinaldi asked them what they were going to do; and he received for an answer that there would be no improper or idolatrous sacrifices, no papers burnt, no libations of wine performed. On this assurance we followed the others . . .[29]

Unfortunately for Ripa, he and his colleagues discover that once the funeral had ended and the emperor's body had been removed to a location outside the clerics' view, great quantities of paper money were burnt such that "the air around was for a time clouded with smoke," and the idolatrous wine libation was also made. His angered reaction ensues: "On hearing that

we had, even unconsciously, taken part in this work of superstition, I was grieved and alarmed to a degree which it would be impossible for me to express; and in order to preclude the recurrence of such a misfortune, I resolved to quit that Babylon at any risk, and as soon as possible."[30]

The good intentions of a second Neapolitan, also commissioned by the *Propaganda Fide* to travel to the Middle Kingdom and aid the troubled missions, again helped to keep infamous Chinese devotions in full view. From his post in Macao Italian papal legate Carlo Mezzabarba wrote and published the "Eight Permissions," a list of concessions for Chinese Christians meant to appease conflicting factions:

52. Buddhist idols and ceremonial. Athanasius Kircher, *China illustrata . . .*, 1677. Permission of Alderman Library, University of Virginia.

1) the Christians may have funeral tablets in their homes simply inscribed with the names of the deceased, provided that beside the tablet there is an apt declaration of the Christian belief on death and provided that all superstition in the construction of the tablets and all scandal are avoided;

. . . .

5) genuflections and prostrations are allowed before the duly corrected tablets and also before the coffin and the deceased;

6) the tables can be prepared with cake, fruit, viands and the customary food in front of the coffin with the corrected tablet, provided there is an explanation that all is done to show respect and piety to the dead;

7) the so-called kowtow prostration is permitted before the corrected tablet on the Chinese New Year and at other times of the year; and

8) all candles and incense can be burned before the corrected tablets as well as before the tombs as long as the required precautions are taken.[31]

The specificity of the permissions demonstrates not only the laser eye of the church watchdogs, but also the immense signifying power in the enactment of the suspect protocols.

By the mid-eighteenth century, the time of the third phase of Buddhist-Catholic rapport (1750–90), the image of Buddhism as pernicious hocus-pocus is picked up by those opposed to Catholic doctrine altogether. The champions of secular truth and natural morality point the finger at Buddhism as corrupting Asian masses with deceit and superstition, just as they claim the unenlightened church corrupts the European faithful. Porter explains how Voltaire sees Confucianism as the only viable choice for any thinking person, inasmuch as it possesses "an exclusive monopoly on a Deist religious truth of which the myriad Christian sects, and especially Jesuit Catholicism, are but sadly degraded variants."[32] Yet again, Buddhism and Catholicism are assimilated as defective in the eyes of Enlightened reformers, who resolutely demote them as unworkable systems in a reasoning society.

Antonio Genovesi, radical Neapolitan economic reformer and leading representative of a new intellectual class, generally had good things to say about China. Among those traits that he disparaged, however, were its people's superstitions, and as noted above in chapter 5, their disturbing degree of naïveté and credulity. Here Genovesi comments on the Chinese lack of powers of discernment with respect to something as elemental as humanness, and in doing so he infers a wide gap on the intellectual plane between Europeans and residents of the Middle Kingdom: "when [the Chinese] saw our clocks and other machines, parts of our science, they thought that the Europeans were men of a far superior nature to others; they nearly judged them to be gods themselves."[33] Another sign for Genovesi of a certain primitivism in the Chinese was the "infinity of fortune tellers and astrologers that keep the greater part of this vast empire enslaved, moreso than do the Tartar troops."[34] As Porter puts it, the "unsettling resemblances between Buddhism and Christianity . . . erupted with a vengeance in the Enlightenment's arsenal of anticlerical barbs, among which was the commonplace substitution in satire of the despised figure of the bonze for the Catholic priest."[35]

The worship scenes in *L'idolo cinese* touch on nearly all the salient aspects of the Buddhist-Catholic synthesis. Tuberone is typically accompanied on stage by a cadre of "ministri" (bonzes/priests) as he rushes about to fulfill his hieratic functions. The exclusivity arrogated by bonzes and Catholic clerics, that is, the privileged intermediary position they claimed between supernal beings and the people, is underscored when Tuberone urges the idol not to labor over his oracle, but simply to deliver up "a little response, let us worry about interpreting it" (1, 7) ("Na respostella, / Ca nce penzammo nuje a 'nterpretarla.").[36] The ostentatious mysticism and superstition upholding the two faiths are evoked in Tuberone's frustrated expla-

nations of proper religious custom to Gilbo and later Ergilla (1, 3; 2, 14).

The cultish excess comes to life, however, with the enactment of the usages. Adoration of the Chinese idol requires a special site with a special staging (umbrellas, tents, pavilion), strict timing (the first light of day), the use of incense ("fussomiggi"), the singing of songs, and studied arrays of food and drink (1, 6; 2, 14–17). The sacrilege at the root of all this calculated ceremony (and, by extension, its doctrine) is inferred in a variety of stage moments. The words and actions of Tuberone, above all, reify the indictments aimed at blasphemous Buddhist bonzes and their Catholic cleric counterparts. As he orders his functionaries to ready the pastoral clearing, the high priest worries that the wrong figure might be taken for the divinity:

> Ministers,
> Raise up the tent, and ready
> The food and wine
> As is our usual practice. And see
> If there are people around,
> So as not to make any mistake,
> And have some streetsweeper show up
> Instead of the idol.
>
> (1, 3)[37]

> [Meniste,
> Schiegate il Paviglione, e preparate
> Lo magnare, e lo vino,
> Comm'è lo rito soleto, e bidete,
> Si nce so gente intorno,
> Che avessimo da prendere quà zaro,
> E pe parte dell'Idolo
> Nce desse mmano quacche monnezzaro.]

That a lowly streetsweeper could be confused with the divinity underscores the fallacy of idol worship, as it simultaneously suggests the credulity of the people, and the ease with which they could be manipulated. If the ministers are not careful, moreover, a solitary streetcleaner who happens upon a sudden feast might help himself to it, upsetting the ritual. Tuberone, naturally, is the most misguided of all. The idol's everyday clothing does not alarm him, and he claims he can see marvelous beams emitting from the deity's forehead: "Rays of light come out of your forehead / It's a miracle!" (1, 7) ("V'escono da la fronte / Cierte raggie, che so na maraviglia."). The idol declares that he can cure a multitude of illnesses, and when Tuberone asks him to diagnose the four "sick" lovers, Kam spouts knowledgeable-sounding nonsense, as well as would the most capable charlatan:

53. **Temple worship. Athanasius Kircher,** *China illustrata . . .,* **1677. Permission of Alderman Library, University of Virginia.**

The diseases sprout from dysentery.
That fellow is phlegmatic, that gal is choleric
This guy is consumptive, this lass is hysterical.
They all need to salivate.

(1, 14)

[I morbi nascono dal vesenterio.
Quello è flemmatico; quella è colerica
Questo è tisico: quest'altra è isterica.
E tutti avrebbero a salivar.]

Gilbo's comical prayer-aria earlier in the act also stresses the venality of the faithful. He intends to petition Kam for some facial hair, so that he is no longer taken for a boy and subject to bullying and taunts (1, 3).[38] The sumptous "lauta mensa" ("lavish meal") arranged for the idol, at which only the priest eats, allegedly on behalf of the deity, directs attention again to the greed and gluttony of the falsely devout, whether they minister to the Buddha or the Christ.

Of course, certain of these scenes constitute standard fixtures in the Italian comic repertoire. The lavish meal, for example, set out before a starving Arlecchino but from which he is always excluded, comprised a stock commedia dell'arte scene. The figure of the unscrupulous ecclesiastic hails back at least as far as Boccaccio, and reached new heights in Machiavelli's well-known comic protagonist Fra' Timoteo. These formulas and characters, however, replayed in a Chinese context, acquire an extra charge. The evolution of the Buddhist-Catholic analogy, and its particular resonance in eighteenth-century Italian Enlightenment centers, effected a shift in meaning, from general condemnation: "The church as disingenuous entity," to the topical: "Church authorities actively flout the best interests of the citizens of today's state." In Naples especially, where from the moment of Carlo's ascendancy in 1734 the Bourbon administration was engaged in a long-running battle of wills with the papacy over the latter's secular authority, the mockery of a priest-figure in the context of Buddhist degeneracy is pregnant with cultural weight.[39] The opera's continuous references to the baseness, deception, and opportunism of Buddhist devotion keeps the analogy and its contingent meaning in front of spectators.

The best example of this occurs in a particular instance of scatological ridicule. The normative use of vulgarities in commedia practice has been mentioned. Like Goldoni's opera, *L'idolo* contains a healthy dose (much more than *Isola*, actually) of bathroom humor. In a series of questions Gilbo poses to Tuberone about the makeup of the idol's body, he asks if the deity defecates, to which the priest answers "And how!" (1, 3).

> [*Gilbo.*   E poi fanno i bisogni?
> *Tuberone.*   E che hanno da crepare!]

In the banquet scene, as Kam commands Tuberone to drink great quantities of water, the priest vomits, whereupon the idol casually remarks that he'll also suffer diarrhea for a month (2, 14). In a third example, the evocation of a rather shocking Buddhist custom with routine scatological wordplay takes degradation of the clergy to a new level. Tuberone cannot master the name by which Ergilla presents herself, Eurina. He continuously mangles it, calling her Aurina (1, 5). In case anyone misses the joke, a brief back-and-forth in the next act between Tuberone and his page Gilbo makes it crystal clear:

Tub.	Her name is
	Sweet Aurine.
Gil.	Urine!
Tub.	Aurine.
Gil.	Sweet?
Tub.	Yes, and then some.
Gil.	Oh go on.
	Don't call such a filthy thing sweet.
Tub.	Aurine filthy?? Oh you poor mongrel,
Tub.	Do you want me to rip you apart? Calling a
	Priestess disgusting?
Gil.	Oh, you mean Eurine.
Tub.	Aurine.
Gil.	Euri . . .
Tub.	Uri . . .
Gil.	Eurine.

(2, 1)

[*Tub.*	Si chiami
	La dolce Aurina.
Gil.	Urina!
Tub.	Aurina.
Gil.	Dolce?
Tub.	Sì: doce e meza.
Gil.	Eh via.
	Non dite dolce questa porcheria.
Tub.	Aurina porcaria? Ohje casa esposito,
	E che buò che te sguarro? Porcaria
	Una sacerdotessa?
Gil.	Ah dir volete, Eurina . . .
Tub.	Aurina.
Gil.	Eurì . . .
Tub.	Urì . . .
Gil.	Eurina . . .]

These lines also remind us that Tuberone has raised Ergilla/Eurina to the position of high priestess of the idol Kam.

The juxtaposition of "sweet urine" with a highly placed religious official and with Buddhist sacerdotal ceremony recalls a practice written about by almost all reporters of Chinese religious culture. Gemelli-Careri narrates as follows, discussing the perverted reverence that the faithful (who he refers to as "those barbarians") make to the Grand Lama: "he is so blindly adored, that whoever is lucky enough to obtain even a small relic of his excrement, purchased at great expense, is thought to be most highly blessed. They believe that if carried in a little gold box worn hanging from the neck, it acts as a sure talisman against all sorts of evils, and a healthy antidote to all sickness. There are even some (oh, such blindness!) who put it in their food as a form of devotion."[40] Associations of the general Chinese population with a penchant for human and animal waste may have obtained also from European writers who commented on the country's prolific cottage industry in manure. The conscientious collection and storage of fecal matter by Middle Kingdom households, and its regular exchange for currency, foodstuffs, and other goods made a marked impression on narrators of Chinese ways.[41]

Scatological tendencies of commedia business notwithstanding, Tuberone's mistaking the name of the woman he loves with a foul bodily fluid highlights the nature of ignorance on two levels. First, as it summons Buddhist conflation of a preposterous (not to mention disgusting) fetish and sacred artifact, it makes fun of absurd ritual. Ultimately, however, the potency of the Buddhist aberration serves to ridicule any sort of religious ritual, including, or especially, those of the church. Emphasizing the inane details of Chinese bonze ceremonial throws an accusatory spotlight on all of Catholicism's purported defects: its exploitative officialdom, the empty mysticism of its "smells and bells," and the incompatibility of its theology with a modern, rational way of thinking.

The church and its many friends occupying government *seggi* wielded a heavy hand in Settecento Naples. In contrast to the Venetian Republic, whose ruling councils effectively kept the church in check, the Kingdom of Naples suffered more than any other Italian state from ecclesiastical abuses, enmeshed in an anarchical tangle of laws. The undermining of Catholicism in *L'idolo cinese* would have resonated with many concurrent efforts aimed at ending the tyrannical reign of the papacy.

Friction between the Bourbon administration and Rome started the minute Carlo took the throne, with the question of his papal investiture. Pope Clement XII, worried about the erosion of his power next to a domineering Spain, delayed for four years this significant "political blessing" of the new king.[42] The profoundly anti-curial bent of Prime Minister Bernardo Tanucci resulted in a number of concordats during the early years of Carlo's reign. Their stipulations included: increased taxation of church properties; reduced immunity for criminals seeking refuge on church grounds; restrictions on the number of vocations, both at the bishop and priest levels; restrictions of benefices and pensions to Neapolitan nationals only; the establishment of a mixed tribune, that is, composed of both priests and laymen, to decide certain jurisdictional matters; and the monarchy's exclusive rights to review and promulgate papal bulls and other official proclamations.[43] With Carlo's transfer to the Spanish throne in 1760, and the start of the regency of his young son Ferdinando IV, Tanucci, who now essentially served as head of state, became even more aggressive in his anticlerical initiatives. Dealing with a much more conservative pope in Clement XIII than his predecessor Benedict XIV had been, gave Tanucci greater impetus. He suppressed convents, confiscated their revenue, and outlawed *mortmain*, or the tradition by which testators could make nontaxable bequests of money and property to the church. He slashed the number of new vocations, expanded the powers of *exequatur*, and declared matrimony a civil bond, over and above its sacramental status. Under Tanucci the regency ordered that clerics could keep only one-third the value of the charitable donations they received, and furthermore "mandated that ecclesiastics limit their alms-seeking to places where benefactors would readily be found, and not assail the poor, the true and legitimate beneficiaries of such alms."[44] This last measure recalls the scene of the idol

Kam's initial appearance, an event which would likely attract a throng of ingenuous targets for money-grubbing curators of the "miracle." Tuberone's reference to a streetcleaner stumbling onto the scene indicates the general socioeconomic status of such a crowd.

Other conflicts between Naples and the papal minions included growing intolerance of the obligatory *chinea*, the showy tribute made to the church in Rome each year by the Neapolitan government, in recognition of papal suzerainty over the Kingdom.[45] The 1750s and '60s also saw the flourishing of the Freemason movement, closely allied with the church. Neapolitan nobility dominated these congregations, and their secretive tendencies and bizarre ceremonies provoked a contemporary anti-Freemason cause. Tanucci's reform objectives thus included the suppression of such clandestine, exclusionary organizations.[46]

As the last statement suggests, Tanuccian reform did not emanate solely from the pragmatic desire to establish Naples's financial and political autonomy. The chief minister's projects originated in the philosophical premises held by the most foremost thinkers of the Neapolitan Enlightenment, and thus he sought to achieve intellectual and spiritual freedoms together with civic strength and independence. A very close friend of Genovesi, Tanucci propounded legislation based in democratizing, demythologizing impulses. His support of the Italian translation of a controversial catechism, François-Philippe Mésenguy's *Exposition de la doctrine Chrétienne, ou Instructions sur les principales vérités de la religion*, is only one example of his interest in the divulgation of accessible, communal, *true* truths, deshrouded of their complicated and cryptic overlays.[47] The opera's ridicule of the elaborately silly religious customs and outlandish beliefs of the Chinese thus touches on this more ideological aspect as well.

The events surrounding the French religious treatise are collectively known as the Mésenguy Affair, since the Naples translation provoked furious rebuttals from the church.[48] The work was placed on the Index and formally denounced by the pontiff, who, as he issued a new edition of a church-sanctioned catechism, reprimanded both Tanucci and the publisher of the heretical text. That the Mésenguy Affair occurred in the years 1758–63 demonstrates the heightened tensions between the monarchy and the church just prior to the creation of *L'idolo cinese*. Although it came to naught, in 1763 Clement XIII listed nearly thirty grievances against Naples in a missive he sent to Carlo in Spain.[49]

The most public church-state conflagration in this period, however, was over the Jesuit order.[50] Among the order's many detractors, Molinists and Jansenists leveled criticism at the showy Jesuit rituals, which they labeled "superfluous vanities" next to the more austere, private spiritual piety they practiced.[51] Certainly Tuberone as an Italian-born, adoptive Chinese high priest must have called the "theatrical," acclimatized China Jesuits to mind.

Tanucci's anti-Jesuit sentiment was but a local drop in an ocean of rancor toward the Society of Jesus for its putative greed and corrupt power. Nonetheless, he did his part to facilitate the order's demise, which had begun officially in Lisbon, with the expulsion of the Jesuits from Portugal and its colonies in 1759. Soon Bourbon factions in France and Parma followed suit, closing Jesuit colleges in 1763, and dissolving the order throughout French dominions in 1764. This same year, Tanucci began endorsing the publication of anti-Jesuit tracts for public consumption.[52] In 1767 Carlo di Borbone joined his dynastic relations and ousted the Jesuits from Spain. To spur Ferdinando to follow in the steps of his father and dissolve the order in the Kingdom of the Two Sicilies, Tanucci obtained permission to convene a special junta on the matter. The resulting decree exposes as well as anything *L'idolo*'s anti-Jesuit coding: "This society is wicked . . . it is above any rule, or better, it has its own living rules, continually changing and arbitrary. It can confirm, repeal, abolish, restrict, and amplify the rules according to its own interests. *It uses its authority to create laws and invent privileges on a whim, and its highest principles and perennially arbitrary legislation are based on its capriciousness*" (italics mine).[53] The phenomenon of invented privileges and capricious laws echoes throughout *L'idolo cinese*. Its very premise, explained in the *Argomento*, involves a Chinese custom which stipulates that should a ruling lord die without an heir, the first foreigner to happen upon that ruler's territory is simultaneously crowned prince and consecrated as high priest. Such a ruling is designed to eliminate disputes among the local citizens, continues the *Argomento*, and thus was Tuberone raised to power in China. The full significance of Tuberone's incongruous status will be discussed further on. For now, suffice it to say that the figure of the deluded Chinese-made priest duly ridiculed the self-importance ascribed to the Jesuit fathers by their enemies. *L'idolo* further attacked the Society by portraying its proclaimed Mecca, that is, the Celestial Empire, as a nation equally deluded—at least enough to elevate fools. Tanucci's decree was obtained in October 1767; *L'idolo* had premiered in spring of the same year. By November, Ferdinando had signed the royal proclamation banishing Jesuits from his realm. The monarchy seized the order's property, and redistributed its real estate to small farmers in accordance with the proposals of Genovesi.[54] The extent to which Lorenzi intended to deliberately pro-

voke the church and/or the Jesuits with his portrayal of an idiot Chinese priest is impossible to determine. Proof that a connection was forged, however, emerges from the fact that some saw in Pilottola and Tuberone irreverent allusions to local clergy, and sacrilegious reflections on the Christian God. In 1813 Lorenzi's editor Vincenzo Flauto wrote, apparently with tongue planted firmly in cheek:

> Of course, with regard to this drama there were some sophists, day-dreamers, and quibblers, who thought they saw things in it which were not there. The idol's apotheosis; his oracles received in a state of transport and submission; a lovesick priest who tricks the deity to obtain his own ends; an idol who starves and a priest who gorges; it was all interpreted as ridiculing the hierarchy and the holy-joe doctrine of our true and sacred religion—I am truly struck that the book was not put on the Index . . . but Lorenzi set his story in China, among a people who at that time were idolatrous, and had no inkling of the true religion, of the true and sacred cult of the Divinity, and therefore the author cannot be accused of atheism.[55]

Both Lorenzi and Paisiello had strong ties to the Bourbon administration, and may reasonably have supported the regalist position in jurisdictional conflicts. The royal commission extended to Lorenzi following King Ferdinand's first viewing of *L'idolo cinese* only reinforced the good relationship the librettist already enjoyed with the Bourbon court.[56] Only a year after appointing him Director of Improvised Comedies, Ferdinand designated Lorenzi director of the Teatrino di Corte. Simultaneously, Lorenzi began a long affiliation with the Teatro San Carlo, the municipal venue for serious opera and at the time the only public theater sanctioned and attended by the crown. Paisiello, who was working as a freelance composer when he collaborated with Lorenzi on *L'idolo*, also appeared well-disposed toward the governing powers. In addition to his settings for comic productions at the Nuovo and Fiorentini theaters, he composed music for opere serie at the San Carlo theater. The fact that three of Paisiello's heroic operas were performed there between the summers of 1767 and 1768 strongly indicates that he too stood in excellent favor with King Ferdinand at the time of *L'idolo*'s debut.[57]

TAKING AIM AT THE ASCENDANT BOURGEOISIE

The figuring of China as objective correlative to a troublesome parvenu is less immediately apparent in *L'idolo cinese* than its evocation of a daft Catholicism. Nonetheless, the former has as incisive a link to local power relations as the latter. For both the monarchy and the Neapolitan grandees, the rising bourgeoisie presented a thorny issue. With the Bourbon charge to reform stagnant and prejudicial economic and legal systems, Prime Minister Tanucci generated initiatives not only in support of the *ceto medio*, but also to institutionalize certain bourgeois systems among the nobility. Tanucci's municipal programs sought to support mid-level families in the metropolis, i.e., those with financial means, skills, and a record of public service, just as his redistribution of clerical lands to smallholders attempted to create a rural bourgeoisie. Likewise, aristocratic families were encouraged to "professionalize" and espouse a "service nobility ethic," in imitation of their non-noble fellows who contributed to society as merchants, magistrates, and civil functionaries.[58]

Baronial opposition to the economic and political expansion of these "modern despots" proved too great to overcome, however. What's more, the administration's financial dependence on resident grandees weakened its effectiveness in founding a new civil society. In the final analysis, the Bourbons were more preoccupied with stabilizing their own position and corseting the gentry's control than with aggrandizing the *borghesia* and achieving social equitability. Tanucci's reforms essentially "intended to consolidate the monarchy, not . . . to introduce a constitutional element."[59] *L'idolo cinese*'s use of China, therefore, to negatively represent bourgeois newcomers and their potential to destabilize the status quo, shows the tight grip exercised by Naples's baronial culture. It reflects the general interest, including within the monarchy, in maintaining rather than revising the current order.

Antipathy toward the parvenu is consolidated in the character of Tuberone, the operatic protagonist most deeply inscribed in Chinese culture. The *Argomento* explains:

> In a certain part of China there was a law that stated that when a Prince died without heirs, his property was to go to the first outsider that happened on the region. Thus were avoided disputes and discord among the nationals. A young Neapolitan, having fled his home, arrived exactly in a place where one of these Lords had died. Adopted by the local people and given the name Tuberone, he was raised according to the customs of the country. He was declared its absolute *Governor*, and *High Priest* of Kam, deity of China. He married, and had a son by the name of Liconatte.

(3)

> [In un certo luogo dell Cina vi era legge, che morendo un Principe senza Eredi, si dassero i beni del Defonto al primo forastiere, che a caso ivi capitato fosse, così ovviandosi le dispute, e le discordie tra' Nazionali. Un gio-

vanotto Napoletano, fuggito dalla sua Casa, pervenne appunto in un luogo, ove morto era uno di tai Signori. E' preso dal Popolo, e col nome di Tuberone viene allevato ne' costumi del Paese, e dichiarato assoluto Padrone di quello, e Sacerdote di Kam Deità della Cina. Si ammoglia questi, ed ha un figliuolo per nome Liconatte.]

As the opera opens then, Tuberone has been in China for many years. In his titled position in the Middle Kingdom he carries out his duties with vigor, especially those related to his religious custodial responsibilities. More than any other character, even his Chinese-born son, Tuberone is portrayed as immersed in Chinese civilization. Nonetheless, as spectators—or at least readers of the libretto—know, he is also a displaced European. Tuberone's buffoon role draws on the absurd incongruities resulting from his accidental entitlements in the Celestial Empire. He is both lord and commoner, Chinese and Neapolitan, legally authorized and utterly illogical as an authority figure.

Tuberone's oxymoronic essence makes him a more dramatically significant buffo protagonist than Pilottola, despite the fact that the bumbling sailor-servant is labeled in the cast list as *primo buffo*. Pilottola's social rank, conventional antics, and vocal performance clearly meet the requirements of the traditional singing stage clown. In his recitatives he intersperses silly errors in comprehension with perceptive observations on the goings-on around him. The text of the arias he sings impersonating the idol Kam shows him boasting that he can lasso the planets if he so desires, or that if he's sufficiently angered, from his outpost on the moon he can let loose a flood to bring all of China down. Musically, Pilottola's lyrical items exhibit the standard elements of the buffa aria: long series of staccato sixteenth-notes to sustain extended patter, octave leaps, strong cadences emphasizing a grandiose sense of self, and multiple tempos within a single piece.[60] He fires off rapid declamation, facilitated by short line lengths, and naturally, he sings in dialect. His lexicon leans toward the concrete, in contrast to the abstract language of the lover's aria. Pilottola's final aria in act 3 offers the best example of all of these buffo conventions. He sings while becoming inebriated, so dramatically and gesturally the scene exemplifies the buffo actor-singer formula par excellence. In this piece his dialect is more pronounced as he drunkenly converses with his flask, referencing material objects and bodily functions, such as his unwieldy, bothersome cloak ("Ca Tabbarrone"), the oppressive heat ("Auf . . . che caudo!"), his rascally, traitorous flask ("Ah bricconciello") and its power to drown him ("Bene mio, ca la fiasca / Mo s'affoga 'nzaneta.") (3, 8).

The very conventionality of Pilottola's buffo performance, however, lessens his dramatic impact. Tuberone, on the other hand, because he combines unexpected and illogical attributes, more meaningfully exploits the role of operatic buffo. In fact, Tuberone may very likely have played the classic Neapolitan commedia role of Pulcinella in his performance. Although Lorenzi states in his *Argomento* only that he referred to histories of China ("Storie della Cina") when writing the opera, the editor of his first published collection of libretti claims that the plot derived from a commedia dell'arte scenario entitled *Pulcinella Re dormendo*.[61] As Naples's flagship commedia mask, Pulcinella had an enormously rich cultural and performative legacy.[62] His characteristic country bumpkin background originated in his alleged birth, or more precisely, his hatching, from a chicken's egg.[63] His movements and psychological makeup thus derive from both the cocky ostentation of the rooster and the base stupidity of the hen. Even when he finds himself in social situations and surroundings far from the barnyard, Pulcinella's "aura" calls up the clowning peasants and animals of that rustic world.

Tuberone's exploitation of this comic heritage is evident from the text of his first musical item. He opens 1, 4 singing a cavatina in which he urges the idol to appear. Since Kam traditionally arrives at daybreak, Tuberone coaxes him by noting that the cricket has finished his nighttime chirping, and by mimicking both the calls of the rooster and other morning creatures:

Tub. The cock's already crowing "Cock-a-doodle-doo"
Come on sun, come to us from Bally-hoo.
Come on Kam-my
Move your gam-mies
The birds are already going "peep-oo, peep-oo."

Coro. The cock's already crowing "Cock-a-doodle-doo"
Come on sun, come to us from Bally-hoo.

Tub. Apollo, let go of all this sleep
The cricket's done with his peep-peep;
Give light to Mr. Kames
You can do it with your flames
Since he's too scared at night to make the leap.
(1, 4)

[*Tub.* Già lo gallo fa chichirichì
Vieni sole da Michirimì.
Vieni Camme,
E botta le gamme,
Ca l'aucielle, già fanno 'nguì 'nguì.
Coro. Già lo gallo fa chichirichì
Vieni sole da Michirimì.

Tub. Lassa Apollo sto tanto dormì.
Ca lo grillo non fa chiù trì trì.
Luce a Camme
Può fa co le sciamme,
Ca de notte se schianta a benì.

Coro. Già lo gallo fa chichirichì
Vieni sole da Michirimì.]

The descent of Tuberone, high priest and governor, to the level of farmyard birds and insects, plainly emphasizes the rural, commoner genesis attached to the Pulcinella role. It would be interesting to know if Tuberone's costume resembled the classic baggy white uniform worn by the Neapolitan fool figure.[64] In any case, one can be fairly certain that some, if not all, of Tuberone's stage business—both his frenzied reactions to the servant-masked-as-idol, and his agitated exchanges with the other characters—replicated the *pulcinellate* known and loved by spectators of the *comici all'impronto*. In a more general sense, Tuberone's precarious relationship with the other characters throughout the opera and his starkly outsider status at the end—when all the other characters appear to be leaving him to return to Naples—reprise the perennial motif of Pulcinella's emargination.[65] For his appropriation of the time-honored commedia role, Tuberone sustains humor throughout the opera at least as much if not more than Pilottola.

Hunter notes that one of the ideologies most intrinsic to opera buffa is non-noble masculinity, aspects of which the buffoon character typically enacts.[66] Again, to a much greater extent than Pilottola, Tuberone engages a host of subjectivities illustrating ignoble masculinity. In his interactions with the others, the Chinese prince-priest shows himself to be a naive, ludicrous disciple, an ineffective father, a deluded lover, an inept captor, a poor matchmaker, and a credulous ruler. Michele Scherillo characterizes Tuberone as an "unmitigated fool" who really believes in his "ill-gotten dignity."[67] Pilottola, on the other hand, knows he is playing a part.[68] When Tuberone insists that Pilottola is the Chinese idol, the servant refers to him in an aside, saying "what a numbskull!" ("che zuccaro!"). When Tuberone refuses to accept Pilottola's professed ignorance of any idols, the latter finally decides to play along, in another aside: "What can I do? Call it craziness [i.e., my playing along with the act]" ("Ch'aggio da fa? pigliammola 'mpazzia"). Pilottola is not only aware of the sham, but also wise enough to think he might profit from the stupidity of Tuberone. The Neapolitan youth-turned-Chinese-governor-and-

54. Giovanni Domenico Ferretti, Italian, 1672–1768. Pulcinella with a Cooking Pot, 18th century. Oil on canvas, 37 ³/₄ x 30 ¹/₂ inches, SN651. Museum purchase, Collection of John and Mable Ringling Museum of Art, the State Art Museum of Florida.

55. **Pulcinella inebriated. Watercolor by Pier Leone Ghezzi. Permission of the Biblioteca e Raccolta Teatrale del Burcardo, Rome.**

ecclesiastic thus epitomizes a collection of social, ethical, familial, and political improprieties.

The most explicit exploitation of Tuberone's essential dissonance, and the clearest linking of his Chinese identity to misguided reformist ideology, occurs at the end of the opera. The lovers have worked through their entanglements and Pilottola's act has been discovered, but he has managed to escape punishment and even convince Parmetella to marry him. Only Tuberone is left hanging—humiliated and marked as dupe extraordinaire. As the three couples (Ergilla and Liconatte, Kametri and Adolfo, and Parmetella and Pilottola), prepare to leave China for Naples, Tuberone asks if he may leave with them, since Naples, he states, is his homeland also. When Adolfo asks how he came to be in China, Tuberone explains his story, reprising the information provided to readers in the *Argomento*:

Tub. They got a law here, that if a Lord
Dies without an heir, the dead guy's
Stuff has to go

To the first outsider
Who shows up . . .

Lic. So that there be no argument
Among the Chinese
As to dividing it.

Tub. Now I, as a youngun,
Ran away from home and ended up
In this country at just the time
That one of these lords had died.
These Alexandrine mummies
Gave me a hand and raised me
According to their crazy laws.

Tub. They turned me from a god-fearin' fellow
Into a High Priest.

Ado. Oh, what a strange mishap!

(3, 9)

[*Tub.* Cca' nc'è na legge, che si more quacche
Signore, senz'arede, ha da passare
La robba de lo muorto

Mmano a chillo frustiero,
Che capeta lo primmo . . .

Lic.   Acciò contrasto
Non vi sia tra Cinesi,
Nel dividersi quella.

Tub.   Or'io fegliuolo
Fujette da la casa, e capetaje
A sto paese'intiempo, ch'era muorto
Uno de sti Segnure.
Ste mummie Alessandrine
Mme dettero de mano, e mme crescettero
Dinto la legge loro a spacca strommola,
E da n'ommo dioto,
Mme facettero Sommo Saciardoto.

Ado.   Oh che strano accidente!]

This recitative exchange speaks volumes. Before examining the dialogue, however, one must first note that by repeating this information from the *Argomento*, Lorenzi ensured that spectators who may not have consulted the libretto did not miss the unusual "exotic" law regarding succession and inheritance. For those who had consulted the libretto, or might do so later, this important contextual element received emphasis.

As Tuberone explains the tradition of awarding the estate of the deceased Prince to the first-to-arrive foreigner, Liconatte interrupts to explain the reasoning behind the practice: "So that there be no argument / Among the Chinese / As to dividing it." His lines are funny, of course, pitched to a crowd all-too-inured to inheritance feuds, but how does the remark function in the opera's plot universe? Does Liconatte explain the Chinese custom because he anticipates puzzlement about it on the part of Adolfo, a European? Is he proud of the well-conceived Chinese system? It is significant that Liconatte, born of Tuberone and a Chinese woman and therefore technically the only native Chinese in the drama, defends the convention, citing its goals of social harmony and equity. His interjection could also have been intended to compensate for a disdainful tone in Tuberone's words. The Chinese-made prince-priest seems now to be dissociating himself from the people who granted him his status. His next lines sharply undercut Liconatte's self-assured commendation. When Tuberone castigates the Chinese as "these Alexandrine mummies" who "raised me / According to their crazy laws," and turned him "from a god-fearin' fellow / Into a High Priest," he enables a crucial interpretative act. He belittles the Chinese as a fossilized society with nonsensical laws and no sense of propriety.[69] The Chinese

have corrupted his original integrity, he says, by elevating him to priestly status. What he does not spell out, but is all-too-apparent, is that the Chinese also granted material substance and power to a nobody—in accordance with a civil code based on fairness and peaceable social relations (as Liconatte has hastened to remind everyone). Tuberone does not enucleate this second impropriety, although it is implied in his reference to "their crazy laws." Nonetheless, the conflation of the bizarre Chinese succession and inheritance procedure with legal reforms being proposed by Ferdinand's administration could hardly have been missed. Tuberone's emphasis on his unearned religious status over his unearned political and financial privilege may have had something to do with the inflammatory atmosphere surrounding issues of patrimony in just that period. At the time of the opera, several pertinent initiatives were on front legislative burners.

Inheritance policy constituted a large part of Enlightenment programs in Italy in general, but in Naples especially, much of Tanucci's work focused on achieving more egalitarian estate distribution. Beginning in 1759, with Charles's departure for Madrid, the chief minister had sought to institute more strident measures with respect to laws governing legacies of land and capital. The above-mentioned confiscation of land from the Jesuits and its reallocation to peasants in the same year of *L'idolo cinese*'s debut was only one of several changes. New laws on wills and testaments were enacted, such as that of 1769 forbidding *mortmain*, and reformers fought for the abolition of *fedecommesso* laws. Even Charles had been caught in the fracas. Owing to an article in the Treaty of Aix-la-Chapelle that restricted his freedom to leave the Kingdom of the Two Sicilies to his heirs, he and his ministers had spent over ten years (1748–59) winning back his legacy rights.[70] Tuberone does not formally denounce his unexpected inheritance in his anti-Chinese diatribe at *L'idolo*'s end, but he doesn't have to. The presence of these issues in contemporary social and political realms would have easily allowed audiences to read the opera's assimilation of Chinese politico-legal nonsense and parvenu privilege.

L'idolo cinese's particular Chinese schema would have been read amidst many positive analogies between the Chinese and the new intermediary class. Genovesi, who saw in the bourgeoisie "the most active and promising element in modern society," admired the pragmatism and political virtue behind the Middle Kingdom's meritocracy.[71] The Chinese mandarin, eighteenth-century incarnation of the ancient philosopher-king, possessed the blend of erudition and civic aptitude that *illuministi* like Genovesi imagined possible in a functioning republic of letters. While Genovesi thought little of the nation's economic isolationism and the superstitions of its populace, he wrote these reverent words describing how China determined ruling competence: "there is an Empire [where] nobility is widespread and remarkable, but not hereditary, nor able to be purchased: it is formed solely from civil wisdom, and does not extend beyond the individual's lifetime. Reign here is more similar to paternal governance than to civil rule: the Sovereign exercises a father's rather than a king's rights . . . He is at once Prince and Priest. This State is China."[72] *Idolo*'s treatment of its prince-priest does not conform in any way to this encomiastic evaluation, however. Rather, Tuberone as Chinese governor represents civil wisdom gone bad, a perversion of the natural and the normal.

Other aspects of the opera's textual and performance conventions support this reading. Adolfo's reaction to Tuberone's story: "Oh what a strange mishap!" corresponds with sentiments about China expressed by other characters at various points in the opera. When Kametri hears the (false) rumor that Ergilla has drowned herself in agony over her thwarted love with Liconatte, she angrily declares:

> . . . China
> produces nothing but monsters! That innocent
>   girl [Ergilla]
> will be avenged this very day!
>
> (3, 5)

> [. . . la Cina
> Non produce, che mostri, e che vendetta
> In questo dì quell'innocente [Ergilla] aspetta.]

The Neapolitan maidservant Parmetella, unwittingly transplanted to China via Tartary, also condemns the Celestial Kingdom and the failure of its resources to resolve problems. Her frequent pleas to return to her homeland imply plenty of resentment toward "this place China" ("sta China"):

> Ah, Naples, where are you?
>
> (1, 8)

> I'm Neapolitan, and by some bad breaks
> I'm now a slave in Tartary. Pilottola
> Is my countryman, and he learns fast
> From those who know lots.
> Together we'll slip out of here
> And get right back to Naples.
>
> (3, 2)

> (*to Ergilla and Pilottola*) Go,
> As soon as it gets dark everybody'll
> March onto Monsieur's ship
> And together we'll leave this China.
>
> (3, 7)

> [Ah, Napole, addò staje?
>
> Io sò Napolitana, e pe' disgrazia
> Mme trovo schiavo 'Ntartaria: Pilottola
> M'è paesano, e a chello
> Che canoscere pozzo è buon allievo.
> 'Nsiemmo ce la sfelammo,
> E a Napole de botta nce ne jammo.
>
> Jate,
> Ca subbeto che scura, tutte quante
> 'Ncoppa a lo bastemiento
> De Monzù nce 'mmarcammo,
> E 'nzieme da sta China nce nne jammo.]

The inadequacy of China's leaders and institutions is pointed up in addition by the fact that those who effectively resolve the lovers' dilemmas are not Chinese. The strategies of Adolfo, a Frenchman, and the smarts of Parmetella, a Neapolitan, fix matters. The efforts of Tuberone, on the other hand, the Neapolitan who "went native," prove completely ineffectual and underscore the impotence of Chinese ways. His ineptitude peaks when French soldiers led by Adolfo send Tuberone's Chinese troops fleeing in the opera's last scene (3, 14). "Let's get to my ship before all of China erupts in tumult," sings Adolfo, upon routing the local army ("Andiamo / Sul bastimento mio, / Pria che in tumulto sia la Cina intera."). Kametri then exhorts Ergilla to hurry, "before it gets more dangerous." ("Pria, che cresca il periglio.") In the hallmark ensemble finale the serious characters celebrate the love that will guide them away from perilous waves toward "safer banks," while the comic characters urge the group's fast escape "from this turf / before we're in big trouble":

[Lic.		
Erg.		Non più si veggan l'onde
Kam.	(*insieme*)	Che in più sicure sponde
Ado.		Amor ci guiderà.
Gil.		
Pil.		Fuimmo da sta terra
Par.	(*insieme*)	Si nò no serra serra
Tub.		Mo nce soccede ccà.

The cast list contributes as well to the stigmatization of Chinese ways, tied so clearly in the opera's last moments to defective judicial and political policy. Although the *Argomento* explains Tuberone's provincial Neapolitan origins, the roster of characters suppresses them. It describes Tuberone only as "Lord of a Chinese territory, and High Priest of the Idol Kam" (9) ("Signore di un luogo della Cina, e Sacerdote dell'Idolo Kam"). One practice, in operas whose plots depended on final surprise revelations of identity, was to preempt the surprise and indicate each character's true identity in the libretto cast list. This habit served to establish class parameters right from the start and reinforce proper social stratification.[73] Defining Tuberone in *L'idolo*'s list of characters only by his important Chinese posts contributed to the opera's comicity, as it exaggerated his eminent standing and hinted at his utter unsuitability for it. Stressing his prestige early on also makes more dramatic his fall, and accentuates the humility (and humiliation?) he expresses at the opera's end, when he has to ask for permisson to quit the very people who empowered him, and return to a familiar status quo. Rather than use the cast list as a reminder of the inflexibility of social and political hierarchy, *L'idolo cinese* communicates the message in its dramatic trajectory. Through his series of failures, and his increasing fear and desperation, pressure builds from within Tuberone's illegitimate standing. Tension deflates only when he renounces the position accorded to him by the Chinese, and meekly requests to reenter his proper sphere.

One bulwark of opera buffa's conservatism consists in the tidy containment of comic social reversals, one of which is the "uncrowning of the king."[74] According to Hunter, the undermining of a ruler's power and authority furnishes risible content in the comic opera, yet skirts any real hierarchical upset inasmuch as the toppled leader is always succeeded by a suitable candidate from the same class and privilege. In such a paradigm the existing power scheme of the dominant class continues unscathed. *L'idolo cinese* alters this paradigm, but yields the same results. Here the comic reversal consists in the *crowning* of a king, a highly inappropriate one. The return to normalcy is predicated on the uncrowning of the Chinese king. The necessary dethroning, however, is not due to decrepitude, or paranoic hanging on, archetypal causes for the downfall of the buffo authority figure. Rather, the system that crowned him is found to be itself dysfunctional. The Chinese, after all, gave their youthful newcomer the name Tuberone, or "big potato"! Tuberone abdicates not to be replaced by a new, more apt replacement who will rule properly. In fact, the business of his replacement is entirely ignored in the group's hurry to leave the strange place and reenter more familiar lands with their more sound and stable political arrangements. Tuberone's nonviability resides in his Chinese acculturation—manifest in an unseemly appropriation of financial, political, and religious power.

Franco Carmelo Greco notes that the 1760s marked a time of crisis for opera buffa in Naples.[75] Timeworn story lines, sloppy, gratuitous comicity, and irrational spectacle, the results of trying to meet competing demands of impresarios, musicians, singer-actors, and the public, figured among the flaws that plagued the genre. Lorenzi, together with other *professionisti* in the arts, entertainment, and intellectual worlds, sought to address these issues by appropriating for opera buffa a sociocultural space midway between those of the aristocracy and the general populace. The reformed opera buffa would manifest the best aspects of both the "royal spectacle," by which was meant opera seria, and "popular spectacle," referring to the farces and burlesque stage antics loved by the masses. It would serve a mediating function between nobility and plebeian audiences.[76] More importantly, however, it would reach out to the public that was beginning to form between the extremes. In his *Avviso* to *L'idolo cinese*, Lorenzi infers the growing numbers of bourgeois spectators when he states that he seeks to compose a drama midway between opera seria and *farsa*. He is even more clear about his intent to provide substantive entertainment to this middle group in his introduction to the libretto for *L'infedeltà fedele*, which inaugurated the Teatro Fondo in 1779. Here he states that he has distanced himself from "that typical vulgar, low-bred clownery, that our small theaters are used to, satisfying myself instead by using moderation . . . my intention, between the wholly serious offerings of the Royal San Carlo Theater, and the wholly comic offerings of the abovementioned theaters [Nuovo and Fiorentino], was to have this opera serve midway between the two, to have it draw uniquely from the one and the other, *so that each person living in the capital city would have a theater corresponding to his liking*" (italics mine).[77]

Lorenzi's professed goals accorded with an important shift in the relationship between bourgeois literary intellectuals and the peasant class, a change expressly evidenced in opera buffa, according to Greco. Where the poet-librettist anchored in official culture traditionally distanced the plebeian universe by ridiculing or arcadizing it in his dramas, he began now to treat it more closely and carefully, to see in it realities crucial to "a reinvention of social and political roles and functions."[78] To put it another way, dramatists started to sense the situation and needs of the *popolo* as representative of a larger set of social needs, needs that demanded reforms if a truly civil society were to form. The "scenic protagonism of the popular class" that emerged from this way of thinking translates therefore into ideological protagonism as well.[79] It deepens Tuberone's Pulcinella dimension, layering upon the cherished but prosaic peasant-fool identity that of a proto–middle class and its aspirations for productive, participatory authority in Neapolitan society.[80]

When one appreciates Tuberone as emblematic of this agenda, then his and his adopted culture's failure in *L'idolo* has a wider scope. It demonstrates what Greco avers as a parallel failure in Naples, that of its theater culture, and its enlightened reform policy.[81] Despite the audience success of *L'idolo cinese*, its bourgeois intellectual vision, like that in other works of Lorenzi and like-minded dramatists, did not take root. Opera buffa more and more exploited its farcical side, neglecting elements that evoked bourgeois concerns (for example, the pathetic), and concentrating only on wholesale *popolano* humor. With Ferdinand taking an increasing interest in and control over the popular theaters in the last quarter of the century, opera buffa evolved as a purely mercantile commodity.[82] At the same time, Neapolitan *illuministi* were whittling down their earlier, more all-embracing reform proposals, to focus on strictly political-economic and/or jurisdictional concerns.[83] Thus, while *L'idolo cinese* plainly raises the concerns of the would-be reformers, it also shows "the failure of a bourgeois ambition to construct an autonomous socio-political space for itself."[84] *L'idolo* simultaneously presents the aspirations and failures of Tanuccian reform, evoked by a non-triumphant, impracticable China.

CONCLUSION

The ideological underpinnings in favor of an emerging middle class in *L'idolo cinese* can be traced to Lorenzi's ambitions for opera buffa, together with his and Paisiello's indebtedness to Bourbon patronage.

However, the administration's hog-tied dependence on the aristocracy conditioned the extent to which any pro-bourgeois policy could flower. Despite the socioeconomic leanings that Tuberone suggested at the end of the opera, Lorenzi's protagonist could not amount to anything other than a laughable Chinese prince-priest.

Insofar as Tanucci's reform efforts were associated with the monarchy, critical assessments of Tuberone as constituting unsavory commentary on Ferdinand IV conform with the notion that, alongside its satire of the church, *L'idolo cinese* wages the battle of the conservative gentry. Luigi Settembrini sees Tuberone as a send-up of the new monarch, especially since Ferdinand came of age only months before the opera's premiere, and during both his regency and formal reign was commonly called the "lazzarone" king.[85] The epithet conflated Ferdinand's nonintellectual nature and his love of outdoor sport with the traits of the *lazzaroni* who clogged the city, "scruffy natives who lived hand-to-mouth and spent the majority of their time in the streets."[86]

The significance of the rhythmic similarity and rhyme of the names "lazzarone" and "Tuberone" can be debated. What cannot be denied, however, is that behind Ferdinando there operated reformists intent on equalizing power over a much greater number of Naples constituents. For those elect who had been used to wielding power exclusively for so long, it must certainly have appeared that Tanucci-led forces sought to put political, economic, intellectual, and other kinds of capital in the hands of undeserving outsiders. In fact, from the point of view of the long-term aristocracy, the ascendancy of Carlo himself, and his progeny, though native to the Kingdom, could be construed as the arrival of ill-suited "foreigners" to power.[87] Returning these strangers to their rightful localities, or better, denuding them of their pretensions and disallowing the culture that encouraged such pretensions, must have made for a most pleasing operatic conclusion.

7
Women Traveling in New Lands:
Giovanni Bertati, *L'inimico delle donne* (1771)

Opera was an important means through which the polemic about women was waged in Venice.[1]

THE TITLE OF GIOVANNI BERTATI'S 1771 COMIC opera *L'inimico delle donne* (*The Misogynist*) strongly suggests that it falls into that group of theater works which exploited antagonistic relations between the sexes for their entertainment effect.[2] The most famous of these productions in eighteenth-century Italy include Goldoni's comedy *La locandiera* (1752), whose crafty innkeeper Mirandolina outwits and humiliates an avowed woman-hater, and Carlo Gozzi's theatrical fable *Turandotte* (1762), where a humble but noble outsider manages to win over a man-hating princess. These were only two among a plethora of spoken and musical works that staged the tensions and antics of wrangling men and women before rapt audiences. Certainly a broad category, whose principal Italian forebears were the Boccaccian *novelle* that pit feminine against masculine wiles in all manner of situations, in the eighteenth century the "battle of the sexes" drama acquired specific meaning, given the period's keen interest in delineating gender roles and duties, primarily those of women, most productive in the service of public utility.[3]

L'inimico delle donne clearly reflects aspects of the ongoing discussion over woman's nature and purpose. Although the initial plot obstacle involves convincing two resistant youths, a Chinese prince and an Italian maiden respectively, of the merits of love and marriage, *L'inimico* concentrates on issues related to women. Feminine beauty, character, friendship, and rivalry are variously treated. Women are alternately portrayed as burdensome to the male guardians charged with procuring spouses for them, and as victims of those eventual spouses: violent, two-faced, cruel, womanizing, neglectful husbands, who, as Agnesina remarks disdainfully, obligate their wives "to give them children at least every year" (2, 3) ("dar loro dei figli almeno ogn'anno").[4] The brand of eighteenth-century misogyny based in physiological principles surfaces in Prince Zon-zon's comparisons between women and dogs, horses, crows, bats, toads, and serpents, and in his comments on women's odor.[5] He even quotes the "Maestro," from whom he learned

> That in knowledge man has no equal,
> That woman is the worst of every animal.
>
> (2, 5)

> [Io dal Maestro appresi,
> Che in saper non aveva un uomo eguale,
> Che la donna è il peggior d'ogni animale.]

The mention of "the Maestro" was likely an allusion to contemporary scientific discourse based on Aristotelian categorizations of the sexes.[6] On the other hand, Zon-zon's ministers spout panegyrics to women, in recitative verse such as this from Si-sin: "How a flesh-and-blood man / Cannot love women, I don't understand" (2, 8) ("Ché un uomo in carne ed ossa / Non so come le donne amar non possa"), and in these lines from one of Lylam's arias:

> Dear women, I can never
> Praise you enough!
>
> (2, 12)

> [Care donne, quanto basta,
> Non vi posso mai lodar!]

These latter sentiments appear to triumph as Zon-zon senses Agnesina's charms and begins to doubt the Master's teachings ("I fear that my Maestro was an ass" [2, 7]; "Temo che il mio Maestro fosse un Asino"). Shortly thereafter he succumbs to the Italian beauty (2, 9), and she too capitulates, although not quite as quickly. Agnesina falls in love with the Chinese prince

56. Frontispiece, *L'inimico delle donne*. Courtesy Schatz Collection of Opera Librettos, United States Library of Congress, Music Division.

two scenes later—but the tug-of-war over her fate as woman is not over. The final act of the opera takes up the circumstances of married women, as the prince orders one of the women of his court to give his Italian fiancée a lesson on how to conduct herself as a loving wife. When as part of this lesson Agnesina learns that polygamy is the Chinese custom, she demands monogamy from Zon-zon or else she will not marry him. He rushes to promise her fidelity, and at the moment of his vow both partners feel a sudden surge of love for each other, borne out, naturally, in a lovers' duet. The opera concludes with their marriage, as well as that of another Italian-Chinese couple, Agnesina's

uncle Geminiano, and Xunchìa, one of the Chinese maidens in the prince's retinue.

By now it is obvious that *L'inimico delle donne* does not merely mirror differing positions in the vociferous Settecento *questione della donna*, but rather takes a stance. In both its formal properties and its content, it demonstrates a clear allegiance to bourgeois values. More to the point, it propounds the idea of woman characterized by the bourgeois domestic ideal.[7]

Hunter notes that the term "bourgeois" with respect to eighteenth-century opera buffa refers at once to aesthetics and sociological message.[8] In terms of aesthetics, *L'inimico* parallels paradigmatic bourgeois dramas (musical and spoken) in their emphasis on stylistic naturalness, expressed by middle-ranking characters who manifest mid-range linguistic registers and sentiment. As discussed above in chapter 5, the social station of operatic protagonists was typically wedded to singing category. The majority of characters in Bertati's opera, including its principals Zon-zon and Agnesina, perform *mezzo carattere* roles. Not only do their language and gestures emanate from a social sphere between that of the nobility and the peasant class, but also, the musical style associated with the *mezzo carattere* singer-actor embraces a wide and versatile middle ground.[9] In terms of sociological content, *L'inimico* advances a specific moral code associated with the rising bourgeoisie and related especially to marriage. To the marital ethos of the aristocracy, which resulted in arranged and often loveless unions, the new morality stressed the power of love, and its role as conduit to consensual, affectionate, companionate marriage, where the different (gendered) virtues of husbands and wives complemented each other.[10] For both partners, the virtues of sincerity and marital fidelity, that is, monogamy, reigned supreme. Women, however, were to function as moral anchors of this familial ship. Bourgeois gender ethics figured women as closer to Nature and therefore privy to an instinctual goodness and happiness different from the contentment that issued from Reason, men's domain.[11] As inherent possessors of such "natural" moral virtue, women were obliged to inculcate it in their less-inclined husbands and children.

Contemporary comic operas that foreground the new familial morality formulaically showed women having to combat a threatening, if not downright misogynistic, world. The drama of a heroine's struggles against immoral, usually masculine forces ended in her ultimate victory over them. Ralph P. Locke has called them "strong woman" operas, the great majority of which can also be termed "Pamela dramas," or eighteenth-century stage versions of Samuel Richardson's best-selling novel.[12] These numerous plays and operas showcased variations of unmarried women's "performance of constancy" in the face of attempted seduction by a man of higher social station.[13] The woman's reward for sustained virtue is love and marriage to the partner of her choosing.[14] *Cecchina, oppure La buona figliuola* (Goldoni-Piccinni, 1760), *Il barbiere di Siviglia* (Petrosellini?-Paisiello, 1782), *La villanella rapita* (Bertati-Bianchi, 1783), and *Nina, o sia La pazza per amore* (Lorenzi-Paisiello, 1789) are only a few of the exemplars. The bourgeois gender ethic required constancy after marriage as well, so operas featuring virtuous wives also abounded. Works such as *La buona figliuola maritata* (Goldoni-Piccinni, 1761), *Gli sposi malcontenti* (Storace-Brunati, 1785), and *La Griselda* (Anelli?-Piccinni, 1793) showed wedded heroines holding up under more or less vicious assaults to their desires and reputations. One might label these operas "Julie dramas," insofar as their oppressed but ever-faithful female protagonists harken to the vision of ideal wifehood described by Jean-Jacques Rousseau in the other best-selling novel of the century, *Julie, ou, La nouvelle Héloïse* (1761). In any case, whether their protagonists originate from the models of bourgeois womanhood put forth by Richardson or Rousseau, and whether they fully exploit the fashionable sentimentality of the moment, the operas listed above depict women whose virtue is sorely afflicted, and who, more often than not, are themselves responsible for confronting and rehabilitating the offensive against them.[15] *Le nozze di Figaro* (Da Ponte-Mozart, 1786) is emblematic of this new feminine agency, insofar as "the efforts of women [Susanna and La Contessa di Almaviva] protect properly individuated love and ensure the 'lawful' institution of bourgeois companionate marriage."[16]

L'inimico delle donne falls somewhere between the two categories identified above. Strictly speaking, Agnesina is not one of "Pamela's daughters," since her maidenhood is not threatened by a man of dubious motive.[17] Still, her persistent premarital moral integrity comes into relief next to the lack of such in her Chinese female peers, and her feminine virtue is rewarded by reciprocal love with the prince. As for her experiences after the wedding, although *L'inimico* technically does not treat Agnesina as a married woman, it clearly evokes wifely trials, in Zon-zon's misogyny and in the heroine's discovery of the Chinese practice of polygamy. When Agnesina learns of the custom of multiple wives and in the next breath forbids it, it is as if the ordeals of the married woman are dramatically foreshortened. Her pronouncement as moral arbiter of the household acknowledges her

betrothed's potential future infractions only long enough to eviscerate them. *L'inimico delle donne* thus offers a streamlined, compressed version of the bourgeois feminine ideal: virtuous maiden capitulates to love, marries, then calls the shots, in terms of sexual respectability and familial decency.

Given *L'inimico*'s relative conventionality in terms of operatic tropes of the model bourgeois woman, one might surmise that its mobilization of China would likewise be fairly predictable. That is to say, the opera would represent one of two canonical paradigms for treating feminine gender in the "exotic" drama. In the first of these the Celestial Empire would be figured as sharp foil—corrupt, licentious, immoral—to wholesome, decent, European bourgeois gender ethics. These kinds of operas essentially reprise the Pamela archetype with one mutation, inasmuch as the seducer/ravisher is the foreign other. The steadfast resistance to exotic captors on the part of virtuous European damsels such as Constanze in *Die Entführung aus dem Serail* results in salvation and union with their preferred mates.[18] The second paradigm assigns the good morals to the foreign observer, who points a critical finger at European shortcomings in male/female relations. Goldoni's "New World" comedies *La bella peruviana* (1754) and *La bella selvaggia* (1758) both reflect their debt to Graffigny's novel insofar as they stress the purity of their uncivilized American heroines against the compromised ethics of the French, Spanish, and Portuguese.[19]

The antithesis in *L'inimico delle donne*, however, is not solely expressed by either of these mechanisms, nor is it as cut-and-dried as one might expect. This is because *L'inimico* traces a trajectory, that is, its heroine's gradual maturation leading to her espousal of bourgeois gender tenets. The valuation of China in relation to this progress is inversely proportionate: as Agnesina evolves from marriage-resistant maiden to staunchly moral wife, China devolves from utopia to dystopia. Taking advantage of multiple and sequential visions of the Celestial Empire allows a fuller exposition of the substance and indeed, the "drama" of the embrace of bourgeois womanhood by Italian girls. In addition, the opera does not show a seamless advancement toward Enlightened womanhood. Points of ambiguity surface in this would-be linear course, and images of China presented in the drama account for these as well.

One of the first perceptions of the Middle Kingdom presented in *L'inimico* is that of a utopian land. When Agnesina and her uncle Geminiano arrive in Kibin-Kin-Ka, a city on an island in the China Sea, neither knows exactly where they've landed. Agnesina is ju-

bilant nonetheless. She immediately invokes her antipathy toward her suitors back home, and her great
joy at having successfully evaded them:

Agnesina.   Oh, how this foreign shore
              Delights me!
              Whoever desires love from me
              I challenge him to follow me here.
                                           (1, 3)

[*Agnesina.*   Oh quanto mi diletta
              Questo straniero lido!
              Qua ad inseguirmi io sfido
              Chi vuole amor da me.]

The young woman perceives the island as an unde-
manding, nonconflictual zone, a place where she will
be free of others' concerns about her betrothal. Much
like the Chinese island in Goldoni's *L'isola disabitata*,
imbued with a sense of unbounded liberty and happy
promise for the Dutch, Bertati's isle symbolizes
carefree ease for Agnesina. When asked by her con-
siderably less confident Uncle Geminiano "What will
become of us?" she flippantly replies "Let the astrologers take care of it / We're here, in any case" (1,
3) (*Gem.* Di noi cosa sarà? . . . *Agn.* Ci pensino gli As-
trologi / Noi siamo intanto qua.).

Geminiano is slower to register optimism about
their prospects, as he fears they've landed among savages. His fright and discomfort rise proportionately
with Agnesina's happiness, expressed in a duet in
which he sings: "Here I always feel full of worry,"
while Agnesina elatedly announces "Here I always
feel free of worry" (1, 3):

[*Gem.*   ⎰ Pien d'affanni ogn'or vi sento,
 a due   ⎱
 Agn.   Senza affanni ogn'or vi sento.]

Geminiano's tension is compounded since as her
guardian, he is responsible for marrying her off. He
chastises his niece for her "stravaganza," that is, her
stubbornness with regard to marriage:

Geminiano.   . . . Every other woman
              Thinks of nothing else but marrying,
              And you, is no catch
              good enough for you?
              . . . .
              What demon has gotten hold of you?
                                           (1, 3)

[*Geminiano.* Ogni altra donna
              Non pensa che al marito,
              E voi nessun partito

Accomodar vi può?
. . . .
Ma qual diavolo è mai che vi prese?]

As soon as he realizes they've arrived in China, however, he thanks the heavens. He has heard that the
Chinese "Are very agreeable, lovable, / And very cer-
emonious" ("Sian benigni, amorosi, / E assai cerimo-
niosi"), and he immediately urges Agnesina to act in
like manner:

Geminiano.   Show that you have a little wit,
              That you're docile, well-mannered,
              Make these courtiers love you!
                                           (1, 5)

[*Geminiano.* Mostratevi un pochino spiritosa,
              Docile, manierosa,
              Fatevi amar da questi Cortigiani!]

For Geminiano, the Celestial Empire is a courtly, elegant place. Its refined ways may make it easier for his
young ward to find a mate than back in Italy, and this
in turn would alleviate his burden.

Geminiano's reassessment of China in terms of its
mildness, sweetness, and courtesies conflates with
Agnesina's initial conjecture of a calm oasis to suggest
that perhaps here, in this remote East Asian region,
reputed for its loving, pacific nature, things will be
possible that are not elsewhere. Just the barest whiff
of sexual utopia wafts through these scenes. It is
worth remembering the eighteenth-century predilec-
tion for sexual and social utopian narratives, many of
which came out around this time. Diderot's fictional
Supplément au Voyage de Bougainville was written in
1772, and in the same year Bertati teamed up with
Gazzaniga on the *dramma giocoso* entitled *L'isola di Alcina*, yet another in the stream of Ariosto-based operas
that, since the seventeenth century, had entranced audiences with the voluptuous promise of pleasure in Alcina's realm.[20] As discussed above in chapter 3, the
chinoiserie phenomenon also transmitted a notion of
China as a soft, effeminate, pliable space, possessed of
its own particular *frisson*.[21]

Agnesina's aria concluding this section tempers the
sense of the risqué, however, allocating to China more
ingenuous attributes of simplicity, peacefulness, and
serenity. Her words call up the classic topoi of innocent youth and its resistance to amorous involvements
as she reasserts her aversion to "Whoever speaks to me
of love" ("Chi mi parla poi d'affetto"), and proclaims
her love of peace and tranquility (1, 5). Agnesina's desire for inner harmony appears to be appeased by her
surroundings. With regard to relations between the

sexes, perhaps in China she can evade restrictive social dictates. Perhaps she has found a land where men
and women see the light, which for her means she will
not have to marry and subject herself to the cruelties
of a neglectful and/or tyrannical husband.

China's potential for civilized outcomes is reinforced by the response of the Chinese to the European
arrivals. In the first scenes of act 1, Bertati utilizes the
foreign observer model, but with an interesting variance. The non-European commentators, that is, the
Chinese, are not disoriented travelers, but rather assured hosts, to whom the newly arrived strangers
seem somewhat odd. Stage directions prescribe that
the Chinese act stupefied (*"facendo atti di meraviglia"*)
in front of the young girl and her guardian, and signal
to their servants to look at the Europeans. In an aside,
Si-sin, the Chinese minister, mutters "What strange
figures!" ("Che figure!"), whereas the humble Agnesina in her aside remarks "What well-dressed people!" ("Che gente ben vestita!") (1, 4). The supposed
superiority of the Chinese persists, as they greet the
Europeans with great ceremony, noting among themselves how the newcomers seem afraid. When Agnesina notices that the islanders speak her language,
Si-sin explains that an Italian had journeyed through
Kibin-kin-ka centuries earlier, and his speech so
pleased the Chinese court that they decided to adopt
it. Again, the Chinese hosts assert their cultural dominance, this time as arbiters of elegance in language
(and as they reduce Marco Polo, who never is named,
to no more than a traveler passing through). Later Si-
sin refers to the Italians' "very strange clothes," and
Zon-zon laughs heartily at the incomprehensible European habit of powdering one's hair, when, as he
notes, nature does its own whitening further along in
time (1, 9–10).

These first scenes figure China as a privileged, cultivated, accommodating place. "Everything you might
wish for / You will find here among us, as we are
friends / To all foreigners, and we love them greatly"
(1, 4) ("Tutto quel che vi aggrada / Troverete fra noi,
ché amici siamo / Di tutti gli stranieri, e assai li ami-
amo"), Si-sin assures the Italians. Audiences must
have at least chuckled at this bit of recitative, given
China's reputation for xenophobia. However, the Italian neophytes onstage don't seem aware of this culture trait, so for them the dream of China's promise
stays alive. For Agnesina, the island is an escape, a
joyful chance to avoid the pains of courtship and marriage. For her guardian uncle Geminiano, it's a felicitous opportunity to dispatch his responsibility as a
man, to affiance his niece to one of these refined persons. Anything is possible—and in this shimmering

vision lies the opera's dramatic tension. Whose utopia
will China be? How will civilized behavior be defined? In what ways will gender be constituted? Does
there exist a realm in which one does not have to com-
ply with social rules? Will Agnesina's idea of utopia
hold sway, whereby she will not have to accede to her
uncle's and society's demands that she marry? Or will
Geminiano's, wherein his niece will learn from experts how to be "Docile, well-mannered," and how to,
as he implores her, "Make these courtiers love you!"?
Agnesina's happiness on arriving in the Celestial
Kingdom hints that she will be rewarded. When her
uncle fears initially that they've landed among savage
cannibals, she answers: "Don't you know the proverb
/ That even if we were to die here, / One cannot escape one's destiny?" (1, 3) ("Non sapete il proverbio,
/ Quand'anche qui dovessimo morire? / Dal destinato
non si può fuggire?"). Her puckish response raises
only the question of what her destiny as a woman will
look like.

Chinese civility in *L'inimico delle donne* starts to slip
at the end of act 1, however, when Geminiano introduces his hosts to Italian wine. The act finale involves
a prolonged royal luncheon during which the diners
may only eat and drink at specified intervals, marked
by the customary gong. In his buffo role, Geminiano
plays up his suffering when he cannot eat or imbibe
except at rare moments. For their part, the Chinese
are so taken with the imported wine that they drink to
excess. Agnesina and Geminiano observe the goings-
on from the sidelines, remarking on their hosts' ignorance of wine and the need for moderation. "Be
careful, Sir, / (our) good wine is not your tea," warns
Agnesina (1, 12) ("Badate, Signor, / Che il buon vino
non è il vostro Thè"). But the Chinese do not heed the
Europeans, and the meal ends in a drunken baccha-
nalia, followed quickly by mass nausea. The two Italians command the servants to bring in plenty of fresh
water, and thus, over the course of the ensemble finale, the Chinese fall from their high perch, and civility reverts back to Europeans.

The shift toward the "exotic as inferior" trope gains
momentum in act 2. Given the opera's focus on the
coming-of-age of the exemplary bourgeois Italian
woman, it follows that the flaws now accruing to
China will concern those obstacles facing the aspiring
virtuous bourgeoise. Apologists of the new feminine
moral order identified the libertine ethos of the elite
ranks as the most insidious threat, both in terms of its
ubiquitous practice by the nobility, and its potential to
corrupt lower classes eager to imitate their social bet-
ters.[22] Thus *L'inimico* now allies the Middle Kingdom
with licentious customs ascribed to the aristocracy.

The most egregious of the Chinese conventions Agnesina learns of is the practice of polygamy. She finds out about Chinese polygamy by accident from Xunchìa, who encourages the Italian maiden to hone her lovemaking skills so as not to lose her new husband to the attractions of another wife. The two are then interrupted, whereupon the next scene begins with Agnesina deep in troubled thought:

Agnesina. If he finds a consort
he likes better than me!
How many can he have?
Could it be that custom permits
More than one wife at a time
To lie upon the nuptial pillow?
(she remains worried)

(3, 8)

[*Agnesina.* Se trova una Consorte
Che più di me gli piaccia!
E quante ne può avere? . . .
Forse più d'una a un tempo
Permetterà il costume
Che occupar possa le nuziali piume?
(resta pensierosa)]

Zon-zon's arrival spurs her to confirm this new information:

Zon-zon. Agnesina, everything is now prepared
To perform the wedding rites . . .
Agnesina. Yes, okay, . . . But tell me, how many
Wives may a man have at one time?
Zon-zon. There is no precise number,
Individual genius dictates the law and
one's own particular situation.
Agnesina. If that is the case, sir,
Cancel the celebration and the ceremony.
Zon-zon. Why?
Agnesina. Because I won't marry that way.
If a wife is barely recognized
In Italy, where men
Have but one apiece,
What will become of her
If a man can have five or six?

(3, 8)

[*Zon-zon.* Agnesina, di già tutto è allestito
Per adempir delli sponsali al rito. . . .
Agnesina. Sì, va bene . . . Ma un uom, ditemi
adesso,
Quante mogli può avere a un tempo stesso?
Zon-zon. Numero in ciò non v'è determinato,
Ma il genio dà la legge e il proprio stato.
Agnesina. Quand'è così, Signore,
Sospendete per me la festa e il rito.
Zon-zon. Perchè?

Agnes. Perchè così non mi marito.
Se in Italia, ove un uomo
Non ne ha che una sola,
La moglie per lo più poco se'n loda,
Or che sarà di lei
Dove un uomo può averne a cinque e sei?]

Agnesina's discovery of the cultural norm and her prompt condemnation of it constitute the most emphatic moment of her allegiance to bourgeois womanhood. She couches her opposition in anxiety over the neglect of wives by Italian husbands, a failing frequently attached to the nobility.

What is most significant in this exchange, however, is Agnesina's veiled recourse to Reason as the backbone of monogamous love. Immediately following her distressed musing over the possibility of a man's having five or six wives, she begins the lovers' duet with Zon-zon. Her initial lyrics are telling:

Agnesina. I admit it, if I were to allow myself
To be imprisoned by genius,
Imagine the pain in store for me
Seeing myself left one day.

(3, 8)

[*Agnesina.* Se dal genio, lo confesso,
Mi lasciassi imprigionar,
Qual dolor per me in appresso
Nel vedermi un dì lasciar.]

Abandonment and sorrow will result if Agnesina allows herself be bound by *genio*. *Genio*, Zon-zon has said—in this context meaning "personal taste," "individual liking," "inclination"—determines Chinese law, as well as one's (husbands' as well as wives') state. But personal inclination is most certainly not working in Agnesina's favor. She construes *genio* as a portal to subjugation, and her rejection of it implicitly proposes that a different logic determine both law and the individual's condition. She doesn't have to intone the words "reasoned, natural love" because it already exists within cultural discourse as the preferable—indeed, the only viable—foundation for social structures, be they states or families. The article *génie* in the *Encyclopédie* defines it as the source of the overpowering passions, imagination, and creative impulses suitable to the arts, but opposes it to the rationalism necessary for the maintenance of stable institutions:

The self-control that subjects the activity of the soul to reason, and that in all events safeguards one from fear, from intoxication, from reckless acts, isn't this a quality that cannot exist in men controlled by imagination? Isn't this quality absolutely opposed to genius? Genius originates in an extreme sensibility that renders it susceptible to a multitude of novel impressions, by which it can be diverted from its primary goal, forced to betray secrecy, to leave behind the laws of reason. Because of the inconsistency of its ways, genius can lose the power it would have had due to the superiority of its intelligence. Men of genius forced to feel and to decide based on their tastes, their revulsions, distracted by a thousand objects, too often guessing and too seldom foreseeing, carrying to excess their desires, their hopes, ceaselessly adding to or taking away from the reality of beings, seem to me men made more for toppling or for founding states, than for maintaining them; they are better for re-establishing order than for submitting to it.

[le sang froid qui soumet l'activité de l'ame à la raison, & qui préserve dans tous les évenemens, de la crainte, de l'yvresse, de la précipitation, n'est-il pas une qualité qui ne peut exister dans les hommes que l'imagination maîtrise? cette qualité n'est-elle pas absolument opposée au génie? Il a sa source dans une extrême sensibilité qui le rend susceptible d'une foule d'impressions nouvelles par lesquelles il peut être détourné du dessein principal, contraint de manquer au secret, de sortir des lois de la raison, & de perdre par l'inégalité de la conduite, l'ascendant qu'il auroit pris par la supériorité des lumieres. Les hommes de génie forcés de sentir, décidés par leurs goûts, par leurs répugnances, distraits par mille objets, devinant trop, prévoyant peu, portant à l'excès leurs desirs, leurs espérances, ajoûtant ou retranchant sans cesse à la réalité des êtres, me paroissent plus faits pour renverser ou pour fonder les états que pour les maintenir, & pour rétablir l'ordre que pour le suivre.][23]

In the article on taste (*goût*), the Encyclopedists emphasize not only Reason's superiority over *genio*, but also its crucial role as regulator of the unpredictable ways of genius:

The philosopher knows that in the moment of production, genius wants no constraint; it loves to run unbridled and unruled, to produce the monstrous next to the sublime, to impetuously roll gold together with silt. Reason therefore gives to genius that which creates complete liberty; reason permits genius to exhaust itself until it needs to rest, like spirited steeds that are broken only when spent. At that moment reason refocuses critically on what genius has produced; it retains that which is the effect of true enthusiasm, and proscribes that which is the work of impulsive ardor. In this way it [reason] draws forth masterpieces. What writer, if he is not without talent and taste, has not remarked that in the heat of composition a part of his spirit remains in some way off to the side, in order to observe reason at work, to give it free rein, and to allow it to mark in advance that which must be erased.

[Le philosophe sait que dans le moment de la production, le génie ne veut aucune contrainte; qu'il aime à courir sans frein & sans regle, à produire le monstrueux à côté du sublime, à rouler impétueusement l'or & le limon tout ensemble. La raison donne donc au génie qui crée une liberté entiere; elle lui permet de s'épuiser jusqu'à ce qu'il ait besoin de repos, comme ces coursiers fougueux dont on ne vient à bout qu'en les fatiguant. Alors elle revient séverement sur les productions du génie; elle conserve ce qui est l'effet du véritable enthousiasme, elle proscrit ce qui est l'ouvrage de la fougue, & c'est ainsi qu'elle fait éclorre les chefs-d'oeuvre. Quel écrivain, s'il n'est pas entierement dépourvû de talent & de goût, n'a pas remarqué que dans la chaleur de la composition une partie de son esprit reste en quelque maniere à l'écart pour observer celle qui compose & pour lui laisser un libre cours, & qu'elle marque d'avance ce qui doit être effacé?][24]

Thus, when Agnesina interprets Zon-zon's *genio* as leading to entrapment, she implicitly summons Reason as a reliable preventative to the damaging effects of runaway personal caprice. Reason functions as a necessary means of moral discrimination and discipline. In the form of monogamous relationship, it promises genuine freedom and individual dignity.[25]

The application of Reason to the institution of marriage (and its manifestation in spousal fidelity) had much to do with social realities of the eighteenth century. Agnesina's announcement to her prince that she would not tolerate multiple wives clearly raised the issue of adultery and concubinage, practices which, if not openly declared as a prerogative of the élites, were in certain circumstances covertly accepted as such.[26] Adulterous liaisons as part of the libidinous culture of *galanteria* came under fire by nearly all moralists and social critics. In terms of the bourgeois familial code, however, the disgrace of marital infidelity was largely imputed to patrician marriages of convenience, where gross mismatches between spouses were common. Unions based on political or economic gain typically conjoined partners whose incompatibility led—shamefully but understandably—to conjugal wandering. Guerci notes that many Italian writings promoting marital compatibility emphasized age conformity, given concerns (and expectations) that the younger member of a married couple very distant in years would "look elsewhere for more appetizing provisions."[27]

Agnesina's indignation referred also to the real threat of polygamy in eighteenth-century Europe, and indirectly, to debates on divorce.[28] Bigamy and polygamy occurred for a number of reasons, many of which can be traced to conjugal laws and procedures that for much of the period were extremely variegated and un-stable. Despite the efforts of Tridentine reformers to systematize matrimony, marital policies remained com-plex and ambiguous even through the eighteenth cen-tury. Divergences in the effective authority of canon law, secular civil law, and the socially sanctioned rights of individual *paterfamilias* resulted in "conflicts, disrup-tions and anxieties that led men to break their promises of marriage, parents to enforce their authority over dis-obedient daughters, husbands to beat their wives and married or adulterous women to abandon the conjugal household."[29] A plethora of marriage formation possi-bilities (clandestine, morganatic, secret, surprise, and false, among others) both contributed to and resulted from this situation.[30] Attempts to regularize the insti-tution were made from mid-century on, but not until the nineteenth century did the legal chaos around mar-ital law and contracts begin to diminish.[31]

Agnesina's stress on faithfulness suggests yet an-other tenet of the middle-class marriage paradigm, the possibility of sexual satisfaction in matrimony. Xunchìa's recitative, wherein she alludes to the sexual enticements in which (it is supposed) Chinese women are accomplished, not only evokes the idea of esoteric bedroom tricks ("l'arte più scaltra"), but also inscribes woman in the universe of pleasure:

Xunchìa. Nature teaches us
The caresses, the loving ways, even skills
To delight the man we adore.
All that I can tell you
Is that you must learn the more crafty tricks
So Zon-zon will never take to another.
(3, 7)

[Xunchìa. Insegna la natura
Le tenerezze, i vezzi, e l'arte ancora
Per allettar un uom quando s'adora.
Solo vi posso dire
Che dovete studiar l'arte più scaltra,
Acciò a Zon-zon giammai non piaccia
un'altra.]

Even if veiled, Xunchìa's mysterious and titillating words suggest at least the potential of women's sexual passion and agency. Likewise, Agnesina's imperative that Zon-zon commit to her alone does not imply per-force that theirs will be a passionless marriage. His quick compliance together with the qualities of their musical piece following raises the possibility of a mu-tually rewarding sexual relationship.

Xunchìa's knowledge about womanly sexual ex-pertise cuts in two directions, however. It functions in

opposition to the bourgeois feminine principle when one recalls that she is Chinese, and the opera assigns to the three Chinese women—in stark contrast to Ag-nesina—negative characteristics with respect to their gender. Here it is helpful to recall the observation that "buffa plots abound with interrogations of woman's nature, and . . . convey an almost obsessive interest in woman's sexual weakness."[32] *L'inimico delle donne* uses the Chinese women in relation to Agnesina to illus-trate the range of feminine morality, from bad to good. Xunchìa's inference about Chinese women's talents in the boudoir align her with a libertine lifestyle, which the Italian woman staunchly rejects. In the first act, contiguous scenes starring the Chinese maidens func-tion as a compendium of womanly defects, as they of-fer themselves to the prince's inspection. Each sings an aria in which she vaunts her attributes. Zyda be-gins, with verse that places her squarely in the camp of libertine women:

Zyda. I am a poor,
rather modest girl,
I am blushingly shy.

If we were here alone . . .
Then I would tell you . . .
Then . . . I would show you
That I'm worthy of love.
(1, 8)

[Zyda. Io sono poverina,
Ragazza modestina,
Son piena di rossor.

Se fossimo qua soli . . .
Allora vi direi . . .
Allor . . . vi mostrerei
Che degna son d'amor.]

Zon-zon fastens not only on her hypocrisy, but also on her wanton ways:

Zon-zon. You wish to pass yourself off
as rather modest. Yes. All women
are quick to blush, but then I see them
commit all sorts of deviltry and even worse.
(1, 8)

[Zon-zon. Tu spacciarti vorresti
Per modestina. Sì. Tutte le donne
Son piene di rossor, ma poi le veggo
Far il diavolo a quattro e ancor di peggio.]

Similarly, following the arias of the other two rivals, he ticks off their defects in short order. When Xunchìa flaunts her beauty and brains, the prince answers that she's not as beautiful as she thinks and needs to grow in wisdom. The youngest of the trio, Kam-si, takes advantage of her youth, calling the prince's attention to her purity and innocence:

> Kam-si.   If you are pleased with me
> I have no grand qualities.
> I'm but a lass; but wait,
> And my intelligence will grow.
>
> I promise you only this
> As I have a sincere heart.
> A poor, simple girl am I . . .
> Come now, take pity on me.
>
>   (1, 8)

> [Kam-si.   Se di me vi contentate
> Io non ho gran qualità.
> Son fanciulla; ma aspettate,
> Che il mio ingegno crescerà.
>
> Questo solo vi prometto,
> Che sincero ho il cor nel petto.
> Poverina, semplicina . . .
> Deh, movetevi a pietà.]

But Zon-zon senses a devious nature behind her claims of guilelessness. "You are not simple; under that / innocent semblance / there's all manner of slyness, visible even now" (1, 8) ("Semplice tu non sei; ma sotto quella / Innocente sembianza / V'è tanta furberia che già n'avanza"). The cortége of women facilitates a sort of extended catalogue aria on unbecoming feminine vices. Agnesina, on the other hand, as the opera's heroine, does not deviate throughout from her virtues of honesty and goodness.

Several scenes in act 2 show a conflict between Chinese and Italian cultures with respect to sincerity and the possibility of friendship between women. When Agnesina arrives on the scene she greets the women with hugs, to which they respond with amazement and suspicion.

> Xunchìa.   Among us women
> We often embrace
> When in our hearts we hide
> Disdain, deceit, and venom.
> . . . .
> Are women in Italy
> Liars perhaps?
>
>   (2, 2)

> Xunchìa.   [Tra noi le Donne
> Ben sovente s'abbracciano
> Quando covano in seno

> Il dispetto, la frode ed il veleno.
> . . . .
> In Italia le Donne
> Sono forse bugiarde?]

Agnesina counters Xunchìa's distrust noting that sincerity is the pride of Italian women. This then leads into a bit of funny business, when the Italian is put to the test and asked to judge the beauty of the Chinese maidens. Since the opera has earlier made the native women out to be ugly, Agnesina must apply all the diplomacy in her power to reply kindly. Her sincerity in this instance is undercut for comic effect, but overall, Agnesina diverges from the Chinese trio in terms of her strong moral and physical graces—qualities which naturally gain her the greatest prize, the love of Prince Zon-zon.

In its instrumentalization of China to embody realities that work against the bourgeois ideal for women, *L'inimico delle donne* has thus far cast the Middle Kingdom in terms of vices associated with the nobility (adultery, polygamy, libertine sexual practices) and with women (dissimulation, sexual wantonness, intellectual lack). Arching over all of these representations, however, is that of China offered in the figure of the prince himself. Zon-zon's—and by extension, all men's—misogyny constitutes another challenge to the bourgeois woman desirous of a peaceful domestic life with a spouse.

Agnesina's ability to vanquish male obstinacy is assimilable to the power of successful heroines in other comic dramas that turn on misogyny, but her power is greater. She doesn't need wiles, as did the conniving chambermaid Serpina in *La serva padrona* (1733), nor does she need a higher masculine authority to step in and correct the bad behavior, as did the noblewoman Lucinda in *Il re alla caccia* (1763).[33] Her power is also more impactful when one carefully examines the nature of Zon-zon's resistance. Ronald J. Rabin distinguishes between male comic operatic protagonists who portray misogyny as an inevitable and unalterable fact, and those who fall into it only momentarily and by accident, suggesting that it can (and should) be avoided.[34] Figaro, for example, belongs to the latter group. His antipathy toward women sprouts only in the final moments of *Le nozze*, when a misunderstanding leads him to doubt Susanna's honesty. Textually and musically, Rabin notes, the opera treats his eleventh-hour venom as a "lapse," a "misstep"—a temporary loss of that nobility of spirit that ordinarily keeps Figaro elevated above the debased clown figure and that much more interesting as a character.[35] Susanna is able to rehabilitate her wayward fiancé, and therein lies her ultimate triumph at the opera's end. In light of Rabin's paradigm, *L'inimico* seems to present a third type of misogynist, that is, the long-term woman-hater who is treatable by woman's intercession. Or, if Zon-zon is relegated to Rabin's first category, Agnesina's power is truly transformative. Her capacity to change Zon-zon's mind not only about women in general, but also with regard to his behavior as a husband, has the feel of a conversion given the embeddedness of his beliefs. *L'inimico* thus presents its heroine's power to correct misogynistic mindsets more emphatically than in similarly themed operas. Agnesina doesn't simply rectify a temporary slip, but extirpates an ingrained habit. The authority of the modern bourgeois feminine ideal (Italian) rises above the erring, outmoded, prejudicial gender ideology of anyone, whatever his class, who scorns women (Chinese).

China, in its vestiges in the last half of the opera, embodies the challenging social and moral terrain that honest, upstanding young women must traverse in order to fully come of age. In this sense it is the opposite of feminized foreign terrain that requires domestication and/or mastering by a masculine agent. Polygamy and misogyny are committed by men, after all, not women. China is revealed to be a misleading, illusory place, as its utopian image gives way to that of a false land of promise, one that Agnesina had risked taking at face value. *L'inimico delle donne* teaches that women, as proper exponents of their gender, must know how to read society properly. The importance of knowing how to accurately read one's surroundings emerges at the very beginning of the opera, in scenes which showcased Geminiano's ineptitude at comprehending the culture before him.[36] Of course, as the *buffo caricato* character, his stupidity is part and parcel of his dramatic function. However, Geminiano's errors also highlight China's complexity, underscoring the need for intelligence in social "travelers," as well as the significance of Agnesina's gradual, judicious self-mentoring. As the Italian girl comes into her own as a bourgeois woman, her earlier penchant to adapt stops. When in the first act Zon-zon announces a wine custom different from the Italian norm, Geminiano rebels, but Agnesina propitiates: "Here it's best to adapt ourselves / to the country's usage / without argument" (1, 13) ("Qua convien senza contese / All'usanza del paese / Adattarci"). Two acts later a very different Agnesina confronts Chinese usages.

The discussion of the Italian *sposa*'s evolution must consider the issue of social class. The confident woman who delimits her betrothed's marital behavior at the opera's end clearly belongs to a sector beneath the aristocracy. At no point in the drama does Agnesina boast royal or noble origins. Her exact social station is actually somewhat misty. Apart from a line or two about their cash-strapped situation, no other textual clues speak to her uncle's status or profession. His buffo antics assimilate him to the clowning peasant or servant character, but his non-dialect, middle-range linguistic traits lift him from purely plebeian ranks. The greatest indicator of the Italians' middle-class collocation lies in the tenor of Agnesina's recitative and lyrical items, which in turn are interdependent with her function as moral arbiter.[37] Like Cecchina in Goldoni's *La buona figliuola*, the heroine of *L'inimico delle donne* "is suspended between the upper and lower classes" and thus partakes in the tradition wherein middle classes model a new morality to both superior and inferior ranks.[38]

Unlike Cecchina, however, to whom Goldoni gave extraordinary character appeal but no substantive moral message, Agnesina is a more didactic protagonist.[39] In *La buona figliuola*, Goldoni suppressed the canonical reward granted to virtuous maidens, i.e., social advancement, since Cecchina is revealed at the opera's end to be equal in rank to her aristocratic suitor.[40] Bertati's low- to middle-class Italian maiden, on the other hand, *is* compensated for her goodness with marrying up. Not only does she win the prince, but she also prevails over the Chinese aspirant Xunchìa, ward of the royal steward Si-sin. Also, in its figuration of Agnesina's psychological dominance over Zon-zon, *L'inimico delle donne* grants an authority to bourgeois women that surpasses that demonstrated by any Goldonian heroine.[41] One can ascribe the increase in authority in part to the times, inasmuch as later decades of the eighteenth century saw a more definitive expression of the bourgeois feminine ideal. Where mid-century operas about the trials of virtuous women moralized that "circumstances can *sometimes* allow natural love to be fulfilled in marriage," *L'inimico* binds marriage *exclusively* to natural (mutual, monogamous) love (italics mine).[42] Agnesina essentially holds Zon-zon hostage to the new morality, and thus demonstrates the more secure footing that bourgeois ideology had attained by the 1770s. She also indicates progressiveness on the part of Bertati, since many of what are considered the most categorical eighteenth-century operatic elaborations of bourgeois womanhood hail from the 1780s and '90s.[43]

Despite its instructive promotion of the bourgeois domestic ethic for women, however, *L'inimico* evidences some ambiguity about the project. Agnesina's acquired subjectivity as proper Italian wife, substantiated by her refusal to tolerate "Chinese" marital practices, does not develop entirely unproblematized. As mentioned above, she does not capitulate to love nearly as quickly nor in as pronounced a fashion as Zon-zon. By the end of act 1 Zon-zon has begun to sense stirrings of love (1, 11); midway through the second act he sings an aria on the inner torment he feels but still cannot explain (2, 7); in 2, 9 he has decided to take the Italian girl as a wife, and in 2, 11 he recognizes that he loves her. This single scene demonstrates his definitive turn to love, since in it he acknowledges that Agnesina possesses a different quality from other women he's known, he declares his love to her, and he admits his error in hating women: "It seems that Nature / now scolds me / for being an enemy to your sex" (2, 11) ("Mi par che la natura / Mi rimproveri adesso / S'io già vissi nemico al vostro sesso"). The correctness of his new attitude comes to the fore as he sings a love aria. Following the aria and still in the same scene, Zon-zon announces joyfully to his servants and officials that he's chosen his mate. He doesn't divulge her identity to them yet, but in an aside to Agnesina he avers that she is the reason for his "sweet jubilation" ("dolce giubilar").

Strangely, Agnesina does not respond to any of these professions of love. Zon-zon's repentance, his aria, and his whispered adoration are met with silence. Earlier in the same scene, Agnesina sings an aria registering her own heart pains and confusion, but unlike the prince, she does not connect her agitation with love. They have a brief angry skirmish; Agnesina is reduced to tears, which precipitates Zon-zon's remorse and outpouring of love. The only textual confirmation of Agnesina's softening occurs when the prince tells her he fears she is still full of antipathy for men. She replies: "Ah! I'm beginning to understand that it's craziness" (2, 11) ("Ah! Comincio a capir ch'è una pazzia").

And yet, even after the momentous change of Zon-zon's heart, Agnesina still is not sure of her feelings. In the idol scene in which Geminiano as the deity authorizes Zon-zon's choice of bride (2, 13), she again confides to the prince that she doesn't understand the unfamiliar sensations in her heart. He tells her they are signs that their marriage will be a happy union, and once more she does not answer. In fact, Agnesina makes no further declaration of her feelings for the prince even when, dressed as a Chinese bride in 3, 6, she awaits her official marriage to him.[44]

Zon-zon meanwhile has recanted a second time, telling Xunchìa he's cured of his antipathy toward women (3, 4). He then orders Xunchìa to teach his betrothed the charms and arts becoming a loving wife,

since in his words, Agnesina is still "rozza" (clumsy, unpolished). He wonders how he will feel with a woman who is no longer "sprezzante" (contemptuous), but "amante" (loving), anticipating a more affectionate Agnesina once she has been schooled by Xunchìa. Zon-zon's characterization of his Italian consort plainly suggests that she is less overcome by the force of love than he is. Without knowledge of actual stage movements and gesture, one can only surmise the meaning of Agnesina's silences. Her reticence could have served to show her deference to the workings of love, and that, like a true *ingénue*, her virtue consists in quiet, humble compliance. On the other hand, it hints at possible ambivalence about the process of bourgeois commitment. Textually, Agnesina comes into her own only when she confronts the polygamy issue, in the lovers' duet of the opera's penultimate scene (3, 8).

Again however, even this duet contains certain lyrics that lace the couple's rapture with doubt. As soon as Zon-zon vows to love only Agnesina ("Sola, sola io v'amerò!"), they sing the following stanza in unison:

> I don't know what
> This new feeling is:
> The closer I get to you
> The more I feel bound
>
> (3, 8)
>
> [Non intendo cosa sia
> Questo nuova simpatia:
> Quanto a voi più m'avvicino
> Più mi sento a vincolar]

Together they express both awe at the new feeling overtaking them, and a sense of tightening. The latter sentiment is enough in fact to stop them in their stage movement toward one another. Stage directions indicate "They stay close a short while," but then they sing "Let's separate a bit," as they pull away from each other. Love draws them close again, and they unite once more, singing in unison that ". . . I can't stay far away."

> [Discostiamoci un pochino . . .
> . . . .
> lontano non posso star.]

Here again, however, short lines by each lover cast an air of indeterminacy over the scene:

> *Zon-zon.*   Enough, enough.
> *Agnesina.*   Now I understand.

In unison.	We've arrived: our hearts are now wounded by love.

(3, 8)

[*Zon-zon.* Basta, basta.
Agnesina. Già ho capito.
a due. Noi ci siamo: già ferito
È d'amore il nostro cor.]

It is difficult to know whether to read the lovers' lyrics solely as happy surrender to the novel and irresistible force of love, or as underpinned with sarcasm, the pinpricks of "reality" popping the balloon of spousal bliss. What has Zon-zon had enough of, distance from his beloved, or marital intimacy? Being ordered around by a wife? What exactly has Agnesina figured out? Does the "wound of love" which afflicts each of them delight or hurt? The minimalism of the words "basta" and "già ho capito" belies their power to undermine the preceding sentimentality. These throwaway lines might well imply that nothing has changed, that life will go on as always—that is, that Zon-zon will soon revive the archetype of intolerant, belittling husband, and Agnesina that of powerless, victimized wife. The position of such potentially cynical taglines is key, right at the end of the opera's most fulgent expression of bourgeois love (the duet) and just before the enactment of their matrimony. It furthermore raises the question of how much weight to give the outcome of a literary or dramatic work, in relation to its other elements and sections.[45] Can one still consider the joyous marriage conclusion and Agnesina's confident assertion of monogamy the primary message of Bertati's libretto?

Charles Ford's analysis of the sexual politics of Mozart's famous comic opera triad offers a helpful interpretative tool at this juncture.[46] According to Ford, the Enlightenment figured gender difference in accordance with its foundational dualism, the "clear . . . distinction between belief [together with feeling, sensibility, desire, instinct] and . . . empirical reason."[47] Binding femininity to the former, and masculinity to the latter resolved a major conundrum of Enlightenment morality, the ineluctable conflict between subjective or individual freedom and objective contingency. To put it another way, despite the Enlightenment's aspirations as to the exercise of Pure Reason, individual subjects could not autonomously "reason upon" other subjects, as if they were non-subjective objects.[48] Establishing the duality of feeling and rational thought, and attaching it to gender, helped mediate the dilemma between Self and Other. However, as Ford notes, women are left "framed" by

this formulation: "Men hold the theoretical, but wholly unreal, promise of scientific moral freedom—to poke, prod, and measure—whilst women, their entire sensibilities irredeemably bound to the vacillations of 'natural' desire, can only be the servants of their whims, or rather, their men."[49] Mozart's *Così fan tutte* affirms this divergence, figuring it as the contrast between (feminine) intention and (masculine) fact: women wish and intend to be faithful, but thanks to their unchangeable natures, simply cannot. In the opera and in the world, women's innate moral frailty, understood as something over which they have no real control, serves both as a foil, to positively highlight men's rationalist potential, and as an explanation for the inevitable failure of that same male potential to fully realize itself. As such, feminine weakness was crucial, indeed, necessary, to Enlightenment epistemological conceptualization and experience.[50]

The interdependent relation between intention and fact can be extended to *L'inimico*. It leads, however, to less misogynist and hermetic conclusions. Agnesina and Prince Zon-zon intend to live the bourgeois ideal, but—as their taglines discussed above subtly insinuate—they may likely fall short of it. Unlike *Così fan tutte*, *Inimico* does not map this disjuncture necessarily onto gender. Here *both* lovers are caught in the slippage between desire and reality. In addition, Bertati's text is less specific as to what drives the wedge between the good intention of the bourgeois gender prescription, and actual marital experience. It cannot be woman's essential nature, since *Inimico* separates women into different categories of greater and lesser virtue. Are men to blame, given that Zon-zon has had to be so severely reined in by a good woman? The discussion above has focused on the aristocracy's corrupt sexual hijinks as chief nemesis of bourgeois reasoned morality, but might the opera also hint at the failure of the ideal itself? Do the moments of ambiguity cast doubt on the feasibility of the moral contract in general, or on its inadequacies for women more so than for men?

The ambivalence at the edges of *L'inimico delle donne* acquires strength from those parts of the libretto that assimilate China and Europe. Certain of these relativistic moments are quite overt. When the prince laughs at the Europeans' powdered wigs, Agnesina observes that "Italy too is like the whole world / It has its good, its bad, its beauty and its ugliness" (1, 10). Zyda universalizes in a sentence aria directed to Agnesina, in which she states that no woman can tolerate another woman's beauty:

Don't think only Chinese women
are so vain:
Because in truth
We are the same in all countries.

(2, 2)

[Né crediate così vane
Solamente le Chinesi:
Perchè in tutti li paesi
Siamo uguali in verità.]

The comparative project continues in the women's perceptions of their maltreatment by men: Agnesina complains of the strictures of marriage to tyrant husbands, while the Chinese women wish their men privileged their wives in the ways European men do (2, 3).

The drive to universalize was ubiquitous in Enlightenment thinking. In an exotic work like *L'inimico delle donne*, it turns China into another Europe, and vice versa. Things are the same the world over; young women and men must learn the right lessons no matter where they're born. When Geminiano exhorts Agnesina to "Make these courtiers love you!" he infers a parallel between Chinese gentlemen and their European counterparts, and thus collapses the distance between the two cultures. The significance of the leveling moments in *L'inimico* is that they weaken the representation of China as either utopia or dystopia. This in turn destabilizes the bourgeois ideology positioned in relation to those constructs.

Within its apparent celebration of the bourgeois model for femininity then, *L'inimico delle donne* also expresses some misgivings. It puts forth a somewhat misanthropic view that is at the same time sympathetic to women. Unlike the protagonists of many other exotic theater works, who at the termination of their adventures quit the hostile foreign territory, Agnesina becomes a Chinese bride. She and Zon-zon will remain in the Celestial Kingdom, a region of familiar and unfamiliar challenges. The Italian woman has laid down the law to her new husband as far as married sexual license is concerned. Yet when her Chinese prince introduces her to his people with these words: "How beautiful, genteel, and well-mannered she is / Following the custom of the country" (3, 9) ("Com'è bella, gentile e manierosa. / Seguitando il costume del Paese"), one is reminded that she has had to—and will continue to have to—adjust to the ways of the strange country. That the strange land is, in the end, one's own home in a moment of profound transformation, now seems the most functional reading of the opera.

The ideological strain in *L'inimico* corresponds with contentious viewpoints in contemporary tracts and public discourse on women. Tommaso Campastri's *La felicità del matrimonio* (1760) presented a fairly liberal view of women's role in marriage, and was reinforced by Melchiorre Delfico's *Saggio filosofico sul matrimonio* (1774), which credited women's wisdom and sensitivity with making them "the linchpin of social stability and happiness."[51] But the same years saw the publication of the century's most brutal and misogynist assessments of women, namely Ferdinando Galiani's *Croquis d'un dialogue sur les femmes* (1772), and the reissue of Antonio Conti's *Lettera dell'Abate Conti . . .* (1773).[52] As Rebecca Messbarger observes, even the most apparently approbatory works contain troublesome contradictions, which betray "the ambivalence at the heart of all Enlightenment discourse about women and their centrality to a properly constituted public sphere."[53]

CONCLUSION

Agnesina's and Prince Zon-zon's capitulation to one another demonstrates the ineluctable power of love and its ideal resolution in monogamous marriage. Since she is portrayed as more resistant to love than the prince, *L'inimico delle donne* suggests that women have a more difficult time conforming and acceding to marriage. The wedding conclusion, of course, is a fixture in comic theatrical works, but *L'inimico* speaks also to women's experience once married. It presents the possibility that husbands, including or especially titled ones, may not be so princely in their comportment. The fact that Agnesina appears so effective in setting her future consort straight in terms of his marital behavior implies that women not only possess the power to enforce moral law with their spouses, but also, that they should actively implement that power. Such is the bourgeois manifesto for women, which animates what looks superficially to be a spare, relatively banal operatic plot line.

Bertati's deployment of China to dramatize the delicate negotiation required of the ideal bourgeois woman takes advantage of a range of expedients regarding the exotic. Thanks to the century's fascination with the Celestial Empire, *L'inimico* could exploit both its utopic and dystopic traits. Figuring China initially as a civilized paradise helped romanticize Agnesina's girlish hopes for freedom and self-reliance. Recasting China as a site of sexual and moral deviation showed the misguidedness of such feminine freedoms, and more importantly, facilitated Agnesina's development into proper bourgeois womanhood, where good wives know the right ways in which to rein in their husbands. The choral ending contains a paean to Prince Zon-zon and men like him, that is, those who give up their distaste for women and learn to love — correctly — the opposite sex:

> *Chorus.* Long live noble Zon-zon,
> Lord of the Land;
> And long live those who know
> How to sincerely love women.
>
> (3, 9)

> [*Coro.* Viva Zon-zon cortese,
> Signore del Paese;
> E viva chi le donne
> Sa di buon cor amar.]

Given the emphasis of the opera, however, it would seem that these lines actually speak more meaningfully to women: "Long live those women who know how to (make themselves) be loved." Through Agnesina, *L'inimico delle donne* models how one becomes first a marriage candidate, and then a morally scrupulous wife who brings honor to her gender.

Finally, the China presented as analogous to the travelers' homeland constitutes the site for the opera's final lesson on the bourgeois familial ideal. With its ethical and domestic provocations, the Middle Kingdom is not much different from the Italian society Agnesina originally attempted to flee. Like all comic operas, *L'inimico delle donne* teaches that there is no escape from social responsibility, and that both sexes must compromise to achieve and maintain social stability. Unlike all comic operas, however, *L'inimico* reveals some of the tension underlying the bourgeois resolution. As the "gentler sex" enters a formidable foreign culture, i.e., the eighteenth-century gender mandate that girls grow gracefully into loving wives and then patrol-guards of familial virtue, women take on the lion's share of the compromise. For them, the inescapable destiny to which Agnesina referred in the opera's early scenes entails a challenging journey indeed.

Conclusion

THE CHINA OPERAS AT THE HEART OF THIS STUDY are not the product of efforts to get to know the other for the other's sake. On the other hand, their spectacular chinoiserie did not amount to mere effect or decoration. More was at stake than, as some critics have put it, a "papier-mâché Orient," or an "exotic backdrop," against which the same old stories took on a newer, fresher look.[1] The ubiquitous presence of Chinese culture in Settecento Italy, and the wealth of information and ideas which circulated about the Middle Kingdom, allowed for notable specificity in operatic representation. Operas, in turn, instrumentalized this information in discrete and productive ways. Not only did well-defined perceptions of Chinese civilization lead to opera's mobilizations of it to avail particular cultural processes, but in eighteenth-century Italy, home to a heterogeneous collection of political, geographical, social, and economic entities, a greater number of diverse elaborations ensued than in other European states.

The Celestial Empire's identity as heir to a supremely venerable heritage allowed for its use by those advocating Italy's return to the solid intellectual and literary foundations of the classical past. Arcadians like Apostolo Zeno represented China in *Teuzzone* to evoke not only the significance of ancient origins, and in particular his own culture's Greco-Roman ancestry, but also the centrality of that legacy to literary achievement. For other early eighteenth-century librettists, like Antonio Salvi, China offered a model of tolerance, pacifism, and levelheadedness, in contrast to the bellicose impulses of less civilized times, and vital to the preservation of the contemporary dynastic state. Salvi's *Il Tartaro nella Cina* spoke also on behalf of peace in the war torn atmosphere of the European succession wars. China could further be wielded to swing the balance in heroic opera from its "heroism" to its less serious, more sentimental side. Domenico Lalli does this in *Camaide, l'imperatore della Cina*, where playful aspects of the opera's love story come to the fore via the addition of "boudoir chinoiserie" within the arc of the drama. Urbano Ricci's *Taican, rè della Cina* demonstrates the least ideologically based mobilization of the Celestial Kingdom. This opera blends China with other Asian cultures in its heady mix of fantasy and the *romanzesco*, epigone of the "untamed" *dramma per musica* of the Seicento.

The Jesuit panegyric of the Middle Kingdom is unstintingly dramatized in Pietro Metastasio's *L'eroe cinese*. In particular, this opera mobilizes the idea of a Christianized populace as prime mover of the enlightened absolute monarchy. Dutiful subjects, Confucius-like in their humility and obedience, and paralleled in the figure of the compliant and ever-loyal state functionary, prove to be the backbone of the new, reform-minded kingdom.

The comic operas make use of still more varied permutations of the Chinese. In the ongoing battle between *Anciennes* and *Modernes*, *tradizionalisti* and *riformisti*, the Celestial Empire serves a multitude of purposes. In *L'isola disabitata*, Carlo Goldoni figures China as hopelessly stuck and enfeebled, much like the Venetian old guard (and all European factions opposed to economic modernization), over which he envisions the victory of a progressive, commerce-savvy *borghesia*. Giambattista Lorenzi's *L'idolo cinese* positions China as a threat, on two fronts. Its spurious religious traditions deter its society from advancement, as its radical governmental policies create total havoc. "Radical" here refers to the Chinese system of political meritocracy, lauded by reform-minded Europeans, but problematic for entrenched players in the old regime. Lorenzi marshals perceptions of China that serve different, and often opposing, Neapolitan identities: anti-Jesuit, anticlerical, and anti-reform. Finally, Giovanni Bertati in *L'inimico delle donne* makes China the moving target in the search for proper gender paradigms. Specifically, Chinese culture functions to delimit the ethos of ideal bourgeois womanhood. First appearing as a no-war zone in the battle of the sexes, the Middle Kingdom then becomes a Babylon of moral challenges, not unlike European society itself, which the virtuous *ingénue* must learn to rise above.

168

PIETRO METASTASIO, *LE CINESI* (1735, 1754)

Should there be any doubt about whether librettists, their sponsors, and their audiences participated in the codification of China to promote or polemicize particular identities, a look at one last opera should suffice to dispel such thoughts. On the surface, Metastasio's *Le cinesi,* a one-act *festa teatrale* with music by Antonio Caldara, looks like one of the more shallow exoticist exercises. Commissioned by the empress Elizabeth in 1735 as part of the carnival festivities at Charles IV's court in Vienna, Metastasio's work was to serve as a lead-in to a *ballo cinese* in which members of the royal family and their entourage would take part.[2] As commonly occurred in princely households, the poet was also charged with casting the young archduchesses Maria Teresa and her sister, Maria Anna. Given these directives and the strictly occasional nature of the production, it would seem likely that China played only a superficial role in Metastasio's invention. However, closer analysis will show that even here, by capitalizing on particular perceptions of the Celestial Kingdom, a discrete agenda could be served.

Set in an unspecified Chinese city, *Le cinesi* had three characters: young Chinese noblewomen who, as the opera begins, sit drinking tea in a room decorated in the Chinese taste ("ornata al gusto cinese").[3] Bored, they seek a diversion with which to while away the afternoon. They decide to put on an operatic piece, and to determine its subject, they agree to act out short scenes in each of the three principal dramatic styles: tragic, pastoral, and comic. Whichever genre most pleases will be chosen for their production. In turn then, each damsel provides a brief context for her scene, and sings an aria in the appropriate style. Besides vaunting the musical and textual virtuosity each aria mode might attain, the individual performances also allow for terse discussions of the poetics associated with the heroic, pastoral, and buffo operatic styles. While the women judge all three worthy, they also note potential pitfalls of each—a comic opera might insult an audience member who perceives his own defects reflected in a certain character, for example. In the end the women opt to undertake a *balletto.* The recitative preceding the final lyrical item states:

> Everyone enjoys a dance,
> everyone understands a dance;

[unlike a tragic *melodramma*] it does not incite tears,
[unlike a pastoral opera] it does not bore,
[unlike an opera buffa] it does not offend.

(353)[4]

> [Ognun ne gode,
> Ognun se ne intende;
> Non fa pianger, non secca e non offende.]

With the concluding musical trio, the actresses thus begin a *ballo cinese* in which the whole audience eventually joined.

As one might surmise from this synopsis, textual references to China in *Le cinesi* are extremely rare. Indeed, the only instance in which one of the women evokes her native land calls attention (rather indirectly) to the Chinese dress worn by the protagonists. Concerned that her costume does not suit her chosen genre and that this will negatively affect her performance, Tangia asks:

> Does it make any difference
> If my dress doesn't quite match?

(346)

> [E non importa al caso
> Se l'abito o non è corrispondente?]

Besides directing eyes to the young archduchess's gown, which must surely have been styled sumptuously *alla cinese,* this line also seems a sardonic side comment by Metastasio, on the topic of appropriate stage costume. Given the fact that the piece itself is predominantly a meditation on operatic genre, the question of aesthetic consistency looms prominently. (One may further recall his complaints about costume restrictions in the case of *L'eroe cinese,* where he was told to dress his neophyte divas properly, that is, in ladylike fashion.)

China thus far takes the stage in terms of the singers' apparel and their tea ware. It displays imperial women partaking in a most fashionable social vogue, tea drinking, and becomes an opportunity to foreground both the custom and the luxury goods. This first performance took place in the imperial apartments of the young princesses, which may have been decorated *alla cinese* even apart from the performance occasion.[5] Finally, the intimate spectacle dissolved into a Chinese masked ball, so that for a while, everyone hailed from the Celestial Kingdom. Little to this point suggests that *Le cinesi* constituted more than a delightful panel of Chinese silk draped over a lighthearted disquisition on opera genres, followed by a frivolous masquerade party.

However, in 1754 the Habsburg court revived *Le cinesi*, and the Chinese exotic resonated in deeper ways.[6] Christoph Gluck's music gave the libretto new life, and Metastasio added a fourth character, Silango, in the part of brother to the *prima donna*, Lisinga. Silango has just returned to China from a European journey and his role as world voyager accounts for much of the way the Middle Kingdom is now coded in *Le cinesi*. The comparativism applied to the operatic genres expands to include competing cultures on the European continent: now Vienna and the Habsburg empire (as China) go up against France and Italy (as Europe).

In keeping with the popular exoticist formula of the foreign observer, Silango has thoughts to impart about the lands to the West with respect to his native China. His comparatist comments are few—but perhaps for that reason it is important to take careful note of them. Silango remarks chiefly on European operatic theater, a cultural form he praises in contrast to its absence in his homeland. China does not know opera, he suggests, because of its provincial, cloistered ways. When Lisinga comes up with the idea of putting on dramatic representations, Silango notes:

> This art is common
> Only in European countries;
> Here in the east,
> Among us Chinese it is still foreign.
>
> (345)

> [E poi quest'arte
> Comune è sol negli Europei paesi;
> Ma qui verso l'aurora
> Fra noi Cinesi è pellegrina ancora.]

When the women discuss which dramatic subject to enact, Silango entreats: "Make it one of those / done on European stages" ("Sia di quegli usati / Su le scene europee"). In a few short lines of recitative he sets up a dichotomy between European operatic theater and its lack in China, an imagined no-man's-land in terms of dramatic achievements. Those who had read Du Halde would have known of China's tradition of musical plays, and that the Jesuit author and others roundly criticized the quality of Chinese theater arts. Moreover, Metastasio's contemporary and very successful opera *L'eroe cinese* (1752) had had clear ties with the Chinese drama contained in Du Halde's work. Thus there was a basis (and built-in tension as well) for using China as a contrasting term in a discussion of European operatic drama. As will be seen however, the question of the worthiness of Chinese stage arts quickly disappears. The real business of the revived *Le cinesi* is to trumpet opera's glory, and to shine attention on the Habsburg court's unique achievements in the genre.

The merit of opera and its connections with dance comprise a principal argument of *Le cinesi*, both in its original and reprised versions. Its expositional discourse with respect to the diverse dramatic types, and its showcasing of the different aria genres, make clear that it is an opera about opera. The addition of a fourth and male voice only enriched the overall quality of the work, as it allowed for a bit of love business between Silango and his sister's friend Sivene, which in turn made room for the performance of yet a fourth aria mode (the amorous). When added to the women's soprano and contralto voices, Silango's tenor also facilitated a stronger closing ensemble in Gluck's composition.

When Silango counters European opera with the Chinese lack thereof, he casts the Middle Kingdom as a site that does not understand, value, or perhaps even permit musical drama, an art form in which the continent far to the west excels. Lisinga refines the antithesis, however. Scolding Silango after he has ridiculed the women's alarm over his presence in their quarters, she sings:

> Remember, here we aren't
> On the Seine or the Po . . .
> . . . and there's no one more comical
> Than you, when you take on
> The authority of reforming customs.
>
> (344–45)

> [Pensa che qui non siamo
> Su la Senna o sul Po . . .
> . . . e che non v'è soggetto
> Più comico di te, quando t'assumi
> L'autorità di riformar costumi.]

Lisinga elides Europe with France, or more precisely, Paris (on the Seine), and Italy, or more specifically northern Italy and its cultivated metropolises Venice and Milan (on the Po). This correspondence makes it possible that China, far to the east of "Europe," can be understood as aligned with east-lying Vienna and the Habsburg empire. These are the real coordinates on the opera's map.

The moral context that Lisinga evokes ratifies these identifications. Her admonishing her brother to protect the modesty of Chinese (Viennese) women from the libertine behaviors endemic to Europe (France and Italy) was not only a commonplace, but also fully accords with the Austrian monarchy's conservatism and strict Catholic culture. In the context of the opera universe, however, the idea that France and Italy far surpass Vienna strikes the height of irony. Not only could Vienna boast one of the most highly accomplished opera cultures in Europe, refulgent with Italian talents, but also, at just this moment, the most authoritative local figures in theatrical music and spectacle had launched an intensive reform program focused especially on opera. These reforms centered on the incorporation of French approaches to spoken and musical drama, especially those deemed successful in French ballet and *opéra-comique*. The desire for spectacles that were more fluid and simple, with better acting and a more integral blending of music and drama, included rejecting those aspects of Italian opera (and opera seria in particular) that had begun to seem overly grandiose and artificial. The timing of the mid-century rendition of *Le cinesi* coincides exactly with the early years of the campaign that would culminate in the famous Viennese theatrical reforms of the 1760s: that of ballet by Gluck and Gasparo Angiolini, and that of opera by Gluck and Ranieri Calzabigi.[7]

So, while the women's characterization of the returned-traveler Silango as a fad-driven, fashion-obsessed French dandy was routine in theater and fiction of the eighteenth century, it also pointed to the concerted importation of well-regarded French modes into the world of Viennese spectacle, up to then dominated by Italians.[8] Lisinga's reproof further functions as a reminder of the importance of discrimination. That is, one must know which "foreign" customs and innovations merit appropriation. When at the end of the piece the group settles on a dance rather than the dramatic performances, Lisinga remarks:

> Someone might say:
> "I find nothing new here";
> But that which is done well is always new.
>
> (353)
>
> [Può dir qualcuno:
> "Novità nella scelta io non ritrovo";
> Ma quel che si fa bene è sempre nuovo.]

She emphasizes the ability to do things well, and to distinguish from among diverse novelties those which should be assayed or discarded. These exchanges remind spectators of the criteria that should be, and, it is inferred, were being applied to the Viennese opera scene. They underscore the efforts of the monarchy's theater leadership to discern and negotiate the "best practices" from Italian and French opera traditions, in the interests of producing the best possible spectacle.

The court-sponsored 1754 production of *Le cinesi* was still very Italian-oriented, given Metastasio's tex-

tual lyricism, the provenance of the singers (Roman sisters Caterina and Francesca Gabrielli among them), and its subject matter, the canonically Italian dramatic/operatic categories of the tragic, comic, and pastoral.[9] However, the playfulness and witticism of the Parisian *opéra-comique* surfaced in Gluck's composition, especially in his "skilful parody of French manners" in the scenes involving the returned traveler Silango.[10] In addition, the work's emphasis on dance, as superior to the three debated opera types, and as an art form that, even if old, could be performed well (i.e., if presented in innovative, reformed ways), plainly evokes the contemporary transformation of old ballet traditions into the new, richly developed *ballet en action*.[11] *Le cinesi* uses China in a vigorous nod to the theater reform programs underway that would soon lead to the great accomplishments of the Viennese opera. Vienna, a supposed "outlier" much like the Celestial Kingdom, ends up besting the "insiders," Europe's French and Italians, as it takes their stage triumphs to new, unseen and unheard-of heights.

In a larger context, Lisinga's sentiments in *Le cinesi* infer Habsburg wisdom and rectitude in other realms: which customs to assume, or to reject; which reforms to institute; which political and social avenues to take. Just as the sensible Chinese women in *Le cinesi* know which aspects of European culture to appropriate and which to steer clear of, the enlightened Austrian monarchy is savvy as to which "foreign" institutions, measures, and methods to adopt.

Le cinesi celebrates Habsburg opera patronage, and the eminence of Viennese courtly culture in general. Its winking presentation of China as a backward hinterland actually capitalizes on prevailing ideas of China as a brilliant empire. It identifies Vienna and the Habsburg realm—the easternmost European power—with the glories of the easternmost world kingdom.[12] *Le cinesi* constitutes a perfect example of how a seemingly banal deployment of Chinese accoutrements belies a more meaningful deployment of the Middle Kingdom. Not simply a trivial exotic embellishment, China in this opera functions as a crucial term in the promotion of Viennese opera and Habsburg power.

❧

The conclusion of this study will address once more the question of orientalism. The brief analysis above has shown a most strategic use of China: on the surface, as a stand-in for the isolated, uncultivated, unsophisticated outsider, ignorant of the exciting and reputedly desirable ways of the world. Then China's true nature is revealed, and the Chinese come to represent decency, good taste, stable foundations, and artistic brilliance: the attributes of a powerful, accomplished empire, just the kind the Austrian Habsburgs fancied themselves as being. That this self-image takes shape in relation to others (in this case the French and Italians), and in the interests of establishing power, is all-important. It raises the thinking about orientalism offered by Arif Dirlik, where "the issue is not orientalism; rather what is at stake is the implication for power . . . in different social and political contexts."[13]

Dirlik concurs with Said's notion that orientalism's sins lie in its "metonymic reductionism," the "portrayal of . . . societies in terms of some cultural trait or other, that homogenize[s] differences within individual societies, and [freezes] them in history."[14] He further sees orientalism evolving in time, insofar as in an early stage of capitalist modernization (i.e., the eighteenth and nineteenth centuries), the sins of the East/West paradigm were indeed perpetrated by Western societies on Asian nations. But as capitalism developed, the dynamic grew more complex, and orientalist practice outpaced geography. Asians themselves began to take part in orientalism, "self-orientalizing" when it benefited them, or "occidentalizing," i.e., making Euro-American culture the enemy, when convenient to different social, cultural, and political agendas.[15] A spectrum of different groups now participates in orientalism in new ways, ways in which place origins are no longer relevant. In the past, Dirlik states, orientalism "articulated a distancing of Asian societies from the Euro-American, [but it] now

appears in the articulation of differences within a global modernity . . . orientalism provides the site for contention between the conflicting ideologies of an elite that is no longer easily identifiable as Eastern or Western, Chinese or non-Chinese."[16] The conflicts of the elites inevitably gravitate around issues of power. Thus, one can, and many do, invent, instrumentalize, deterritorialize, re-territorialize, manipulate essentialisms—in short, practice orientalism (metonymic reductionism) to abet plays for power in various situations. Dirlik calls this newer condition "the reification of orientalism at the level of a global ideology."[17]

What is interesting, is that the new global orientalism Dirlik sees as developing after, and owing to, the more ethnic, territory-based orientalism of previous centuries, appears already operative in the eighteenth-century China operas. As the operas show so many "Chinese" characteristics appropriated by so many diverse Italian subcultures, they evidence the same articulation of "deterritorialized" differences that Dirlik attributes to a twentieth-century world. Might it be that what Dirlik sees as a defensive, and in some ways natural response to the disruptive consequences of globalized capitalism, that is, the proliferation of national and ethnic reification of cultures —our age's celebrated multiculturalism—has had an earlier genesis, in eighteenth-century Italy? Did appropriations of so many diverse kinds of "Chineseness" observable in the operas chiefly serve the rapidly growing number of new identities in the somewhat disconcerting global world of the Settecento? The Italian China operas present convincing evidence in the affirmative.

Appendix 1: List of Documented 18th-Century European Dramatic and Performed Works Featuring China

Note: It is impossible to establish with certainty the exact number and the titles of dramatic works based on China written and/or performed in the eighteenth century. Clarence D. Brenner explains the difficulties in the prefatory section of his *A Bibliographical List of Plays in the French Language 1700–1789* (Berkeley: n.p., 1947), iii–iv. Among the obstacles is the fact that many performances and/or texts were simply never documented. Some of those for which there exist references are yet to be found in manuscript or printed form, while archives remain that have not yet been perused. Add to these lacunas the fact that play titles were often changed for revivals, or for new venues, or, in the other direction, original titles were retained for heavily adjusted material. The possibility of a partial and simultaneously redundant inventory looms large; the list of works below likely falls prey to at least a few of these pitfalls.

It is also limited by certain deliberate choices. The chart does not include Jesuit theater which featured China, primarily because it was written and performed in Latin, and this study concerns itself with vernacular drama. Because the majority of eighteenth-century China dramas known to scholars were penned by Italian, French, and English theater writers, I have not attempted to account for the works of other European traditions. In making the chart I consulted the most reliable bibliographers of Italian, French, and English dramas and stage productions in the period; for France and England there exist works that attempt to enumerate the China dramas issuing from those countries, Guy and Clark, respectively. My French sources were Guy and Brenner; for England, Clark, Appleton, and Nicoll. For the Italian works I used Sartori and Mamcsarz principally, as well as histories of eighteenth-century theaters and theatrical dance. Cross-referencing was possible with the use of *Grove Music Online*, Oscar Sonneck's libretto catalogue, *Enciclopedia dello spettacolo*, and the unpublished but ongoing bibliography compiled by independent scholar Aaron Cohen. Where the work's author is listed as the source, the reader is directed to the primary sources in the bibliography.

Guy, combing through Brenner's long bibliography, notes approximately twenty-four China theater works by French authors, which he further divides into categories by dramatic genre (182 n7). However, he never identifies the individual works, so it is difficult to know which ones he considered vaudevilles, comédies, pantomimes, ballets, and the like. Given the rather porous boundaries among French theatrical genres, especially those labeled *opéra-ballet*, *comédie-ballet*, *opéra-comique*, *comédie*, *ballet-pantomime*, *divertissement*, *interméde*, *vaudevilles*, or simply *piéce*, trying to pin Guy's findings down has proven challenging. My own careful cross-referencing yields only twenty French works.

Italian, French, and English Theater Productions Featuring China Written and/or Performed in the Eighteenth Century

	Year first written or performed	Title	Genre	Author/ Choreographer	Composer	Place/date of premiere	First known publication	Source
1	ca. 1700	Le metamorfosi di Pulcinella	commedia dell'arte scenario	Father Placido Adriani	NA	Naples?	Selva, overo Zibaldone di concetti comici . . . 1734 Perugia, 1734, Biblioteca Augusta	Adriani
2	1700	Mascarade du roi de la Chine	mascarade	Anon.	André Danican Philidor, aîné	Marly, 7–8 Jan. 1700	Paris, 1700, Christophe Ballard	Brenner, Grove
3	1704	Le Prince de Cathay	entertainment	Nicolas de Malézieu	Jean-Baptiste Matho	Paris, Château de Chatenay, 16–17 Aug. 1704		Brenner, Grove
4	1704	The Biter	comedy	Nicholas Rowe	NA	London, Lincoln's Inn Fields	London, 1705, Jacob Tonson	Clark, Appleton, Nicoll
5	1706	Il Teuzzone	dramma per musica	Apostolo Zeno	Paolo Magni (Act 1); Clemente Monari (acts 2–3)	Milan, Teatro Regio Ducale, 1706	Milan, 1706, Marc Antonio Pandolfo Malatesta	Sartori
6	1707	Taican, rè della Cina	dramma per musica	Urbano Ricci	Francesco Gasparini	Venice, San Cassiano, 4 Jan. 1707	Venice, 1707, Marino Rossetti	Sartori
7	1707	Lisetta cinese e Astrobolo indiano	intermezzo in Taican rè della Cina	Conte N. H. Ludovico Vidimann	Francesco Gasparini	Venice, San Cassiano, 4 Jan. 1707	?	Mamczarz, Ericani "Impero"
8	1713	I Taimingi	tragedy	Pier Jacopo Martello	NA	Modena, Collegio dei Nobili, 1732	Teatro italiano di Pier Jacopo Martello, Rome, 1715	Martello
9	1713	Arlequin invisible chez le roi de Chine	one-act vaudeville piece	Alain-René Lesage	Jean-Claude Gillier	Paris, St. Laurent fair theater, 30 July 1713	Théâtre de la foire, t. 1, Paris, 1721	Brenner, Lesage TF
10	1715	Il Tartaro nella Cina	dramma per musica	Antonio Salvi	Francesco Gasparini	Teatro dell'illus- trissimo pubblico di Reggio, 1715	Reggio, 1715, Ippolito Vedrotti	Sartori
11	1716	Fatal Vision	tragedy	Aaron Hill	NA	London, Lincoln's Inn Fields theater, Feb. 1716	London, 1716, E. Nutt	Appleton, Nicoll

No.	Year	Title	Type	Author/Librettist	Composer	Place, Date	Publication	Source
12	1718	Arlequin Major Ridicule, aka Arlequin docteur chinois	harlequinade	Anon?	?	London, prob. Haymarket, 1718	?	Nicoll
13	1718	La Princesse de Carizme	comic opera	Alain-René Lesage (w/ Joseph La Font?)	Louis Lacoste	Paris, St. Laurent theater, July 1718	Théâtre de la foire, t. 3, Paris, 1721	Brenner, Lesage TF
14	1722	Camaide, l'imperatore della China, ovvero Li figliuoli rivali del padre	dramma per musica	Domenico Lalli	Antonio Caldara	Salzburg, Hoftheater, 4 Oct. 1722	Salzburg, 1722, Giovanni Gios. Mayr	Sartori
15	1722	La marchesina di Nanchin	intermezzo in Camaide, imperatore della Cina	Domenico Lalli	Antonio Caldara	Salzburg, Hoftheater, 4 Oct. 1722	Salzburg, 1722, Giovanni Gios. Mayr	Sartori
16	1722	Rutzvanscad il giovine	burlesque tragedy (parody of Ulisse il giovane, Domenico Lazzarini)	Zaccaria Valaresso	NA	?	Bologna, 1722, Costantino Pisarri	Sartori
17	1723	Arlequin barbet, pagode et médecin	pantomime	Alain-René Lesage & Jacques-Phillipe d'Orneval		Paris, St. Germain fair theater, 1723	Théâtre de la foire, t. ?, Paris, 17??	Brenner, Lesage TF
18	1724	Harlequin invisible, or; The Emperor of China's Court	harlequinade	?		London, Lincoln's Inn Fields theater, April, 1724	?	Appleton, Nicoll
19	1729	La Princesse de Chine	comic opera	Alain-René Lesage & Jacques-Phillipe d'Orneval	Jean-Claude Gillier	Paris, St. Laurent fair theater, 15 Jun, 1729	Théâtre de la foire, t. 7, Paris, 1731	Brenner, Lesage TF
20	1731	The Emperor of China Gran Volgi, or The Constant Couple Rewarded	drama	William Rufus Chetwood,	NA?	London, Bartholomew Fair, Aug. 1731	Never printed?	Clark, Appleton, Nicoll
21	1735	Le cinesi	dramatic composition for music in one act	Pietro Metastasio	Antonio Caldara or Georg Reutter	Vienna, imperial chambers, Carnival, 1735	Milan, 1750, Malatesta	Sartori, Grove
22	1735	Les Indes galantes	opera-ballet	Louis Fuzelier	Jean-Philippe Rameau	Paris, Théâtre Opéra, 23 Aug. 1735	Paris, 1735, J. B. C. Ballard	Brenner
23	1741	The Chinese Orphan, interpers'd with songs, after the Chinese manner	historical tragedy	William Hatchett	NA?	Never performed?	London, 1741, Charles Corbett	Clark, Appleton, Nicoll

(continued)

Italian, French, and English Theater Productions Featuring China Written and/or Performed in the Eighteenth Century (*continued*)

	Year first written or performed	Title	Genre	Author/Choreographer	Composer	Place/date of premiere	First known publication	Source
24	1747	*La finta tartara*	musical farce	?	Niccoló Conforto	Rome, Teatro della Valle, 1747	Rome, 1747, San Michele a Ripa Grande	Sartori
25	1747	*The Chinese Triumph*	pantomime	?	?	?	?	Nicoll
26	1748 (or earlier)	*Il cinese rimpatriato / Le chinois de retour*	intermezzo	?	Giuseppe Sellitti	?London, King's Theatre, ?1748	Paris, 1753, Veuve Delormel (libretto in French and Italian)	Sartori, Grove, Mamczarz
27	1748	*Les fêtes chinoises*	ballet	Jean-George Noverre	?	Strasbourg or Marseilles, 1748	?	Guy, Brenner, Grove, Appleton
28	1748	*L'opérateur chinois*	ballet-pantomime	Jean Baptiste François Dehesse	Louis-Gabriel Guillemain	Paris, Marchionesse de Pompadour's theater, 12 Dec. 1748; also Versailles, Chez Mme. de Marck, 1748	?	Brenner, Grove
29	1752	*L'eroe cinese*	dramma per musica	Pietro Metastasio	Giuseppe Bonno	Vienna, Schonbrunn palace garden theater, 13 May 1752	Vienna, 1752, Van Ghelen (also 1752 in Milan, Naples, Palermo, Rome)	Sartori, Grove
30	1753	*La schiava cinese*	comedy	Pietro Chiari	NA	Venice, Teatro San Samuele, autumn 1753	*Commedie in versi…*, Venezia, 1756, Bettinelli	Chiari, Alberti
31	1754	*Le sorelle cinesi*	comedy	Pietro Chiari	NA	Venice, Teatro San Samuele, autumn 1754	*Commedie in versi…*, Venezia, 1756, Bettinelli	Chiari, Alberti
32	1754	*Le Chinois poli en France*	intermezzo, parody of *Le chinois de retour*	Louis Anseaume	Giuseppe Sellitti?	Paris, St. Laurent fair theater, 20 July 1754	Paris, 1754, Duchesne	Sartori, Mamczarz, Brenner
33	1754	*Les jardins Chinois*	ballet-pantomime	Jean Baptiste François Dehesse (also attributed to Antoine Pitrot)	?	Paris, Théâtre italien, 24 June 1754	?	Brenner

No.	Year	Title	Genre	Author	Composer	Premiere	Publication	Source
34	1755	*Marco Polo*	tragedy	Gasparo Gozzi	NA	Venice, Teatro San G. Grisostomo	*Opere in versi e in prosa . . .*, Venice, 1758, Bartholomew Occhi	Gozzi, G.
35	1755	*L'Orphelin de la Chine*	tragedy	Voltaire	NA	Paris, Comédie-Française, 20 Aug. 1755	London?, 1756, Jean Nourse	Guy, Brenner
36	1755	*Le Ballet turc et chinois*	ballet-pantomime	Jean Baptiste François Dehesse	?	Paris, Théâtre italien, 12 June 1755	?	Brenner
37	1755	*Les Tartares*	ballet-pantomime	Jean Baptiste François Dehesse and Antoine Pitrot	?	Paris, Théâtre italien, 14 Aug. 1755		Brenner
38	1755	*Proteus, or Harlequin in China*	pantomime	Henry Woodward	NA	London, Drury Lane, 4 Jan. 1755		Appleton, Nicoll
39	1756	*Le Chinois*	intermezzo, parody of *Le chinois de retour*	Charles-Simon Favart and Jacques André Naigeon	Sellitti?	Paris, Théâtre italien, Feb/March 1756	Paris, 1756, Veuve delormel et fils	Sartori, Mamczarz, Brenner
40	1756	*Les Noces chinoises*	ballet-pantomime, in *Le Chinois*	Jean Baptiste François Dehesse	?	Paris, Théâtre italien, 18 March 1756		Brenner
41	1756	*Les Magots*	comic parody of *Orphelin de la Chine*, Voltaire	Antoine François Riccoboni and/or Boucher	?	Paris, Théâtre italien, 19 March 1756	Paris, 1756, Veuve delormel et fils	Brenner
42	1757	*L'isola disabitata*	dramma giocoso	Carlo Goldoni	Giuseppe Scarlatti	Venice, Teatro San Samuele, 20 Nov. 1757	Bologna, 1752?; Venice, 1757, Modesto Fenzo	Sartori
43	1758	*Fiera di mercanti cinesi*	ballo in *Arianne*, Stanzani?-Ciampi	Gaetano Pugnani (w/ Claudio Le Comte?)	Gaetano Pugnani (at least arias for ballo)	Turin, Teatro Regio, carnevale, 1758	Turin, 1758, Zappata and Avondo	Grove
44	1759	*The Orphan of China*	tragedy	Arthur Murphy	NA	London, Drury Lane, 21 April 1759	London, 19 April, P. Vaillant	Appleton, Nicoll
45	1762	*Turandot*	favola teatrale	Carlo Gozzi	NA	Venice, Teatro San Samuele, 22 Jan. 1762	*Opere*, Venice, 1772, Colombani	Gozzi, C.
46	1762	*L'orfano della Cina*	ballo	Gasparo Angiolini	Gasparo Angiolini	Vienna, court opera theater, 1762	?	Tozzi

(continued)

Italian, French, and English Theater Productions Featuring China Written and/or Performed in the Eighteenth Century (*continued*)

	Year first written or performed	Title	Genre	Author/ Choreographer	Composer	Place/date of premiere	First known publication	Source
47	1764	Le rencontre imprévue ou Les pèlerins de la Mecque	comic opera	Charles-Simon Favart or Louis Hurtaut Dancourt?	Christoph von Gluck	Vienna, Burgtheater, 7 Jan. 1764	Vienna, 1763, Van Ghelen	Brenner, Grove
48	1764	La Matrone chinoise	comedy-ballet	Pierre-René Lemonnier	?	Paris, Théâtre italien, 2 Jan. 1764	Paris, 1764, Claude Hérissant	Brenner, Grove
49	1767	L'idolo cinese	commedia per musica	Giambattista Lorenzi	Giovanni Paisiello	Naples, Teatro Nuovo, 1 April 1767	Naples, 1767, Gennaro Migliaccio	Sartori
50	1767	Il tiranno cinese	tragicomedy	Francesco Cerlone	NA	Naples, Teatro Nuovo or dei Fiorentini, 1767	*Commedie* . . . Naples, 1772, Flauto?	Cerlone
51	1767	I cinesi in Europa (Les Chinois en Europe)	ballo	Gasparo Angiolini	Gasparo Angiolini	St. Petersburg palace theater, 31 Jan. 1767	?	Tozzi
52	1768	Le Gesuitiche arricchite	?	?	?	?	?	Ericani, "Impero"
53	1768	I Gesuiti mercanti	?	?	?	?	?	Ericani, "Impero"
54	1771	L'inimico delle donne	dramma giocoso	Giovanni Bertati	Baldassare Galuppi	Venice, Teatro San Samuele, 1771	Venice, 1771, Modesto Fenzo	Sartori
55	1777	Gengis-Kan	dramma per musica	?	Pasquale Anfossi	Turin, Teatro Regio, carnevale, 1777	Turin, 1777, Onorato Dorossi	Sartori, Grove
56	1777	Il matrimonio cinese	ballo in Gengis-Kan	P. Franchi	Vittorio Amedeo Canavasso	Turin, Teatro Regio, carnevale, 1777	Turin, 1777, Onorato Dorossi	Sartori
57	1779	Lo sposalizio cinese (aka La Solennità del primo giorno dell'anno in China?)	ballo in Achille in Sciro, Metastasio-Sarti	Domenico Rossi	Giuseppe Sarti?	Florence, Teatro Pergola, 1779	Florence, 1779	Sartori See also Muraro, Scenografie, Tozzi, Pallerotti

58	1782	*Il Teatro italiano alla Chinese*	ballo	F.(Francesco?) Beretti	J. Starz?	Parma, Teatro Ducale, 1782	?	*Muraro, Scenografie*
59	1783	*The Temple of Confucius (=Harlequin the Phantom of the Day?)*	pantomime?	Charles Dibdin	?	London, Royal Circus, 1783	?	Clark, Appleton
60	1786	*Cublai, Gran Can de' Tartari*	opera eroicomico-fantastica	Gianbattista Casti	Antonio Salieri	Never performed	Pisa, *Opere varie*, 1821	Casti, Grove
61	1787	*L'Orfano cinese*	dramma per musica	?	Francesco Bianchi	Venice, Teatro San Benedetto, carnevale and fiera dell'ascensione, 1787 (also Florence, music by various composers, Teatro Pergola, autumn, 1787)	Venice, 1787, Modesto Fenzo (Florence, 1787, Stamperia Albizziniana)	Sartori
62	1787	*Gengis-Kan Conquistatore della Cina*	ballo eroico	?	?	?	Genoa	Sartori
63	1788	*Il finto giardiniere chinese*	ballo	?	?	Milan, Teatro alla Scala, 1788	?	*Muraro, Scenografie*
64	1789	*The Mandarin, or, Harlequin Widower*	entertainment	unknown	?	London, Sadlers Wells, winter or 13 April, 1789		Appleton, Nicoll
65	1790	*La compagnia d'opera a Nanchin (aka L'ouverture du Grand Opéra Italien à Nankin)*	dramma giocoso	Antonio Filistri de' Carmondani	Felice Alessandri	Berlin, small Royal theater, 16 Oct. 1790	Berlin, 1790, Haude and Spener	Sartori, Grove
66	1793	*Il cinese in Italia*	dramma giocoso	Alessandro Pepoli	Francesco Bianchini	Venice, Teatro San Moisé, autumn 1793	Venice, 1793, Modesto Fenzo	Sartori, Grove

Appendix 2: Opera Plots, Information on Sources, History of Composition, Libretto Publication, and Performance

TEUZZONE, APOSTOLO ZENO

Plot

IN KEEPING WITH HIS COMMITMENT TO SIMPLIFY AND purify the seventeenth-century *dramma per musica*, which, in the view of many, had spun out of control on so many fronts, Zeno gave *Teuzzone* a very straightforward plot. More to the point, he borrowed from straightforward plots—Racine's *Bajazet* and Corneille's *Le Comte de Essex*. The incidents leading up to the action of the opera, as outlined in the *Argomento*, are these: Troncone, Chinese emperor, has won a battle against rebel forces, but dies shortly after returning to court. He has specified his heir—his son Teuzzone—in a sealed testament entrusted to his ministers, Cino and Sivenio. Zidiana, betrothed but not yet married to Troncone (she was due to become one of his wives), plots with Cino and Sivenio to forge her name on the testament. Secretly, she swears love to each of the ministers in separate, vowing to marry them once she ascends to the throne. This is a lie, however, since Zidiana actually loves the imperial heir Teuzzone. More than the power to govern, she desires the power to sway him to marry her, so that they both may rule over China. When Zelinda, Tartar princess and Teuzzone's betrothed, overhears the plot, she quietly plans to disrupt it.

Act 1 centers on the deceased emperor's funeral, at which the false successor is announced. Teuzzone, who knew he was to take the throne, is outraged at this turn of events and vows to rise up against Zidiana and the two ministers, with the Chinese populace in tow. Zelinda, meanwhile, disguises herself as the virgin-priestess to the Chinese god Amida, so that she may confer unknown with Zidiana, and convince her to defer punishment of the obstinate Teuzzone.

The tension builds in act 2, as Teuzzone refuses to cede to Zidiana. She therefore imprisons him, but delays punishment thanks to the intercessions of Zelinda, and her abiding hope that he will come to love her. Eventually Zidiana is pushed to her limit, however, and the act ends on her ultimatum to Teuzzone: "Love me or be killed." Zelinda makes a last plea to Zidiana that she give Teuzzone one more chance.

In act 3 Zelinda, desperate but still thinking clearly, seeks to foil Zidiana's plan by telling Cino he's been de-

ceived. Teuzzone continues to hold firm against Zidiana. With regard to Zelinda, who begs him to save his life by joining the conniving Zidiana, Teuzzone pleads with her to accept their fate and leave the kingdom without him. In her anguish Zelinda confesses her true identity to Zidiana, as well as her love for Teuzzone. Zidiana condemns both to die. Their sacrifice will be a part of the Chinese "Festival of the Mare" to be celebrated that very day, a commemoration of the birth of the universe. At the moment of the lovers' sentencing, the betrayed Cino reads the correct testament. Simultaneously, the enormous golden mare that had appeared on the stage as part of the festivities erupts with soldiers loyal to Teuzzone. They rout the factions loyal to Zidiana and reinstate Teuzzone, now free to unite with his beloved Zelinda. Offstage, the defeated Sivenio kills himself, while Teuzzone grants clemency to Zidiana.

Source / History of Composition and Performance

Zeno states in his *Argomento* that he based *Teuzzone* on information found in the first part of Martino Martini's *Sinicae historiae deca*, as well as in the works of other writers—who he does not specify—treating the Chinese empire.

Teuzzone was the first serious opera in Europe to treat China. It premiered during carnival season at the Regio Ducal Teatro of Milan, with music by Paolo Magni (act 1) and Clemente Monari (acts 2 and 3). Composed most likely on commission under the impresarios the Piantanida brothers, it has been classified as a "mercenary job," meaning only that Zeno apparently did not consider it artistically deserving enough to mention in his contemporary correspondence with other *literati* (Strohm, *Dramma*, 125). In contrast to its author's silence, however, *Teuzzone* raised quite a clamor among both composers and audiences, both in Italy and other European centers. Extant librettos indicate at least nine different settings in the eighteenth century, eight of which are dated before 1730. Librettos further show that *Teuzzone* saw eighteen performance runs in sixteen cities (it enjoyed two runs in both Naples and Livorno). Outside Italy it was produced in London (1727), Prague (1734), and Vienna (1735). All but one of its eighteenth-century performances in Italian cities took place by 1721.

TAICAN, RÈ DELLA CINA, URBANO RICCI

Plot

The *Argomento* situates the opera's conflict on the contest for the throne between imperial brothers Taican and Vanlio. The former is the emperor's firstborn son, begotten of Gemira, a foreigner of unknown origins and the emperor's favorite. Vanlio, born after Taican, is the son of one of the emperor's queen wives. Chinese custom states that should the empress bear no sons, the firstborn male from the emperor's union with any woman in his entourage, no matter her lineage, becomes the legitimate heir. Vanlio militates against this, however, claiming that Taican's questionable bloodline disqualifies him for the throne. Vanlio is supported by his servant Sunone, who represents the mandarins of arms. Pitted against them are the mandarins of letters, who support Gemira and Taican, based on the emperor's privileging her among his wives. They also have imperial protocol on their side. All of this functions as a sort of background plot, however, to the business of Gemira's tragic past and her thwarted love story with Zuliano, king of Japan.

Gemira is actually Selene, an Indian princess, who in her younger days was the beloved of Zuliano. When he suspected her of adultery (reported to him by his servant Ruteno, who had concocted her affair to counter the possibility that Selene would tell the ruler of his amorous attentions toward her), he plunged a sword in her side, then ordered Ruteno to put her to sea. Although it was long thought that she died, Selene was instead found floating on the back of a dolphin by the Chinese literary mandarin Mitrane. Her magnificent jewels implied royal status, but she kept her origins secret, and as Gemira, quickly became the emperor's favorite.

As it happens Zuliano (disguised as a secretary) is in China with his country's ambassador (Ruteno in disguise), ostensibly to pay respects to the recently deceased emperor. He has actually come to ask for Gemira's hand, since he's gone unmarried for many years following Selene's betrayal and banishment. The Indian princess Elmirena is also in China to marry the new Chinese emperor, by virtue of a formerly arranged agreement. The Selene tragedy comes to the fore, first when Gemira recognizes Zuliano as her past consort and accuser/attacker, and then when Elmirena, Selene's cousin, hears talk of Zulian, and, enraged, vows vengeance on him for murdering her cousin.

Shortly thereafter both Gemira and Zuliano discover the truth, as to Selene's innocence and Ruteno's treachery. Zuliano attacks Ruteno but is taken by locals as an insolent servant and imprisoned. In the meantime Gemira forgives and revives her love for him. To save him from death, however (Elmirena has discovered that the impudent servant is Zulian and condemns him to death), she must prove her identity as Selene. Gemira does this by making Ruteno recount the details of his abandonment of the princess at sea. She then has Mitrane bring out the recovered jewels and regal clothing, garments torn from her sword wound by

Zuliano. All is well: Gemira/Selene reunites with Zuliano, king of Japan; her daughter Aglatide will marry Vanlio (the two have been in love and squabbling throughout the tragedy), and become heirs to the Japanese throne; Taican and Elmirena will marry and rule the Chinese kingdom.

Source / History of Composition and Performance

Ricci tells readers of his libretto that *Taican* is founded on historical episodes related in the accounts of Father Semedo, Portuguese Jesuit and author of *Relação da grande monarquia da China* (1638); (published in 1643 in Rome as *Relatione della grande monarchia della Cina*). The many particular customs and practices of the Chinese referenced in the opera he attributes to the works of Jesuit fathers Athanasius Kircher (*La China illustrata . . .*), Daniello Bartoli (*La Cina*), and Louis Le Comte (*Nouveaux Mémoires sur l'état present de la Chine*).

Records indicate only one setting, by Venetian composer Francesco Gasparini. The only extant libretto documents a performance at the Tron Theater at San Cassiano, in Venice in 1707.

IL TARTARO NELLA CINA, ANTONIO SALVI

Plot

The *Argomento* states that the Chinese king had had a premonition that his infant son would cause the downfall of the kingdom as well as his own death. To prevent such a disaster, he asks Colao, one of his mandarins, to do away with the child, either by killing him or leaving him to fate. Colao gives him to a Tartar lord, who passes the baby on to the Tartar emperor, Licungo. Licungo has no offspring, so adopts the infant, naming him Arturo. About the time that Arturo is twenty years old, the Tartars have moved against the Chinese, successfully breaching the Great Wall that divides the two empires. In short order the invaders overtake all but the capital city, Peking. The opera begins as Licungo's troops ready themselves to conquer Peking and the imperial Chinese family, enclosed within its walls.

Act 1 begins as Colao, stationed with the Tartar forces as Chinese ambassador, asks Licungo to suspend fighting and spare Peking. The brutal Licungo sees this request as treachery, and imprisons Colao. Within the Chinese imperial palace, the mandarin's son Vanlio and daughter Timurta hear of their father's captivity and despair. The Chinese emperor loses hope also. With the enemy so close at hand, and fearing slavery under the Tartars, he kills himself, after trying (unsuccessfully) to persuade his daughter Assuana to do the same.

In act 2 Timurta tells Assuana about the dream she's had of her true love who will one day rule China. She draws his portrait to better recognize him when the moment arrives. Her jealous lover Taicungo steals the portrait so he can kill the rival should he encounter him. Ermanda, daughter of a

Tartar general killed in the recent battle, confesses her love for Arturo. Licungo meanwhile admits his love for Ermanda. The Tartars advance to the city walls and find Vanlio standing guard upon them. Licungo threatens that if Peking is not ceded, he will kill Colao, Vanlio's father. Vanlio won't budge, whereupon Licungo sentences Colao to a gruesome, violent death, to be executed by Arturo. Back in the Tartar encampments, Arturo suspends the death order, for reasons he cannot quite explain.

In the Chinese palace Assuana assumes the vacant throne. Taicungo tells her the Chinese people want her to partner as they need a king. The royal funeral for her father is about to take place, and Assuana states she will follow her father's advice and kill herself. Vanlio, who loves her, can't bear this news and convinces her to stay alive. He later confesses that his love for Assuana motivates his courageous actions, not his loyalty to his country. Arturo wants to grant Colao freedom to return to Peking, but the steadfast mandarin, dictated to by a sense of duty and fate, will not leave Licungo's service. Arturo decides then to exchange himself for Colao as a hostage in Peking. There he meets Timurta and falls inexplicably and deeply in love. She recognizes him as the man from her dream.

The events of act 3 include several love scenes between Arturo and Timurta. Taicungo spies them together and identifies Arturo as the portrait subject. Filled with a jealous rage he attacks Arturo. Timurta enters the fray to break it up, and announces that Arturo will become both her husband and China's next ruler. Back in the Tartar battle camp, Licungo discovers Arturo's betrayal, in having freed Colao. Enraged, he rants that all his conquests have been for Arturo, his would-be son, to whom he intended to give the whole combined Tartar and Chinese kingdom. He asks Ermanda for love, to help mitigate his fury.

Taicungo, having lost Timurtina to Arturo, goes to Licungo and orchestrates a secret entry into Peking to attack from the inside, precisely during the imminent funeral. The Chinese discover the plan and devise a counterattack. Arturo and Vanlio fight together in China's defense as if they were brothers. Ever the loyal son, Arturo also asks Vanlio to spare his father Licungo if he should be captured. The battle between Tartars (Licungo with Taicungo's aid) and Chinese (Arturo and Vanlio) is speedily reprised, with the Chinese emerging victorious. Arturo thinks he's killed Taicungo but when the latter shows up a prisoner, Arturo realizes he's killed his father, Licungo. He wishes to die, as he cannot bear to have so dishonored his father. In the nick of time Ermanda reveals that Licungo was not Arturo's real father. She had learned of his authentic origins from her father before he died. The documents attached to the foundling reveal that he is actually Zunteo, son of the former Chinese king. Assuana rejoices at having found her lost brother; Colao, who has returned to Peking, will act as Zunteo's counsel; Zunteo and Timurta will marry and rule over China; Vanlio and Assuana will marry and rule Tartary; Taicungo will be pardoned and marry Ermanda, to whom Zunteo owes so much, for having explained his true

lineage. He postpones his father's funeral, to celebrate the good news and joyous resolutions.

Source / History of Composition and Performance

Salvi notes in his *Argomento* that he has plumbed the story of the Tartar conquest of China from *Giro del Mondo*, by Giovanni Gemelli-Careri.

Il Tartaro nella Cina was commissioned by Rinaldo I, Duke of Reggio (Emilia), and performed during the 1715 fair period at the Teatro Pubblico di Reggio Emilia. This performance marks its only setting, by Francesco Gasparini.

CAMAIDE, L'IMPERATORE DELLA CINA, DOMENICO LALLI

Plot

Background information in the *Argomento* allows that Camaide, emperor of China, had been escorting his soon-to-be-wife Lovamia back to the capital Nanking from her home on the island of Sonda. Tartar invasions in a Chinese province called him away to battle, however, whereupon Chinese ministers safeguarded Lovamia in the royal palace. The combat went badly and to save himself Camaide spread the rumor of his death. His two sons Tico and Cambice rushed back to Nanking from their posts in outlying provinces.

Act 1 begins with Cambice's boastful claims that he will take Lovamia and the throne, now that his father has passed on. Amane, Cambice's betrothed, vows revenge for his impudence. Tico, the younger brother, and Lovamia virtually admit their love for one another. Tico then challenges Cambice for his arrogance, and the two nearly come to blows. At this moment Amane announces that Camaide is alive after all. The brothers, who have broken their father's law by returning so quickly to their homeland on news of his death, differ sharply in their reactions: Tico hopes for mercy and forgiveness, Cambice anticipates cruel punishment. Camaide is angered, as expected, accusing his sons of greediness to govern. Like good vassals, they should have remained where they were and awaited more intelligence. He then discusses with his minister Orda Tico's meekness and obedience, versus Cambice's effrontery. From Amane he learns of Cambice's earlier intentions, so now he is upset at both Cambice and Lovamia, believing that she returns his elder son's affections.

Act 2 opens with Lovamia's lament of her difficult situation, constrained to honor her betrothal with Camaide. He, on the other hand, entrusts her temporarily to Tico, since he reads her reluctance as a sign of her feeling for Cambice. Again, Tico and Lovamia bemoan their predicament. Amane continues to fail at making Cambice respect their betrothal. Camaide devises a strategy: Tico will go fight the Tartars, while Cambice will marry Amane and return to his province. Tico is eager to follow his father's orders, but Cambice bristles. He and his father get into a fight, whereupon Camaide sends his son away in chains. To sound out Lovamia, Camaide tells her she's no longer bound to marry him, but shall wed Tico, more fitting in age. She rejoices, telling him of her love for his younger son. The rejected Camaide now feels betrayed by both Cambice and Tico. Lovamia realizes her outburst may have been a mistake and despairs. Orda and Amane try to dissuade Cambice from his wrath, but are unsuccessful. He plots to join with the Tartars against China. Amane despairs.

In act 3 Tico and Lovamia still fret about their now-public sentiments for one another. Camaide pardons Lovamia by reinstating his marriage to her. She refuses, claiming she is now betrothed to Tico, at which point Camaide erupts in rage. Orda announces that Cambice has escaped and advances toward China with the Tartar enemy. Camaide imprisons Lovamia and runs to join Tico against the Tartars. From high upon the city walls Tico encourages his army in the name of loyalty to their king. Cambice appears with the Tartar regiments, and Camaide, who has been taken prisoner. The two brothers rail against each other. Back in the palace, Amane and Lovamia bewail the news that Cambice has won and Tico is dead. A page arrives with a note from Camaide, ordering that Lovamia drink poison to prevent her marrying Cambice. Orda appears just in time to dispel the rumor: Tico has in fact triumphed, and saved his father Camaide. To reward him, Camaide grants him Lovamia, and inheritance of the throne. The remorseful enchained Cambice requests just punishment, but upon the cries for mercy from Amane, Lovamia, and Tico, Camaide forgives his wicked son and awards him Amane in marriage.

Source / History of Composition and Performance

No source is specified in the libretto. *Camaide* may have loosely derived its story of brothers' rivalry from an episode during the Manchu takeover. In 1651 the regent Dorgon had died, and the incumbent Ch'ing emperor Zungteus III was still only thirteen years old. Nieuhof reports that a fight broke out for the regency between two brothers (Zungteus's uncles?), fifteen-year-old Xunchius and Quintus (unspecified). The fact that the libretto specifies Nanking as the capital could situate the opera in the early Ming period, when the first Ming ruler inaugurated it as the official imperial city (1368–1421). However, even when the capital moved to Peking in 1421, and well into the eighteenth century in fact, Nanking was still recognized as a "capital" of the southern Chinese regions.

Only one setting is documented, by Salzburg Kappelmeister Antonio Caldara, for the one known performance at the archiepiscopal Court Theater in Salzburg. *Camaide* was performed under the auspices of Francesco Antonio, Archbishop and Prince of Salzburg. The libretto does not indicate a precise date, although New Grove indicates 1722 for the Caldara setting. Lalli evidently was in Venice in

1722, under the protection of Zeno, so he must have written the libretto for export to Salzburg.

L'EROE CINESE, PIETRO METASTASIO

Plot

During an insurrection which forced the Chinese emperor, Livanio [Li-vang], into exile, his son, Svenvango [Swen-vang], was saved by Leango [Le-ang], who wrapped his own infant son in the royal garments and left him for the mob. Later, as regent, Le-ang raised the royal heir as his own child under the name of Siveno [Si-veng].

Act 1: Si-veng and Lisinga [Li-sing], a captive Tartar princess, are in love. Li-sing is reminded by her sister, Ulania [U-lan], that Si-veng is not only a commoner but also her enemy: for these reasons, U-lan claims, she will leave Minteo [Min-ti], Si-veng's friend and a mandarin in the Chinese army. Si-veng and Li-sing despair when her father sends word that she must marry the unknown heir to the Chinese throne. With this opportunity for an alliance with the Tartars, Le-ang feels ready to reveal Si-veng's identity; Si-veng, however, announces that the populace call for Le-ang himself as emperor. Le-ang's response leads Li-sing to suspect that Si-veng is indeed the heir.

Act 2: Since Le-ang will not accept the throne, but insists on revealing the true heir, Si-veng resolves to flee. Le-ang, however, explains all to Si-veng and, bidding him remain silent, departs to explain to Li-sing. Meanwhile, Min-ti is summoned by Alsingo [Al-sing], an old man who, having found Min-ti wrapped as a royal baby, had raised him in the belief that he was Li-vang's son. Min-ti, now convinced that he is the heir, informs Si-veng, who is thrown into confusion and shows little reaction to Li-sing's delight at Le-ang's revelation.

Act 3: Si-veng departs to suppress an insurrection; U-lan enters to announce that Min-ti is its leader. Challenged by Le-ang, Min-ti reveals that he is the true heir and has prevented the mob from entering the palace. Le-ang corrects his mistake and, learning from U-lan of Si-veng's mission, Min-ti rushes to his friend's aid. Rumors that Si-veng is dead are then dispelled by his arrival with Min-ti, who has rescued him. Appropriate reunions follow as Si-veng is officially identified as Swen-vang and Min-ti as the son of Le-ang.[1]

Source / History of Composition and Performance

Metastasio states in the libretto that he based *L'eroe cinese* on an episode of ancient Chinese imperial history ("La storia Tchao-kong"), related in the popular Jesuit compilation, *Description géographique, historique, chronologique, politique et physique de l'Empire de la Chine et de la Tartarie chinoise* (1735). Many scholars also cite as a source the Chinese music drama *Tchao chi cou ell* (*Orphan of the Family Tchao*), contained as well in Du Halde's work. Little evidence of this can be found in Metastasio's libretto, however. See the chapter on *L'eroe cinese* for more detailed information on the source question.

Including Giuseppe Bonno's setting, composed for the premiere performance by young members of the royal family in the garden theater at the Schönbrunn palace, *L'eroe cinese* was set nineteen times over the course of the eighteenth century. The illustrious crowd of composers who put Metastasio's libretto to music included Galuppi (1753), Hasse (1753, 1773), Perez (1753), Conforto (1754), Ballabene (1757), Piazza (1757), Uttini (1757), T. Giordani (1766), ?Majo (1770), Sacchini (1770), Colla (1771), Mango (1771), Bertoni (1774 as *Narbale*), Bachschmidt (1775), Checchi (1775), Cimarosa (1782), and Rauzzini (1782).

Thirty published librettos imply thirty different productions, although not every libretto specifies a composer, so one cannot match the performances to exact musical settings. On the flip side, one libretto for a 1774 production lists music by Bertoni, but does not indicate a performance site. If each libretto indicates a single performance run, then *L'eroe cinese* enjoyed thirty showings in at least twenty-four cities in just over thirty years (1752–84).[2] Over half of these runs (eighteen) took place by 1760, followed by a flurry of eight stagings in 1770–75. Naples saw three different productions (1752, 1753, 1782), and the following cities had two runs apiece: Milan (1752, 1758), Munich (1770, 1771), and London (1782, 1784). Fifteen of the productions were mounted in peninsular centers, including Palermo, while *L'eroe cinese* ran fourteen times in cities outside Italy.[3]

L'ISOLA DISABITATA, CARLO GOLDONI

Plot

L'isola disabitata opens as a crew of Dutch sea merchants land on an uninhabited island off the coast of China. The island, according to the ship's admiral Roberto, has been granted to them by the Chinese. The Dutch sailors quickly set about establishing a settlement; in the process they discover Gianghira, a beautiful Chinese maiden who has been banished from the mainland by her father for resisting the marriage he had arranged. Gianghira captivates Roberto, as well as his top commanders Valdimonte and Garamone. Roberto declares himself her defender and pledges to restore her peace of mind; his commanders have less virtuous designs on the *cinesina*. But Valdimonte and Garamone are already affianced, to two young women also present in the ship's company. Nonetheless, they contend for Gianghira, each contriving to win her for himself. Their jealous consorts, Carolina and Giacinta, mount their own ruses to foil their wayward lovers. The height of these machinations is the scene of the "finti cinesi" (make-believe Chinamen) in which the four youths, disguised as Chinese ambassadors, stage a fake embassy on behalf of Gianghira's father and would-be husband, in an attempt to make Roberto release

Gianghira. The opera ends with the proper pairing of the two commanders with their partners, and the announcement of Roberto's forthcoming marriage to Gianghira. At this point Chinese ships are sighted on the horizon: this time a real envoy seeking restitution of Gianghira. A battle ensues and in short order the Dutch overcome the Chinese. The opera closes with an elaborate, festive dance, conflating the naval victory with the nuptials.

Source / History of Composition and Performance

It is difficult to establish a clear source(s) for the Chinese material in *Isola*. The libretto does not include prefatory material, nor does Goldoni refer in any way to the opera in the usual locus for self-assessment of his work, his *Mémoires*. The most likely sources were Du Halde's famous compilation *Description géographique, historique, chronologique, politique et physique de l'Empire de la Chine et de la Tartarie chinoise* (Paris, 1735) and Prévost's *Histoire générale des voyages* (Paris, 1746–91). A similar multivolume collection by the English historian Thomas Salmon must also be considered, *Modern History, or Present State of All Nations* (London, 1725–38). Translation of this work into Italian began in Venice in 1731 (*Lo stato presente di tutti i paesi, e popoli del mondo naturale, politico e morale* [Venice: Albrizzi, 1731–65]), and Goldoni specifically cites it as a source for his Persian trilogy (1753–56). As Salmon dedicated a long section of *Modern History* to China, it may well have furnished some data about the Middle Kingdom to the Venetian playwright.

L'isola disabitata was set to music only once, by Neapolitan composer Giuseppe Scarlatti. The progeny of the famous Scarlatti musical dynasty had composed scores for two previous Goldoni librettos, *I portentosi effetti della Madre Natura* (Venice, 1752), and *De gustibus non est disputandum* (Venice, 1754). Although Scarlatti's gifts were not equal to those of Galuppi and Piccinni, with whom Goldoni had reached earlier pinnacles of success, he had distinctive talents, indicated by the opera's success.

L'isola disabitata appears to have been first performed in Venice, at the Teatro San Samuele, in autumn of 1757. Some records, however, suggest an earlier 1752 performance in Bologna. The 1752 date appears on the libretto cover featured in *Il teatro illustrato nelle edizioni del Settecento*, ed. Cesare Molinari and Filippo Pedrocco (Venice: Marsilio, 1993), as well as in Oscar Sonneck's *Catalogue of Opera Librettos Printed Before 1800*, and in Claudio Sartori's *Indice degli autori dei testi*, one of the indexes in his *I libretti italiani a stampa dalle origini al 1800*. Sonneck, however, states that the composer is unknown and does not list a theater. In addition, neither Sartori's actual catalogue of libretti nor his *Indice delle località e delle sedi delle esecuzioni* reference a 1752 production. Both of these records instead indicate the 1757 performance in Venice as the comic opera's premiere. This discrepancy could be owing to the difference between the date of libretto publication and the date of operatic performance. Since Goldoni never refers to the opera in his *Mémoires*, it is difficult to be more precise.

With Francesco Carattoli, Caterina Ristorini, and other members of the hugely popular Baglioni family starring in the Venice debut, *L'isola disabitata* was very well received by audiences. Its immediate success has been cited as one of the reasons for Scarlatti's subsequent lucrative employment contract in Vienna. Reprised immediately in Venice, *L'isola disabitata* also ran the same year in Vienna, followed by performances in Cologne (1758), Trieste (1759), Turin and Genoa (where it was renamed *La cinese smarrita* [1760]), Klagenfurt (1765), Prague (1767), Dresden (1767, 1770), and again in Vienna (1773).

In recent years, *L'isola disabitata* has been performed in Venice in 1991, at the Teatro Arsenale during Festival Venezia, under the direction of Ida Kuniaki (http://www.teatroarsenale.org/arsenale/il_teatro/cv/scheda_cv?id=31).

L'IDOLO CINESE, GIAMBATTISTA LORENZI

Plot

The plot of *L'idolo cinese* revolves around the usual travails of two sets of lovers, now set amid the obsessive interest of the local ruler, Tuberone (big potato), in the oracles and rituals surrounding the Chinese idol Kam, chief among national deities. We learn from the libretto's *Argomento* that Tuberone was a young Neapolitan whose flight from home brought him to China just as a native ruler had died without an heir. Chinese law prescribes that in such a situation, to avoid local squabbles over inheritance, the first foreigner to arrive is crowned prince, and also named high priest in charge of worship of Kam. Thus Tuberone ascended to power, eventually married, and had a son, Liconatte. Liconatte has fallen in love with the Tartar damsel Ergilla, but the long-standing enmity between their fathers prevents their union. The lovers' plans to run away together are foiled by a meddling third party, who convinces each separately of the other's perfidy. They have a violent encounter, where Liconatte stabs Ergilla and leaves her for dead. She survives, of course, and wanders China seeking revenge. In the meantime Tuberone has arranged for Liconatte to marry Kametri, a different Tartar maiden. Kametri, unfortunately, pines for the French chevalier Adolfo, who once visited her lands and when pressed to leave on other business, vowed to return for her. The opera opens as Adolfo comes back, as promised. He chances into Ergilla, and vows to help her avenge her wrong by Liconatte. When Ergilla and Adolfo enter Tuberone's province and discover the betrothal of their respective consorts, Liconatte and Kametri, the melee begins. To complicate things further, Tuberone, who has been given to believe that the newcomers Ergilla and Adolfo are siblings from France, falls for Ergilla. He forthwith begins plans for a double wedding, alongside his son and Kametri.

At this point Tuberone mistakes Pilottola, Adolfo's bumbling sailor-servant, for the Chinese idol Kam, and seeks his help to cure what seems to be a profound malady affecting the four young people. Not only are they in a stupefied state, but Liconatte will not obey his commands to marry Kametri, and appears to be thwarting his father's proposed union with Ergilla. The opera's comicity hinges on Pilottola's mishap-ridden performance as the idol, and on Tuberone's neurotic and idiotic reverence for him. Tuberone's exasperation peaks when he discovers he's been duped: Ergilla is not who he thought she was, nor is Pilottola. He orders their punishment, along with that of his insubordinate son Liconatte. In the end, the strategies of Adolfo and Kametri's servant Parmetella, a sharp Neapolitan girl somehow become a Tartar slave, untangle the confusion among the four lovers and save them from Tuberone's reprisals. Adolfo manages their escape, by surprising Tuberone's Chinese guards with his own naval militia. As the French troops rout the Chinese warriors, three pairs of lovers prepare to leave the tumultuous Middle Kingdom and sail to Naples. For the servants Pilottola and Parmetella, the departure signifies a longed-for return to their homeland; for Liconatte and Ergilla, and Adolfo and Kametri, Naples means the chance to love as they wish. Tuberone meekly asks if he too may go with them—a request that signals the end of his Chinese adventure.

Source / History of Composition and Performance

Lorenzi refers only to various "Chinese histories" ("Storie della Cina") as having provided data for *L'idolo cinese*. Certain episodes point convincingly to Kircher's *China illustrata* and Martini's *Deca* as likely candidates, both works frequently cited by other dramaturgs. The Flautina editor states that the idea for the opera was provided by a popular commedia dell'arte canovaccio, entitled *Pulcinella Re dormendo*.

L'idolo cinese was an early work for both Lorenzi and Paisiello and their first collaboration. For Lorenzi, it was only his fifth libretto, and the fourth of thirty comic opera librettos he would author over his lifetime. For Paisiello, *Idolo* numbered twelve out of two hundred eventual opera scores, but was only his third opera buffa composition. After finishing his training at the Conservatorio di Sant' Onofrio in Naples, Paisiello spent two years in northern Italian cities, during which time he set two *drammi giocosi*. *L'idolo cinese* was the first comic opera he composed when he returned to Naples.

L'idolo cinese premiered at Naples's Teatro Nuovo in spring of 1767. The brothers Giuseppe and Antonio Casaccia played the parts of buffos Tuberone and Pilottola, respectively, with Nicoletta Mendorsi and Nicolò Grimaldi in the roles of the lovers Ergilla and Liconatte. The opera was performed in Naples again the next year, in addition to performances in Lecce (1768) and Palermo (1773). In 1773 *Idolo* was staged in Venice to a setting by Giovanni Rust. Rust's music was also featured in productions in Bologna (1774), Pisa (1777), and again in Venice (1774, 1777). A score by Schuster served performances in Dresden (1774) and Prague (1776), but Paisiello's setting again took the fore in the later part of the century, with performances in Turin (1777), Fermo (1779), Paris (1779), St. Petersburg (1779), and Naples (1783).

The opera has been revived relatively recently, for the Settimane Musicali Internazionali in Naples in 1991 and 1992 (Teatro Mercadante), and in Verona in 1996 and 1997 (Teatro Filarmonico). Roberto de Simone directed the Naples performances, with Peter Maag and Lorenza Codignola directing the Verona revivals respectively. All productions used scenery and costumes designed by Emanuele Luzzati. For more information, see http://nautilus.tv/9705it/musica/idolo.htm.

L'INIMICO DELLE DONNE, GIOVANNI BERTATI

Plot

L'inimico delle donne takes place on an island in the Chinese sea, where ministers to Prince Zon-zon pressure him to choose a mate, since according to law, he must marry on this day or lose the crown. Zon-zon hates all women, however, and duly criticizes the prospective brides brought before him, including the Chinese damsels Xunchìa and Kam-si (cousins, related to the prince's steward, Si-sin) and Zyda (daughter of Ly-Lam, the high priest). He unexpectedly meets the Italian girl Agnesina, who, together with her uncle Geminiano, has been shipwrecked on the island after fleeing her suitors back home. Agnesina detests all men, and is grateful to have arrived safely in a land far from the problems of love. But her encounter with Zon-zon sets in motion the inevitable process by which they become mutually enamored. The prince has at last found a consort. To counter possible objections that Agnesina is a foreigner, Zon-zon convinces Geminiano to pose as the Chinese idol that, according to custom, must publicly affirm his choice of mate. Geminiano reluctantly agrees, and makes the desired pronouncement just before fleeing the scene, afraid of

being found out and subjected to painful corporal punishments. Zon-zon's ministers see through the ruse but decide to play along. The last obstacle to overcome is Agnesina's potential lack of skills in terms of wifely affections, and Zon-zon assigns Xunchìa to instruct her in this area. In the course of her lesson Agnesina learns of the likelihood that Zon-zon will take other wives, whereupon she gives him an ultimatum: monogamy or nothing. He immediately and willingly conforms to her terms. Preparations then ensue for not only Zon-zon and Agnesina's marriage, but, by Zon-zon's decree, that of Geminiano and Xunchìa as well.

Source / History of Composition and Performance

No written testimony has thus far been uncovered as to sources Bertati may have consulted for his version of China in *L'inimico delle donne*. One specification for scenery points to the standard sources: the first act opens on a coastal country landscape, at the center of which stands a pedestal supporting the idol Ca-na-gà. The exact name of the deity suggests that Bertati was aware of Martini and/or Kircher. All other directives for sets are less precise, however, naming only the by-then commonplace fixtures: the palace adorned "all'uso de' Cinesi," the magnificent banquet table, the Chinese garden and the illuminated Chinese temple. By 1771, the year of the opera's premiere, the rage for things Chinese on the stage was firmly established.

Following *L'inimico delle donne*'s first performance at Venice's Teatro San Samuele in fall of 1771, it was staged in seven other cities, over a period of eight years. Galuppi's original setting was used in all but one of the performances of what became more or less a repertory work. With certain textual changes, the opera played in Turin (1772), Lisbon (1774), Parma (1774), Dresden (1775), Vienna (1775, as *Nemico delle donne*), and again in Venice (1779). In 1773 Gazzaniga wrote the only alternative musical score to Galuppi's, for a production at the Ducal Palace of Milan, where the opera was titled *Zon-zon, principe di Kibinkin-ka*.

Notes

INTRODUCTION

1. Mary K. Hunter, *The Culture of Opera Buffa in Mozart's Vienna* (Princeton: Princeton University Press, 1999), 53.

2. Reinhard Strohm states: "It is the very first opera libretto known to me with a Chinese subject." *Dramma per Musica: Italian Opera Seria of the Eighteenth Century* (New Haven: Yale University Press, 1997), 125. The following works featuring Chinese settings or characters are known to have been performed and/or published in the seventeenth century: *Ballet des Chevaliers des Indes et de la Chine* (ballet, author unknown, 1604); Chappuzeau, *Armetzar ou Les Amis Ennemis* (tragicomedy, 1658); Elkanah Settle, *The Conquest of China by the Tartars* (heroic drama, 1676); Elkanah Settle, *The Fairy Queen* (opera pastiche, music by Henry Purcell, 1692); Jean Regnard and Charles Dufresny, *Les chinois* (comedy performed by the Théâtre Italien, Paris, 1692). Comparing the records, it would appear that these productions did not involve quite the stage extravagance, in combination with more developed perceptions about China, evidenced in the eighteenth-century works. See Pierre Leprohon, "Esotismo," *Enciclopedia dello spettacolo*, vol. 4 (Rome: Le Maschere, 1957), 1614; William Worthen Appleton, *A Cycle of Cathay* (New York: Columbia University Press, 1951); Hugh Honour, *Chinoiserie. The Vision of Cathay* (New York: E. P. Dutton, 1961); Aaron Cohen, "Euro-Oriental Works for Performance: Timeline up to 1900," unpublished list, 2005. My thanks to Mr. Cohen for providing me with this list.

3. The discrepancy between number of runs and number of cities occurs because *Teuzzone* had two runs each in Naples (1708, 1720), and in Livorno (1721, 1753).

4. From now on the expressions "China dramas," "China theater," and the like will be used, rather than "Chinese dramas," to indicate European works that treated China.

5. See appendix 1 for a list of works.

6. Settle-Purcell's 1692 *The Fairy Queen* cannot rightly be considered an opera concentrating on China, as it essentially comprises a musical patchwork version of Shakespeare's *A Midsummer Night's Dream*, with a Chinese *divertissement* tacked on at the end. See Appleton, *Cycle*, 70–71; Honour, *Chinoiserie The Vision*, 77–78.

7. Metastasio's opera was preceded by several Jesuit productions on the topic in Latin, and an English adaptation, written but never staged, by William Hatchett in 1741. On the Jesuit plays, see Adrian Hsia, "The Transformation of Chinesia from Jesuitical Fiction to Jesuit College Drama: A Preliminary Survey," in *Chinesia: The European Construction of China in the Literature of the 17th and 18th Centuries* (Tübingen: Niemeyer, 1998), 55–74. For Hatchett, see Appleton, *Cycle*, 82–87. See chapter 4 for detailed treatment of *L'eroe cinese*.

8. Hsia never mentions it in " 'The Orphan of the House Zhao' in French, English, German, and Hong Kong Literature," in *The Vision of China in the English Literature of the Seventeenth and Eighteenth Centuries*, ed. Hsia (Hong Kong: Chinese University Press, 1998), 383–99, although he corrects the lacuna (with several inaccuracies) in "The Transplanted Chinese Orphan in England, France, Germany, Italy, and His Ripatriation to Hong Kong," in Hsia, *Chinesia*, 75–98. See also Shouyi Chen, "The Chinese Orphan: A Yuan Play," in Hsia, *Chinesia*, 359–82. To my knowledge, Metastasio's opera has been studied by only: Antonio Caroccia, " 'Ve le canto in cinese': rivendicazioni e fascino esotico nell'*Eroe cinese* di Domenico Cimarosa," in *Pietro Metastasio. Il testo e il contesto*, ed. Marta Columbro and Paologiovanni Maione (Naples: Altrastampa, 2000), 203–24; Elena Sala di Felice, "Delizie e saggezza dell'antica Cina secondo Metastasio," in *Opera e Libretto II*, ed. Maria Teresa Muraro and Giovanni Morelli (Florence: Olschki, 1993), 85–106; Nicola Savarese, *Teatro e spettacolo fra Oriente e Occidente* (Rome-Bari: Laterza, 1992), 129–44.

9. Interestingly, Guy notes that the appropriation of the Chinese topos by increasingly reputable theatrical genres contrasted with developments in the domain of French fiction. Basil Guy, *The French Image of China before and after Voltaire* (Geneva: Institut et musée Voltaire, 1963), 182.

10. French, Dutch, English, Prussian, Italian, and Spanish chinoiseries are distinguished from one another, as are Baroque, rococo, and neoclassical chinoiseries. See Honour, *Chinoiserie The Vision*; Dawn Jacobson, *Chinoiserie* (London: Phaidon Press, 1993); Madeleine Jarry, *Chinoiserie: Chinese Influence on European Decorative Art, 17th and 18th Centuries*, trans. Gail Mangold-Vine (New York: Vendome, 1981); Oliver Impey, *Chinoiserie: The Impact of Oriental Styles on Western Art and Decoration* (New York: Charles Scribner's Sons, 1977).

11. Enrico Fubini, *Music and Culture in Eighteenth-Century Europe*, trans. Wolfgang Freis, Lisa Gasbarrone, and Michael Louis Leone, trans. ed. Bonnie J. Blackburn (Chicago: University of Chicago Press, 1994), 2; Strohm, *Dramma per Musica*, 4.

12. The *ballo* was an Italian (or even more precisely, Venetian) form of dance with its own marked differences from the French *ballet* in the same period. See Irene Alm, "Winged Feet and Mute Eloquence: Dance in Seventeenth-Century Venetian Opera," *Cambridge Opera Journal* 15, no. 3 (2003): 217.

13. Among the best-known theater works by non-Italians— France: Jean-Georges Noverre, *Les Fêtes chinoises* (ballet, 1752), Voltaire, *L'Orphelin de la Chine* (tragedy, 1755); England: Aaron Hill, *The Fatal Vision* (1716), William Hatchett, *The Chinese Orphan* (tragedy, 1741), David Garrick, *The Chinese Festival* (ballet after Noverre, 1755), Arthur Murphy, *The Orphan of China* (tragedy, 1759); Germany: Johann Wolfgang von Goëthe, *Elpinor* (one-act fragment, 1781–83). See appendix 1 for more complete list.

14. Strohm, *Dramma per Musica*, 6.

15. Ibid., 6. On Italian opera outside of Italy in the eighteenth century, see Reinhard Strohm, ed., *The Eighteenth-Century Diaspora of Italian Music and Musicians* (Turnhout: Brepols, 2001); Alberto

Basso, ed., *Musica in Scena: Storia dello Spettacolo Musicale*, vol. 3, 3–54 (Austro-German states), 329–37 (Russia); 469–77 (Spain) (Turin: UTET, 1995).

16. The bibliography on the Jesuit mission to China and its repercussions in Europe is mammoth. For a general introduction, see George Dunne, *Generation of Giants: The Story of the Jesuits in China in the Last Decades of the Ming Dynasty* (Notre Dame: University of Notre Dame Press, 1962); René Etiemble, *Les Jesuites en Chine: La querelle des rites (1552–1773)* (Paris: Julliard, 1966); David E. Mungello, *Curious Land: Jesuit Accommodation and the Origins of Sinology* (Stuttgart: Franz Steiner Verlag Wiesbaden, 1985); Charles E. Ronan and Bonnie B. C. Oh, eds., *East Meets West: The Jesuits in China 1582–1773* (Chicago: Loyola University Press, 1988); Arnold H. Rowbotham, *Missionary and Mandarin: The Jesuits at the Court of China* (New York: Russell & Russell, 1966).

17. See Donald F. Lach and Edwin J. Van Kley, *Asia in the Making of Europe*, 3 vols. (Chicago: University of Chicago, 1965–93), for best coverage of the literature on China in early modern Europe; also John Lust, *Western Books on China Published up to 1850 in the Library of the School of Oriental and African Studies, University of London: A Descriptive Catalogue* (London: Bamboo Publishing, 1987).

18. See Maxine Berg, "Manufacturing the Orient: Asian Commodities and European Industry, 1500–1800," in *Prodotti e tecniche d'oltremare nelle economie europee secc. XIII–XVIII*, ed. Simonetta Cavaciocchi (Prato: Istituto internazionale di storia economica F. Datini, 1998), 385–419; also Honour, *Chinoiserie The Vision*; Jacobson, *Chinoiserie*; Jarry, *Chinoiserie Chinese Influence*; Impey, *Chinoiserie The Impact*.

19. Tragedies: Pier Jacopo Martello, *I Taimingi* (1712), Gasparo Gozzi, *Marco Polo* (1755); tragic parody: Zaccaria Vallaresso, *Rutzvanscad il giovine* (1722); comedies: Pietro Chiari, *La schiava cinese* (1753), *Le sorelle cinesi* (1754), and Carlo Gozzi's "favola teatrale" *Turandotte* (1762).

20. Mita Choudhury, *Interculturalism and Resistance in the London Theater, 1660–1800* (Lewisburg, PA: Bucknell University Press, 2000), 16. See also Paula Backscheider, *Spectacular Politics: Theatrical Power and Mass Culture in Early Modern England* (Baltimore: Johns Hopkins University Press, 1993).

21. Martha Feldman, *Opera and Sovereignty* (Chicago: University of Chicago Press, 2007), 6.

22. I believe the apparent inconsistency in Fido's article stems only from an emphasis on spoken theater versus its musical counterpart. He appears to put opera in a separate category; thus, if one concentrates on non-operatic genres, he is correct in observing that Italy has no match for the centralized, consolidated theatrical institutions of eighteenth-century France (the *Comédie Française*, *Comédie italienne*, *Théâtre de foire et de boulevard*, etc.). I would assert, however, that Italian opera comes very close to filling this role, despite not tracing its core production to a nationally recognized capital. Franco Fido, "Il pubblico dei teatri e la questione dei generi drammatici nel Settecento," *Italiana* 9 (2000): 161–72.

23. Strohm, *Dramma per Musica*, 6.

24. Franco Piperno, "Opera Production to 1780," in *Opera Production and Its Resources*, ed. Lorenzo Bianconi and Giorgio Pestelli, trans. Lydia G. Cochrane (Chicago: University of Chicago Press, 1998), 28. On the rampant growth of opera as business, starting in the last quarter of seventeenth century, see this chapter by Piperno (1–79); also Alberto Basso, ed., *Musica in Scena: Storia dello Spettacolo Musicale*, vols. 1–3 (Turin: UTET, 1995–). On opera's cultural and commercial foundations in Venice, see Beth L.

Glixon and Jonathan E. Glixon, *Inventing the Business of Opera* (Oxford: Oxford University Press, 2006).

25. Nathaniel Burt, "Opera in Arcadia," *The Musical Quarterly* 41, no. 2 (1955): 146.

26. Strohm, *Dramma per Musica*, 5.

27. The reference to the "citizenry" and students comes from documents relating to a seventeenth-century operatic production sponsored by a noble family in Padua. Opera in centers such as Padua, where there was no court, exhibited earlier on certain traits more common to the eighteenth-century commercial opera tradition. The presence of students at an opera in a famous university center is one such example. Piperno, "Opera Production," 8, 37.

28. Ibid., 45.

29. Ibid., 69.

30. Strohm, *Dramma per Musica*, 4; Piperno, "Opera Production," 67–71.

31. Piperno, "Opera Production," 70.

32. For France see Henri Cordier, *La Chine en France au XVIIème siècle* (Paris: H. Laurens, 1910); Virgile Pinot, *La Chine et la formation de l'esprit philosophique en France, 1640–1740* (Geneva: Slatkine, 1971); Guy, *The French Image*; for England see Appleton, *Cycle*; Hsia, *Vision*; T. Blake Clark, *Oriental England* (Shang-Hai: Kelly and Walsh, 1939); David Porter, *Ideographia: The Chinese Cipher in Early Modern Europe* (Stanford: Stanford University Press, 2001); for the Netherlands see John E. Wills, *Embassies and Illusions: Dutch and Portuguese Envoys to K'ang hsi, 1666–1687* (Cambridge: Council on East Asian Studies, Harvard University, 1984); Charles R. Boxer, *The Dutch Seaborne Empire 1600–1800* (London: Hutchinson, 1965); for Germany see Todd Kontje, *German Orientalisms* (Ann Arbor: University of Michigan Press, 2004); Willy Richard Berger, *China-Bild und China-Mode im Europa der Aufklärung* (Cologne: Böhlau, 1990); Mungello, *Curious Land*; Hsia, *Chinesia*; for Russia see Barbara Widenor Maggs, *Russia and "le rêve chinois": China in Eighteenth-Century Russian Literature* (Oxford: Voltaire Foundation, 1984); Daniel J. Brower and Edward J. Lazzerini, *Russia's Orient: Imperial Borderlands and Peoples, 1700–1917* (Bloomington: Indiana University Press, 1997); for Spain see A. Owen Aldridge, "China in the Spanish Enlightenment," *Proceedings of the XIIth Congress of the International Comparative Literature Association* (Munich: Iudicium, 1990), 404–9; Michael Schlig, "Spain as Orient in Juan Pablo Forner's *Los Gramáticos*: Historia chinesca," *Dieciocho: Hispanic Enlightenment* 23, no. 2 (2000): 313–25; for the United States, see A. Owen Aldridge, *The Dragon and the Eagle: The Presence of China in the American Enlightenment* (Detroit: Wayne State University Press, 1993); John Kuo Wei Tchen, *New York Before Chinatown: Orientalism and the Shaping of American Culture, 1776–1882* (Baltimore: Johns Hopkins University Press, 1999); Henry Trubner, ed., *Catalog: China's influence on American culture in the 18th and 19th centuries: A special Bicentennial exhibition drawn from private and museum collections, China Institute in America/China House Gallery . . . April 8 through June 13, 1976* (Seattle: Seattle Art Museum, 1976).

33. Sergio Zoli, *Europa libertina tra Controriforma e Illuminismo: l'Oriente dei libertini e le origini dell'Illuminismo* (Bologna: Cappelli, 1989); "La Cina nella cultura italiana del 700," in *La Conoscenza dell'Asia e dell'Africa in Italia nei secoli XVIII e XIX*, ed. Ugo Marazzi, vol. 1 (Naples: Istituto Universitario Orientale Collana "Matteo Ripa" III, 1984), 211–57; "L'immagine dell'Oriente nella cultura italiana da Marco Polo al Settecento," in *Storia d'Italia. Annali 5 Il Paesaggio*, ed. Cesare de Seta (Turin: Einaudi, 1982), 4–123; "Il mito settecentesco della Cina in Europa e la moderna storiografia," *Nuova rivista storica* 3–4 (1976): 335–66; *La Cina e l'età del-*

l'Illuminismo in Italia (Bologna: Pàtron, 1974); *La Cina e la cultura italiana dal Cinquecento al Settecento* (Bologna: Pàtron, 1973); "Le polemiche sulla Cina nella cultura storica, filosofica, letteraria italiana della prima metà del 700," *Archivio Storico Italiano* 130 (1972): 409–67.

34. Giuliana Ericani, "L'immagine della Cina a Venezia nel Settecento," in *Venezia e l'Oriente,* ed. Lionello Lanciotti (Florence: Olschki, 1987), 161–88; "L'impero della Cina sulle scene e nella festa veneziana tra '600 e '700," in *La scenografia barocca. Atti del Convegno Internazionale di Storia dell'Arte,* ed. Antoine Schapper (Bologna: CLUEB, 1982), 95–104; "Della Cina o del Commercio dello stato. Immagini di un sogno nel declino della Serenissima," in *I linguaggi del sogno,* ed. Vittore Branca, et al. (Florence: Sansoni, 1984), 325–39.

35. The study of exoticism in early modern Italian theater has gained ground very recently, however. See for example Marco Catucci, *Il teatro esotico dell'abate Chiari* (Rome: Robin, 2007); Elena Sala di Felice, "Esotismo goldoniano," *Rivista di letteratura italiana* 25, no. 1 (2007): 115–42; and Francesco Cotticelli and Paologiovanni Maione, eds., *Le arti della scena e l'esotismo in età moderna / The Performing Arts and Exoticism in the Modern Age* (Naples: Turchini, 2006). (This scholarship will be referred to in greater detail in chapter 1.) With regard especially to the East and to China, the following provide general overviews: Franco Fido, "L'oriente sui palcoscenici veneziani del Settecento: età dell'innocenza?" in *Viaggi in Italia di don Chisciotte e Sancio e altri studi sul Settecento* (Florence: Società Editrice Fiorentina, 2006), 73–92; Anna Bujatti, "Cina e cineserie nel teatro Italiano del Settecento," in *La Conoscenza dell'Asia e dell'Africa in Italia nei secoli XVIII e XIX,* ed. Aldo Gallotta and Ugo Marazzi, vol. 3, part 1 (Naples: Istituto Universitario Orientale Collana "Matteo Ripa" VIII, 1989), 451–72.

36. For example, Appleton, *Cycle;* Maggs, *Russia;* Adolph Reichwein, *China and Europe* (New York: Barnes and Noble, 1968).

37. On the good/bad Chinese, see Fido, "L'oriente sui palcoscenici."

38. Sala di Felice, "Delizie e saggezza dell'antica Cina secondo Metastasio," *Accademia Clementina. Atti e memorie* 30–31 (1992): 213.

39. Giambattista Vico, *Scienza nuova seconda,* ed. Fausto Nicolini, Parte prima, book 1 (Bari: Laterza, 1953), 141.

40. Pietro Verri, "Elementi di commercio," in *Il Caffè,* ed. Sergio Romagnoli (Milan: Feltrinelli, 1960), 27.

The idea of identifying national superiority with "having one's eyes open" was expressed also in a 1752 letter by Francesco Algarotti, this time in relation to his native land. After pointing out that Italians taught the French (not the other way around) the finer aspects of living, such as culinary skills, dancing, fashion, and manners, he noted: "The fact is that after Europe's shared period of barbarism, the Italians opened their eyes before all other nations. When the others were still sleeping, we were wide awake." *Lettere varie,* in *Opere del conte Algarotti edizione novissima,* vol. 9, pt. 1 (Venice: Carlo Palese, 1792), 236–37.

41. Franco Venturi, "Oriental despotism," in *Italy and the Enlightenment,* ed. Stuart Woolf, trans. Susan Corsi [this article trans. Lotte F. Jacoby and Ian M. Taylor] (London: Longman, 1972), 41–51.

42. For examples of how the Italian Enlightenment is sidelined in relation to the dynamism of the movement in other European countries, see Owen Chadwick, "The Italian Enlightenment," in *The Enlightenment in a National Context,* ed. Roy Porter and Mikulas Teich (Cambridge: Cambridge University Press, 1981), 90–105.

43. See note 16 above, and Paul A. Rule, *K'ung-tzu or Confucius? The Jesuit Interpretation of Confucianism* (Sydney: Allen and Unwin, 1986).

44. "Era lo spirito del Rinascimento che con i gesuiti scopriva l'Oriente." *La cina e l'età,* 57. Mungello also credits the neo-Platonic humanist tradition of the Italian early modern period for the Italian Jesuits' success in China. *Curious Land,* 28–30.

45. Henry Kamen, *Rise of Toleration* (New York: McGraw Hill, 1967), 81. J. S. Cummins notes that a Portuguese Jesuit missionary remarked "the Italians understand so much better than us things which so little concern them"; as late as the last decades of the eighteenth century, Lord McCartney commented that the Italian fathers in Peking were "more learned and liberal than the Portuguese who still retain a considerable share of ancient bigotry and rancour." Cummins, *A Question of Rites* (Hants, England: Scolar Press, 1993), 66–67.

46. Lach and Kley, *Asia in the Making,* vol. 1, book 1, 799–800; vol. 3, book 1, 388–89.

47. Cummins refers to the "supra-nationalism" of the early Jesuits, who encouraged each individual member to "make his homeland a foreign country to himself, and every country his fatherland, so as to be at home everywhere." *A Question,* 63–67.

48. Ibid., 66.

49. Giovanni Iannettone, *Presenze italiane lungo le vie dell'Oriente nei secoli XVIII e XIX* (Naples: Edizioni Scientifiche Italiane, 1984), 16, 20, 33.

50. See Lach and Kley, *Asia in the Making,* and Adrienne Ward, "China in 17th and 18th-Century Italy: Travel Literature, Scholarly/Reformist Writings, Theater" (PhD diss., University of Wisconsin–Madison, 1998), for more on the publication and circulation of works on China by Italians and other Europeans in the seventeenth century.

51. Lach and Kley, *Asia in the Making,* vol. 3, book 1, 388.

52. Ibid., 389.

53. Venturi, *Italy and the Enlightenment; Settecento riformatore* (Turin: Einaudi, 1969); *Utopia e riforma nell'Illuminismo* (Turin: Einaudi, 1970). A standard text for eighteenth-century Italian history is Dino Carpanetto and Giuseppe Ricuperati, *L'Italia del Settecento: crisi, trasformazioni, lumi* (Rome: Laterza, 1986), although it has been augmented by Alberto Postiglia, ed., *Un decennio di storiografia italiana sul secolo XVIII* (Naples: Officina Tipografica, 1995). Other newer studies include John A. Marino, ed., *Early Modern Italy, 1550–1796* (Oxford: Oxford University Press, 2002); and Christopher F. Black, *Early Modern Italy: A Social History* (London: Routledge, 2001). One is also advised to seek the many recent and established regional and cultural histories for more thorough treatments.

54. To that end, Ricuperati cites the "other Enlightenment identities" brought to light in the work of eighteenth-century scholars Margaret Jacob, J. G. A. Pocock, and Luciano Guerci. Giuseppe Ricuperati, "Illuminismo e Settecento dal dopoguerra ad oggi," in *La reinvenzione dei lumi,* ed. Ricuperati (Florence: Olschki, 2000), 220.

55. Ibid. For more on recent assessments of Italian Enlightenment studies, see Guido Santato, ed., *Letteratura italiana e cultura europea tra Illuminismo e Romanticismo. Atti del Convegno Internazionale di Studi Padova-Venezia, 11–13 maggio 2000* (Geneva: Droz, 2003). The welcome extended toward Enlightenment research on subjects outside of high culture parallels the kinds of newer work being encouraged in French and English Enlightenment studies. See for example Felicity Nussbaum, ed., *The Global Eighteenth Century* (Baltimore: Johns Hopkins University Press, 2003), and Felicity Nussbaum and Laura Brown, eds., *The New Eighteenth Century* (New York: Methuen, 1987).

56. Lisa Lowe, *Critical Terrains* (Ithaca: Cornell University Press, 1991), and James Clifford, "On Orientalism," in *The Predicament of Culture* (Cambridge: Harvard University Press, 1988), 255–76, are only two of many responses of this kind. For details on the reception of Said's concepts, see Alexander Lyon Macfie, ed., *Eastern Influences on Western Philosophy: A Reader* (Edinburgh: Edinburgh University Press, 2003); "Edward W. Said," in *The Norton Anthology of Theory and Criticism*, ed. Vincent B. Leitch (New York: Norton, 2001), 1986–2011.

57. Stephen J. Greenblatt, "Toward a Poetics of Culture," in *Learning to Curse* (New York: Routledge, 1990), 158.

58. André Helbo, *Theory of Performing Arts* (Amsterdam: John Benjamins, 1987), 110.

59. See Strohm on the different subgenres of the *dramma per musica. Dramma per Musica*, 2–4.

60. Strohm notes that it had no poetics. On the different currents of eighteenth-century opera theory and criticism, see *Dramma per Musica*, 23–29.

61. Helbo, *Theory of Performing Arts*, vii. On present-day clarifications and confusions over theater semiotics, see Marvin Carlson, "Theories of Drama, Theatre, and Performance," in *The Oxford Encyclopedia of Theatre and Performance*, ed. Dennis Kennedy, vol. 2 (Oxford: Oxford University Press, 2003), 1355–61; Paul Hernardi and Adriana Popescu, "Dramatic Theory," in *The Cambridge Guide to Theatre*, ed. Martin Banham (Cambridge: Cambridge University Press, 1995), 302–7.

62. Umberto Eco, "Semiotics of Theatrical Performance," *Drama Review* 21, no. 1 (1977): 107–17.

63. Ibid., 112.

64. Ibid., 112.

65. Ibid., 116.

66. Ibid., 116.

67. Ibid., 117.

68. Patrice Pavis, *Analyzing Performance*, trans. David Williams (Ann Arbor: University of Michigan Press, 2003); Jean Alter, *A Sociosemiotic Theory of Theatre* (Philadelphia: University of Pennsylvania Press, 1990).

69. Consensus on the nature of the dramatic text and its relationship to stage performance is even more elusive than agreement about legitimate semiotic systems for theater. The most extreme positions define text and performance as mutually exclusive, and entirely inimical to one another (De Marinis, Lehmann). Less drastic approaches oppose them still, but admit each one's role, however minimal, in the genesis or functioning of the other (Ubersfeld, Elam). See Carlson, "Theories of Drama."

70. Pavis, *Analyzing Performance*, 12, 8–9.

71. Ibid., 216.

72. Ibid., 198.

73. Ibid., 198.

74. Ibid., 8–9; see also Helbo's conception of the playscript in relation to three subsets: dramatic text (written signs meant for reading), production text (written signs comprising stage directions, i.e., the "scenic annotations destined particularly for actualization through staging"), and theatrical text (a combination of the two above). *Theory of Performing Arts*, 44–45.

75. Pavis, *Analyzing Performance*, 8–9, 11.

76. Ibid., 208.

77. Ibid., 11.

78. Ibid., 209.

79. Alter, *A Sociosemiotic Theory*, 31–90.

80. Ibid., 82.

81. Ibid., 82. Alter refines this argument with the notion of *performance* as involving properties in excess of the coded properties belonging to the ideal signifier, which are normally apprehended right away by the spectator: "spectators intent on deconstructing stage signs, focusing on performance styles and techniques, can truly appreciate what excess properties bring to the referential world, how they help concretize it, why they infuse its vision with magic. A charismatic, muscular Hamlet, evoked by a charismatic muscular Olivier, will have a special power in excess of the meaning projected by coded Olivier acting," 84–87.

82. Ibid., 85.

83. Ibid., 71–79.

84. Ibid., 71–72.

85. Ibid., 78.

86. Ibid., 81–82.

87. Ibid., 85.

88. Pavis, *Analyzing Performance*, 24.

89. Andrea Perrucci's famous treatise *Dell'arte rappresentativa* (Naples: Mutio, 1699), predates the works Pavis quotes as being at the origins of dramaturgical analysis: Diderot, *De la poésie dramatique* (1758), and Lessing *Die Hamburgische Dramaturgie* (1767). *Analyzing Performance*, 7.

90. An example of the former is Ellen Rosand, *Opera in Seventeenth-Century Venice* (Berkeley: University of California Press, 1991), and Linda Hutcheon, "Interdisciplinary Opera Studies," *PMLA* 121, no. 3 (2006): 802–10. Examples of the latter include David J. Levin, who promotes the study of all aspects of opera that can be read (poetry, drama, stage directions, performance, reception, social occasionality/contingency), as opposed to the narrow and at times spurious interpretations that result from labeling opera a musical art first and foremost. David J. Levin, *Opera Through Other Eyes* (Stanford: Stanford University Press, 1994), 1–18. See also Arthur Groos and Roger Parker, "Introduction," in *Reading Opera*, ed. Groos and Parker (Princeton: Princeton University Press, 1988), 1–11.

91. Paul Robinson, "A Deconstructive Postscript: Reading Libretti and Misreading Opera," in *Reading Opera*, ed. Groos and Parker (Princeton: Princeton University Press, 1988), 328–46.

92. Several essays in Cotticelli and Maione, *Le arti della scena*, evidence this, as well as Elena Sala di Felice and R. Caira Lumetti, eds., *Il melodramma di Pietro Metastasio* (Rome: Aracne, 2001); and Marta Columbro and PaolGiovanni Maione, eds., *Pietro Metastasio. Il testo e contesto* (Naples: Altrastampa, 2000).

93. See Mary Hunter and James Webster, eds., *Opera buffa in Mozart's Vienna* (Cambridge: Cambridge University Press, 1997) for several examples of this approach, including Edmund J. Goehring, "The Sentimental Muse of *Opera buffa*," 115–45, and Marvin Carlson, "*Il re alla caccia* and *Le Roi et le fermier*: Italian and French Treatments of Class and Gender," 82–97. See also Thomas Bauman and Marita McClymonds, eds., *Opera and the Enlightenment* (Cambridge: Cambridge University Press, 1995).

94. Strohm, *Dramma per Musica*, 1. For a full treatment of issues surrounding eighteenth-century libretti, see Richard Macnutt, "Libretto (i)," *Grove Music Online*, ed. L. Macy, http://www.grovemusic.com; Brian Trowell, "Libretto (ii)," *Grove Music Online*, ed. L. Macy, http://www.grovemusic.com; Fabrizio Della Seta, "The Librettist," in Bianconi and Pestelli, *Opera Production*, 229–90; and Patrick J. Smith, *The Tenth Muse: A Historical Study of the Opera Libretto* (New York: Knopf, 1970).

95. On the paucity of printed scores and the difficulty of interpreting them, see Lorenzo Bianconi and Thomas Walker, "Production, Consumption and Political Function of Seventeenth-Century Opera," in *Early Music History 4, Studies in Medieval and Early Modern Music*, ed. Iain Fenlon (Cambridge: Cambridge University Press, 1984), 244. Hunter notes the challenges of re-

searching settings of late eighteenth-century comic opera. Scores were rarely published in their whole form, extant autograph scores are largely nonauthoritative, and the patched-together state of practical scores, i.e., scores used for rehearsals and ongoing performances of an opera, render it "essentially impossible to tease out distinct or internally consistent 'layers' of performance history." *Culture,* 16–17. Della Seta talks about seventeenth-century opera scores being printed primarily to commemorate individual performances, not to inspire future work. Della Seta, "The Librettist."

96. Strohm, "Towards an Understanding of the *opera seria,*" in *Essays on Handel and the Italian Opera* (Cambridge: Cambridge University Press, 1985), 97.

97. Strohm, "Towards," 96.

98. The traditional order of the steps in the process of staging a commercial opera were as follows: theater was rented, singers were procured, librettist wrote text, composer wrote music. Piperno, "Opera Production," 26–27.

99. Fubini, *Music and Culture,* 20.

100. Ibid., 5–6.

101. Strohm, "Towards," 97.

102. Ibid., 102.

103. Ibid., 96–97. Hunter concurs with Strohm's notion of the effacement of the "individual" operatic work when she says that to speak of a "single" work is a gross simplification. *Culture,* 18.

104. Hunter observes that the shape and trajectory of the plots in most of the operas she studies (Viennese comic repertory, 1770–90) were identical to their originals, *Culture,* 18.

105. Pietro Metastasio, *Tutte le opere di Pietro Metastasio,* ed. Bruno Brunelli (Milan: Mondadori, 1953); Carlo Goldoni, *Tutte le opere,* ed. Giuseppe Ortolani (Milan: Mondadori, 1935–55).

106. See note 1 for full citation.

107. Hunter, *Culture,* 22.

108. See Hunter on *opera buffa*'s conservative frameworks, *Culture,* 52–70.

109. On Salvi, see Francesco Giuntini, *I drammi per musica di Antonio Salvi* (Reggio Emilia: Società Editrice Il Mulino, 1994).

CHAPTER 1. EIGHTEENTH-CENTURY EXOTICISM

1. David Mungello, *The Great Encounter of China and the West, 1500–1800* (Lanham, MD: Rowman & Littlefield, 1999), 83–84.

2. The contact between Europe and China in the sixteenth century was actually a reencounter, given the medieval travels of Western ecclesiastics and merchants in the thirteenth and fourteenth centuries. In 1368, however, the new Ming rulers inaugurated a ban on travel both into and out of the Middle Kingdom, so that aside from limited land expeditions, the European (Portuguese) sea voyages to the south coast of China in the first half of the 1500s marked the West's first contact with the country in nearly two centuries. See Charles O. Hucker, *China's Imperial Past* (Stanford: Stanford University Press, 1975).

3. The first early works include: Augustinian friar and diplomat Juan Gonzalez de Mendoza, *Historia de la cosas mas notables, ritos y costumbres del gran Reyno de la China* (Rome, 1585); Jesuit Giovanni Pietro Maffei, description of China in book 6 of his *Historiarum Indicarum libri XVI* (Florence, 1588); Nicholas Trigault, *De christiana expeditione apud sinas* (Augsburg, 1615); Alvarez Semedo, *Relação da propagação da fé no regno da China e outras adjacentes* (Goa, 1638).

4. *Novus atlas Sinensis* was first published in 1655 as the sixth volume in Dutch cartographer Johann Blaeu's famous world cosmography *Theatrum orbis terrarum* (Amsterdam, 1635–55). It was quickly reprinted and translated into the major Western tongues. Two anastatic editions were prepared on the occasion of a 1980s conference on Martini: *Novus atlas Sinensis* (Trent: Museo Tridentino di Scienze Naturali, 1981); and a separate text containing the prefatory chapter: *Ad Lectorem Praefatio,* edited by Giorgio Melis and translated into Italian, English, French, and German, by Pietro Nicolao (Trent: Museo Tridentino di Scienze Naturali, 1981). On Martini's life and works, see Giorgio Melis, ed., *Atti del convegno Internazionale su Martino Martini* (Trent: Museo Tridentino di Scienze Naturali, 1983).

5. *Ad Lectorem,* 117–19.

6. Johannes Nieuhoff, *An Embassy from the East-India Company of the United Provinces, to the Grand Tartar Cham, Emperor of China . . .* (London?: White Friers, 1673), trans. of *Het gezantschap der Neêrlandtsche Oost-Indische Compagnie aan den grooten tartarischen cham, den tegenwoordigen keizer van China* (Amsterdam, 1665).

7. First printed in Latin as *China monumentis qua sacris qua profanis, nec non variis naturæ & artis spectaculis, aliarumque rerum memorabilium argumentis illustrata . . .* (Amsterdam: Johannes Jansson von Waesberg & Elizeum Weyerstraet, 1667).

8. The work was originally written in 1668 by Portuguese Jesuit Gabriel Magalhães, but Couplet brought the manuscript to France, where he reorganized and published it.

9. Jean-Baptiste Du Halde, *Description geographique, historique, chronologique, politique et physique de l'Empire de la Chine et de la Tartarie chinoise* (Paris, 1735).

10. See Isabel Landry Deron, *La preuve par la Chine: La "Description" de J.-B. Du Halde, Jésuite, 1735* (Paris: Editions de l'Ecole des hautes études en sciences sociales, 2002); Theodore Foss, "Reflections on a Jesuit Encyclopedia: du Halde's *Description . . . de la Chine* (1735)," *Actes du IIIe Colloque International de Sinologie, Chantilly, 1980,* vol. 6 (Paris: Belles Lettres, 1983), 67–77.

11. For a concise but solid overview of China's place in the chief intellectual concerns and developments in seventeenth-century Europe, see Mungello, *Curious Land,* and *Great Encounter;* see also Thomas H. C. Lee, ed., *China and Europe: Images and Influences in Sixteenth to Eighteenth Centuries* (Hong Kong: Chinese University Press, 1991); Jonathan Spence, *The Chan's Great Continent: China in Western Minds* (New York: Norton, 1998); Guy, *The French Image;* Lach and Kley, *Asia in the Making.*

12. Lach states that Martini's work was the first serious European attempt to write Chinese history, beginning with the earliest times and spanning to the mid-Han dynasty at the time of the birth of Christ. Lach and Kley, *Asia in the Making,* vol. 1, 527. See Mungello, *Great Encounter,* 66–67.

13. Isaac de la Peyrère, *Pre-Adamitae sive . . .* (Leyden, 1655); *Men Before Adam* (London, 1656).

14. Kircher's *China illustrata* (1667), for example, maintained that the Chinese descended from Noah. Theologian and bishop Jacques-Benigne Bossuet rejected the new chronological findings by not even including East Asia in his study *Discours sur l'histoire universelle* (1679). Orientalist Eusebius Renaudot in *Anciennes relations* (1718) attacked the Jesuit affront to sacred scriptures.

15. See Edwin J. Van Kley, "Europe's 'Discovery' of China and the Writing of World History," *American Historical Review* 76 (1971): 358–85.

16. See Mungello, *Great Encounter,* 66–67; Antonello Gerbi, *The Dispute of the New World; the History of a Polemic, 1750–1900,* trans. Jeremy Moyle, rev. and enl. ed. (Pittsburgh: University of Pitts-

burgh Press, 1973); León Poliakov, *The Aryan Myth*, trans. Edmund Howard (Edinburgh: Sussex University Press, 1974).

17. "De Confucius, le Socrates de la Chine" was a chapter title in François de La Mothe-Le-Vayer's *De la vertu des payens* (1641–42), a treatise advancing religion as reasoned (not revealed) morality.

18. Gerbi, *Dispute*, 152.

19. François Fénelon, *Dialogues des morts* (Paris: Nelson/Lutetia, 1933), 170, 176–78.

20. John Webb, *An Historical Essay Endeavoring a Probability that the Language of the Empire of China is the Primitive Language* (London, 1669).

21. Isaac Vossius, *De vera aetate mundi* (The Hague, 1659). Voltaire, hugely admiring of China, referenced it in a great many works. The most well-known citations occur in: *Le siècle de Louis XIV* (1752), *Essai sur les moeurs et l'esprit des nations* (1756), *Le traité sur la tolerance* (1763), *Le Dictionnaire philosophique* (1764), and *Les lettres chinoises* (1776). Voltaire also based his 1755 tragedy, *L'Orphelin de la Chine*, on the Chinese. On Voltaire and China, see Guy, *The French Image*, 214–84, 440–41. *L'Orphelin de la Chine* is discussed at greater length in chapter 4 of the present study.

22. See Jonathan D. Spence and John E. Wills, eds., *From Ming to Ching* (New Haven: Yale University Press, 1979).

23. Martino Martini, *De bello tartarico historia* (Milan, 1654). Concomitant with the Italian edition, four Latin editions were issued in Antwerp, Amsterdam, Cologne, and Vienna.

24. Lorenzo Magalotti, *Relazione della China*, ed. Teresa Poggi Salani (Milan: Adelphi, 1974), 51. This brief work by the Florentine academician and polygraph comprised the transcription of Magalotti's interview with Austrian Jesuit Johann Grueber just after the latter's return to Europe from Peking. Written in 1666, *Relazione della China* circulated in manuscript form for several years before being published in 1672. Magalotti sent it to peers in Rome, Bologna, and other cities. Gravina, presiding over the Academy of the Crusca and one of Magalotti's colleagues, is said to have read the pithy relation three times in a row. It was first published as part of the fourth and final volume of Thévenot's famous travel collection, *Rélations de divers voyages curieux*, 4 vols. (Paris, 1663–72). See Teresa Poggi Salani, Introduzione, *Relazione della Cina* by Magalotti, ed. Salani (Milan: Adelphi, 1974), 9–32.

25. Ibid., 83–91.

26. Jean-Jacques Rousseau, *Discours sur les sciences et les arts* (London: Oxford University Press, 1946), 113.

27. *Confucius Sinarum Philosophus*, ed. Philippe Couplet (Paris, 1687). Mungello provides a detailed examination of its contents, *Curious Land*, 247–99.

28. François Bernier, "Introduction à la lecture de Confucius," *Le Journal des Sçavans*, 7 June 1688: 17–26. Jean de Labrune's popularization entitled *La morale de Confucius* was published in Amsterdam in 1688. Mungello, *Great Encounter*, 84–85.

29. The many groups antagonistic to the Jesuits included Pietists, Quietists, Molinists, Jansenists, and reform Catholics.

30. See Domingo Navarrete, *Tratados historicos, politicos, ethicos y religiosos de la monarchia de China* (Madrid, 1676); Noël Alexander, *Conformité des ceremonies chinoises avec l'idolatrie Grecque et Romaine* (Cologne, 1700); Matteo Ripa, *Storia della fondazione della Congregazione e del Collegio de' Cinesi* (Naples: Manfredi, 1832).

31. Gottfried Wilhelm Leibniz, *Novissima sinica* (1697). For Voltaire, see note 21 above.

32. Pietro Verri, "Dialogo fra un Mandarino Chinese e un Sollecitatore," in *Il Caffè*, ed. Sergio Romagnoli (Milan: Feltrinelli, 1960), 324–26.

33. Daniello Bartoli, *Della geografia trasportata al morale* (Milan: Malatesta, 1664), 45–46.

34. William Temple, *Of Heroic Virtue* (London, 1690).

35. Jean-Baptiste Du Halde, *The General History of China*, trans. John Watts (London: John Watts, 1736), vol. 2, 211–12.

36. Bernier, "Introduction," 22–23. Translation by Guy, *The French Image*, 132–33.

37. Guy, *The French Image*, 135.

38. Ibid., 137.

39. Scipione Maffei, *Della scienza chiamata cavalleresca . . .* (Rome: F. Gonzaga, 1710).

40. See Massimo Petrocchi, "Il mito della Cina in Scipione Maffei," *Miti e suggestioni nella storia europea* (Florence: Sansoni, 1950), 23–26.

41. In this way one understands the statement that the Chinese Sage could be seen as "either a tool in the defense of orthodoxy or a weapon in the service of revolt," that he was a figure that could be all things to all men. Guy, *The French Image*, 149.

42. Ibid., 144.

43. Bartoli, *Della geografia*, 44–45.

44. Francesco Algarotti, "Dialoghi sopra l'ottica Neutoniana," in *Opere di Francesco Algarotti e di Saverio Bettinelli. Illuministi Italiani*, ed. Ettore Bonora, vol. 2 (Milan: Ricciardi, 1969), 11–77.

45. Fénelon, *Dialogues*, and Jean-Baptiste de Boyer, Marquis D'Argens, *Lettres chinoises; ou, Correspondance philosophique, historique et critique, entre un chinois voyageur à Paris & ses correspondans à la Chine, en Moscovie, en Perse & au Japon* (The Hague: Pierre Paupie, 1756), for example.

46. Alessandro Verri, "Lo spirito di società," *Il Caffè*, ed. Sergio Romagnoli (Milan: Feltrinelli, 1960), 278–82.

47. On Montesquieu and China, see Ward, "China in 17th," 203–9.

48. Vico, *Scienza nuova*; Renaudot, *Ancienne relations*.

49. The account of Anson's 1744 voyage to China offers a good example of this. Lord George Anson, Richard Walter, and Benjamin Robins, *A Voyage Round the World . . .* (London, 1748).

50. See Ward, "China in 17th," 181–86.

51. The engraving was published in Kircher's 1667 *China illustrata*.

52. Giovanni Francesco Gemelli-Careri, *Giro del mondo*, vol. 4 (Naples: Rosselli, 1699–1700), 523–24.

53. Francesco Carletti, *Ragionamento del mio viaggio intorno al mondo*, ed. Paolo Collo (Turin: Einaudi, 1989), 156.

54. Jacobson, *Chinoiserie*, 23–24. Starting in the mid-to-late sixteenth century, Florentine factories of the Medici also attempted to reproduce the beautiful Chinese porcelain that had arrived in Europe. See Honour, *Chinoiserie The Vision*, 36–39; Clare Le Corbellier, *Eighteenth-Century Italian Porcelain* (New York: Metropolitan Museum of Art, 1985).

55. Honour, *Chinoiserie The Vision*; Jacobson, *Chinoiserie*; Impey, *Chinoiserie The Impact*; Jarry, *Chinoiserie Chinese Influence*.

56. Jacobson, *Chinoiserie*, 32–34.

57. Honour, *Chinoiserie The Vision*, 56.

58. Ibid., 53–56.

59. Ibid., 61–63.

60. Six Jesuits organized by the French Academy of Sciences were subsidized by Louis XIV to go to the K'ang hsi emperor's court.

61. There seems to be some discrepancy as to the dating of these tapestries: Jacobson says 1690, then 1700, 56, 62; Honour says as late as the end of the 1720s, 92. Porter says early eighteenth century, *Ideographia*, 147. On the story of the tapestries, see Jarry, *Chinoiserie Chinese Influence*, 15–31.

62. Porter notes that the tapestries convey a degradation in the European (French) view of the authority of the Chinese monarch, compared to images produced in the preceding century. Interestingly, however, even these chinks serve to aggrandize the French crown. The cameo appearance of a Western missionary in the tapestry depicting the Dragon King on a journey denotes a "shift in the perceived balance of power within the history of the encounter [of China and Europe]. China, once the fount of privileged and universal forms of knowledge, has succumbed to the greater epistemological power of the Western [specifically French] scientific gaze." *Ideographia*, 153. In Honour's view, the tapestries still convey the "pomp and circumstance of the East," *Chinoiserie The Vision*, 93.

63. Ibid., 93.

64. Appleton, *Cycle*, 93.

65. The king of Sweden constructed a Chinese Pavilion at Drottningholm as a birthday present for his queen, sister to Frederick the Great (1753). Outside Madrid, Charles III of Spain commissioned a Chinese room in the Palace at Aranjuez, in imitation of the porcelain extravaganza he had left behind in Naples at Portici (1760).

66. See Le Corbellier, *Eighteenth-Century Italian Porcelain.*

67. Carlo Cresti, *Orientalismi nelle architetture d'Occidente* (Florence: Angelo Pontecorboli, 1999), 78.

68. Jacobson, *Chinoiserie*, 162–63.

69. *Schole-house for the Needle*, ibid., 31.

70. The following are only the most prominent among these works: John Stalker and George Parker, *A Treatise of Japaning and Varnishing* (Oxford, 1688); Johann Bernhard Fischer Von Erlach, *Entwurf einer historischen Architectur* (Vienna, 1721); William Halfpenny and John Halfpenny, *New Designs for Chinese Temples, Triumphal Arches, Garden Seats, Palings, &c.* (London, 1750); *Chinese and Gothic Architecture, Properly Ornamented* (London, 1752); William Chambers, *Designs of Chinese Buildings, Furniture, Dresses, Machines, and Utensils* (London, 1756).

71. Best-known examples include Jean Pillement's *The Ladies Amusement; or, Whole Art of Japanning Made Easy* (London, 1762), and the collections of engraving patterns for use in making *lacca contrafatta*, published by the Remondini firm in the Veneto. See for example Giuseppe Remondini, *Catalogo delle stampe in rame e delle varie qualità di carte privilegiate dall'eccellentissimo senato: le quali si lavorano in Bassano presso la dita di Giuseppe Remondini e figli di Venezia* . . . (Bassano del Grappa: Remondini, 1770). Honour, *Chinoiserie The Vision*, 121.

72. Guy, *The French Image*, 161; see also David Porter's insightful discussion of the ideology at work behind porcelain statues in English society. *Ideographia*, 181–92.

73. Katie Scott, *The Rococo Interior* (New Haven: Yale University Press, 1995), 131.

74. Jacobson, *Chinoiserie*, 64, 68–70; Honour, *Chinoiserie The Vision*, 90–92.

75. Lach and Kley, *Asia in the Making*, vol. 3, book 1, 382.

76. Honour, *Chinoiserie The Vision*, 58–59; Guy, *The French Image*, 158–60; Appleton calls him "Shen Fo Tsung," *Cycle*, 35.

77. See Guy, *The French Image*, 158–60, 354–56; Reichwein, *China and Europe*, 102–3.

78. This famous institution later became the Istituto Orientale di Napoli, today one of the foremost European centers for the study of Asian cultures.

79. Mungello, *Great Encounter*, 79.

80. Honour, *Chinoiserie The Vision*, 118. On pages 118–19 Honour refers to another monumental China gala, the 1769 Festival at Colorno to celebrate the marriage of the Duke of Parma with the Archduchess Maria Amalia, daughter of Maria Teresa. As for his mention of Rome's *Festa della Cinea*, I believe he mispells the word *chinea*. The Festa della Chinea refers to the extravagant celebrations surrounding the annual delivery of a white mare (the *chinea*) as a tribute offering to the Pope by the King of Naples. On chinoiserie as part of the chinea festivities in Rome, see Guido Magnoni, "La moda cinese e le 'cineserie' in Europa nei secoli XVII e XVIII," *Arte tra Cina e Europa*, http://www.italiacina.org/cultura/arte/arte_cineu1.htm.

81. For a general introduction to the topic, see Victor Segalen, *Essay on Exoticism: An Aesthetics of Diversity*, trans. and ed. Yaël Rachel Schlick (Durham: Duke University Press, 2002); Tzvetan Todorov, *On Human Diversity: Nationalism, Racism, and Exoticism in French Thought*, trans. Catherine Porter (Cambridge: Harvard University Press, 1993); Chris Bongie, *Exotic Memories* (Stanford: Stanford University Press, 1991); Isabel Santaolalla, ed., *"New" Exoticisms* (Amsterdam: Rodopi, 2000); Leprohon, "Esotismo."

82. The most important of which may be that the term and the very idea of exoticism is a Western European-conceived phenomenon.

83. Mario Praz sees exoticism here. *The Romantic Agony* (Oxford: Oxford University Press, 1970).

84. Leprohon, "Esotismo," 1612.

85. G. S. Rousseau and Roy Porter, eds., *Exoticism in the Enlightenment* (Manchester: Manchester University Press, 1990), 14.

86. Todorov, *On Human Diversity*, 394.

87. Rana Kabbani, *Imperial Fictions: Europe's Myths of Orient* (London: HarperCollins, 1994), 6–7.

88. Edward Said, *Orientalism* (New York: Random House, 1978).

89. Rousseau and Porter, *Exoticism*, 1–2.

90. I am interpreting Orientalism broadly here, but this definition is typically accepted. A. L. Macfie offers this: "an ideology, justifying and accounting for the subjugation of blacks, Palestinian Arabs, women and many other supposedly deprived groups and peoples." *Orientalism* (London: Longman, 2002), 4. On the question of accuracy and representation, Said states: "the phenomenon of Orientalism as I study it . . . deals principally, not with a correspondence between Orientalism and Orient, but with the internal consistency of Orientalism and its ideas about the Orient . . . despite or beyond any correspondence, or lack thereof, with a 'real' Orient." *Orientalism*, 5.

91. See for example, Richard Barbour, *Before Orientalism* (Cambridge: Cambridge University Press, 2003).

92. Choudhury, *Interculturalism and Resistance*; Tchen, *New York Before Chinatown*.

93. See chapter 2, "Gesture and Dance," for more on the *ballet des nations.*

94. Gioseffa Cornoldi Caminer, *La donna galante ed erudita*, ed. Cesare de Michelis (Venice: Marsilio, 1983), Plate 1, 11.

95. Cresti, *Orientalismi*, 36 fn11.

96. Regnard and Dufresny, *Le chinois*, 234–35.

97. Guy, *The French Image*, 11.

98. On the history of European and Turkish relations, see Lucette Valensi, *The Birth of the Despot: Venice and the Sublime Porte*, trans. Arthur Denner (Ithaca: Cornell University Press, 1993); Mustafa Soykut, *Image of the Turk in Italy* (Berlin: Klaus Schwarz, 2001); Carlo Pirovano, ed., *Venezia e i Turchi* (Milan: Electa, 1985); Charles A. Frazee, *Catholics and Sultans* (Cambridge: Cambridge University Press, 1983); Paolo Preto, *Venezia e i turchi* (Florence: Sansoni, 1975); A. N. St. Clair, *The Image of the Turk in Europe* (New York: Metropolitan Museum of Art, 1973); G. E. Von Grunebaum, ed., *English and Continental Views of the Ottoman Em-*

pire, 1500–1800 (Los Angeles: Williams Andrew Clark Memorial Library, 1972); Dorothy M. Vaughn, *Europe and the Turk* (Liverpool: Liverpool University Press, 1954).

99. P. J. Marshall and Glyndwr Williams, *The Great Map of Mankind* (Cambridge: Harvard University Press, 1982), 13.

100. Soykut, *Image of the Turk*, 148.

101. See Nora Kathleen Firby, *European Travellers and Their Perceptions of Zoroastrians in the 17th and 18th Centuries* (Berlin: Dietrich Reimer, 1988).

102. Preto, *Venezia e i Turchi*, 467.

103. Soykut, *Image of the Turk*, 113.

104. From the late fifteenth century on, these included histories, travelers' accounts, ambassadorial and diplomatic reports, and proto-sociological treatises.

105. Pierre Martino, *L'Orient dans la littérature française au XVIIe et au XVIIIe siècle* (New York: Burt Franklin, 1971), 27–46.

106. Soykut, *Image of the Turk*, 119, 127.

107. Martino, *L'Orient*, 173–76.

108. Metastasio, *Il re pastore*, in *Tutte le opere*, ed. Brunelli, vol. 1, 1137.

109. Qtd. Marshall and Williams, *The Great Map*, 17.

110. Ibid., 18.

111. Ibid., 9.

112. See chapter 2, "Characters," and chapter 3.

113. Paul Hazard, *The European Mind, 1680–1715* (Cleveland: World Pub. Co., 1963), 31.

114. Marshall and Williams, *The Great Map*, 21.

115. Nieuhof, qtd. in ibid., 22.

116. Marshall and Williams, *The Great Map*, 15–16.

117. Carpanetto and Ricuperati, *L'Italia*, 176.

118. Jeremy Black, *The British and the Grand Tour* (London: Croom Helm, 1985), 174, 176.

119. See Porter, *Ideographia*.

120. Herbert Lindenberger compares eighteenth- and nineteenth-century opera in terms of European perceptions of the East: in the first period, the Orient signifies violence, barbarism, primitivism, and a male, military-centered essence, while in the successive epoch, Orient connotes the feminine, sensual, soft, passive, enchanting, and langorous. Lindenberger does not explore the implications of these characterizations, however. He falls back on the idea that the exotic in eighteenth-century opera primarily served a need for novelty, and as a respite from classical convention. His statement that "the Orient has continued to provide an icon for various modes of 'otherness' " (181) is certainly applicable to the China operas, and this study aims to examine the substance and processes behind this iconization. Lindenberger, "Opera / Orientalism / Otherness," *Opera in History* (Stanford: Stanford University Press, 1998), 160–90. Analyses of orientalism in nineteenth-century opera include: Paul Robinson, "Is Aida an Orientalist Opera?" *Opera, Sex, and other Vital Matters* (Chicago: University of Chicago Press, 2002), 123–33; Mary K. Hunter, "The *Alla Turca* style in the Late Eighteenth Century: Race and Gender in the Symphony and the Seraglio," in *The Exotic in Western Music*, ed. Jonathan Bellman (Boston: Northeastern University Press, 1998), 43–73; Ralph P. Locke, "Cutthroats and Casbah Dancers, Muezzins and Timeless Sands: Musical Images of the Middle East," in Bellman, *The Exotic*, 104–36, and "Constructing the Oriental 'Other': Saint-Saëns's *Samson et Dalila*," *Cambridge Opera Journal* 3 (1991): 261–302; Edward Said, "The Empire at Work: Verdi's *Aida*," *Culture and Imperialism* (New York: Vintage Books, 1994), 111–32; Fabrizio Della Seta, "*O cieli azzurri*: Exoticism and Dramatic Discourse in *Aida*," *Cambridge Opera Journal* 3 (1991): 49–62.

121. See Cotticelli and Maione, *Le arti della scena e l'esotismo in età moderna*. Interestingly, of the more than thirty contributions to this volume, only four cite orientalism directly; of these, only one deals with Italian works: Melania Bucciarelli, "Echi tassiani e rappresentazioni dell'Oriente al Teatro S. Angelo di Venezia," in Cotticelli and Maione, *Le arti della scena*, 217–33.

122. See Jean-François Lattarico, "Il soggetto esotico nei melodrammi veneziani del Seicento," in Cotticelli and Maione, *Le arti della scena*, 157–73; Wendy Heller, "Venezia in Egitto: Egyptomania and Exoticism in Seventeenth-Century Venetian Opera," in Cotticelli and Maione, *Le arti della scena*, 141–55; Rosand, *Opera in Seventeenth-Century Venice*, 143–51; Angelo Michele Piemontese, "Persia e persiani nel dramma per musica veneziano," in *Opera e libretto II*, ed. Maria Teresa Muraro and Giovanni Morelli (Florence: Olschki, 1993), 1–34.

123. Secondary factors that generated exotic Settecento comedies include: contemporary events involving distant places, rivalries and competition among dramatists, moves to larger theaters requiring more expansive scenery and sound, and the need to make a comeback after bombing with a particular performance. See Marzia Pieri, "Introduzione," *La sposa persiana. Ircana in Julfa. Ircana in Ispaan*, by Carlo Goldoni, ed. Pieri (Venice: Marsilio, 1996), 9–85; Manlio Stocchi, "Introduzione," *La trilogia di Ircana*, by Carlo Goldoni, ed. Stocchi (Vicenza: Neri Pozza, 1993), vii–xxxiv; Catucci, *Il teatro esotico dell'abate Chiari*, and Marco Catucci, "Introduzione," *La schiava chinese. Le sorelle chinesi*, by Pietro Chiari, ed. Catucci (Rome: Vecchiarelli, 1999), 7–36; Sala di Felice, "Esotismo goldoniano," and Elena Sala di Felice, "L'esotismo americano: seduzioni edonistiche e implicazioni etico-politiche," in Cotticelli and Maione, *Le arti della scena*, 507–30; Franco Fido, *Nuova guida a Goldoni* (Turin: Einaudi, 2000), 121–35.

124. Other observations about the exotic in early modern opera include the notion that thematics of travel, distance, and battles between exotic archenemies served primarily to metaphorize love. See Lattarico, "Il soggetto esotico"; Silvia Carandini, "L'Oriente in maschera nelle 'invenzioni' dei comici dell'Arte," in Cotticelli and Maione, *Le arti della scena*, 23–44. For Marina Mayrhofer, operatic exoticism offered a means to flee a reality changing too quickly, "Ideologia ed evasione, due occasioni esotiche per Salieri: *Tarare* (Parigi 1787) e *Axur Re d'Ormus* (Vienna 1788)," in Cotticelli and Maione, *Le arti della scena*, 588. Bruce Alan Brown speaks somewhat to the idea that the exotic facilitated aesthetic experimentation, when he avers that the foreign subject allowed composers to enrich and intensify their musical language, "Gli Sciti di Gluck," in Cotticelli and Maione, *Le arti della scena*, 572.

125. On the first point, i.e., that exoticism allowed playwrights to try new poetics, Goldoni furnishes the foremost example. Scholars characterize his exotic plays as highly strategic to his aesthetic aims, chiefly his desire to legitimize in the bourgeois comedy a new kind of drama that surpassed traditional comic and tragic genres, as it drew from each. See Pieri, "Introduction," 18–19.

126. Stocchi, "Introduzione," xxi. See xviii–xxi for a longer discussion of the above.

127. Rosalind Ballaster, *Fabulous Orients: Fictions of the East in England, 1662–1785* (Oxford: Oxford University Press, 2005), 145.

128. Eighteenth-century Italian plays that fall partly in this category include Carlo Goldoni's *La peruviana* (1754) and *La bella selvaggia* (1758), and Pietro Chiari's Chinese diptych of 1753–54. See Goldoni, *Tutte le opere*, ed. Giuseppe Ortolani, vol. 9 (Milan: Mondadori, 1935–55), 737–813, 815–85; Chiari, *La schiava chinese. Le sorelle chinesi*, ed. Marco Catucci (Rome: Vecchiarelli, 1999).

129. The novel and the oriental tale are the two most prominent of four categories Ballaster identifies for eighteenth-century fictional narratives treating the foreign other.

130. Ballaster, *Fabulous Orients*, 12; see 10–12.

131. McClymonds is speaking of Metastasian operas; see McClymonds (with Daniel Heartz), "Opera seria."

132. Bellman, introduction, xii–xiii.

133. This is the term Feldman uses in her magisterial *Opera Seria and Sovereignty*.

Chapter 2. From Page to Stage

1. Marialuisa Angiolillo, *Storia del costume teatrale in Europa* (Rome: Lucarini, 1989), 66–67.

2. "Pagoda," *WordReference.com*, http://wordreference.com.

3. Guy, *The French Image*, 177n5.

4. Mazouer notes this distinction in regard to *Les bains de la porte Saint-Bernard*, 1698, one of the final plays of the *Ancien Théâtre Italien*, before Italians were banned from the French theaters. The singers in this play represented East Asian idols, just as Mezzetin had impersonated a large idol in *Les chinois*, 1692. Charles Mazouer, ed., *Le Théâtre italien*, by Évariste Gherardi, vol. 1 (Paris: Société des Textes Français Modernes, 1994), 411n225.

5. Richard Martin and Harold Koda, *Orientalism: Visions of the East in Western Dress* (New York: Harry Abrams, 1994), 17.

6. In English, "pagoda" indicated the temple, and "pagod" was used to refer to the deity, its official icon, or the household knickknack.

7. Anonymous, *Il cinese rimpatriato, divertimento scenico da rappresentarsi in Parigi, nel Teatro dell'Opera, l'anno 1753* (Paris: Delormel, n.d.). Giuseppe Sellitti is listed as the composer.

8. The plot of the one-act intermezzo is as follows: two Chinese sisters, one serious, one spirited, have been promised by their mandarin-father to a pair of Chinese brothers, one of whom has just returned from France. The traveler-brother returns full of gay and enthusiastic energy, in sharp contrast to his sober sibling. Unfortunately, the sisters have been assigned to their personality opposites. The entreaties the happy, lively sister makes to her father prevail, however, and the *fidanzati* are switched. Louis Anseaume, *Le Chinois poli en France* (1754), in *Histoire du Théâtre de l'Opera Comique*, 2 vols. (Paris: Des Ventes Deladoué, 1770), 250.

9. Reinhard Strohm talks about Zidiana's differences from Roxane in "Towards."

10. Anonymous, *Il cinese rimpatriato*, 9–11.

11. Historians also note that the successors to the K'ang hsi emperor were not as effective with their subjects, nor as congenial to the Jesuits.

12. Regnard and Dufresny, *Les chinois*, 230.

13. Ibid., 231–32.

14. Ibid., 232.

15. Ibid., 234.

16. Martino points out that it is also a delicate time (1692) for the Jesuits, in China as well as in Europe, *L'Orient*, 231. Interestingly, Guy disagrees with Martino's identification of a Jesuit critique in *Les chinois*. He says that besides the title and a few episodes, there is little to do with China in the piece. Instead he sees "perhaps an early popular reference to bizarre, disorderly or refractory qualities of mind and body under the name [chinoiseries] which is still current in France whenever disparagement is the object." *The French Image*, 178.

17. Technically, deities belonging to a number of East Asian civilizations took material form in plump, Buddha-like carved statues and sculpted figurines. However, because these images and idols were so associated with the other Chinese commercial products flooding the European marketplace, they came to be known mainly as of Chinese origin.

18. Placido Adriani, *Selva, ovvero Zibaldone di concetti comici . . . 1734* (Perugia: Biblioteca Augusta, 1734); "Le metamorfosi di Pulcinella," *Sipario* 82 (1954): 32–34.

19. Anonymous, "Arlequin, rival du docteur," in *Histoire du Théâtre de l'Opera Comique*, 2 vols. (Paris: Des Ventes Deladoué, 1770), 180.

20. Unfortunately, I have not been able to find a plot description for this nor for another harlequinade in which the Middle Kingdom appears—*Arlequin invisible chez le roi de la Chine*, by Alain Lesage—to see how it instrumentalized its subject, and if it too poked fun at Chinese beliefs and/or Jesuit aspirations. *Histoire du Théâtre de l'Opera Comique*, 2 vols. (Paris: Des Ventes Deladoué, 1770), 166, 172.

21. Much earlier however, clothing indigenous to foreign peoples had appeared in theater genres outside of high culture, such as the commedia dell'arte. These costumes, so to speak (for they were most likely rough and rudimentary) would have belonged to relatively nearby eastern others, most especially the Turks. *Isabella, astrologa*, for example, one of the sketches in Flaminio Scala's 1611 published collection of commedia scenarios, indicates that the female protagonist dresses as a Syrian (268), and that her female friend Rabbya wears "Turkish clothes" (270). Most often the props lists ("Robbe per la Comedia") for the scenarios call for foreign merchants' robes and/or slave attire. See scenarios 1, 26, and 36, in Flamino Scala, *Il teatro delle favole rappresentative*, ed. Ferruccio Marotti, 2 vols. (Milan: Polifilo, 1976).

22. Other reasons for the slow evolution of authentic exotic costume included 1) still-limited knowledge of foreign dress, and 2) actors' personal tastes, especially given the tradition by which they themselves had responsibility for conceiving of and providing their stagewear. Performers often wore what they wanted to, not what was recommended to them by the *capocomico* or *costumista*. Angiolillo, *Storia*, 69–70; James Laver, *Drama: Its Costume and Décor* (London: Studio Ltd., 1951).

23. Most often the wish to present contemporary fashion on stage meant the contamination of dress codes proper to dramas based in antiquity. Roman senators and military captains for example, commonly strode forth in powdered wigs, glittering jewels, sumptuous brocade drapery, and crinolines—habits derided by increasingly discerning theater critics. Angiolillo, *Storia*, 68, 71.

24. Laver, *Drama*, 151.

25. Martin and Koda, *Orientalism: Visions*, 13, 15, 53.

26. According to Boucher's designs, Angiolillo, *Storia*, 71.

27. Angiolillo, *Storia*, 74.

28. Laver, *Drama*, 156. Marvin Carlson cites a true costume reform in France, and credits *Orphelin de la Chine* with its more-or-less official beginnings. *Voltaire and the Theatre of the Eighteenth Century* (Westport, CT: Greenwood Press, 1998), 101–5.

29. Carlson, *Voltaire*, 100; Angiolillo, *Storia*, 74.

30. "Alla Contessa di Sangro, Napoli," Lettera 616, Vienna 29 Gennaio 1753, in Brunelli, *Tutte le opere*, 3:789–90. The sack gown (il sacchetto) was one of the more popular styles in eighteenth-century Europe; the *palatina* was a kind of fur collar worn by women, named after the Princess Palatina, sister-in-law to Louis XIV. Joan Nunn, *Fashion in Costume 1200–2000*, 2nd ed. (Chicago: New Amsterdam Books, 2000), 87.

31. See Schuyler Cammann, *China's Dragon Robes* (New York: Ronald Press, 1952).

32. On Chinese concern with hair, Valerie Steele and John S. Major, *China Chic: East Meets West* (New Haven: Yale University Press, 1999), 16–17.

33. Angiolillo, *Storia*, 71.

34. On Marini see Mercedes Viale Ferrero, *La scenografia del '700 e i fratelli Galliari* (Turin: Pozzo, 1963), 68–70.

35. Marcello, *Il teatro alla moda* (Venice, 1720); Algarotti, "Il saggio sopra l'opera in musica" (Venice?, 1762).

36. Francesco Algarotti, *Saggio sopra l'opera in musica*, ed. Annalisa Bini (Bologna: Libreria Musicale Italiana, 1989), 22–23.

37. Milizia, *Trattato Completo, Formale e Materiale del Teatro* (Bologna: Forni, 1969), 69–70. First published in 1771 in Rome.

38. On the Mauro family, see Ferrero, *La scenografia*, 13–14 and 17n9; Laver, *Drama*, 145.

39. Martin and Koda characterize eighteenth-century Chinese dress as conceived by Europeans as "ebullient and inventive Chinoiserie," in contrast to the "deliberate and self-conscious use of Chinese materials and symbols" in the nineteenth, *Orientalism: Visions*, 16–17.

40. Castiglione lived in China from 1715 to his death in 1766. See Cécile and Michel Beurdeley, *Giuseppe Castiglione, A Jesuit Painter at the Court of the Chinese Emperors* (Rutland, VT: Tuttle, 1971), Hui-ting Kwok, "Imperial Encounters: Giuseppe Castiglione, An Italian Painter at the Chinese Court" (master's thesis, University of Auckland, 1998), Marie-Catherine Rey, *Les Très Riches Heures de la Cour de Chine: Chefs-d'œuvre de la Peinture Impériale des Qing, 1662–1796: Exposition Présentée au Musée Guimet du 26 avril au 24 juillet 2006* (Paris: Musée Guimet, 2006).

41. Ferrero notes the progression from indiscriminate scenic exotica to more and more distinct, accurate replicas of foreign, i.e., non-European environments. *La scenografia*, 2.

42. On the fame and achievements of the Galliari family in the area of theater and stage design, see ibid.; and Rossana Bossaglia, *I fratelli Galliari, pittori* (Milan: Ceschina, 1962).

43. The dance was the first of two performed between acts of the serious opera *Giulio Sabino*. See Ferrero, *La scenografia*, 223–79 for references to more Galliari designs and sketches for chinoiserie scenes in the productions mentioned (*Arsinoe*, 1758; *Gengis-Kan*, 1777, *L'orfano della Cina*, 1790), as well as for performances of Metastasio's *L'eroe cinese* (Genoa, 1771), Vittorio Cigna's *Tamas-Kouli-Kan* (Turin, 1772) and Bertati's *Zon-Zon, principe di Kibin-kin-ka* [*L'inimico delle donne* under a different title] (Milan, Regio Ducal Teatro, 1773). Ferrero also remarks on the mediocrity of Giovannino's design talent with respect to the creations of his father Fabrizio. *La scenografia*, 59–60.

44. Maria Ida Biggi, "La scenografia," in *Teatro Malibran*, ed. Biggi and Giorgio Mangini (Venice: Marsilio, 2001), 137–38.

45. The dozen sets specified in Salvi's libretto (four for each of three acts) noticeably outnumbers the number of scenery changes in the other serious operas under consideration in this study. However, twelve falls within the norm for the genre. See Mercedes Viale Ferrero, "Stage and Set," trans. Kate Singleton, in Bianconi and Pestelli, *Opera on Stage*, 1–48.

46. Antonio Salvi, *Il Tartaro nella Cina, Drama per musica . . . dedicato all'Altezza Serenissima di Rinaldo I, Duca di Reggio, Modona . . .* (Reggio: Vedrotti, 1715).

47. On the Bibiena family, see Deanna Lenzi and Jadranka Bentini, eds., *I Bibiena. Una famiglia europea* (Venice: Marsilio, 2000); Maria Teresa Muraro and Elena Povoledo, eds., *Disegni teatrali dei Bibiena* (Venice: Fondazione Cini, 1970); A. Hyatt Mayor, *The Bibiena Family* (New York: H. Bittner, 1945); Corrado Ricci, *I Bibiena* (Milan: Alfieri & Lacroix, 1915).

48. Jean-Denis Attiret, "A Particular Account of the Emperor of China's Gardens near Pekin . . .," trans. Joseph Spence (London, 1752).

49. See the rave review given Quaglio's staging by Karl Ditters von Dittersdorf in *The Autobiography of Karl Von Dittersdorf* (New York: Da Capo, 1970), 70–72.

50. The Villa Valmarana and the Villa Giustiniani in Noventa Padovana, and the Castello Grimani-Marcello at Montegalda. See the catalogue by Lucio Grossato, *Andrea Urbani (1711–1798), scenografo e frescante* (Padua: Antoniana, 1972).

51. See *L'idolo cinese* 1, 5; 1, 8, for examples.

52. Claudia Celi, "Italy," in "Dance Traditions Before 1800," in *International Encyclopedia of Dance*, ed. Selma Jeanne Cohen, vol. 3 (New York: Oxford University Press, 1998), 542.

53. Miriam K. Whaples, "Early Exoticism Revisited," in Bellman, *The Exotic*, 6.

54. Ibid., 6. Note that ballet became entirely silent only in the eighteenth century. Before that it regularly included dialogue and/or monologues, spoken or sung. See Celi, "Italy"; Mary Clarke and Clement Crisp, *Ballet: An Illustrated History* (London: A. and C. Black 1973); Ivor Guest, *The Dancer's Heritage. A Short History of Ballet* (London: Dancing Times, 1977).

55. Edmund Fairfax, *The Styles of Eighteenth-Century Ballet* (Lanham, MD: Scarecrow Press, 2003).

56. Whaples, "Early Exoticism," 7.

57. Qtd. Mark Franko, *Dance as Text: Ideologies of the Baroque Body* (New York: Cambridge University Press, 1993), 127.

58. Ibid., 127.

59. See Miriam Whaples, *Exoticism in Dramatic Music, 1600–1800* (PhD diss. Indiana University, 1958), 23–27.

60. Leprohon, "Esotismo," 1616.

61. This perspective differed from the former, Renaissance aesthetic, which focused on humans' place in the larger universe, the order of that world, and how to read that order. In the eighteenth century humans were looking at other humans, and attempting to realize perfected visions of social intercourse. See Susan Leigh Foster, *Reading Dancing* (Berkeley: University of California Press, 1986), 121–45.

62. On the Turkish entrée of *Les Indes galantes*, see Lincoln Kirstein, *Movement and Metaphor: Four Centuries of Ballet* (New York: Praeger, 1970), 114–17.

63. Forty-five out of 292 pages (16 percent) treat dance customs of different European and global regions, beginning with the section entitled "A Summary Account of various Kinds of Dances In different Parts of the World." Gallini, *A Treatise on the Art of Dancing*, 181. Gallini was a Florentine dancer and dance master who emigrated to England when he was twenty-five years old. His *A Treatise on the Art of Dancing* was reprinted several times (1765, 1772). Scholars maintain that Gallini borrowed heavily from others. See Judith L. Schwartz and Christena L. Schlundt, *French Court Dance and Dance Music. A Guide to Primary Source Writings, 1643–1789* (Stuyvesant, NY: Pendragon Press, 1987), 35–36. I am very grateful to Madison Sowell for bringing Gallini's text and engraving to my attention.

64. Gallini, *A Treatise on the Art of Dancing*, 201–7.

65. Ibid., 201–2.

66. Ibid., 207. He states that he took the plate "from the description of a traveller into that country" (202), but I have not yet found the text.

67. Originally titled *Les Métamorphoses chinoises*, and first performed in 1751 or earlier, in Marseilles or Strasbourg. It played again at the Opéra Lyons in 1751–52, but did not enjoy its

resounding success until the July 1754 production at the Opéra-Comique. Deryk Lynham, *The Chevalier Noverre* (London: Chameleon Press, 1972), 20–24, 53, 165, 177.

68. Honour, *Chinoiserie The Vision*, 100; see also Kirstein, *Movement and Metaphor*, 110–13.

69. Lynham, *The Chevalier*, 20–24; Appleton, *Cycle*, 78–79; Clarke and Crisp, *Ballet*, 46.

70. Fairfax, *The Styles of Eighteenth-Century Ballet*, 142.

71. Ibid., 141–42.

72. Fairfax notes that this step was "evidently used in the 'Chinese' ballet *Das Fest des porzellanenen Turms zu Peking*." See ibid., 142, for a complete description.

73. Italian style takes shape between 1559 and the 1630s, then becomes extremely popular in the seventeenth century. Celi, "Italy," 543. On the history of Italian dance, see Celi; also "500 Years of Italian Dance," an online exhibition offered by the New York Public Library, http://www.nypl.org/research/lpa/italian-dance/.

On dance especially related to opera, see Kathleen Kusmick Hansell, "Theatrical Ballet and Italian Opera," in Bianconi and Pestelli, *Opera on Stage*, 177–308; Basso, *Musica in Scena*, vol. 5, *L'arte della danza e del balletto* (Turin: UTET, 1995); Alm, "Winged Feet," and "Theatrical Dance in Seventeenth-Century Venetian Opera" (PhD diss., University of California at Los Angeles, 1993).

74. First published in Nuremberg as *Neue und Curieuse Theatralische Tantz-Schul*, with text in German and Italian. See the modern edition: Gregorio Lambranzi, *New and Curious School of Theatrical Dancing*, ed. Cyril W. Beaumont, trans. Derra De Moroda (New York: Dance Horizons, 1966).

75. I have thus far been unable to locate the original work containing this engraving, nor determine exactly which member of Paris's Bonnart family of engravers and printers produced it (Henri II [1642–1711] or his son, Jean-Baptiste Henri [1678–1726]?) A reproduction of the engraving, labeled " 'A Chinese,' From the engraving by H. Bonnart" appears in Cyril W. Beaumont, *Ballet Design* (London: Studio Publications, 1946), 16.

76. Lambranzi, *New and Curious*, 16.

77. In fact, very little authentically non-European music was produced in the seventeenth and eighteenth centuries. Commenting on the score for Rameau's 1735 *opéra-ballet Les Indes galantes*, Locke says "Despite the title and other extra-musical signals, many of these [works] are musically indistinguishable from nonexotic compositions of the day." Ralph P. Locke, "Exoticism," *Grove Music Online*, ed. L Macy, http://www.grovemusic.com. Another example exists in the libretto for *Le chinois* by Regnard and Dufresny. It includes musical notation for Mezzetino's song (titled "Air des chinois"), but the melody reveals nothing outside the bounds of the standard French vaudeville line. My thanks to Richard Will for advising me on this matter. See Regnard, *Les chinois*, 1–3 (these pages are at the very end of the volume). See also "Exoticism" [Opera], *Grove Music Online*, ed. L Macy, http://www.grovemusic.com; Cotticelli and Maione, *Le arti della scena*; Whaples, *Exoticism*, and "Early Exoticism"; Bellman, *The Exotic*; Heidi Lee, "Musical *Chinoiserie*: Representation of China in Western European Music of the Eighteenth and Early Nineteenth Centuries" (master's thesis, University of Washington, 2001).

78. Jean-Jacques Rousseau, *A Complete Dictionary of Music*, trans. William Waring (London: AMS, 1975) anastatic rpt. of 1779 London ed., 265.

79. Lee, "Musical *Chinoiserie*," 31. Joseph-Marie Amiot, *Mémoire sur la musique des Chinois* (Geneva: Minkoff, 1973).

80. Whaples calls attention to the contemporary term *Türkenoper* to designate an opera on any oriental subject (Turkish, Arab, Persian, Tartar, even Indian and Chinese). She says the word is proof of the naïveté, unwillingness, or inability of seventeenth- and eighteenth-century composers to differentiate among disparate cultures, and also points to the problematics of Western musical representation of Eastern others, "Early Exoticism," 3–4, 15.

81. Heidi Lee also mentions the use of flute and other wind instruments to create a pastoral atmosphere, since chinoiserie was associated in the minds of many with a pastoral, idyllic state. "Musical *Chinoiserie*," 16–25.

82. Ibid., 10n17.

83. Dittersdorf, *The Autobiography*, 71.

84. Gerhard Croll, "*Le cinesi*. An opera-serenade by Christoph Willibald Gluck," booklet, *Le cinesi*, by Christoph Willibald Gluck (Munich: Orfeo, 1989), 16.

85. Rose A. Pruiksma discusses Lully's use of the *chaconne* (a musical piece associated with the Spanish dance called the *chacona*, thought to be derived from North African and/or New World cultures and connoting a strong exoticism and sensuality) in various court spectacles requiring a non-French presence, be it of Moorish slaves, Egyptian royalty, indigenous Americans, Turks, Italians, even Chinese. Rose A. Pruiksma, "Music, Sex, and Ethnicity: Signification in Lully's Theatrical Chaconnes," *Gender, Sexuality and Early Music*, ed. Todd M. Borgerding (New York: Routledge, 2002), 227–48.

86. Bellman, introduction to *The Exotic*, ix.

87. Hunter, "The Alla Turca Style," 51.

88. Alm, "Winged Feet," 255–56.

89. Lee, "Musical *Chinoiserie*," 16.

90. Lee's analysis of Domenico Corri's 1806 opera *The Travellers* explains how he integrates several of the Chinese musical elements introduced by Amiot. This work amounted to more or less a musical version of the "ballet des nations," in other words, an orchestral pastiche of different music from different nations. Ibid., 27–28, 52.

Chapter 3. Opere serie

1. Antonio Salvi, "Dedica," *Il Tartaro nella Cina*, 3–4.

2. See appendix 2 for plot synopses of all the operas.

3. The term "opera seria" didn't come into being until the late eighteenth century, however. Other modern appellations include "aria opera," "Neapolitan opera," and "number opera." Strohm, *Dramma*, 1–2; Thomas Bauman, "The Eighteenth Century: Serious Opera," in *Oxford Illustrated History of Opera* (Oxford: Oxford University Press, 1994), 47–83.

4. "Monstrosities" is a term Gianmario Crescimbene uses in his reprobation of opera, *La bellezza della volgar poesia* (1700). For detailed discussions of opera seria, see Strohm, *Dramma per Musica* and "Towards"; Marita McClymonds and Daniel Heartz, "Opera seria," *Grove Music Online*, ed. L. Macy, http://www.grovemusic.com; Don Neville, 'Metastasio, Pietro," *Grove Music Online*, ed. L. Macy, http://www.grovemusic.com; Burt, "Opera in Arcadia"; Richard Freeman, "Opera Without Drama: Currents of Change in Italian Opera, 1675–1725" (PhD diss., Princeton University, 1967), and "Apostolo Zeno's Reform of the Libretto," *Journal of the American Musicological Society* 21, no. 3 (1968): 321–41. On seventeenth-century opera, see Bianconi and Walker "Production, Consumption and Political Function;" Rosand,

Opera in Seventeenth-Century Venice; Tim Carter, "The Seventeenth Century," *Oxford Illustrated History of Opera* (Oxford: Oxford University Press, 1994), 1–46.

5. On the Arcadian Academy and its poetics, see Walter Binni, *Classicismo e neoclassicismo nella letteratura del Settecento* (Florence: Nuova Italia, 1976); *L'Arcadia e il Metastasio* (Florence: Nuova Italia, 1968); Amedeo Quondam, *Cultura e ideologia di Gian Vincenzo Gravina* (Milan: Mursia, 1968), and "L'istituzione Arcadica. Sociologia e ideologia di un'accademia," *Quaderni storici* 23 (1973): 389–438.

6. See Emilio Bertana, *La tragedia. Storia dei generi letterari italiani* (Milan: Vallardi, 1904); Walter Binni, "Il Settecento letterario," in *Il Settecento,* ed. Natalino Sapegno (Milan: Garzanti, 1988), 323–1040.

7. For the French influence on Italian opera seria see Strohm, *Dramma per Musica;* Bianconi and Walker, "Production"; and Melania Bucciarelli, *Italian Opera and European Theatre, 1680–1720* (Brepols: Turnhout, 2000). Bucciarelli includes tables of Italian operas and their sources in French tragedy.

8. Strohm provides a very helpful explanation of how operas more and less successfully integrated the rules of classical tragedy, *Dramma per Musica,* 202–10.

9. Ibid., 204.

10. Ibid., 17.

11. Frederick W. Sternfeld provides several reasons for the traditional happy ending of seventeenth-century opera: dramatically, it furnished a potent contrast to the solo lament by the *prima donna* or *primo uomo* that typically preceded it; musically, it was preferred by composers, who liked the opportunity it provided for more expressive variety; and the occasional nature of many operas, that is, their express purpose of celebrating signal events in European courts, favored festive, joyous conclusions. Frederick W. Sternfeld, "Lieto fine," *Grove Music Online,* ed. L. Macy, http://www.grovemusic.com.

12. Antonio Planelli, *Dell'opera in musica* (Naples: Donato Campo, 1772), 72–74. Modern edition by Francesco Degrada, ed. (Fiesole: Discanto, 1981), 42–43. My thanks to Marita McClymonds for bringing this citation to my attention.

The *lieto fine* also acquired support as part of a larger, progressive aesthetic championed by the "moderns," in their polemics against the "ancients," in the eponymous literary debate that peaked in the mid-eighteenth century. The former cheered the creation of a modern literature freed from the restraints of what they felt was a pedantic classicism, which in its most uncompromising stance argued for the tragic ending of Greek drama.

13. Sternfeld, "Lieto fine."

14. Just one example of the problems attending dynastic succession were the challenges facing Charles VI and the Habsburg empire. See Jean Bérenger, *A History of the Habsburg Empire 1700–1918,* trans. C. A. Simpson (London: Longman, 1997), 26–39.

15. See for example, Sala di Felice, "Osservazioni sulla meccanica drammaturgica di Metastasio," in Sala di Felice and Lumetti, *Il melodramma di Pietro Metastasio,* 127–59.

16. Neville, "Metastasio." See also Feldman, *Opera and Sovereignty.*

17. See Burt, "Opera in Arcadia."

18. Hunter, *Culture,* 27–51.

19. Or "art" and "non-art." Ibid., 4.

20. Ibid., 45.

21. Strohm, *Dramma per Musica,* 18.

22. Hunter, *Culture,* 21–22.

23. Strohm, *Dramma per Musica,* 6.

24. See for example, Freeman, "Opera Without Drama"; Joseph Kerman, *Opera as Drama* (Berkeley: University of California Press, 1988).

25. Strohm suggests as much when he states that opera seria has survived to the present day, "perhaps even into the age of the Hollywood cinema." *Dramma per Musica,* 29. To the objection that spectators were in the theater only for socializing and rarely gave their attention to the activity on stage, McClymonds notes that repeat audiences tuned in to the most affective scenes, and the climactic moments, "Opera seria."

26. The others were either comic or pastoral. Strohm states that these statistics were likely true for all other major cities, though Piperno speaks of a greater number of productions of opera buffa as early as the 1750s. Strohm, *Dramma per Musica,* 4, 29; Piperno, "Opera Production," 67.

27. Strohm, *Dramma per Musica,* 7.

28. See appendix 2 for plot synopsis.

29. Zoli, *La Cina e l'età,* 58. See for example, assessments of China in Scipione Maffei, *Della scienza chiamata cavalleresca* (1710), Paolo Maria Doria, *La vita civile* (1710), and Vittorio Silvio Grandi, *Le vite degli imperatori* (1716).

30. The issue of three major publications by French Jesuit missionaries at the very end of the seventeenth century contributed greatly to heightening the debates. *Nouveaux Mémoires sur l'état présent de la Chine* (Paris, 1696), by Father Louis Le Comte, argued that the Chinese had known God for longer than had European Christians; Bouvet's *Portrait historique de l'Empereur de la Chine* (Paris, 1697); Father Charles Le Gobien in *L'Histoire de l'édit de l'empereur de la Chine* (Paris, 1698) observed that Chinese ancestor worship not only was not heretical, but was socially beneficial, insofar as it provided Europeans a model of filial piety and respect for authority. See also the sections above in chapter 1 on "Chinese Antiquity" and "Religion in China."

31. See Mungello, *Curious Land;* Ronan and Oh, *East Meets West.*

32. "In un certo giorno dell'anno, che qui si accenna essere il primo di Maggio, si fa nella Cina la solennità della Giumenta, con ornarsi la Sala, ò il Cortile Regio di addobbi pastorali: e ciò in memoria della nascita del Mondo creduta da'Cinesi, in tal giorno pel calcio, che diede una Vacca ad un'uovo, onde e'dicono, che quest'Universo sortisse." Zeno, *Teuzzone,* 3–4.

33. The Milan production featured a white horse. Strohm, *Dramma per Musica,* 129.

34. A minor point: to respect Arcadian dictates that the use of grandiose theatrical contraptions be reduced if not eliminated, Zeno confined his truly grand spectacle to the finale. Troncone's funeral in act 1 constituted the other instance of spectacle.

35. Strohm notes that this motive served Zeno as a reinforcement to Cino's change of mind, should critics have deemed it insufficiently verisimilar. *Dramma per Musica,* 131–32.

36. Piperno also notes that Venetian opera (and Zeno was Venetian) traditionally included a reference to Troy, site of Venice's mythic origins. "Opera Production," 30.

37. See Poliakov, "Italy: The Seed of Aeneas," in *The Aryan Myth,* 54–70. Interestingly, given our Chinese context, Poliakov refers to "that particularly Italian form of ancestor worship which is Romanism (*Romanità*)," 59.

38. Sala di Felice, "Osservazioni," 144–48.

39. *Nell'aprirsi della nuova Colonia d'Arcadia in Verona. S'accennano i migliori Poeti italiani.* In *Rime e prose del Sig. marchese Scipione Maffei...* (Venice: Coleti, 1719), 132–37.

40. See Antonio Franceschetti, "L'Arcadia veneta," in *Storia della Cultura Veneta*, ed. Girolamo Arnaldi and Manlio Pastore Stocchi, vol. 5, part 1, *Dalla Controriforma alla fine della Repubblica* (Vicenza: Neri Pozza, 1985), 131–70.

41. Quoted in Franceschetti, "L'Arcadia veneta," 135.

42. See Quondam, "L'istituzione Arcadica"; "La crisi dell'Arcadia," *Palatino: Rivista Romana di Cultura* 12 (1968): 160–70; Susan Dixon, "Forum: Women and the Academy," *Eighteenth-Century Studies* 32, no. 3 (1999): 371–390.

43. Franceschetti, "L'Arcadia veneta," 169.

44. See for example, Daniello Bartoli, *La Cina*, ed. Bice Garavelli Mortara (Milan: Bompiani, 1975), 37–38.

45. Martino Martini, *Bellum Tartaricum, or, The History of the Warres of the Tartars in China*, in Alvaro Semedo, *The History of that Great and Renowned Monarchy of China . . .* (London: E. Tyler, 1655), 294–95.

46. Ibid., 259.

47. Nieuhof, *An Embassy from the East-India Company*, 255.

48. Ibid., 250.

49. Martini, *Bellum Tartaricum*, 285.

50. Nieuhof, *An Embassy from the East-India Company*, 249. Gemelli-Careri's take on the Ming defeat also casts a shadow over the Chinese. He sees it as just desserts, since the Ming line had been founded by lowly criminals:

> Considering the miserable end of this Family, it seems to have made good the saying in the book of Wisdom, *In the same that he Sins, in the same shall he be punish'd*. Because from the common sort it rais'd itself to the Throne, through the Industry of one of his Fore-fathers, who from a mean servant to the *Bonzes*, becoming a Captain of Robbers, put down the Family *Yven* of the Western Tartars, which had rul'd 89 years, and set up the Family *Mim* [Ming], which continu'd in the Throne, during the Reigns of 21 Emperors, for the space of 276 years, till another Captain of Robbers utterly destroy'd it.
>
> *A Voyage Round the World*, in *Collection of Voyages and Travels*, ed. Awnsham Churchill, vol. 4 (London, 1704), 387.

51. Martini, *Bellum Tartaricum*, 266–67. It should be remembered that the Jesuits, most favored of all European interlocutors with respect to the Chinese, enjoyed a fruitful relationship as well with the new Manchu administration, at least for several decades. See Pamela K. Crossley, *The Manchus* (Oxford: Blackwell, 1997).

52. Nieuhof, *An Embassy from the East-India Company*, 298.

53. Martini, *Bellum Tartaricum*, 264.

54. He proves this fact noting that the father of the last Chinese empress had maintained himself making shoes of straw, *An Embassy from the East-India Company*, 294.

55. Martini, *Bellum Tartaricum*, 263.

56. *Il Tartaro nella Cina*, 9–10. I have been unable thus far to locate designs for these scenes.

57. Text in the opera's *finale* reprises nearly all of these roles (*padre, signore, giudice, genitore, figlio, rè*), as the characters right all the previous wrongs and reestablish proper relationships among themselves. For example, upon hearing Cambice's apology and Tico's request for clemency toward his brother, Camaide tells his wayward son

> Your beautiful remorse
> Disarms me on the one hand; and on the other
> Incites justice's wrath. Yet I do return
> From judge to father.

Son, I grant you mercy:
I take pleasure in being unjust; and I pardon you.

(3,15)

> [Il tuo bel pentimento
> Mi disarma in un punto; e da la destra
> Il fulmine mi strappa. Ecco ritorno
> Già da giudice in padre.
> Figlio, pietà ti dono:
>
> Godo d'essere ingiusto; e ti perdono.]

58. Lalli, *Camaide*, no page number.

59. Porter, *Ideographia*, 135.

60. Ibid., 135–36.

61. For detailed treatment of chinoiserie as a threatening sexual metaphor and the "dominant aesthetic backdrop to tropes of gender transgression," see Porter, *Ideographia*, 181–92. See also Scott, *The Rococo Interior*.

62. On the poetics and history of the eighteenth-century intermezzo, see Charles Troy, *The Comic Intermezzo* (Ann Arbor: UMI Research Press, 1979); Irène Mamczarz, *Les intermèdes comiques italiens au XVIIIe siècle en France et en Italie* (Paris: Centrenational de la recherche scientifique, 1972).

63. *Camaide*, 25–26.

64. Ibid., 64.

65. Porter, *Ideographia*, 189.

66. Ibid.

67. Honour notes that Watteau "set the pattern and tone for rococo chinoiserie decorations not only in France but throughout Europe." This painting was part of a series entitled *Figures chinoises et tartares*, adorning the *cabinet du roi*. Impey dates them as early as ca. 1707, while Honour claims ca. 1719—in either case they are contemporaneous with Lalli's drama. Only the engravings by Aubert remain. See Honour, *Chinoiserie The Vision*, 88–90; Impey, *Chinoiserie The Impact* 80; Porter, *Ideographia*, 158–59.

68. Porter, *Ideographia*, 159.

69. Porter, *Ideographia*, 158. For the whole discussion of chinoiserie's penchant for hybridity, and its transformational and reductive powers, see Porter, 155–60.

70. Ibid., 139.

71. Impey, *Chinoiserie The Impact*, 9–10.

72. Ricci, *Taican, rè della Cina*, 32, 42.

73. Burt, "Opera in Arcadia," 132. See also Lattarico, "Il soggetto esotico."

74. Ricci, *Taican*, 2, 3.

CHAPTER 4. *L'EROE CINESE*

1. Sandro Magister, "In China, Obedience Isn't a Virtue Anymore," www.chiesa, http://chiesa.espresso.repubblica.it/articolo/112861?&eng=y.

2. Pietro Metastasio, *L'eroe cinese*, 1:1154. All citations are taken from the Brunelli edition.

3. "Ad Antonio Tolomeo Trivulzio, Milano," Lettera 542, Vienna 9 Gennaio 1752, in Brunelli, *Tutte le opere*, 3:707–8.

4. Marita McClymonds, "Myth of Metastasian Dramaturgy," Inaugural Conference for the Ricasoli Collection: Patrons, Politics, Music, and Art in Italy, 1738–1859, University of Louisville, March 14–18, 1989; Strohm, *Dramma per Musica*, 165–98.

5. Bérenger, *A History of the Habsburg Empire*, 80–98.

6. Ibid., 65.

7. Ibid., 67–79.

8. Ibid., 72.

9. See Carpanetto and Ricuperati, *L'Italia*, 122–23, and 132–36, on Muratori's role in the campaign for moderate religiosity in Italian states.

10. Ibid., 132.

11. Ibid., 136. Bérenger notes the positive effect Muratori had on Austrian *Reformkatholizismus*, beginning with his book *Della carità cristiana* (1723), translated into Czech and Hungarian. *A History of the Habsburg Empire*, 70.

12. Ibid., 79, 53–54.

13. Du Halde, *The General History*, vol. 2, 203.

14. Ibid., vol. 2, 211–12.

15. *Alessandro nelle Indie* and *Semiramide* have a few exotic touches in their stage directions, but not as extensive nor as interpretive as those in *L'eroe cinese*.

16. Sala di Felice, "Delizie," 214; Michael E. Yonan, "Veneers of Authority: Chinese Lacquers in Maria Theresa's Vienna," *Eighteenth-Century Studies* 37, no. 4 (2004), 672 n. 47.

17. See Yonan, "Veneers," 653–72.

18. Sala di Felice notes that Metastasio's stage directions indicate he is familiar with Montesquieu's work. "Delizie," 209.

19. Montesquieu, *De l'esprit des lois;* see also Walter Watson, "Montesquieu and Voltaire on China," *Comparative Civilizations Review* 2 (1979): 38–51.

20. Sixty works covering a span of fifty-six years (1722–78), see Guy, *The French Image*, appendix D, 440–41.

21. Metastasio notes this episode "and others" ("et altri"). He refers to the section of Du Halde's work in which he found the Tchao-kong story as "Fasti della monarchia cinese." This corresponds to the chapter heading "Fastes de la Monarchie chinoise" in the original work, and, in the contemporary English translation, to the section called "Annals of the Chinese Monarchy, or, A Chronological History of the most remarkable Events that happen'd during the Reign of every Emperor." See Du Halde, *The General History*, vol. 1, 269.

22. Ibid., 319–20. As for the original Chinese historical sources, Hsia states that the rescue of the son of King Li (r. 878–842 BC) by the king's loyal official Shao-gong/Duke Shao, occurred in the Western Chou era of the Zhou/Chou dynasty period (1122–256 BC), and was first documented in an extremely brief passage—twelve lines—in the *Chunqiu*, or *Spring and Autumn annals*. These annals were believed to have been compiled and edited by Confucius, ca. 500 BC.

According to Hsia, the legend next appears in Shima Qian's *Shih-chi*, described by Hucker as the earliest major historical work of the early empire period and "one of the most prized works of all East Asian literature." In this work, written 150?–87? BC, the averted murder of the imperial heir takes place in a different context. The royal infant is no longer the emperor's son, but his grandson, born to the emperor's daughter and her husband Zhao Suo. The son-in-law Zhao Suo is a member of the Chao family, cherished by the emperor for its long years of faithful service to the dynasty. The Chaos have enemies, however, in the rival Tu clan. The ruthless Tu'angu, head of the rival clan, slyly manages to have all Chao members assassinated. To make sure he also rids the realm of the infant heir, he forges orders to kill all children under two. Chen Ying, a retainer loyal to the Chao family, saves the baby by substituting his own son. Later, at a propitious moment, court officials tell the ruler of the wrongs done to the Chao family by the Tu'angu and his clan. The emperor reinstates the orphan

and has the entire Tu clan executed. When the orphan is of majority age, his protector Chen Ying commits suicide so as to be reunited in the netherworld with a former associate who helped him greatly in the rescue attempt of the baby heir. (Hsia explains that Chinese culture revered loyalty to friends just after loyalty to sovereign.)

Some discrepancies have yet to be resolved. For example, Hucker conforms with Hsia as far as locating King Li's reign in the mid-800s BC, but states that the *Chunqiu* covered events throughout China only from 722 to 481 BC. Du Halde's version of the orphan story has more (and some conflicting) details compared to Hsia's description of the *Chunqiu* entry. Also, Du Halde's account has none of the embellishments of the *Shih-chi* version. Might Du Halde and/or his co-Jesuit contributors have derived their dynastic history from yet another Chinese or European source? See Hsia, "The Transplanted Chinese Orphan"; Hucker, *China's Imperial Past*, 224–27.

23. Du Halde, *The General History of China*, vol. 1, 321.

24. The pre-story in Metastasio's *Argomento* recaps even more concisely the historical incident:

> In tutto il vastissimo impero cinese è celebre anche a' dì nostri dopo tanti e tanti secoli l'eroica fedeltà dell'antico Leango (nella Storia Tchao-kong).
>
> In una sollevazione popolare da cui fu costretto a salvarsi con l'esilio l'Imperadore Livanio suo Signore; per conservare in vita il picciolo Svenvango, unico resto della trucidata famiglia Imperiale, offerse Leango con lodevole inganno alle inumane ricerche de' sollevati, in vece del Reale Infante, il proprio figliuolo ancor bambino, da lui nelle regie fasce artificiosamente ravvolto. E sostenne a dispetto delle violenti tenerezze paterne di vedarselo trafigger su gli occhi, senza tradire il segreto.
>
> *L'eroe cinese*, 1155.

25. Premaré's translation greatly abridged the Chinese drama, although he retained the fundamental outlines of the plot. Shouyi Chen, "The Chinese Orphan," in Hsia, *Chinesia*, 361.

26. See note 22.

27. Some critics say it covers twenty-five years, e.g., Shouyi Chen. Carlson, however, citing Voltaire's astonishment at the excessive length of the Chinese drama, mentions seventy-five. Carlson, *Voltaire*, 99.

28. Spence, *The Chan's Great Continent*, 75.

29. As a side note, though I have not come across any direct documentation to verify this, Metastasio may have been influenced by interpretations of the orphan account in contemporary Jesuit theater. The Chao family saga counted among the more popular "Chinese" events and themes that the Jesuits adapted for their school theater in German states in the eighteenth century. In fact, in a list of twenty-eight Jesuit works produced in German-speaking states in the eighteenth century, at least four treat the orphan story, beginning with *Chaocungus Tragoedia*. It was produced in Ingolstadt in 1736, only one year after Du Halde's Paris publication (and sixteen years before Metastasio's opera). Hsia observes that even though "plays dramatizing Chinese martyrs and virtuous non-Christians were staged regularly in Germany, Switzerland, and Austria from the beginning of the eighteenth century . . . to the year of the suppression of the Societas Jesu," extant playtexts are extremely rare. In any case, as mentioned in this book's introduction, I am concerned with Italian dramas in the vernacular. See Hsia, "The Transformation of Chinesia"; and William H. McCabe, S.J., *An Introduction to the Jesuit Theater*, ed. Louis J. Oldani, S.J. (St. Louis: The Institute of Jesuit Sources, 1983).

30. In the pre-story part of the *Argomento*, Metastasio leaves out that the emperor was a tyrant, and replaces the throat cutting (in

the historical account the rebellious crowds cut the throat of the alleged imperial orphan—the minister's son—right in front of him) with a less vicious general stabbing: "despite the violent pangs of his paternal love, he managed to watch [his son] be slain before his eyes, without giving away the secret" ("sostenne a dispetto delle violenti tenerezze paterne di vederselo trafigger su gli occhi, senza tradire il segreto"). *L'eroe cinese*, 1155.

31. On the century's reverence for high voices, see Margaret Reynolds, "Ruggiero's Deceptions, Cherubino's Distractions," in *En Travesti: Women, Gender Subversion, Opera*, ed. Corinne E. Blackmer and Patricia Juliana Smith (New York: Columbia University Press, 1995), 132–51.

32. Only rarely did singing prominence not correspond to story prominence. That is, the two performers comprising the first-ranked singing couple were normally linked romantically as the most significant lovers in the opera plot. Likewise, the second-ranked vocalists constituted the secondary pair of *innamorati*, and by the opera's end, each pair of lovers was happily united. Such were the "the conventions of rank as related to first and second couples," according to McClymonds. She points to the following operas which deviated from the norm: *Issipile* (1732), where the *secondi* are son and mother; *Ciro riconosciuto* (1736), which added to the traditional cast members a dominant mother figure who not only surpassed the principal couple in aria allotment, but also was paired within the narrative with the second-ranking *uomo*, for whom she was too strong a performative consort; *Zenobia* (1740), where the *prima donna* loves the *primo uomo* but stays faithful to the tenor, and *Attilio Regolo* (1750). "Myth," 11–12, 16.

33. It should be noted, however, that here too, the lovers situation does not follow convention. The principal woman Attilia is paired with the third-ranking Licinio, a highly unusual arrangement.

34. McClymonds notes that Metastasio established this ranking system in 1733 and it held sway only until around 1750, when he returned to giving all protagonists equal musical weight, that is, the same number of arias. *L'eroe cinese* seems to deviate from this finding. "Myth," 9–10, 16.

35. Ibid., 12.

36. Neville, "Metastasio," 354. McClymonds says that most heroes of *opere serie* do not triumph by their wills, but rather, virtuous endings occur despite the hero's actions. "Myth," 12.

37. This practice from the French tragedy was known as the "liaison-des-scenes," and became a vital convention of opera seria.

38. This apparently takes place offstage, in the time between acts 1 and 2.

39. On the aria-oriented dramaturgy of eighteenth-century opera, see Ronald J. Rabin, "Mozart, Da Ponte, and the Dramaturgy of Opera Buffa: Italian Comic Opera in Vienna, 1783–1791" (PhD diss., Cornell University, 1996); Peter Kivy, *Osmin's Rage* (Princeton: Princeton University Press, 1988); Marita McClymonds, "Aria," (Part 2, The Eighteenth Century), *Grove Music Online*, ed. L. Macy, http://www.grovemusic.com.

40. Kivy, *Osmin's Rage*, 175–76.

41. On the terms polemic, see Rule, *K'ung-tzu or Confucius?* and the works in note 16 from introduction.

42. Sala di Felice, "Delizie," 138–39.

43. Zoli, *La Cina e l'età dell'illuminismo*, 231.

44. Preface, *The Orphan of China*, 179–80. This and all subsequent English translations of *Orphelin* are from *The Orphan of China*, by Voltaire, in *The Works of Voltaire*, ed. and trans. Tobias George Smollett and William F. Fleming (Paris: E. R. Du Mont, 1901), 15:175–237.

Voltaire likely knew of Metastasio's opera by reading the libretto, hearing about it in printed works and/or his correspondence, or via conversations with fellow luminaries who had attended or otherwise knew of the production. It appears unlikely that he ever saw *L'eroe cinese* before penning his spoken tragedy, since in the few years between the première of the *dramma per musica* in 1752 and the completion of his work (1755), the opera never played in the areas to which Voltaire confined himself (Berlin, Geneva, and environs). Documented performances of *L'eroe cinese* in this period include: Vienna, Naples, Palermo, and Rome [all in 1752]; Venice, Naples, Dresden, Lisbon, Hamburg, Madrid, and Warsaw [1754]. Some scholars maintain the reverse, i.e., that Metastasio was inspired by Voltaire's play, but offer no supporting information. See Hsia, "The Transplanted Orphan," and Chen, "The Chinese Orphan."

45. Preface, *The Orphan of China*, 176.

46. Preface, *The Orphan of China*, 176.

47. Ibid., 177.

48. Ibid., 176.

49. Quoted in William H. Sun, "The Orphan of Chao and China: A Comparative Study of Three Revenge Plays by Ji Junxiang, Voltaire and Shakespeare," *Text and Presentation: The Journal of the Comparative Drama Conference* 11 (1991): 25.

50. Carlson, *Voltaire*, 43–44.

51. It has been said that Voltaire used theater as an "école de moeurs," and a too-blatant vehicle for Enlightenment propaganda.

52. Voltaire, *The Orphan of China*, 216.

53. Claudia Marie Kovach, "Reconsidering the 'Victor Vanquished': Panoplies of Power in Voltaire's *L'Orphelin de la Chine*," *Studies in Language and Literature* 5 (1992): 59–76.

54. Voltaire, *The Orphan of China*, 224.

55. Ibid., 198.

56. The spotlight on Idamé's emotionalism might also have been due to Voltaire's anticipating the outrageously famous actress Mme. Clairon in the role, and/or to the new fashion in France for pathos on the stage. The vogue for theatrical sentimentality manifested itself particularly in comedies classified as *attendrissante*, or *larmoyante*, that is, that mixed tragic elements with comic, and were expressly designed to bring their spectators to tears. See Carlson, *Voltaire*, 49–50.

57. Voltaire, *The Orphan of China*, 236–37.

58. Carlson notes that *Orphelin de la Chine* was "much closer [than his other tragedies] to Voltaire's own philosophy of the natural connection between reason and morality, and in fact much more subversive of a conservative ecclesiastical position than the few supposed references to deism dutifully excised by Crébillon." *Voltaire*, 99. Guy observes: "Voltaire would always pretend to study China as a philosophical representation, and as such, a weapon in his ideological armoury." *The French Image*, 226.

59. Voltaire, preface, *The Orphan of China*, 179.

60. Although he offers no supporting documentation, William H. Sun claims that "the repressive [Tartar] laws, which could kill a play and its authors and performers immediately, . . . forced playwright Ji Junxiang to disguise his very timely political play as a history saga attacking an ancient dictator." He notes Voltaire's mistake in assessing the play as emblematic of an accomplished Chinese theater culture: "It is true that the Yuan dynasty marked the first peak in the history of Chinese drama. Ironically, this achievement . . . illustrates not the rulers' mercy to artists in particular but their cruelty to Chinese intellectuals in general. Their new racial discrimination laws cast all Chinese in the lowest social status and banned them from entering government services.

This compelled many intellectuals who could have become officials in the previous system to write plays—a profession as inferior as prostitution according to the law." "The Orphan of Chao and China," 109.

61. Kovach, "Reconsidering."

CHAPTER 5. *L'ISOLA DISABITATA*

Originally published in a slightly different form in *Theatre Journal* 54 (2002): 203–21. Reprinted by permission of the author and the publisher. I wish to thank Marita McClymonds for her helpful comments and suggestions in the revision of this chapter.

1. Tom Denison, Dharmalingam Arunachalam, Graeme Johanson, and Russell Smyth, "The Chinese Community in Prato" (paper presented at Communities and Action: Prato CIRN Conference, Prato, Italy, November 5–7, 2007).

2. While Carlo Goldoni's fame among theater scholars rests primarily or even solely on his prose comedies, fully one-third of his theatrical production (eighty out of approximately 240 works) was written for the musical stage. Comic opera was his privileged musical genre, accounting for fifty-four of his eighty librettos. By 1757, the year in which he collaborated with Neapolitan composer Giuseppe Scarlatti on *L'isola disabitata*, Goldoni had already written more than thirty comic librettos, three-fifths of his lifetime total. On Goldoni's career as a librettist, see Piero Weiss, "Goldoni, Carlo," *Grove Music Online*, ed. L. Macy, http://www.grovemusic.com; Piero Weiss, "Opera buffa," *Grove Music Online*, ed. L. Macy, http://www.grovemusic.com. The most recent studies on Goldoni's musical theater include Domenico Pietropaolo, ed., *Goldoni and the Musical Theatre* (New York: Legas, 1995), and Ted Emery, *Goldoni as Librettist: Theatrical Reform and the Drammi Giocosi* (New York: Peter Lang, 1991). While Emery ably demonstrates how Goldoni's reform interests emerge in his comic operatic works, neither his nor Pietropaolo's volume gives much attention to *L'isola disabitata*.

3. See Giorgio Padoan, "L'impegno civile di Carlo Goldoni," in *Il punto su: Goldoni*, ed. Giuseppe Petronio (Bari: Laterza, 1992), 146–52; Sergio Romagnoli, "Goldoni e gli illuministi," in *Carlo Goldoni 1793–1993. Atti del Convegno del Bicentenario. Venezia, 11–13 aprile 1994*, ed. Carmelo Alberti and Gilberto Pizzamiglio (Venice: Regione del Veneto, 1995), 55–78.

4. Franco Fido hypothesizes as much when he notes that *L'isola disabitata* suggests its author's engagement in certain kinds of intensive and important European cultural experiences which the Venetian bourgeois spoken comedy by its nature tended to exclude. *Nuova guida a Goldoni* (Turin: Einaudi, 2000), 70.

5. See Weiss, "Goldoni, Carlo," and "Opera buffa"; Daniel Heartz, "Goldoni, *Don Giovanni* and the Dramma Giocoso," in *Mozart's Operas* (Berkeley: University of California Press, 1990), 195–205; Heartz, "The Creation of the Buffo Finale in Italian Opera," *Proceedings of the Royal Musical Association* 104 (1977–78): 67–78; Renato Bossa, "Goldoni e l'opera buffa," *Sipario* 537 (1993): 65–68; Donald J. Grout, *A Short History of Opera* (New York: Columbia University Press, 1988), 287.

6. According to Piero Weiss, the "dramma giocoso" designation, along with all others in use ("dramma bernesco," "dramma comico," "divertimento giocoso," "commedia per musica," etc.) is virtually meaningless. See "Opera buffa." Heartz, however, makes a case for Goldoni's intervention in giving the *dramma giocoso* a "specific complexion" that strongly influenced certain subsequent

comic operatic masterpieces, among them *Don Giovanni*. See "Goldoni, *Don Giovanni*, and the Dramma Giocoso."

7. Daniel Heartz, "Poet as Stage Director: Metastasio, Goldoni, and Da Ponte," in *Mozart's Operas* (Berkeley: University of California Press, 1990), 96.

8. Although McClymonds notes that the baritone voice was seldom used in eighteenth-century opera. Heartz, "Goldoni, *Don Giovanni*, and the Dramma Giocoso," 197. For more on the buffo aria, see Hunter, *The Culture of Opera Buffa*, 110–26.

9. Marita McClymonds, "Opera seria? Opera buffa? Genre and Style as Sign," in *Opera buffa in Mozart's Vienna*, ed. Mary Hunter and James Webster (Cambridge: Cambridge University Press, 1997), 197–231. See also McClymonds, "Style as Sign in Some Opere Serie of Hasse and Jomelli," International Musicological Symposium: Johann Adolf Hasse in Seiner Zeit, Hamburg, 1999. I thank Professor McClymonds for sharing this paper with me.

10. This is a retraction of what I have asserted in an earlier analysis of *L'isola disabitata*, where I maintained that these four characters played buffo, not *mezzo carattere* parts (Ward, " 'Imaginary Imperialism,' " 214). Upon closer examination it seems that they occupy a more middle vocal and dramatic ground.

11. Heartz, "Poet as Stage Director," 96. With respect to Goldoni's interest in commercial gain from his libretti, his denigration of them in his *Mémoires* leads Piero Weiss to refer to them as "merely lucrative by-products" of his more committed work, the spoken plays. See "Opera buffa."

12. One of Goldoni's most successful *drammi giocosi*, *Il filosofo di campagna* (1754), shows the earnestness with which Goldoni committed to the *parti serie* Rinaldo and Eugenia, where Galuppi goes full throttle with the heroic style in their arias. Heartz, "Goldoni, *Don Giovanni*, and the Dramma Giocoso," 197.

13. "the two books on which I've meditated most, and which I'll never regret using, were World and Theater. The first shows me many, many diverse types of people, it paints them for me so naturally that they seem made on purpose to supply me with abundant topics for pleasant and instructive comedies; it puts in front of me the signs, the substance, the effects of all the human passions, it provides me with interesting events, it informs me about current customs, it instructs me on the most common vices and defects of our century and of our Nation; . . . at the same time it points out to me, via certain virtuous persons, the means with which Virtue resists these corruptions." From the preface of the first volume of Goldoni's works, published by Bettinelli in Venice in 1750. See Goldoni, http://www.classicitaliani.it/goldoni/goldo58.htm.

14. General consensus with regard to Venice (and the Italian peninsula as a whole) is that a true middle class was only beginning to take shape in the Settecento. Recent scholarship points to the more accurate division of society into two orders: a higher, yet heterogeneous social tier, comprised of the nobility and wealthy non-nobles (including professionals, state officials, and, most notably, merchant *borghesi*), and an equally composite lower tier, containing but not limited to small shopkeepers, artisans, servants, manual workers, peasants, and the disenfranchised. A full-fledged *borghesia*, or middle class, only eventually consolidated from groups at a nebulous intermediary position between the upper and lower orders.

For bibliography and a very good summary discussion of the complexity attached to the question of social class in eighteenth-century Venice, see Maggie Günsberg, *Playing with Gender: The Comedies of Goldoni* (Leeds: Northern Universities Press, 2001), 10–13.

15. Dino Carpanetto, "Reforms without Enlightenment: the Papal States, the republics and Charles Emanuel III's Piedmont," in *Italy in the Age of Reason, 1685–1789*, Carpanetto and Giuseppe Ricuperati, trans. Caroline Higgitt (London: Longman, 1987), 198–202; Paolo Preto, "L'Illuminismo veneto," in *Il Settecento*, vol. 5, part 1, *Storia della cultura veneta*, ed. Girolamo Arnaldi and Manlio Pastore Stocchi (Vicenza: Neri Pozza, 1985), 1–45.

16. Carpanetto refers to this group as the "merchant aristocracy" or "merchant oligarchy," in view of the fact that the majority of Venetian nobility derived their wealth from their forebears engaged in sea trade in centuries past. The terminology should not be understood as affirming the inclusion of merchants in eighteenth-century Venetian aristocracy. On the contrary, ensconced in lives of idle and wasteful luxury, most of these élites disdained the idea of working in trade or commerce, and associated the merchant with a less socially prestigious rank.

17. Although Venetian conservatism and tight bonds between the patricians and the church forestalled major jurisdictionalist reforms, ecclesiastical domain lessened to some measure. Carpanetto notes, "There were few other cities in Italy where the [jurisdictionalist] debate reached such radical and liberal heights as it did in Venice." "Reforms without Enlightenment," 201.

18. Ibid., 201.

19. Competition from other nations quashed the recovery and rehabilitation of Venetian sea markets, and the state's own calcified land policies prevented attempts at modernizing agriculture in the provinces. As an example of the reform attempts that failed, a new customs law in 1754 whose provisions included free export of grain "seemed to be ushering in a system of free trade much earlier than other similar Italian provisions." Unfortunately it came to naught, since traditional structures and legal provisions were never revamped to conform with new edicts. Ibid., 200–201.

20. Isser Woloch, *Eighteenth-Century Europe: Tradition and Progress, 1715–1789* (New York: Norton, 1982), 124.

21. Ortolani, Note, *Il medico olandese*, in *Tutte le opere*, vol. 6, 1244.

22. *Tutte le opere*, vol. 6, 367–440.

23. The Netherlanders had apparently feared an uprising on the part of the Chinese. See Boxer, *The Dutch Seaborne Empire 1600–1800*, 236.

24. In *China and the Foreign Powers: The Impact of and Reaction to Unequal Treaties* (Dobbs Ferry, NY: Oceana, 1970), 1–4, William L. Tung discusses the Chinese disdain for trade and traders, who came in at the bottom of a traditional hierarchy of professions.

25. Binding of the Chinese woman's feet is likened to the cramped narrowness of the Chinese mind, for example. See Porter, *Ideographia*, 211–26.

26. "Sarebbe'egli utile, perciò espediente il mettersi nello stato di una totale indipendenza. A che dico, che no. Prima non si potendo per la natura; e volendolo ottenere per legge, si verrebbe a perdere, anzi che a guadagnare. E poi, perchè si priverebbe la nazione de' lumi degli altri popoli; e per questa via verrebbe col tempo ad essere di tutte la più bisognosa di dipendere siccome accadde agli Ebrei, prima de' tempi di Salomone e avverrà senza dubbio ai Cinesi, dove non cambino metodo politico." Antonio Genovesi, *Delle lezioni di commercio*, part 1 (Naples: Fratelli Simone, 1765–67), 118.

27. "La China . . . mi pare ancora molto distante dall'essere una nazione dotta, e di uomini pervenuti alla loro maturità e v'è tuttavia di gran fanciullaggine." Ibid., part 2, 207.

28. "Di' un poco che una nave da guerra cinese, se quelle mezze femmine n'hanno alcuna, attraversi i nostri mari come noi attra-

versiamo loro? Tanto ardirebbero di berseli! E se si desse il caso che qualcuna il facesse, vogliam dire che il suo capitano farebbe in uno de' porti nostri quel che gli paresse e piacesse, come fece il caposquadra Anson quando giunse in Cantone con la sua nave?" Giuseppe Baretti, *La scelta delle lettere familiari*, ed. Luigi Piccioni (Bari: Laterza, 1912), part I, letter XXVI, 111.

29. A caveat for my translation: I can only hope to approximate both the sense and nonsense of the Italian wordplay. The Italian makes extensive use of the occlusive phoneme /k/ and truncated syllables at the end of lines, perhaps to imitate the perceived clipped sound of Chinese speech, but also highly conventional in low-style operatic diction. I have tried to imitate this flavor in an English parody as closely (and creatively) as possible.

30. See chapter 2, "Characters," and "Gesture/Dance."

31. Allardyce Nicoll, *World of Harlequin* (Cambridge: Cambridge University Press, 1963), 16–18.

32. Ibid., 44–46.

33. From the diary entry of a spectator of Andreini's command performance at the Medici wedding of 1589, qtd. in John Russell Brown, ed., *The Oxford Illustrated History of Theatre* (Oxford: Oxford University Press, 1995), 121.

34. Antonio Scuderi, *Dario Fo and Popular Performance* (Ottawa: Legas, 1998), 8.

35. Antonio Scuderi, *Dario Fo: Stage, Text and Tradition* (Carbondale: Southern Illinois University Press, 2000), 58. For more on the history of *grammelot* and its manifestations in twentieth-century theater, see the aforementioned works by Scuderi, as well as Dario Fo, *Tricks of the Trade*, trans. Joseph Farrell (New York: Routledge, 1991).

36. For a modern-day version of this technique, one might consider the sounds used to convey the parents' voices issuing from offscreen in the animated *Peanuts* movies.

37. The language business in the turqueries episode consists actually of several levels, or modes of expression, all of them inferior to the standard French of the rest of the text. The majority of the Turkish talk is a Mediterranean *lingua franca*, a sort of dumbed-down Romance blended from French, Spanish, Italian, and Arabic. It would have been understandable to French, Italian, and Spanish-speaking audiences. Slightly more nonsensical Turkish phrases mix authentic Turkish, Arabic, and Hebrew with gibberish words; finally, some terms appear to be wholly invented, with the occasional scatological reference typical of commedia wordplay thrown in (the term "Cacaracamouchen" is explained as meaning "My darling" in Turkish). See Morris Bishop, trans. and ed., *The Would-Be Gentleman*, in *Eight Plays by Molière*, by Molière, trans. Morris Bishop (Mattituck, NY: Aeonian Press, 1957), 387.

38. Greenblatt faults New World colonizers not only for denying speech to the American natives, but also for perpetrating the exact opposite, i.e., for denying *any difference at all* between indigenous and European language. Recorders of encounters between Europeans and Americans often documented absolute understanding between the two parties, neither of which spoke the other's language—another instance of obliterating the other's reality. Goldoni's use of Chinese-sounding gibberish to cloak clearly intelligible Italian harkens as well to this colonial practice. See Greenblatt, "Learning to Curse: Aspects of Linguistic Colonialism in the Sixteenth Century," *Learning to Curse: Essays in Early Modern Culture* (London: Routledge, 1990), 26–32.

39. See Alessandro Verri, "Lo spirito di società," *Il Caffè 1764–1766*, ed. Gianni Francioni and Sergio Romagnoli (Turin: Bollati Boringhieri, 1993), 396–402.

40. Thanks to Jonathan Shiff for bringing this to my attention.

41. Michael Seidel, *Robinson Crusoe: Island Myths and the Novel* (Boston: Twayne, 1991), 36–54.

42. See Greenblatt's discussion of this colonialist attitude in "Learning to Curse," 17.

43. Fido, *Nuova guida a Goldoni*, 70. Other notable "island story" ancestors include Thomas More's *Utopia* (1516), Tommaso Campanella's *La città del sole* (1623), and Francis Bacon's *The New Atlantis* (1627).

44. Daniel Defoe, *La vita e le avventure di Robinson Crusoe*, trans. D. Occhi (Venice, 1757–62). The National Union Catalog contains records of Italian translations (largely from the French) beginning in 1734 and continuing with regularity throughout the eighteenth century. *National Union Catalog Pre-1956 Imprints*, vol. 136 (London: Mansell, 1971), 635–36.

45. Mary Louis Pratt, *Imperial Eyes: Travel Writing and Transculturation* (London: Routledge, 1992), 125.

46. Julia Douthwaite, *Exotic Women: Literary Heroines and Cultural Strategies in Ancien Régime France* (Philadelphia: University of Pennsylvania Press, 1992), 11.

47. See chapter 2, section on "Gesture and Dance."

48. A familiar instance of the *ballet des nations* occurs as the last dance interlude in Molière's comedy-ballet *Le Bourgeois gentilhomme* (1670). It featured Spaniards, French, and Italians. In 1697 André Campra produced his famous opéra-ballet *L'Europe galante*, with four *entrées*: French, Spanish, Italian, and Turkish.

49. Foster, *Reading Dancing*, 135.

50. Qtd. in Franko, *Dance as Text*, 44.

51. Ibid., 129.

52. Emery, *Goldoni as Librettist*, 83–93.

53. Michael Hays, "Representing Empire: Class, Culture and the Popular Theatre in the Nineteenth Century," *Imperialism and Theatre*, ed. J. Ellen Gainor (London: Routledge, 1995), 133.

54. Ibid., 136.

55. Fido, *Nuova guida a Goldoni*, 72–73.

56. Carlo Goldoni, *The Coffeehouse*, trans. Jeremy Parzen (New York: Marsilio, 1998), 176.

57. The publications of these political economists, statesmen and *filosofi* include: Pompeo Neri, *Osservazioni sopra il prezzo legale delle monete e le difficoltà di prefinirlo e di sostenerlo* (1751); Gian Francesco Pagnini (together with Angelo Tavanti), translation of John Locke's writings on economics as *Ragionamento sopra la moneta, l'interesse del denaro, le finanze, il commercio*, to which was added as an appendix Pagnini's essay *Sopra il giusto pregio delle cose* (1751); Girolamo Belloni, *Del commercio* (1750, 1757); Ferdinando Galiani, *Della moneta* (1751); Genovesi, *Lezioni di commercio*; François Quesnay, the articles "Fermiers" and "Grains" in the *Encyclopédie* (1756–57), *Tableau économique* (1758), *Physiocratie* (1768); Anne-Robert-Jacques Turgot, *Réflections sur la formation et la distribution des richesses* (1766), *Lettres sur la liberté du commerce des grains* (1770); Adam Smith, *An Inquiry into the Nature and Causes of the Wealth of Nations* (1776).

58. Carpanetto, "Reforms without Enlightenment," 198.

59. Ibid., 199.

Chapter 6. *L'idolo cinese*

1. The *Protesta* following the *Argomento* in Domenico Lalli's libretto for the *dramma per musica Camaide, l'imperatore della Cina*, 3.

2. See appendix for more information on Lorenzi's authorship and Paisiello's composition of *L'idolo*. For more extended biographical data on Lorenzi and his works, see the editorial comments in Vincenzo Flauto, ed., *Opere teatrali di Giambattista Lorenzi napolitano . . .*, 4 vols. (Naples: Flautina, 1806–20); Vanda Monaco, *Giambattista Lorenzi e la commedia per musica* (Naples: Berisio, 1968).

3. On the danger of engaging in political satire on the Neapolitan comic stage, see Michael F. Robinson, *Naples and Neapolitan Opera* (Oxford: Clarendon Press, 1972), 191–92.

4. Luciano Maggi, "L'idolo cinese," *Nautilus* (Musica), May 1997, http://nautilus.tv/9705it/musica/idolo.htm.

5. Pietro Martorana, *Notizie biografiche e bibliografiche degli scrittori del dialetto napolitano* (Naples: Chiurazzi, 1894), 287.

6. Michele Scherillo, *L'opera buffa napoletana* (Bologna: Arnaldo Forni, 1975), 321–23.

7. On the prevalence in Neapolitan theater of the performative over the literary, on the orientation around actors—or what Francesco Cotticelli refers to as the centrality of acting ("centralità attorica")—rather than theoretical and textual dimensions, see Franco Carmelo Greco, *Teatro napoletano del '700* (Naples: Libreria Tullio Pironti, 1981), LXXIII–LXXIV, and a fairly recent study of the interpenetration of improvisational theater and musical stage performance in Neapolitan spectacle: Alessandro Lattanzi and Paologiovanni Maione, eds., *Commedia dell'Arte e spettacolo in musica tra Sei e Settecento* (Naples: Editoriale Scientifica, 2003). See especially the contribution by Cotticelli, "Splendori e miserie dell'Arte nel Settecento napoletano," in Lattanzi and Maione, *Commedia dell'arte e spettacolo*, 365–78. Greco further notes that in Neapolitan opera buffa neither libretto nor music was subordinate to the other, as much as both were subordinate to the talents and propensities of the comic singer-actor. *La tradizione e il comico a Napoli dal XVIII secolo ad oggi* (Naples: Guida, 1982), 44.

8. The question of why reform failed in Naples is rather complex: some blame it on the baronial stronghold, others on Tanucci's own inefficacy. See Stuart Woolf, *La storia politica e sociale (dal primo Settecento all'Unità)*, trans. A. Serafini and E. Negri, in *Storia d'Italia*, ed. Stuart Woolf (Turin: Einaudi, 1973), 3:84–85. For general histories of Settecento Naples, see also Benedetto Croce, *Storia del regno di Napoli* (Bari: Laterza, 1972); Antonio Ghirelli, *Storia di Napoli* (Turin: Einaudi, 1992); Girolamo Imbruglia, ed., *Naples in the Eighteenth Century* (Cambridge: Cambridge University Press, 2000); Anna Maria Rao, *Il Regno di Napoli nel Settecento* (Naples: Guida, 1983).

9. Venturi, *Italy and the Enlightenment*, 218. Gregory Hanlon explains that many of the initiatives ostensibly on behalf of the bourgeoisie constituted tactical moves against the barons more than they did advancements of middle-class solidarity. For example, the reallocation of church-held lands to smallholders sought to create a rural *borghesia* that would function as "a countervailing economic force to the barons in the countryside." But lack of capital and other obstacles prevented this class from succeeding. *Early Modern Italy, 1550–1800* (New York: St. Martin's Press, 2000), 331–32; 342.

10. Venturi, *Italy and the Enlightenment*, 220; see also Ghirelli, *Storia di Napoli*; Hanlon, *Early Modern Italy*; Imbruglia, *Naples in the Eighteenth Century*.

11. Hunter, *Culture*, 52–92. In Hunter's words, "with remarkable uniformity the abstract configurations of characters (whose relative rank and status are emphasized by the music) and the trajectories of the plots in these works repeatedly affirm two important and socially relevant conservative principles: that hierarchy is inevitable and necessary, and that social stability is always to be desired," 56.

12. Hucker, *China's Imperial Past*, 207–20.

13. I am borrowing here from Porter's study in his *Ideographia* of the European response to Chinese religious thought in the seventeenth and eighteenth centuries. Porter is chiefly interested in the dynamics of a representational order based on the concept of legitimacy, and his three phases center on the intricacies of European attempts to legitimize Confucianism. As he deftly illustrates, Buddhism is necessarily implicated in this process. I wish to explicate the three phases in terms more squarely focused on Buddhism, and on popular Italian understandings of Buddhist practice and orthodoxy, especially those that made their way to the eighteenth-century Italian stage. See Porter, *Ideographia*, 78–132.

14. Although Porter notes that the strict appropriation of the different systems by disparate classes was not as rigid as sometimes portrayed. See also Hucker, *China's Imperial Past*, 359–60.

15. Ibid., 362.

16. Mungello, *Great Encounter*, 14, 17.

17. Jumping ahead to the *philosophes'* extrapolation of the China Jesuits' philosophical and theological strides, Mungello notes, "The European Enlightenment's use of Confucianism to support its goal of replacing Christianity with natural religion found its parallel in China in the [Chinese] literati's use of Christianity in an attempt to remove Buddhist and Daoist influences from Confucian teaching." Ibid., 6.

18. "bu Ru yi Fo," coined by Xu Guangqi. Ibid., 17.

19. See chapter 1, note 24 on Magalotti.

20. Citations from *Relazione della China*, ed. Salani, 61.

21. Gemelli-Careri published the account of these trips in *Viaggi per l'Europa* (1693).

22. Giovanni Francesco Gemelli-Careri, *Giro del mondo*, 6 vols. (Naples: Rosselli, 1699–1700). The first two volumes, on Turkey and Persia respectively, were published in 1699, and the following year the next four were issued, on India, China, the Philippines, and "Nuova Spagna." All six volumes were reprinted almost immediately in Venice (1700), and were quickly translated into French, German, and English. *Giro del mondo* was expanded and republished again several times in Naples and Venice in the eighteenth century.

23. For the history of Buddhism in China, see Hucker, *China's Imperial Past*, 207–20, 357–62.

24. *Giro del mondo*, 4:153–54.

25. In addition to sources cited in the introduction, notes 16 and 43, see George Minamiki, *The Chinese Rites Controversy: From Its Beginning to Modern Times* (Chicago: Loyola University Press, 1985).

26. Today it is known as the Istituto Orientale di Napoli, one of the foremost world centers for study of Asian cultures.

27. The three-volume account was not published until 1832 (Naples: Manfredi), but given Ripa's high standing and activity, it must certainly have circulated among the most important church, education, and government leaders.

28. Rowbowtham, *Missionary and Mandarin*, 167.

29. Fortunato Prandi, ed. and trans., *Memoirs of Father Ripa* (London: John Murray, 1844), 119–20.

30. Ibid., 120. Ripa's China-Babylon metaphor recalls the vicious attacks on Buddhism launched by the first Jesuit missionary to penetrate China, Matteo Ricci. See Porter, *Ideographia*, 83–108.

31. Quoted in Minamiki, *The Chinese Rites Controversy*, 62–67.

32. Porter, *Ideographia*, 128.

33. Antonio Genovesi, *Discorso sopra il vero fine delle lettere e delle scienze*, in *Antonio Genovesi, scritti*, ed. Franco Venturi (Turin: Einaudi, 1977), 65.

34. *Delle lezioni di commercio*, part 2, 207.

35. Porter, *Ideographia*, 129.

36. This and all following libretto citations from Giambattista Lorenzi, *L'idolo cinese operetta giocosa per musica, da rappresentare nel Real Teatrino di Caserta, per divertimento delle Maestà Loro nel felicissimo arrivo di S. M. La Regina* (Naples: Vincenzo Flauto, 1768).

37. Many thanks to Francesco Cotticelli for his help with this and subsequent translations of parts of this libretto.

38. This focus on Gilbo's hoped-for whiskers also ties in directly with the Chinese, whose customs regarding hair were especially emphasized in narrative accounts. It was commonly written that Chinese men wore a very unusual style of moustache, and that they valued their hair excessively. Given Gilbo's servant status and a subsequent instance in the opera where he is concerned with grammatical gender, he might also serve as an evocation of the eunuch class and/or opera's castrati.

39. Jill Deupi sees Naples's cultural identity in the eighteenth century as determined largely by the Bourbons' contentious relationship with Rome. Conflict over religious authority and temporal power comprised only one facet of the complicated rivalry between the royals and papal factions, however. Other areas of concern to both papacy and monarchy in this period, among them erudition, economic standing, public image, and aesthetic influence, led to interactions wherein Naples alternately emulated and rejected Roman solutions to these issues. "Cultural Identity in Bourbon Naples, 1734–99: Academies, Antiquities, and Rivalries with Rome" (PhD diss., University of Virginia, 2005).

40. *Giro del mondo*, 4:154–55.

41. Porter discusses eighteenth-century Englishman John Barrow's reaction to the Peking manure market. *Ideographia*, 214–15. The operation of this still-essential business among small farming families in modern China is referenced by Da Chen, in his keynote address "From China to Wall Street to Random House," New York Conference on Asian Studies (NYCAS), Sept. 30–Oct. 1, 2005, New Paltz, NY.

42. For the full story of the vexed papal investiture, see Ludwig Von Pastor, *The History of the Popes* (London: Routledge & Kegan Paul; St. Louis: Herder, 1936–53); Owen Chadwick, *The Popes and European Revolution* (Oxford: Clarendon Press, 1981); Emilio Casa, *Controversie fra la Corte di Parma e la Santa Sede nel secolo XVIII* (Modena: T. Vincenzi, 1881). My thanks to Jill Deupi, *Cultural Identity in Bourbon Naples, 1734–1799*, for her organization and presentation of much of the following material on Naples's interactions with Rome.

43. See Von Pastor, *The History of the Popes*.

44. Dated 20 July 1762, Naples; Libro 254c, Archivio General di Simancas; quoted in Deupi, *Cultural Identity*, 81.

45. Although the chinea was not officially terminated until 1788, rancor over this act of forced tribute brewed for many decades preceding. See John E. Moore, "Prints, Salami and Cheese: Savoring the Roman Festival of the Chinea." *Art Bulletin* 77 (1995): 584–906.

46. Hanlon, *Early Modern Italy*, 320.

47. Genovesi also supported the translations of the catechism, although Venturi hastens to note that in this case the support derived less from theological considerations and more from his regalist advocacy, in an anti-Rome, anti-Jesuit context. On this and Tanucci's relationship with Genovesi, see Franco Venturi, *Settecento Riformatore* (Turin: Einaudi, 1969–90), 2:163–65.

48. On the incident see Von Pastor, *The History of the Popes*, 37:18ff.

49. Deupi, *Cultural Identity*, 82.

50. On the fall of Jesuits in the eighteenth century, see Chadwick, *The Popes*, 345–90.

51. Hanlon, *Early Modern Italy*, 312.

52. Venturi, *Settecento Riformatore*, 2:167.

53. Quoted in Bernardo Peluso, *Documenti diplomatici inediti intorno alle relazioni fra la Sede Apostolica e il Regno di Napoli dal 1734 al 1818* (Naples: Officina Cronotipografica Aldina, 1917), 1:273; see also Von Pastor, *The History of the Popes*, 37:228.

54. See Francesco Renda, *Bernardo Tanucci e i beni gesuiti* (Catania: Università di Catania, Facoltà di Lettere e Filosofia, 1970).

55. Flauto, "L'editore ai lettori," 2:xiii–xv. Scherillo also sees an easy likening of Pilottola to the pope, in the scenes where he is both being ministered to and executing functions. To verify *L'idolo*'s references to local personages and institutions, Scherillo notes the scene in which Tuberone begs for the idol's help with his son, and Pilottola tells him to "Write to Pontannecchino!" ("Scrive a Pontannecchino!")—Pontannecchino was in fact a famous executioner at the time. Scherillo, *L'opera buffa napoletana*, 334, 336.

56. Greco notes that Lorenzi had been part of a group of dilettante writers and dramatists more literary than professional (though Lorenzi also had an acting background) that Ferdinand had brought to his court starting in 1763. *Teatro*, CIII. On Lorenzi's life and career see also Gordana Lazarevich, "Lorenzi, Giambattista," *Grove Music Online*, ed. L. Macy, http://www.grovemusic.com.

57. Soon afterward, however, this favor diminishes, due perhaps to a skirmish over a marriage contract Paisiello attempted to disavow. He would not regain court favor until 1774. See Michael F. Robinson, "Paisiello, Giovanni," *Grove Music Online*, ed. L. Macy, http://www.grovemusic.com.

58. See Hanlon, *Early Modern Italy*, 331–32, 342.

59. Harry Hearder, *Italy: A Short History* (New York: Cambridge University Press, 2001), 141–42.

60. See Hunter, *Culture*, 110–26.

61. Flauto, "L'editore ai lettori," 2: xiii–xv; quoted in Greco, *Teatro*, 563–64.

I have been unable to find a scenario bearing this exact title. However, several scenarios in the Casamarciano collection seem similar: *Policinella finto regente* (*Pulcinella Pretends to be a Governor*), *Il finto Re* (*The Make-Believe King*), *Il finto Prencipe* (*The Make-Believe Prince*), and *Nuovo finto principe* (*The False Prince*). All of them turn on reversals of social status, with Pulcinella in the starring role. Francesco Cotticelli, Anne Goodrich Heck, and Thomas F. Heck, trans. and eds., *The Commedia dell'Arte in Naples: A Bilingual Edition of the 176 Casamarciano Scenarios*, 2 vols. (Lanham, MD: Scarecrow Press, 2001).

62. See Romualdo Marrone, ed., *Il paese di Pulcinella* (Naples: Bellini, 1991); Franco Carmelo Greco, ed., *Pulcinella, maschera del mondo* (Naples: Electa, 1990); Romeo De Maio, *Pulcinella: il filosofo che fu chiamato pazzo* (Florence: Sansoni, 1989); Franco Carmelo Greco, ed., *Quante storie per Pulcinella / Combien d'histoires pour Polichinelle* (Naples: Edizioni scientifiche italiane, 1988); Carmine Coppola, *Pulcinella: la maschera nella tradizione teatrale* (Naples: Edizioni scientifiche italiane, 1987).

63. The name "Pulcinella" comes from the Italian "pulcino," which means "chick" in English. Other evocations in the opera of Tuberone's association with chickens include his characterization of Ergilla, to whom he has taken a liking, and of whom he sings "The little hen is nuts [about me], and I get / To pluck her" ("È cotta la pollanca, ed a mme attocca / De spollecaremella" [1, 5]); he also mentions the upcoming Chinese "festival of the egg" ("festa dell'ova" [1, 11]).

As for his anthropomorphic birth, see Giandomenico Tiepolo's pen-and-ink drawing of the purported "miracle of nature," entitled *Pulcinella nasce da un uovo di tacchino* (*Punchinello is Hatched by a Turkey*), from the artist's series *Divertimento per li regazzi*, in Greco,

ed., *Pulcinella: maschera del mondo*, 306–10. Another illustration of the phenomenon appears in the frontispiece of Pietro Fabris's 1773 *Raccolta di varii Vestimenti ed Arti del Regno di Napoli*, ed. Franco Mancini (Naples: Guida, 1985), 9.

64. One can surmise a positive answer here, based on a circuitous but nonetheless compelling set of circumstances. Critics have seen a reflection of King Ferdinando in Tuberone; Ferdinando was called the "lazzarone king" (see chapter conclusion for more on these comparisons); the *lazzaroni* of Naples (poor street people of peasant origins, to whom was attributed a devil-may-care spirit) allegedly put on tattered white tunics for the 1647 Masaniello uprising, so as to resemble both cadavers readied for burial, but also the sickly Lazarus ("Lazzaro"). On this episode, and the *lazzaroni* as a social phenomenon in Settecento Naples, see Atanasio Mozzillo, "I figli della cuccagna," in *La frontiera del Grand Tour: viaggi e viaggiatori nel Mezzogiorno borbonico* (Naples: Liguori, 1992), 9–54. Harold Acton compares the *lazzaroni*'s "open-air existence" to "a perpetual comic opera, for those who did not peer too close [sic]." *The Bourbons of Naples, 1734–1825* (London: Prion Books, 1998), 8–9.

65. "il motivo dell'emarginazione pulcinellesca." Cotticelli, "Proposte per una lettura e interpretazione degli scenari Casamarciano," in Cotticelli, Heck, and Heck, eds., *The Commedia dell'Arte in Naples*, 7.

66. *Culture*, 110.

67. "puro sciocco"; "malacquistata dignità." Scherillo, *L'opera buffa napoletana*, 344.

68. See Ronald J. Rabin on the important difference, for the buffo role, between playing a part and becoming a part. "Figaro as Misogynist: On Aria Types and Aria Rhetoric," in Hunter and Webster, *Opera Buffa in Mozart's Vienna*, 258.

69. The reference to Egyptians also shows the divulgation of theories in scholarly discussions of world history and the original language, that the Chinese descended from Egyptians. Kircher's *China illustrata* was one of the first works to explore these ideas.

70. See Carpanetto and Ricuperati, *Italy in the Age of Reason*, 187–88; Woolf, *La storia politica e sociale*, 84–5.

71. Venturi, *Italy and the Enlightenment*, 204.

72. Genovesi, *Lezioni di commercio*, part 1, 61.

73. Hunter, *Culture*, 35, 58–60.

74. Ibid., 73–79.

75. Greco, *Teatro*, XCIII.

76. Ibid., LXXXVII.

77. Lorenzi, *L'infedeltà fedele, commedia per musica / di Giambatista Lorenzi P.A.; da rappresentarsi nell'apertura del real Teatro del Fondo di Separazione; nella està del corrente anno 1779*. Naples, 1779.

78. Greco, *Teatro* LXXXIII.

79. Ibid., LXXXVIII–LXXXIX.

80. Writing of Pulcinella in Lorenzi's works, Monaco writes: "it is possible to reconstruct the sort of Pulcinella figure which must have been popular in Naples in the last years of the seventeenth and in the eighteenth century: a Pulcinella who, even with his foolish fantasy worlds, his presumptions, his nonsense, even between funny business and grimaces, increasingly acquired a sense of the sentimental, something more palpably human." *Giambattista Lorenzi*, 140.

81. Greco, *Teatro* XCIV–XCV.

82. Ibid., XCIII–XCIV, CV.

83. Ibid., XCIV–V.

84. Ibid., XCIV–V.

85. Luigi Settembrini, *Lezioni di letteratura italiana*, vol. 2, lesson 86 (Florence: Sansoni, 1964), 914–15. Lorenzi's first editor Flauto also affirms the opera's antimonarchical valence, paradoxically in his statements to the contrary. He attributes to Lorenzi's genius

and skillful handling the fact that *L'idolo* did not communicate libel toward the king, the potential for which he says existed in the commedia dell'arte source (*Pulcinella, Re dormendo*), where "in a sideways manner they ridiculed the decorum of a character who, just after God, should merit men's respect, obedience, and veneration." According to Flauto, only because the scenario was written and performed in barbaric times ("quei tempi barbari"), did people not notice the danger. *Opere teatrali*, 563.

86. Again, on *lazzaroni* see Mozzillo, "I figli della cuccagna." This definition comes from Deupi, *Cultural Identity*, 192n5.

87. See Deupi on the response of the Caroline court to accusations of provincialism. *Cultural Identity*, 64.

CHAPTER 7. *L'INIMICO DELLE DONNE*

1. Wendy Heller, *Emblems of Eloquence* (Berkeley: University of California Press, 2003), 1.

2. English title from Dale E. Monson: "L'inimico delle donne," *Grove Music Online*, ed. L. Macy, http://www.grovemusic.com.

3. The bibliography on the eighteenth-century Italian discussion of women has been updated significantly in recent years. Luciano Guerci's works still prove fundamental: *La discussione sulla donna nell'Italia del Settecento* (Turin: Tirrenia, 1987), and *La sposa obbediente: Donna e matrimonio nella discussione dell'Italia del Settecento* (Turin: Tirrenia, 1988), and they've been augmented. Citing only those works published since the turn of the current century, see Paula Findlen, Wendy Wassyng Roworth, and Catherine M. Sama, eds., *Italy's Eighteenth Century: Gender and Culture in the Age of the Grand Tour* (Stanford: Stanford University Press, forthcoming); Maria Gaetana Agnesi, Giuseppa Eleonora Barbapiccola, et al., *The Contest for Knowledge*, ed. Rebecca Messbarger and Paula Findlen (Chicago: University of Chicago Press, 2005); Paula Findlen, "Becoming a Scientist: Gender and Knowledge in Eighteenth-Century Italy," *Science in Context* 16 (2003): 59–87; "The Scientist's Body: The Nature of a Woman Philosopher in Enlightenment Italy," in *The Faces of Nature in Enlightenment Europe*, ed. Gianna Pomata and Lorraine Daston (Berlin: Berliner Wissenschafts-Verlag, 2003), 211–36; Rebecca Messbarger, *The Century of Women* (Toronto: University of Toronto Press, 2002); Luisa Ricaldone and Adriana Chemello, eds., *Geografie e genealogie letterarie. Erudite, biografe, croniste, narratrici, "épistolières," utopiste tra Settecento e Ottocento* (Padua: Il Poligrafo, 2000). Karen Offen's *European Feminisms 1700–1950* (Stanford: Stanford University Press, 2000) presents a good overview of the key polemics in the "woman question" throughout Europe in the eighteenth century, 27–76.

4. All citations are taken from Giovanni Bertati and Baldassare Galuppi, *L'inimico delle donne*, ed. Helen Geyer-Kiefl, vol. 1 (Milan: Ricordi, 1986), cccvii–cccxxvii. This edition contains the first version of Bertati's libretto, in contrast to a number of textual variants issued in the eight years following the opera's Venice premiere and corresponding to performances in various cities in Italy and Europe. In her introduction, Geyer-Kiefl explains that these reworked librettos flattened the characters and generally rendered *L'inimico* a much less complex and innovative work than in its initial text. My study focuses on this original libretto. Helen Geyer-Kiefl, "L'Italiana in Pechino," (L'inimico delle donne, 1771)," in Bertati and Galuppi, *L'inimico*, ed. Geyer-Kiefl, vol. 1 (Milan: Ricordi, 1986), viii–xxxii.

5. 1, 6; 1, 8; 1, 9; 1, 11.

Animal metaphors to describe women derived especially from the foundational line of thought that associated women solely with physical materiality (body), while it granted men both body and intellect (mind). Various modes of thinking about women generated various animal figures. Guerci points out that to emphasize the importance of women's chastity, for example, writers compared women to hedgehogs (who kept outsiders out thanks to their protective spines); to stress the value of segregating women, some assimilated them to bees, who work diligently in private, hidden spaces, versus wasps, who work out in the open. The business of women's stink comes from the association of women with lust and dirtiness, propounded mainly by devout Catholic writers of both the seventeenth and eighteenth centuries. On the many contemporary works by men treating the woman question from religious and biological determinist points of view, see Guerci, *Discussione sulla donna*; Ludmilla Jordanova, *Sexual Visions: Images of Gender in Science and Medicine between the Eighteenth and Twentieth Centuries* (Madison: University of Wisconsin Press, 1989).

6. Guerci notes especially a seminal letter by Venetian patrician and philosopher Antonio Conti, published in Venice in 1756 but circulating since 1721. The letter reprises all the themes and arguments at the base of the Settecento's misogyny, many of which stemmed from Aristotle's originary theories equating women's physiological difference from men with intellectual and moral inferiority. *Discussione sulla donna*, 141–60. See also Messbarger, *Century of Women*, 49–68.

7. The degree and nature of gender consciousness in comic opera derives from both the genre's formal properties and its evolution in time, although opinions vary on precisely when a bourgeois feminine ethos began to emerge. Margaret Reynolds sees opera seria as more gender neutral and thus more sexually transgressive than comic opera, insofar as it deified the high voice, no matter who generated it. Its revue-like form, i.e., its focus on a series of virtuoso aria performances, also rendered it less susceptible to ideological gender concerns. Comic opera, on the other hand, because it rose later in the century when bourgeois gender schematization had taken stronger root, because its form was more associative and developmental than opera seria's, and because it treated love more often than opera seria, presented more rigidly distinct gender roles. For Wendy Heller, however, a more systematic and narrow treatment of the feminine started *with* the birth of opera seria, in contrast to the fullness and diversity of the feminine expressed by female operatic characters in seventeenth-century opera. She imputes to Arcadian reforms opera seria's consistent parade of admirable, stoic, "proper" women, who contained their passions and gently but steadfastly resisted all questionable essays on their virtue. Reynolds, "Ruggiero's Deceptions," 132–51; Heller, *Emblems*, 295–300. See also Mary K. Hunter, *Culture*; "Bourgeois values and opera buffa in 1780s Vienna," *Opera Buffa in Mozart's Vienna*, ed. Mary Hunter and James Webster (Cambridge: Cambridge University Press, 1997), 165–96; "Pamela: The Offspring of Richardson's Heroine in Eighteenth-Century Opera," *Mosaic* 18, no. 4 (1985): 61–76. On more general issues of gender in opera, see Susan McClary, *Feminine Endings* (Minneapolis: University of Minnesota Press, 1991); Ruth Solie, ed., *Musicology and Difference* (Berkeley: University of California Press, 1993).

8. Hunter, "Bourgeois values."

9. See discussion of middle style music in chapter 5.

10. The best primary source expressing women's role in this conceptualization of the ideal familial partnership is the article "Femme" in the *Encyclopédie*, especially the subsection "Morale." See M [Joseph-François-Edouard de Corsembleu] Desmahis, "Femme (Morale)," *Encyclopédie ou dictionnaire raisonné des sciences, des arts et des métiers* (Paris, 1751–72), The ARTFL Encyclopédie Project (page 6:472–75), ARTFL Project, University of Chicago,

2001, http://www.lib.uchicago.edu/efts/ARTFL/projects/encyc/. Nancy Armstrong offers a thorough treatment of the (politicized) gender principles constructed to uphold the notion of the bourgeois companionate marriage in *Desire and Domestic Fiction* (New York: Oxford University Press, 1987). See also Cissie Fairchilds, "Women and Family," in *French Women and the Age of Enlightenment*, ed. Samia I. Spencer (Bloomington: Indiana University Press, 1984), 97–110; and Bridget Hill, *Eighteenth-Century Women: An Anthology* (London: George Allen and Unwin, 1984). Few studies focus specifically on the workings of the new ideology in Italian marriage, but Guerci's *La sposa obbediente* refers to its infiltration in contemporary texts treating women and courtship, marriage and family. For descriptions of the customs surrounding the courtly and/or patrician marriage, against which the new morality asserted itself, see Margaret H. Darrow, "French Noblewomen and the New Domesticity 1750–1850," *Feminist Studies* 5, no. 1 (1979): 41–65; and Elena Brambilla, "La storia di Mie Mie. e condizione della donna fra Antico Regime e Rivoluzione," *Acme* 52 (1999): 63–93.

11. Dena Goodman, "Women and the Enlightenment," in *Becoming Visible: Women in European History*, ed. Renate Bridenthal, Susan Mosher Stuard, and Merry E. Wiesner, 3rd ed. (Boston: Houghton Mifflin, 1998), 246–59.

12. Ralph P. Locke, "What Are These Women Doing in Opera?" in Blackmer and Smith, *En Travesti*, 59–98; see also Hunter, "Pamela."

13. Gretchen A. Wheelock uses this phrase in her contribution to Wye Jamison Allanbrook, Mary Hunter, and Gretchen A. Wheelock, "Staging Mozart's Women," in *Siren Songs*, ed. Mary Ann Smart (Princeton: Princeton University Press, 2000), 50–57.

14. In Richardson's novel (*Pamela, or Virtue Rewarded*) the chosen partner is the seducer himself, once his "tyranny" has been transformed into love. In other works, the heroine's triumph over the seducer includes rejection of him, in favor of socially sanctioned marriage to her preferred consort, often a man of lower class than the seducer.

15. On the culture of sensibility and sentimentality in eighteenth-century Europe, see Bernadette Fort, "Exploring Sentiment," *Eighteenth-Century Studies* 37, no. 1 (2003): 1–89; Patricia Meyers Spacks, "Ambiguous Practices," in *Eighteenth-Century Genre and Culture: Serious Reflections on Occasional Forms: Essays in Honor of J. Paul Hunter*, ed. Dennis Todd and Cynthia Wall (Newark: University of Delaware Press, 2001), 150–64; Franco Piva and Jean Sgard, eds., *La Sensibilité dans la littérature française au XVIIIe siècle* (Fasano, Italy: Schena, 1998); Anne Vila, *Enlightenment and Pathology: Sensibility in the Literature and Medicine of Eighteenth-Century France* (Baltimore: Johns Hopkins University Press, 1998); G. J. Barker-Benfield, *The Culture of Sensibility: Sex and Society in Eighteenth-Century Britain* (Chicago: University of Chicago Press, 1992).

For the dynamics of sensibility in bourgeois drama see James R. Foster, "Sentiment from Afra Behn to Marivaux," in *The Eighteenth-Century English Novel*, ed. Harold Bloom (Philadelphia, PA: Chelsea House, 2004), 43–69; Roger Gautier, "Le Thème de l'amour dans le théâtre de Jean-Jacques Rousseau," *Revue d'Histoire du Theatre* 38, no. 3 (1986): 281–92; Julie C. Hayes, "A Theater of Situations: Representation of the Self in the Bourgeois Drama of La Chaussée and Diderot," in *The Many Forms of Drama*, ed. Karelisa V. Hartigan (Lanham, MD: University Presses of America, 1985), 69–77.

16. Tia DeNora, "The Biology Lessons of Opera Buffa: Gender, Nature, and Bourgeois Society on Mozart's Buffa Stage," in Hunter and Webster, *Opera Buffa*, 160.

17. Robert Palfrey Utter and Gwendolyn Bridges Needham, *Pamela's Daughters* (New York: Macmillan, 1937).

18. Referring to the libretto upon which Mozart's opera was based, Thomas Bauman notes: "Bretzner's story of attempted escape by Westerners in an exotic setting joined an extensive family tree of plays and operas with various traits in common (principally Dryden, *Don Sebastian*, 1689; Favart, *Soliman II*, 1761; Martinelli, *La schiava liberata*, 1768; Bickerstaffe, *The Captive*, 1769; and Grossmann, *Adelheit von Veltheim*, 1780)." "Belmont und Constanze (i)," *Grove Music Online*, ed. L. Macy, http://www.grovemusic.com.

19. Adrienne Ward, " 'New Worlds' and Theatre: Goldoni's Exotic Comedies," *Annali d'Italianistica* 11 (1993): 213–24.

20. Although not published until 1796, Diderot's manuscript circulated widely and created quite a sensation. See Dena Goodman, *Criticism in Action: Enlightenment Experiments in Political Writing* (Ithaca: Cornell University Press, 1989). The first known operatic version of the Alcina-Ruggiero episode goes back to the 1625 Florence performance of *La liberazione di Ruggiero dall'isola d'Alcina*, libretto by Ferdinando Saracinelli, music by Francesca Caccini (incidentally, the first woman to compose opera, according to Suzanne G. Cusick). The most well-known eighteenth-century adaptation is George Frideric Handel's opera seria *Alcina* of 1735 (librettist unknown), itself adapted from A. Fanzaglia's libretto for Riccardo Broschi's *L'isola di Alcina* (Rome, 1728). For a list of the many operas on this theme, see Tim Carter, "Ariosto, Ludovico," *Grove Music Online*, ed. L Macy, http://www.grovemusic.com. On Francesca Caccini, see Suzanne G. Cusick: "2) Francesca Caccini [Francesca Caccini Signorini; 'La Cecchina'; Francesca Raffaelli]," *Grove Music Online*, ed. L Macy, http://www.grovemusic.com.

21. See chapter 3, section on Lalli's *Camaïde*.

22. Guerci, *La sposa obbediente*, 12.

23. Louis de Jaucourt [Saint-Lambert?], "Génie," (subsection "Philosophie & Littér."), *Encyclopédie ou dictionnaire raisonné des sciences, des arts et des métiers* (Paris, 1751–72), The ARTFL Encyclopédie Project (page 7:583), ARTFL Project, University of Chicago, 2001, http://www.lib.uchicago.edu/efts/ARTFL/projects/encyc/.

I thank Jenny Tsien for her help with the English translation for this and the following citation.

24. Jean-le-Rond d'Alembert, "Goût," *Encyclopédie ou dictionnaire raisonné des sciences, des arts et des métiers* (Paris, 1751–72), The ARTFL Encyclopédie Project (page 7:769–70), ARTFL Project, University of Chicago, 2001, http://www.lib.uchicago.edu/efts/ARTFL/projects/encyc/.

25. Earlier Agnesina has referred to men's "tyrannical . . . inclination" ("genio . . . tiranno"), lamenting married women's burden of having to give their husbands children at least every year (2, 3).

26. On adultery associated with cicisbeismo, see Guerci, "Le conversazioni e il cicisbeismo," in *Discussione sulla donna*, 89–140; Paola Giuli, "Noblewomen and the Crisis of Traditional Marriage," in *Enlightenment, Arcadia, and Corilla: The Inscription of Eighteenth-Century Italian Women Writers in Literary History* (PhD diss., Rutgers University, 1994), 50–54. Darrow notes that adultery among French noblewomen was "indulged, if not positively encouraged, if it could increase a woman's influence" within courtly circles. "French Noblewomen," 47; see also Gabriele Martini, "La donna veneziana del '600 tra sessualità legittima ed illegittima: Alcune riflessioni sul concubinato," *Atti dell'Istituto Veneto di Scienze, Lettere ed Arti 145* (1986–87): 301–39. The nature and intensity of the arguments in the *Encyclopédie* pertaining to adultery, monogamy, and marriage clearly point to the prevalence of infractions. See Terry Smiley Dock, *Woman in the Encylopédie* (Potomac: Studia Humanitatis, 1983), 120–34.

27. Guerci, *La sposa obbediente*, 77–78.

28. Although the divorce polemic blazed more brightly in France than on the peninsula, it nonetheless threw flares into Italy. See Luca De Biase, "Problemi ed osservazioni sul 'divorzio' nel patriziato veneziano del XVIII: Un tentativo di analisi storica seriale," *Atti dell'Istituto Veneto di Scienze, Lettere ed Arti* 140 (1981–82): 143–62; Gaetano Cozzi, "Note e documenti sulla questione del 'divorzio' a Venezia (1782–1788)," *Annali dell'Istituto Italo-Germanico in Trento* 7 (1981): 275–360; Luciano Guerci, "Tra scogli e fiori: una guida alla felicità coniugale per le donne del Settecento," *Studi di storia della civiltà letteraria francese* (Paris: Editions Honoré Champion, 1996), 549–87.

29. Daniela Hacke, *Women, Sex and Marriage in Early Modern Venice* (Aldershot: Ashgate, 2004), 230. See also Lorella Tessarotto, "Promesse e inganni: seduzione e matrimonio dopo il Concilio di Trento," in *Madri pervasive e figli dominanti*, ed. Luisa Accati (Florence: European Press Academic Publishing, 2003), 33–103; David I. Kertzer and Marzio Barbagli, *Family Life in Early Modern Times 1500–1789* (New Haven: Yale University Press, 2001); Roberto Bizzocchi, *In famiglia. Storie di interessi e affetti nell'Italia moderna* (Rome: Laterza, 2001); Daniela Hacke, "Non lo volevo per marito in modo alcuno," in *Time, Space, and Women's Lives in Early Modern Europe*, ed. Anne Schutte et. al. (Kirksville: Truman State University Press, 2001), 203–21; Brambilla, "La storia di Mie Mie"; Michela De Giorgio and Christiane Klapisch-Zuber, *Storia del matrimonio* (Rome: Laterza, 1996); Marzio Barbagli and David I. Kertzer, *Storia della famiglia italiana 1750–1950* (Bologna: Il Mulino, 1992); Marzio Barbagli, *Sotto lo stesso tetto* (Bologna: Il Mulino, 1984). For contemporary marriage issues in England and France, see Lawrence Stone, *Uncertain Unions* (Oxford: Oxford University Press, 1992); James F. Traer, *Marriage and the Family in Eighteenth-Century France* (Ithaca: Cornell University Press, 1980); Fauchery, *La destinée féminine*, 352–99.

30. Daniela Lombardi, "Fidanzamenti e matrimonio dal Concilio di Trento alle riforme settecentesche," in De Giorgio and Klapisch-Zuber, *Storia del matrimonio*, 215–50; Gunda Barth-Scalmani, "Eighteenth-Century Marriage Contracts," in Schutte, *Time, Space*, 265–81; Beatrice Gottlieb, "The Meaning of Clandestine Marriage," in *Family and Sexuality in French History*, ed. Roberto Wheaton and Tamara K. Hareven (Philadelphia: University of Pennsylvania Press, 1980), 49–83.

31. In England, for example, Hardwicke's Marriage Act of 1753 was instituted. See Hill, *Eighteenth-Century Women*, 89–93, 99–100. Barth-Scalmani implies the nineteenth-century time frame when she remarks that "neither [modern-day] legal experts nor historians have been interested in the legal regulations of marriage in the time before the great codifications of private law in Europe (that is the Prussian *Allgemeines Landrecht* in 1794, the *Code Napoléon* in France in 1803, or in 1811 the *ABGB* or *Allgemeines Bürgerliches Gesetzbuch*—the General Civic Law—in the Habsburg territories)." "Eighteenth-Century Marriage Contracts," 267. See also Hacke, *Women, Sex and Marriage*, 234–35.

32. DeNora, "The Biology Lessons of Opera Buffa," 160.

33. Gordana Lazarevich, "La serva padrona," *Grove Music Online*, ed. L. Macy, http://www.grovemusic.com. In Goldoni's *Il re alla caccia*, the noblewoman appeals to the king for resolution when the cruel Milord refuses to make good on his promise to marry her. See Carlson, "Il re alla caccia," in Hunter and Webster, *Opera Buffa in Mozart's Vienna*, 90, 95.

34. That is, their misogyny is an essential part of their natures, so much so that over the course of their operatic adventures no others, including women, are able to rid them of it. They will continue to be misogynists even after their story has ended. Ronald J. Rabin, "Figaro as Misogynist."

35. Ibid., 249.

36. In 1, 3 Geminiano thinks he and his niece have arrived among cannibals:

> I'm deathly afraid
> That we're among savages, and I can already see
> We'll both be roasted on a spit and eaten!
>
> [Io temo assai
> Che siam qui tra selvaggi, e già prevedo
> Ch'ambi sarem mangiati arrosti a spiedo.]

In 3, 2 Geminiano again misreads the intentions of the two Chinese ministers Ly-lam and Si-sin. Geminiano thinks they've come to punish him for his fraudulent imitation of the deity, whereas they announce (as they simultaneously have some fun at the expense of his obtuse and gullible nature) that he is to be raised to the highest mandarin position.

37. On the touching, affective, sweet qualities of the typical Pamela-heroine's music, and "the use of distinctions in social class for emotive purposes," see Hunter, "Pamela," 63–66; also *Culture*, 84–92.

38. Hunter, "Pamela," 65.

39. Ibid., 67.

40. Goldoni's other work based on Richardson's novel, the spoken play *La Pamela nubile* (1750), also denied social advancement to its protagonist, insofar as Pamela's noble ancestry is unexpectedly discovered at the comedy's end, allowing her to marry Milord Bonfil.

41. Studies of Goldoni's female characters generally concur in asserting the dramatist's conservatism with respect to women's voice, agency, and happiness. Even those protagonists to whom Goldoni granted the most apparent command (Rosaura in *La donna di garbo*, Mirandolina in *La locandiera*, Giacinta in the *Villeggiatura* trilogy, for example), ultimately bow to patriarchal imperatives, when they are not admonished by them. The ideal Goldoni heroine is as virtuous as Agnesina, but is not permitted the latitude Agnesina has to dictate the rules of domesticity, nor the happiness she ostensibly will enjoy as a married woman. See Giuseppina Scognamiglio, *Ritratti di donna nel teatro di Carlo Goldoni* (Naples: Edizioni Scientifiche Italiane, 2002); Günsberg, *Playing with Gender*; Norbert Jonard, "L'image de la femme dans les comedies de Goldoni," *Problemi di critica goldoniana* (1996): 179–98; Kristine Hecker, "Le donne in Goldoni ovvero: trappole da evitare. Considerazioni sul personaggio femminile nelle commedie goldoniane. Appunti per una ricerca," in *Carlo Goldoni 1793–1993: Atti del Convegno del Bicentenario (Venezia 11–13 aprile 1994)*, ed. Carmelo Alberti and Giorgio Pizzamiglio (Venice: Regione del Veneto, 1995), 341–56; Pamela D. Stewart, "Le femmes savantes e la poetica della 'naturalezza,' " in *Goldoni fra letteratura e teatro* (Florence: Olschki, 1989), 161–94; Franca Angelini, "Le personnage féminin dans le théâtre de Goldoni," in *Le Théâtre dans l'Europe des Lumières: Programmes, pratiques, échanges*, ed. Mieczslaw Klimowicz (Warsaw: Wydanawnictwo Uniwersytetu Wroclawskiego, 1985), 125–31; Franco Fido, "Giacinta nel paese degli uomini: interpretazione delle *Villeggiature* e del 'femminismo' goldoniano," in *Da Venezia all'Europa: Prospettive sull'ultimo Goldoni* (Rome: Bulzoni, 1984), 11–58.

42. Mary Hunter, "Buona figliuola," *Grove Music Online*, ed. L. Macy, http://www.grovemusic.com.

43. Hunter notes that "open didacticism was not the rule in opera buffa in the 1760s and '70s," and identifies *Nina, o sia La pazza per amore* by Lorenzi-Paisiello (1789) as the first comic opera

in the virtuous maiden subgenre to present "constancy . . . in a specifically and overtly moral light." "Pamela," 67, 72.

44. She speaks only to thank her Chinese rivals for their good wishes on her imminent wedding (3, 6).

45. Locke refers to this in "What Are These Women Doing?" 64–65.

46. Charles Ford, *Così? Sexual Politics in Mozart's Operas* (Manchester: Manchester University Press, 1991).

47. Ibid., 230.

48. Ford, *Così?* especially chapters 1 and 2.

49. Ibid., 230.

50. Ibid., 8–9.

51. See Messbarger, *Century of Women,* 16. On Campastri see Guerci, *Discussione sulla donna,* 138.

52. Galiani, *Croquis d'un dialogue sur les femmes* (1772). In *Opere di Ferdinando Galiani,* ed. Furio Diaz and Luciano Guerci, vol. 6, *Illuministi Italiani* (Milan: Ricciardi, 1975), 615–33.

53. Messbarger, *Century of Women,* 16–17.

CONCLUSION

1. Giuseppe Ortolani, "Notes" to *La sposa persiana,* in Ortolani, *Tutte le opere,* vol. 9, 1332–38; Paolo Bosisio on Gasparo Gozzi's tragicomedy *Marco Polo,* "Gasparo Gozzi poeta e traduttore drammatico," *Gasparo Gozzi. Il lavoro di un intellettuale nel Settecento Veneziano. Atti del convegno (Venezia-Pordenone 4–6 dicembre 1986),* ed. Ilaria Crotti and Ricciarda Ricorda (Padua: Editrice Antenore, 1989), 306.

2. Jeremy Hayes points out that *Le cinesi* was Metastasio's only comic work. "Gluck, Christoph Willibald Ritter von (2. 1746–61)," and "Le Cinesi," *Grove Music Online,* ed. L. Macy, http://www.grovemusic.com.

3. A noblewoman and friend of the royal sisters took the third role.

4. All citations are from the Brunelli edition.

5. For information on the Chinese interior decoration of the Habsburg residence, see Yonan, "Veneers of Authority."

6. Actually two performances took place in 1754. The first was arranged for the royal family by Field Marshal Joseph Friedrich, Prince of Saxe-Hildburghausen, in the theater of his summer palace at Schlosshof. *Le cinesi* was one of a group of spectacles in honor of Maria Teresa's visit there to discuss purchasing the property. The production so impressed the imperial entourage that Francis I had it produced at the Burgtheater the same year — since the Schlosshof spectacle debuted late in the year (September 24), the Habsburgs must have mounted their performance rather soon afterward. Hayes, "Gluck."

7. The mid-century revamping of Viennese musical spectacles and its constituent francophilia can be traced to a number of factors, not the least of which was the fact that France had become Austria's new ally in 1748, at the end of the war of Austrian succession. Francis I's embrace of a French aesthetic paralleled the efforts of Wenzel Kaunitz (appointed Imperial Chancellor in 1753) and Count Giacomo Durazzo (Director of Court Theaters as of 1752) to reorganize the theater scene. In 1752 they began a concerted plan, importing French actors, librettists, and their native conventions, and integrating them with still viable Italian modes and performers (mainly singers, musicians, and dancer-choreographers). They concentrated on performances in the Burgtheater, a relatively new and more intimate royal venue, founded by Maria Teresa in 1748 to replace the large, baroque-styled Hoftheater. Bruce Alan Brown observes that Kaunitz and Durazzo wished to reintegrate "into dramma per musica the spectacle, dance and choral forces that had once been a part of that genre, and that French opera still retained." Other events that conditioned the revisionist program included Gluck's arrival in Vienna in 1751 and definitive settling there as of 1752, choreographer Gasparo Angiolini's arrival in 1753, and the contemporary and very fertile musical environment nurtured by Viennese melomane Prince Joseph Friedrich von Sachsen-Hildburghausen. Bruce Alan Brown, "Gluck, Christoph Willibald Ritter von (11. Italian reform operas)," "Angiolini, Gasparo," and "Durazzo, Count Giacomo," *Grove Music Online,* ed. L. Macy, http://www.grovemusic.com; Theophil Antonicek et al., "Vienna," *Grove Music Online,* ed. L. Macy, http://www.grovemusic.com; Hayes, "Gluck"; Fubini, *Music and Culture,* 1–36, 69–127; Basso, *Musica in Scena,* vol. 3, 3–54.

8. Regarding the ridicule of "Frenchified" Europeans, Brunelli draws a comparison between Silango and Parini's "Giovin signore." Brunelli, Notes to *Le cinesi,* 1317.

9. It is difficult to establish the precise singers for each of the two 1754 performances. The Schlosshof rendition starred the Italian virtuosa and contralto Vittoria Tesi as Lisinga, and Austrian tenor Joseph Friebert as Silango; the Burgtheater performance seems to have featured soprano Caterina Gabrielli as Lisinga, and probably her sister, Francesca, as the *seconda donna* Sivene. In one or possibly both productions, Catharina Starzer, sister of composer and violinist Joseph Starzer, played the role of Tangia. Most if not all of these singers were part of the stable of musical talents cultivated by Prince von Sachsen-Hildburghausen, and were also court-employed soloists. Gerhard Croll, "Tesi, Vittoria," *Grove Music Online,* ed. L. Macy, http://www.grovemusic.com; Robert N. Freeman, "Friebert, Joseph" *Grove Music Online,* ed. L. Macy, http://www.grovemusic.com; Gerhard Croll and Irene Brandenburg, "Gabrielli, Caterina," *Grove Music Online,* ed. L. Macy, http://www.grovemusic.com; Bruce Alan Brown and Julian Rushton, "Gluck, Christoph Willibald Ritter von (3. Vienna, 1752–60)," *Grove Music Online,* ed. L. Macy, http://www.grovemusic.com; Brown, "Gluck (8. Early Italian operas)."

10. Brown, "Gluck (3. Vienna, 1752–60) and (8: Early Italian Operas)."

11. Bruce Alan Brown, "Angiolini, Gasparo," and "Gluck (10. Ballets)."

12. Again Yonan, "Veneers of Authority."

13. Arif Dirlik, "Chinese History and the Question of Orientalism," *History and Theory* 35, no. 4 (1996): 110.

14. Ibid., 111.

15. See Xiaomei Chen, *Occidentalism: Theory of Counter-Discourse in Post-Mao China,* 2nd ed. (Lanham, MD: Rowman and Littlefield, 2002).

16. Dirlik, "Chinese History," 108.

17. Ibid.

APPENDIX 2

1. Synopsis by Don Neville, "Eroe cinese," *Grove Music Online,* ed. L. Macy, http://www.grovemusic.com.

2. Twenty-five cities if the libretto indicating Bertoni as composer was for a production in a locale not yet counted.

3. Again, because no performance locale is mentioned in the Bertoni libretto, it cannot be placed.

Bibliography

PRIMARY SOURCES

Adriani, Placido. "Le metamorfosi di Pulcinella." *Sipario* 82 (1954): 32–34.

———. *Selva, ovvero Zibaldone di concetti comici . . . 1734*. Perugia: Biblioteca Augusta, 1734.

Agnesi, Maria Gaetana, Giuseppa Eleonora Barbapiccola, et al. *The Contest for Knowledge*. Edited by Rebecca Messbarger and Paula Findlen. Chicago: University of Chicago Press, 2005.

Alexander, Noël. *Conformité des ceremonies chinoises avec l'idolatrie Grecque et Romaine*. Cologne, 1700.

Algarotti, Francesco. "Dialoghi sopra l'ottica Neutoniana." In *Illuministi Italiani*. Vol. 2, *Opere di Francesco Algarotti e di Saverio Bettinelli*, edited by Ettore Bonora. Milan: Ricciardi, 1969. First published 1737.

———. In *Opere del conte Algarotti edizione novissima*. Vol. 9, pt. 1, *Lettere varie*. Venice: Carlo Palese, 1792.

———. *Saggio sopra l'opera in musica*. Edited by Annalisa Bini. Bologna: Libreria Musicale Italiana, 1989. First published 1762.

Amiot, Joseph-Marie. *De la musique moderne des Chinois*. 1780 ca.

———. *Mémoire sur la musique des Chinois*. Paris: Nyon, 1779. A facsimile of the first edition. Geneva: Minkoff, 1973.

Anelli, Angelo. *La Griselda*. Music by Piccinni. 1793.

Angiolini, Gaspare. *Les chinois en Europe*. 1767.

———. *L'orfano della Cina*. 1762.

Anonymous. *Alcina*. Music by Handel. 1735.

———. *Arlequin Barbet, pagode et médecin*. In *Histoire du Théâtre de l'Opera Comique*. 2 vols. Paris: Des Ventes Deladoué, 1770.

———. *Arlequin, rival du docteur*. In *Histoire du Théâtre de l'Opera Comique*. 2 vols. Paris: Des Ventes Deladoué, 1770.

———. *Ballet des Chevaliers des Indes et de la Chine*. 1604.

———. *Il cinese rimpatriato, divertimento scenico da rapresentarsi in Parigi, nel Teatro dell'Opera, l'anno 1753*. Paris: Delormel, n.d.

———. *Feste Persiane e Chinesi*. 1772.

———. *Fiera di mercanti cinesi*. 1757.

———. *I Gesuiti mercanti. Opera illustrata con note interessanti indirissata al reverendissimo Padre Ricci*. Venice, 1768.

———. *Le Gesuitiche arricchite con note curiose*. Venice, 1767.

———. *Le Grand bal de la douairière de Billebahaut*. 1626.

———. *Lo Sposalizio dell'imperatore della China*. 1785.

———. *Stanzas written hastily for the Ballet of the Princes of China*. 1600–1601.

———. *Schole-house for the Needle*. London, 1624.

Anseaume, Louis. *Le chinois poli en France*. In *Histoire du Théâtre de l'Opera Comique*. 2 vols. Paris: Des Ventes Deladoué, 1770.

Anson, Lord George, Richard Walter, and Benjamin Robins. *A Voyage Round the World . . .* London, 1748.

Argens, Jean-Baptiste de Boyer, Marquis d'. *Lettres chinoises; ou, Correspondance philosophique, historique et critique, entre un chinois voyageur à Paris & ses correspondans à la Chine, en Moscovie, en Perse & au Japon*. The Hague: Pierre Paupie, 1756. First published anonymously 1742.

Attiret, Jean-Denis. "A Particular Account of the Emperor of China's Gardens near Pekin: in a Letter from F. Attiret, a French Missionary, Now Employ'd by that Emperor to Paint the Apartments in Those Gardens, to his Friend at Paris." Translated by Joseph Spence (Sir Harry Beaumont). London, 1752. First published in *Lettres édifiantes et curieuses*. Paris: Guerin, 1749.

Bacon, Francis. *The New Atlantis*. 1627.

Baretti, Giuseppe. *La scelta delle lettere familiari*, edited by Luigi Piccioni. Bari: Laterza, 1912.

Bartoli, Daniello. *La Cina*, edited by Bice Mortara Garavelli. Milan: Bompiani, 1975. First published Rome, 1663.

———. *Della geografia trasportata al morale*. Milan: Malatesta, 1664.

Belloni, Girolamo. *Del commercio*. 1750, 1757.

Bernier, François. "Introduction à la lecture de Confucius." *Le Journal des Sçavans*, 7 June 1688: 17–26.

———. *Voyage dans les Etats du Grand Mogol*. 1670.

Bertati, Giovanni. *L'inimico delle donne. Dramma giocoso per musica di Giovanni Bertati da rappresentarsi nel Teatro di San Samuel l'autunno dell'anno 1771*. Venice: Modesto Fenzo, n.d.

———. *L'isola di Alcina*. Music by Gazzaniga. 1772.

———. *La villanella rapita*. Music by Bianchi. 1783.

Bertati, Giovanni, and Baldassare Galuppi. *L'inimico delle donne*, edited by Helen Geyer-Kiefl. 3 vols. Milan: Ricordi, 1986.

Bickerstaffe, Isaac. *The Captive*. 1769.

Bonarelli, Prospero. *Il Solimano*. Florence: Pietro Cecconelli, 1620.

Bossuet, Jacques-Benigne. *Discours sur l'histoire universelle*. Paris, 1681.

Bouvet, Joachim. *Portrait historique de l'Empereur de la Chine*. Paris, 1697.

Bretzner, Christoph Friedrich. *Belmont und Constanze, oder Die Entführung aus dem Serail*. 1780.

Caminer, Gioseffa Cornoldi. *La donna galante ed erudita: giornale dedicato al bel sesso*, edited by Cesare de Michelis. Venice: Marsilio, 1983. First published 1786–88.

Campanella, Tommaso. *La città del sole*. 1623.

Campastri, Tommaso. *La felicità del matrimonio*. 1760.

Campra, André. *L'Europe galante*. Paris?, 1697.

Carletti, Francesco. *Ragionamento del mio viaggio intorno al mondo*, edited by Paolo Collo. Turin: Einaudi, 1989. First published 1701.

Casti, Gianrinaldo. *Cublai, gran Kan de' tartari, Imperador de' mogolli*. In *Opere varie di G. Casti*, vol. 6. Paris [Pisa?]: Luigi Tenré, 1821.

———. *Melodrammi giocosi*, edited by Ettore Branca. Modena: Mucchi, 1998.

Cerlone, Francesco. *Il tiranno cinese*. In *Opere*. Naples, 1772.

Cervantes, Miguel. *Don Quixote*. 1605.

Chambers, William. *Designs of Chinese Buildings, Furniture, Dresses, Machines, and Utensils*. London, 1756.

Chappuzeau, Samuel. *Armetzar ou Les Amis Ennemis*. 1658.

Chardin, Jean. *Voyages de monsieur le chevalier Chardin en Perse et autres lieux de l'orient*. 1711.

Cherry, A. *The Travellers, or Music's Fascination*. Music by Domenico Corri. London, 1806.

Chiari, Pietro. *La schiava chinese. Le sorelle chinesi*, edited by Marco Catucci. Rome: Vecchiarelli, 1999. First published Bologna/Venice, 1759–62.

Churchill, John. *Collection of Voyages and Travels*. London, 1704.

Conti, Antonio. *Prose e poesie del signor abbate Antonio Conti, patrizio veneto*. 2 vols. Venice: Giambattista Pasquali, 1756.

Couplet, Philippe, ed. *Confucius Sinarum philosophus*. Paris, 1687.

———, ed. *Nouvelle relation de la Chine*. By Gabriel Magalhães. Paris, 1688.

Crébillon, Claude. *Le Sopha*. 1742.

Crescimbene, Gianmario. *La belleza della volgar poesia*. 1700.

Croubelis, Simoni dall. *Dans Le Gout asiatique*. 1780 ca.

———. *Simphonie chinoise*. 1780 ca.

D'Aglié, Filippo. *La Primavera trionfante dell'inverno*. 1657.

———. *Il tabacco*. 1650.

D'Alembert, Jean-le-Rond. "Goût." *Encyclopédie ou dictionnaire raisonné des sciences, des arts et des métiers* (Paris, 1751–72). The ARTFL Encyclopédie Project (page 7:761–70). ARTFL Project, University of Chicago, 2001. http://www.lib.uchicago.edu/efts/ARTFL/projects/encyc/.

Da Ponte, Lorenzo. *Così fan tutte*. Music by Mozart. 1790.

———. *Don Giovanni*. Music by Mozart. 1787.

———. *Le nozze di Figaro*. Music by Mozart. 1786.

David, Domenico. *La forza di virtù*. 1693.

Defoe, Daniel. *La vita e le avventure di Robinson Crusoe*, translated by D. Occhi. Venice, 1757–62. First published 1719.

Delfico, Melchiorre. *Saggio filosofico sul matrimonio*. 1774.

Desmahis, M [Joseph-François-Edouard de Corsembleu]. "Femme (Morale)." *Encyclopédie ou dictionnaire raisonné des sciences, des arts et des métiers* (Paris, 1751–72). The ARTFL Encyclopédie Project (page 6:472–75), ARTFL Project, University of Chicago, 2001. http://www.lib.uchicago.edu/efts/ARTFL/projects/encyc/.

Diderot, Denis. *De la poésie dramatique*. 1758.

———. *Supplément au Voyage de Bougainville*. 1796.

Dittersdorf, Karl Ditters von. *The Autobiography of Karl Von Dittersdorf*. New York: Da Capo, 1970. First published 1896.

Doria, Paolo Maria. *La vita civile*. 1710.

Dryden, John. *Don Sebastian*. 1689.

Du Halde, Jean-Baptiste. *Description geographique, historique, chronologique, politique et physique de l'Empire de la Chine et de la Tartarie chinoise*. Paris, 1735.

———. *The General History of China*, translated by John Watts. 4 vols. London: John Watts, 1736.

Fabris, Pietro. *Raccolta di varii Vestimenti ed Arti del Regno di Napoli*, edited by Franco Mancini. Naples: Guida, 1985. First published 1773.

Favart, Charles Simon. *Les amours de Bastien et de Bastienne*. Paris: Veuve Delormel, 1753.

———. *Soliman II*. 1761.

Favart, Charles, and J. A. Naigeon. *Le chinois. Parodie de Il cinese rimpatriato*. 1754.

Federico, Gennaro Antonio. *La serva padrona*. Music by Pergolesi. 1733.

Fénelon, François de Salignac de La Mothe. *Dialogues des morts*. Paris: Nelson/Lutetia, 1933. First published 1712.

Fischer Von Erlach, Johann Bernhard. *Entwurf einer historischen Architectur*. Vienna, 1721.

Fuzelier, Louis. *Les Indes galantes*. Music by Jean-Philippe Rameau. 1735.

Galiani, Ferdinando. *Croquis d'un dialogue sur les femmes*. In *Illuministi Italiani*. Vol. 6, *Opere di Ferdinando Galiani*, edited by Furio Diaz and Luciano Guerci. Milan: Ricciardi, 1975. First published 1772.

———. *Della moneta*. 1751.

Gallini, Giovanni-Andrea. *A Treatise on the Art of Dancing*. London, 1762.

Garrick, David. *The Chinese Festival*. 1755.

Gemelli-Careri, Giovanni Francesco. *La Cina*. Vol. 4 of *Giro del mondo*. 6 vols. Naples: Rosselli, 1699–1700.

Genovesi, Antonio. *Delle lezioni di commercio*. Naples: Fratelli Simone, 1765–67.

———. *Discorso sopra il vero fine delle lettere e delle scienze*. In *Antonio Genovesi, scritti*, edited by Franco Venturi, 40–87. Turin: Einaudi, 1977. First published 1754.

Gherardi, Evaristo. *Le Theatre italien de Gherardi ou Le recueil general de toutes les comedies et scénes françoises jouées par les Comediens Italiens du Roi, pendant tout le temps qu'ils ont été au service*. Paris: Chez Briasson, 1741.

Goëthe, Johann Wolfgang von. *Elpinor*. 1781–83.

Goldoni, Carlo. *L'Arcadia in Brenta*. In Ortolani, *Tutte le opere*, 10:583–634.

———. *Le avventure della villeggiatura*. In Ortolani, *Tutte le opere*, 7:1077–1144.

———. *La bella selvaggia*. In Ortolani, *Tutte le opere*, 9:815–85.

———. *La bottega del caffè*. In Ortolani, *Tutte le opere*, 3:1–80.

———. *La buona figliuola maritata*. In Ortolani, *Tutte le opere*, 12:55–107.

———. *La Cecchina, oppure La buona figliuola*. In Ortolani, *Tutte le opere*, 11:511–59.

———. *La donna di garbo*. In Ortolani, *Tutte le opere*, 1:1013–84.

———. *La famiglia dell'antiquario*. In Ortolani, *Tutte le opere*, 2:879–962.

———. *Il filosofo di campagna*. In Ortolani, *Tutte le opere*, 11:157–212.

———. *Ircana in Julfa*. In Ortolani, *Tutte le opere*, 9:595–663.

———. *Ircana in Ispaan*. In Ortolani, *Tutte le opere*, 9:665–736.

———. *L'isola disabitata*. In Ortolani, *Tutte le opere*, 11:661–711.

———. *La locandiera*. In Ortolani, *Tutte le opere*, 4:773–858.

———. *Il medico olandese*. In Ortolani, *Tutte le opere*, 6:367–440.

———. *Pamela nubile*. In Ortolani, *Tutte le opere*, 3:327–409.

———. *La peruviana*. In Ortolani, *Tutte le opere*, 9:737–813.

———. Prefazione. In first volume of Goldoni's works, published by Bettinelli in Venice in 1750. See Goldoni, http://www .classicitaliani.it/goldoni/goldo58.htm.

———. *Il re alla caccia*. In Ortolani, *Tutte le opere*, 12:161–219.

———. *Il ritorno dalla villeggiatura*. In Ortolani, *Tutte le opere*, 7:1145–1215.

———. *I rusteghi*. In Ortolani, *Tutte le opere*, 7:617–96.

———. *Le smanie per la villeggiatura*. In Ortolani, *Tutte le opere*, 7:1005–76.

———. *La sposa persiana*. In Ortolani, *Tutte le opere*, 9:515–93.

———. *La trilogia della villeggiatura*. In Ortolani, *Tutte le opere*, 7:1005–1215.

———. *Tutte le opere*, edited by Giuseppe Ortolani. 14 vols. Milan: Mondadori, 1935–55.

Gozzi, Carlo. *Turandot*. In *Opere*. Venice, 1772.

———. *Fiabe teatrali*, edited by Paolo Bosisio. Rome: Bulzoni, 1984.

Gozzi, Gasparo. *Marco Polo*. 1755.

Grandi, Vittorio Silvio. *Le vite degli imperatori*. 1716.

Grossmann, Gustav Friedrich Wilhelm. *Adelheit von Veltheim*, 1780.

Halfpenny, William, and John Halfpenny. *Chinese and Gothic Architecture, Properly Ornamented*. London, 1752.

———. *New Designs for Chinese Temples, Triumphal Arches, Garden Seats, Palings, &c.* London, 1750.

Hatchett, William. *The Chinese Orphan*. London, 1741.

Hill, Aaron. *The Fatal Vision*. 1716.

Howard, R., and J. Wilmot. *The Conquest of China by the Tartars*. 1670.

Jaucourt, Louis de [Saint-Lambert?]. "Génie." *Encyclopédie ou dictionnaire raisonné des sciences, des arts et des métiers* (Paris, 1751–72). The ARTFL Encyclopédie Project (page 7:581–83), ARTFL Project, University of Chicago, 2001. http://www.lib.uchicago .edu/efts/ARTFL/projects/encyc/.

Ji Junxiang. *Tchao chi cou ell*. 13th century.

Kircher, Athanasius. *China Illustrata: with Sacred and Secular Monuments, Various Spectacles of Nature and Art and Other Memorabilia*. Edited and translated by Charles D. Van Tuyl. Bloomington: Indiana University Research Institute for Inner Asian Studies, 1987. First published as *China monumentis qua sacris qua profanis, nec non variis naturæ & artis spectaculis, aliarumque rerum memorabilium argumentis illustrata . . .* Amsterdam: Johannes Jansson von Waesberg & Elizeum Weyerstraet, 1667.

Labrune, Jean de. *La morale de Confucius*. Amsterdam: P. Savouret, 1688.

La Chaussée, Nivelle de. *Amour castillan*. Paris: Prault, 1747.

La Mothe le Vayer, François de. *De la vertu des payens*. Paris, 1641–42.

Lalli, Domenico. *Camaide, l'imperatore della Cina, ovvero li figliuoli rivali del padre, Dramma per Musica da rappresentarsi nel Teatro di Corte per ordine di S. A. R. Monsignor Francesco Antonio, Arcivescovo e Prencipe di Salisburgo . . .* Salzburg: Mayr, n.d.

———. *La marchesina di Nanchin, Il Conte di Pelusio*. In Lalli, *Camaide, l'imperatore della Cina . . .* Salzburg: Mayr, n.d.

Lambranzi, Gregorio. *New and Curious School of Theatrical Dancing*, edited by Cyril W. Beaumont. Translated by Derra De Moroda. New York: Dance Horizons, Inc., 1966. First published as *Neue und Curieuse Theatralische Tantz-Schul*. Nuremberg, 1716.

Le Comte, Louis. *Nouveaux mémoires sur l'état présent de la Chine*. 2 vols. Paris, 1696.

Le Gobien, Charles. *L'Histoire de l'édit de l'empereur de la Chine en faveur de la religion chrétienne*. Paris, 1698.

Leibniz, Gottfried Wilhelm. *Novissima sinica*, 1697.

Lesage, Alain. *Arlequin invisible chez le roi de la Chine*. In *Histoire du Théâtre de l'Opera Comique*. 2 vols. Paris: Des Ventes Deladoué, 1770.

Lesage, Alain-Rene, and Jacques-Philippe d'Orneval. *Le Théâtre de la Foire, ou L'opéra-comique*. 9 vols. Paris, 1721–37.

Lessing, Gotthold Ephraim. *Die Hamburgische Dramaturgie*. 1767.

Lorenzi, Giambattista. *L'idolo cinese. Operetta giocosa per musica, Da rappresentarsi nel Real Teatrino di Caserta, per divertimento delle Maesta Loro nel felicissimo arrivo di S. M. La Regina*. Naples: Vincenzo Flauto, 1768.

———. *L'infedeltà fedele, commedia per musica / di Giambatista Lorenzi P.A.; da rappresentarsi nell'apertura del real Teatro del Fondo di Separazione ; nella està del corrente anno 1779*. Naples, 1779.

———. *Nina, o sia La pazza per amore*. Music by Paisiello. 1789.

———. *Opere teatrali di Giambattista Lorenzi napolitano [. . .]*, edited by Vincenzo Flauto. 4 vols. Naples: Flautina, 1806–20.

Maffei, Giovanni Pietro. *Historiarum Indicarum libri XVI*. Florence, 1588.

Maffei, Scipione. *Della scienza chiamata cavalleresca, libri tre . . .* Rome: F. Gonzaga, 1710.

———. *Rime e prose del Sig. marchese Scipione Maffei*. Venice: S. Coleti, 1719.

Magalhães, Gabriel. *Nouvelle relation de la Chine*, edited by Philippe Couplet. Paris, 1688.

Magalotti, Lorenzo. *Relazione della China*, edited by Teresa Poggi Salani. Milan: Adelphi, 1974. First published 1672.

Marana, Giovanni Paolo. *L'Espion du Grand Seigneur*. 1684.

Marcello, Benedetto. *Il teatro alla moda*. Venice, 1720.

Marini, Leonardo. *Abiti antichi di diverse nazioni d'Europa e d'Asia, inventati e disegnati da Leonardo Marini, torinese ed eseguiti al Real Teatro di Torino*. Turin, 1771.

Marlowe, Christopher. *Tamburlaine*. London, 1587.

Martello, Pier Jacopo. *I Taimingi*. In *Teatro*, edited by Hannibal S. Noce. Vol. 2. Bari: Laterza, 1981. First published 1712–13.

Martinelli, Gaetano. *La schiava liberata*. 1768.

Martini, Martino. *Ad Lectorem Praefatio*, edited by Giorgio Melis. Translated by Pietro Nicolao. Trent: Museo Tridentino di Scienze naturali, 1981.

———. "Bellum Tartaricum, or, The History of the Warres of the Tartars in China." In *The History of that Great and Renowned Monarchy of China* ... by Alvaro Semedo. London: E. Tyler, 1655.

———. *De bello tartarico historia*. Milan, 1654.

———. *Novus atlas Sinensis*. Trent: Museo Tridentino di Scienze naturali, 1981. First published Amsterdam: Blaeu, 1655.

———. *Sinicae historiae decas prima*. Munich, 1658.

Mendoza, Juan Gonzalez de. *Historia de las cosas mas notables, ritos y costumbres del gran Reyno de la China*. Rome, 1585.

Mésenguy, François-Philippe. *Exposition de la doctrine Chrétienne, ou Instructions sur les principales vérités de la religion*. 1744.

Metastasio, Pietro. "Ad Antonio Tolomeo Trivulzio, Milano." Lettera 542, Vienna 9 Gennaio 1752. In Brunelli, *Tutte le opere*, 3: 707–8.

———. *Alessandro nelle Indie*. In Brunelli, *Tutte le opere*, 1:307–54.

———. *Artaserse*. In Brunelli, *Tutte le opere*, 1:355–414.

———. *Attilio Regolo*. In Brunelli, *Tutte le opere*, 1:971–1021.

———. *La clemenza di Tito*. In Brunelli, *Tutte le opere*, 1:693–750.

———. *Le cinesi*. In Brunelli, *Tutte le opere*, 2:341–54.

———. "Alla Contessa di Sangro, Napoli." Lettera 616, Vienna 29 Gennaio 1753. In Brunelli, *Tutte le opere*, 3:789–90.

———. *Demetrio*. In Brunelli, *Tutte le opere*, 1:415–77.

———. *L'eroe cinese*. In Brunelli, *Tutte le opere*, 1:1153–93.

———. *Il re pastore*. In Brunelli, *Tutte le opere*, 1:1115–52.

———. *Siroe, re della Persia*. In Brunelli, *Tutte le opere*, 1:67–123.

———. *Tutte le opere di Pietro Metastasio*, edited by Bruno Brunelli. 5 vols. Milan: Mondadori, 1953–54.

Mezzabarba, Carlo. "Eight Permissions." 1721.

Milizia, Francesco. *Trattato Completo, Formale e Materiale del Teatro*. Bologna: Forni, 1969. First published Rome, 1771.

Molière, Jean-Baptiste Poquelin. *Le bourgeois gentilhomme*. Paris, 1670.

Montesquieu, Charles Louis Secondat de. *De l'esprit des lois*. Paris: Garnier, 1973. First published 1748.

———. *Lettres persanes*. Paris, 1721.

More, Thomas. *Utopia*. 1516.

Muratori, Ludovico. *Della carità cristiana*. 1723.

———. *Della pubblica felicità*. 1749.

Murphy, Arthur, and J. B. Du Halde. *The Orphan of China: a Tragedy, as it is Perform'd at the Theatre-Royal, in Drury-Lane*. London: P. Vaillant, 1759.

Navarrete, Domingo. *Tratados historicos, politicos, ethicos y religiosos de la monarchia de China*. Madrid, 1676.

Neri, Pompeo. *Osservazioni sopra il prezzo legale delle monete e le difficoltà di prefinirlo e di sostenerlo*. 1751.

Nieuhoff, Johannes. *An Embassy from the East-India Company of the United Provinces, to the Grand Tartar Cham, Emperor of China . . .* London: White Friers, 1673. Trans. of *Het gezantschap der Neêrlandtsche Oost-Indische Compagnie aan den grooten tartarischen cham, den tegenwoordigen keizer van China*. Amsterdam, 1665.

Noverre, Jean-Georges. *Les Fêtes chinoises*. Music by Jean-Philippe Rameau. 1752.

Pagnini, Gian Francesco. *Ragionamento sopra la moneta, l'interesse del denaro, le finanze, il commercio*. 1751.

Pepoli, Alessandro. *Il cinese in Italia*. 1793.

Perrucci, Andrea. *Dell'arte rappresentativa*. Naples: Mutio, 1699.

Petrosellini, Giuseppe. *Il barbiere di Siviglia*. Music by Paisiello. 1782.

Peyrère, Isaac de la. *Men Before Adam*. London, 1656.

———. *Pre-Adamitae sive . . .* Leyden, 1655.

Pillement, Jean. *The Ladies Amusement; or, Whole Art of Japanning Made Easy*. London, 1762.

Planelli, Antonio. *Dell'opera in musica*, edited by Francesco Degrada. Fiesole: Discanto, 1981. First published Naples: Donato Campo, 1772.

Quesnay, François. "Fermiers." *Encyclopédie ou dictionnaire raisonné des sciences, des arts et des métiers* (Paris: 1751–72). The ARTFL Encyclopédie Project (page 6:528–40), ARTFL Project, University of Chicago, 2001. http://www.lib.uchicago.edu/efts/ARTFL/projects/encyc/.

———. "Grains". *Encyclopédie ou dictionnaire raisonné des sciences, des arts et des métiers* (Paris: 1751–72). The ARTFL Encyclopédie Project (page 7:812–31), ARTFL Project, University of Chicago, 2001. http://www.lib.uchicago.edu/efts/ARTFL/projects/encyc/.

———. *Physiocratie*. 1768.

———. *Tableau économique*. 1758.

Racine, Jean. *Bajazet*. Paris, 1672.

Reade, Charles. *It's Never Too Late to Mend*. London: Clowes and Sons, 1856.

Regnard, Jean-François, and Charles Rivière Dufresny. *Les chinois*. In *Théâtre italien*, edited by Evariste Gherardi. Vol. 2, pt. 4, 199–260. Geneva: Slatkine, 1969. Facsimile of 1741 edition.

Remondini, Giuseppe. *Catalogo delle stampe in rame e delle varie qualità di carte privilegiate dall' eccellentissimo senato: le quali si lavorano in Bassano presso la dita di Giuseppe Remondini e figli di Venezia . . .* Bassano del Grappa: Remondini, 1770.

Renaudot, Eusebius. *Anciennes relations*. Paris, 1718.

Ricci, Urbano. *Taican rè della Cina. Tragedia per Musica da rappresentarsi nel Teatro Tron di S. Cassano l'anno MDCCVII*. Venice: Rossetti, 1707.

Riccoboni, Francesco. *Les magots. Commedia dell'arte parodia di L'orphelin de la Chine di Voltaire*. 1756.

Richardson, Samuel. *Pamela, or Virtue Rewarded*. London, 1740.

Ripa, Matteo. *Memoirs of Father Ripa, during thirteen years' residence at the court of Peking in the service of the emperor of China with an account of the foundation of the college for the education of young Chinese at Naples*. Translated and edited by Fortunato Prandi. London: John Murray, 1844.

———. *Storia della fondazione della Congregazione e del Collegio de' Cinesi*. Naples: Manfredi, 1832.

Rousseau, Jean-Jacques. *Dictionnaire de musique*. Paris, 1768.

———. *Discours sur les sciences et les arts*. London: Oxford University Press, 1946. First published 1750.

———. *Julie, ou la nouvelle Héloïse*. Paris: Garnier, 1960. First published 1761.

Salmon, Thomas. *Modern History, or Present State of All Nations*. 20 vols. London, 1725–38.

———. *Lo stato presente di tutti i paesi, e popoli del mondo naturale, politico e morale*. 26 vols. Venice: Albrizzi, 1731–66.

Salvi, Antonio. *Il Tartaro nella Cina, Dramma per musica da rappresentarsi nel teatro dell'ill.mo Pubblico di Reggio in occasione della fiera l'anno MDCCXV. Dedicato all'Altezza Serenissima Rinaldo I, Duca di Reggio, Modona, Mirandola, ecc.* Reggio: Vedrotti, 1715.

Saracinelli, Ferdinando. *La liberazione di Ruggiero dall'isola d'Alcina*. Music by Francesca Caccini. Florence, 1625.

Scala, Flaminio. *Il teatro delle favole rappresentative*, edited by Ferruccio Marotti. 2 vols. Milan: Polifilo, 1976. First published 1611.

Semedo, Alvarez. *The History of that Great and Renowned Monarchy of China . . .* London: E. Tyler, 1655.

———. *Relação da propagação da fé no regno da China e outras adjacentes*. Goa, 1638.

Settle, Elkanah. *The Conquest of China by the Tartars*. 1676.

Settle, Elkanah, and Henry Purcell. *The Fairy Queen*. 1692.

Smith, Adam. *An Inquiry into the Nature and Causes of the Wealth of Nations*. 1776.

Soave, Francesco. *Novelle morali*. Milan: Motta, 1782.

Stalker, John, and George Parker. *A Treatise of Japaning and Varnishing.* Oxford, 1688.

Stephanie, Gottlieb. *Die Entführung aus dem Serail.* Music by Mozart. Vienna, 1782.

Storace, Stephen. *Gli sposi malcontenti.* Music by Brunati. 1785.

Tasso, Torquato. *Gerusalemme liberata.* 1581.

Temple, William. *Of Heroic Virtue.* London, 1690.

Thévenot, Melchisédec. *Rélations de divers voyages curieux, qui n'ont point este publiées, et qu'on a traduit ou tiré des originaux des voyageurs françois, espagnols, allemands, portugais, anglois, hollandois, persans, arabes et autres originaux.* 4 vols. Paris, 1663–72.

Trigault, Nicholas. *De christiana expeditione apud sinas.* Augsburg, 1615.

Turgot, Anne-Robert-Jacques. *Lettres sur la liberté du commerce des grains.* 1770.

———. *Réflections sur la formation et la distribution des richesses.* 1766.

Valaresso, Zaccaria. *Rutzvanscad il giovine.* 1722.

Verri, Alessandro. "Lo spirito di società." *Il Caffè ossia brevi e vari discorsi distribuiti in fogli periodici (dal giugno 1764 a tutto il maggio 1765),* edited by Sergio Romagnoli, 278–82. Milan: Feltrinelli, 1960.

Verri, Pietro. "Dialogo fra un Mandarino e un Sollecitatore." *Il Caffè ossia brevi e vari discorsi distribuiti in fogli periodici (dal giugno 1764 a tutto il maggio 1765),* edited by Sergio Romagnoli, 324–26. Milan: Feltrinelli, 1960.

———. "Elementi di Commercio." In *Il Caffè ossia brevi e vari discorsi distribuiti in fogli periodici (dal giugno 1764 a tutto il maggio 1765),* edited by Sergio Romagnoli, 27–29. Milan: Feltrinelli, 1960.

Vico, Giambattista. *Scienza nuova seconda,* edited by Fausto Nicolini. Bari: Laterza, 1953. First published 1730.

Vidimann, N. H. *Lisetta cinese e Aristobolo Indiano. Intermedj rappresentati in musica nel Teatro di San Cassiano nell'Opera Taican Re della Cina, Anno MDCCVII.* In *Taican re della Cina. Tragedia per Musica da rappresentarsi nel Teatro Tron di S. Cassano l'anno MDCCVII.* By Urbano Ricci. Venice: Rossetti, 1707. 1–11.

Voltaire, François Arouet de. *Alzire.* 1736.

———. *Le Dictionnaire philosophique.* 1764.

———. *Essai sur les moeurs et l'esprit des nations.* 1756.

———. *Les lettres chinoises.* Paris, 1776.

———. *Mahomet.* 1742.

———. *The Orphan of China.* In *The Works of Voltaire: A Contemporary Version with Notes.* Edited and translated by Tobias George Smollett and William F. Fleming. Délices edition. 15:175–237. Paris: E. R. Du Mont, 1901.

———. *Le siècle de Louis XIV.* 1752.

———. *Le traité sur la tolerance.* 1763.

———. *Zaïre.* 1732.

Vossius, Isaac. *De vera aetate mundi.* The Hague, 1659.

Webb, John. *An Historical Essay Endeavoring a Probability that the Language of the Empire of China is the Primitive Language.* London, 1669.

Zeno, Apostolo. *Ormisda.* 1721.

———. *Teuzzone, Dramma per Musica nel Regio Ducal Teatro di Milano l'anno MDCCVI. Consecrato al Serenissimo Prencipe di Vaudemonte.* Milan: Malatesta, 1706.

Zini, Franceso Saverio. *Dal finto il vero.* Music by Paisiello. 1776.

Secondary Sources

"500 Years of Italian Dance." Online exhibition offered by the New York Public Library. http://www.nypl.org/research/lpa/italiandance/.

Acton, Harold. *The Bourbons of Naples, 1734–1825.* London: Prion Books, 1998.

Alberti, Carmelo, and Gilberto Pizzamiglio, eds. *Carlo Goldoni, 1793–1993. Atti del Convegno del Bicentenario. Venezia, 11–13 aprile 1994.* Venice: Regione del Veneto, 1995.

Aldridge, A. Owen. "China in the Spanish Enlightenment." In *Proceedings of the XIIth Congress of the International Comparative Literature Association,* 404–9. Munich: Iudicium, 1990.

———. *The Dragon and the Eagle: The Presence of China in the American Enlightenment.* Detroit: Wayne State University Press, 1993.

Allanbrook, Wye Jamison. "Mozart's Happy Endings: A New Look at the 'Convention' of the 'lieto fine.' " *Mozart-Jahrbuch* (1984–85): 1–5.

Alm, Irene. "Theatrical Dance in Seventeenth-Century Venetian Opera." PhD diss., University of California at Los Angeles, 1993.

———. "Winged Feet and Mute Eloquence: Dance in Seventeenth-Century Venetian Opera." *Cambridge Opera Journal* 15, no. 3 (2003): 216–80.

Alter, Jean. *A Sociosemiotic Theory of Theatre.* Philadelphia: University of Pennsylvania Press, 1990.

Angelini, Franca. "Le personnage féminin dans le théâtre de Goldoni." In *Le Théâtre dans l'Europe des Lumières: Programmes, pratiques, échanges,* edited by Mieczyslaw Klimowicz, 125–31. Warsaw: Wydanawnictwo Uniwersytetu Wroclawskiego, 1985.

Angiolillo, Marialuisa. *Storia del costume teatrale in Europa.* Rome: Lucarini, 1989.

Antonicek, Theophil, et al. "Vienna." *Grove Music Online,* edited by L. Macy. http://www.grovemusic.com.

Appleton, William Worthen. *A Cycle of Cathay.* New York: Columbia University Press, 1951.

Armstrong, Nancy. *Desire and Domestic Fiction.* New York: Oxford University Press, 1987.

Backscheider, Paula. *Spectacular Politics: Theatrical Power and Mass Culture in Early Modern England.* Baltimore: Johns Hopkins University Press, 1993.

Ballaster, Rosalind. *Fabulous Orients: Fictions of the East in England, 1662–1785.* Oxford: Oxford University Press, 2005.

Barbagli, Marzio. *Sotto lo stesso tetto.* Bologna: Il Mulino, 1984.

Barbagli, Marzio, and David I. Kertzer. *Storia della famiglia italiana, 1750–1950.* Bologna: Il Mulino, 1992.

Barbour, Richard. *Before Orientalism.* Cambridge: Cambridge University Press, 2003.

Barker-Benfield, G. J. *The Culture of Sensibility: Sex and Society in Eighteenth-Century Britain.* Chicago: University of Chicago Press, 1992.

Barth-Scalmani, Gunda. "Eighteenth-Century Marriage Contracts." In Schutte, Kuehn, and Seibel, *Time, Space,* 265–81.

Basso, Alberto, ed. *Musica in Scena: Storia dello Spettacolo Musicale.* 6 vols. Turin: UTET, 1995.

Bauman, Thomas. "Belmont und Constanze (i)." *Grove Music Online,* edited by L. Macy. http://www.grovemusic.com/.

———. "The Eighteenth Century: Serious Opera." In Parker, *The Oxford Illustrated History of Opera,* 47–83.

———. *W. A. Mozart: Die Entführung aus dem Serail.* Cambridge Opera Handbooks. Cambridge: Cambridge University Press, 1987.

Bauman, Thomas, and Marita Petzoldt McClymonds, eds. *Opera and the Enlightenment.* Cambridge: Cambridge University Press, 1995.

Beaumont, Cyril W. *Ballet Design.* New York: Studio Publications, 1946.

Bellman, Jonathan, ed. *The Exotic in Western Music.* Boston: Northeastern University Press, 1998.

———. Introduction to Bellman, *The Exotic,* ix–xiii.

Bérenger, Jean. *A History of the Habsburg Empire, 1700–1918.* Translated by C. A. Simpson. London: Longman, 1997.

Berg, Maxine. "Manufacturing the Orient: Asian Commodities and European Industry, 1500–1800." In *Prodotti e tecniche d'oltremare nelle economie europee secc. XIII–XVIII,* edited by Simonetta Cavaciocchi, 385–419. Prato: Istituto internazionale di storia economica F. Datini, 1998.

Berger, Willy Richard. *China-Bild und China-Mode im Europa der Aufklärung.* Cologne: Böhlau, 1990.

Bertana, Emilio. *La tragedia. Storia dei generi letterari italiani.* Milan: Vallardi, 1904.

Beurdeley, Cécile, and Michel Beurdeley. *Giuseppe Castiglione, A Jesuit Painter at the Court of the Chinese Emperors.* Rutland, VT: Tuttle, 1971.

Bianconi, Lorenzo, and Giorgio Pestelli, eds. *Opera on Stage.* Translated by Kate Singleton. Part 2, vol. 5 of *The History of Italian Opera.* Chicago: University of Chicago Press, 1998.

———, eds. *Opera Production and Its Resources.* Translated by Lydia G. Cochrane. Part 2, vol. 4 of *The History of Italian Opera.* Chicago: University of Chicago Press, 1998.

Bianconi, Lorenzo, and Thomas Walker. "Production, Consumption and Political Function of Seventeenth-Century Opera." In *Early Music History 4. Studies in Medieval and Early Modern Music,* edited by Iain Fenlon, 209–96. Cambridge: Cambridge University Press, 1984.

Biggi, Maria Ida. "La scenografia." In *Teatro Malibran,* edited by Biggi and Giorgio Mangini, 137–47. Venice: Marsilio, 2001.

Binni, Walter. *L'Arcadia e il Metastasio.* Florence: Nuova Italia, 1968.

———. *Classicismo e neoclassicismo nella letteratura del Settecento.* Florence: Nuova Italia, 1976.

———. "Il Settecento letterario." In *Il Settecento,* vol. 6 of *Storia della letteratura italiana,* edited by Emilio Cecchi and Natalino Sapegno, 323–1040. Milan: Garzanti,1988.

Bishop, Morris, trans. and ed. *The Would-Be Gentleman.* In *Eight Plays by Molière* by Molière. Translated by Morris Bishop. Mattituck, NY: Aeonian Press, 1957. 324–99.

Bizzocchi, Roberto. *In famiglia. Storie di interessi e affetti nell'Italia moderna.* Rome: Laterza, 2001.

Black, Christopher F. *Early Modern Italy: A Social History.* London: Routledge, 2001.

Black, Jeremy. *The British and the Grand Tour.* London: Croom Helm, 1985.

Blackmer, Corinne E., and Patricia Juliana Smith, eds. *En Travesti: Women, Gender Subversion, Opera.* New York: Columbia University Press, 1995.

Blichmann, Diana. " 'So che un barbaro sei, né mi spaventi.' Spunti esotici nella *Didone Abbandonata* di Metastasio." In Cotticelli and Maione, *Le arti della scena,* 235–70.

Bongie, Chris. *Exotic Memories.* Stanford: Stanford University Press, 1991.

Bosisio, Paolo. "Gasparo Gozzi poeta e traduttore drammatico." In *Gasparo Gozzi. Il lavoro di un intellettuale nel Settecento Veneziano. Atti del convegno (Venezia-Pordenone 4–6 dicembre 1986),* edited by Ilaria Crotti and Ricciarda Ricorda, 281–213. Padua: Antenore, 1989.

Bossa, Renato. "Goldoni e l'opera buffa." *Sipario* 537 (1993): 65–68.

Bossaglia, Rossana. *I fratelli Galliari, pittori.* Milan: Ceschina, 1962.

Boxer, Charles R. *The Dutch Seaborne Empire, 1600–1800.* London: Hutchinson, 1965.

Brambilla, Elena. "La storia di Mie Mie. «Spirito di famiglia» e condizione della donna fra Antico Regime e Rivoluzione." *Acme* 52 (1999): 63–93.

Brenner, Clarence D. *A Bibliographical List of Plays in the French Language, 1700–1789.* Berkeley: n.p., 1947.

Brower, Daniel J., and Edward J. Lazzerini. *Russia's Orient: Imperial Borderlands and Peoples, 1700–1917.* Bloomington: Indiana University Press, 1997.

Brown, Bruce Alan. "Angiolini, Gasparo." *Grove Music Online,* edited by L. Macy. http://www.grovemusic.com.

———. "Durazzo, Count Giacomo." *Grove Music Online,* edited by L. Macy. http://www.grovemusic.com.

———. "Gluck, Christoph Willibald Ritter von." *Grove Music Online,* edited by L. Macy. http://www.grovemusic.com.

———. "Gli Sciti di Gluck." In Cotticelli and Maione, *Le arti della scena,* 555–73.

Brown, Bruce Alan, and Julian Rushton. "Gluck, Christoph Willibald Ritter von (3. Vienna, 1752–60)." *Grove Music Online,* edited by L. Macy. http://www.grovemusic.com.

Brown, John Russell, ed. *The Oxford Illustrated History of Theatre.* Oxford: Oxford University Press, 1995.

Brunelli, Bruno. Notes to *Le cinesi.* In Brunelli, *Tutte le opere,* 2: 1317.

———. Notes to *L'eroe cinese.* In Brunelli, *Tutte le opere,* 1:1509.

Bucciarelli, Melania. "Echi tassiani e rappresentazioni dell'Oriente al Teatro S. Angelo di Venezia." In Cotticelli and Maione, *Le arti della scena,* 217–33.

———. *Italian Opera and European Theatre, 1680–1720.* Brepols: Turnhout, 2000.

Bujatti, Anna. "Cina e cineserie nel teatro italiano del Settecento." In Gallotta and Marazzi, *La Conoscenza dell'Asia,* 451–72.

Burt, Nathaniel. "Opera in Arcadia." *The Musical Quarterly* 41, no. 2 (1955): 145–70.

Cammann, Schuyler. *China's Dragon Robes.* New York: Ronald Press, 1952.

Camporesi, Piero. *Exotic Brew.* Translated by Christopher Woodall. Cambridge: Polity Press, 1994.

Carandini, Silvia. "L'Oriente in maschera nelle 'invenzioni' dei comici dell'Arte." In Cotticelli and Maione, *Le arti della scena,* 23–44.

Carlson, Marvin. "*Il re alla caccia* and *Le Roi et le fermier:* Italian and French Treatments of Class and Gender." In Hunter and Webster, *Opera Buffa in Mozart's Vienna,* 82–97.

———. "Theories of Drama, Theatre, and Performance." In *The Oxford Encyclopedia of Theatre and Performance,* edited by Dennis Kennedy, 2:1355–61. Oxford: Oxford University Press, 2003.

————. *Theories of the Theatre*. Ithaca: Cornell University Press, 1984.

————. *Voltaire and the Theatre of the Eighteenth Century*. Westport, CT: Greenwood Press, 1998.

Carluccio, Luigi, ed. *Il teatro Regio di Torino*. Turin: Aeda, 1970.

Caroccia, Antonio. " 'Ve le canto in cinese': rivendicazioni e fascino esotico nell'*Eroe cinese* di Domenico Cimarosa." In Columbro and Maione, *Pietro Metastasio*, 203–24.

Carpanetto, Dino. "Reforms without Enlightenment: the Papal States, the republics and Charles Emanuel III's Piedmont." In *Italy in the Age of Reason, 1685–1789*, edited by Dino Carpanetto and Giuseppe Ricuperati, translated by Caroline Higgitt, 198–202. London: Longman, 1987.

Carpanetto, Dino, and Giuseppe Ricuperati. *L'Italia del Settecento: crisi, trasformazioni, lumi*. Rome: Laterza, 1986.

Carter, Tim. "Ariosto, Ludovico." *Grove Music Online*, edited by L. Macy. http://www.grovemusic.com.

————. "The Seventeenth Century." In Parker, *Oxford Illustrated History of Opera*, 1–46.

Casa, Emilio. *Controversie fra la Corte di Parma e la Santa Sede nel secolo XVIII*. Modena: T. Vincenzi, 1881.

Catucci, Marco. Introduction to *La schiava chinese. Le sorelle chinesi*, by Pietro Chiaris, edited by Catucci, 7–36. Rome: Vecchiarelli, 1999.

————. *Il teatro esotico dell'abate Chiari*. Rome: Robin, 2007.

Chadwick, Owen. "The Italian Enlightenment." In *The Enlightenment in a National Context*, edited by Roy Porter and Mikulas Teich, 90–105. Cambridge: Cambridge University Press, 1981.

————. *The Popes and European Revolution*. Oxford: Clarendon Press, 1981.

Chen, Da. "From China to Wall Street to Random House." Keynote address, annual meeting of the New York Conference on Asian Studies (NYCAS), New Paltz, NY, Sept. 30–Oct.1, 2005.

Chen, Shouyi. "The Chinese Orphan: A Yuan Play." In Hsia, *Chinesia*, 359–82.

Chen, Xiaomei. *Occidentalism: Theory of Counter-Discourse in Post-Mao China*. 2nd ed. Lanham, MD: Rowman and Littlefield, 2002.

Choudhury, Mita. *Interculturalism and Resistance in the London Theater, 1660–1800*. Lewisburg, PA: Bucknell University Press, 2000.

Clark, T. Blake. *Oriental England. A Study of Oriental Influences in Eighteenth Century England as Reflected in the Drama*. Shanghai: Kelly & Walsh, 1939.

Clarke, Mary, and Clement Crisp. *Ballet: An Illustrated History*. London: A. and C. Black, 1973.

Clifford, James. "On Orientalism." Chap. 11 in *The Predicament of Culture*. Cambridge: Harvard University Press, 1988.

Cohen, Aaron. "Euro-Oriental Works for Performance: Timeline up to 1900." Unpublished list, 2005.

Columbro, Marta, and Paologiovanni Maione, eds. *Pietro Metastasio. Il testo e il contesto*. Naples: Altrastampa, 2000.

Coppola, Carmine. *Pulcinella: la maschera nella tradizione teatrale*. Naples: Edizioni scientifiche italiane, 1987.

Cordier, Henri. *La Chine en France au XVIIIème siècle*. Paris: H. Laurens, 1910.

Cotticelli, Francesco. "Problemi della drammaturgia di Francesco Cerlone. Appunti sui drammi esotici." In Cotticelli and Maione, *Le arti della scena*, 383–420.

————. "Proposte per una lettura e interpretazione degli scenari Casamarciano." In *The Commedia dell'Arte in Naples*, edited and translated by Francesco Cotticelli, Anne Goodrich Heck, and Thomas F. Heck. Vol. 2, 3–13. Lanham, MD: Scarecrow Press, 2001.

————. "Splendori e miserie dell'Arte nel Settecento napoletano." In Lattanzi and Maione, *Commedia dell'Arte e spettacolo*, 365–78.

Cotticelli, Francesco, Anne Goodrich Heck, and Thomas F. Heck, trans. and eds. *The Commedia dell'Arte in Naples: A Bilingual Edition of the 176 Casamarciano Scenarios*. 2 vols. Lanham, MD: Scarecrow Press, 2001.

Cotticelli, Francesco, and Paologiovanni Maione, eds. *Le arti della scena e l'esotismo in età moderna/The Performing Arts and Exoticism in the Modern Age*. Naples: Turchini, 2006.

Cozzi, Gaetano. "Note e documenti sulla questione del 'divorzio' a Venezia (1782–1788)." *Annali dell'Istituto Italo-Germanico in Trento* 7 (1981): 275–360.

Cresti, Carlo. *Orientalismi nelle architetture d'Occidente*. Florence: Angelo Pontecorboli, 1999.

Croce, Benedetto. *History of the Kingdom of Naples*, edited by H. Stuart Hughes. Translated by Frances Frenaye. Chicago: University of Chicago Press, 1970.

————. *Storia del regno di Napoli*. Bari: Laterza, 1972.

Croll, Gerhard. "*Le cinesi*. An opera-serenade by Christoph Willibald Gluck." Booklet. *Le cinesi*, by Christoph Willibald Gluck. Orfeo, 1989.

————. "Tesi, Vittoria." *Grove Music Online*, edited by L. Macy. http://www.grovemusic.com.

Croll, Gerhard, and Irene Brandenburg. "Gabrielli, Caterina." *Grove Music Online*, edited by L. Macy. http://www.grovemusic.com.

Crossley, Pamela K. *The Manchus*. Oxford: Blackwell, 1997.

Cummins, J. S. *A Question of Rites*. Hants, England: Scolar Press, 1993.

Cusick, Suzanne G. "Caccini, Francesca." *Grove Music Online*, edited by L. Macy. http://www.grovemusic.com.

Darrow, Margaret H. "French Noblewomen and the New Domesticity, 1750–1850." *Feminist Studies* 5, no. 1 (1979): 41–65.

De Biase, Luca. "Problemi ed osservazioni sul 'divorzio' nel patriziato veneziano del XVIII: Un tentativo di analisi storica seriale." *Atti dell'Istituto Veneto di Scienze, Lettere ed Arti* 140 (1981–82): 143–62.

De Giorgio, Michela, and Christiane Klapisch-Zuber, eds. *Storia del matrimonio*. Rome: Laterza, 1996.

De Maio, Romeo. *Pulcinella: il filosofo che fu chiamato pazzo*. Florence: Sansoni, 1989.

De Marinis, Marco. *The Semiotics of Performance*. Translated by Áine O'Healy. Bloomington: Indiana University Press, 1993.

De Nora, Tia. "The Biology Lessons of Opera Buffa: Gender, Nature, and Bourgeois Society on Mozart's Buffa Stage." In Hunter and Webster, *Opera Buffa in Mozart's Vienna*, 146–64.

De' Paoli, Domenico. "Il librettista Carlo Goldoni e l'opera comica veneziana." In *Studi goldoniani*, edited by Vittore Branca and Nicola Magnini, 571–91. Venice-Rome: Istituto per la collaborazione culturale, 1957.

Della Seta, Fabrizio. "*O cieli azzurri:* Exoticism and Dramatic Discourse in Aida." *Cambridge Opera Journal* 3 (1991): 49–62.

———. "The Librettist." In Bianconi and Pestelli, *Opera Production and Its Resources*, 229–90.

Denison, Tom, Dharmalingam Arunachalam, Graeme Johanson, and Russell Smyth. "The Chinese Community in Prato." Paper presented at Communities and Action: Prato CIRN Conference, Prato, Italy, November 5–7, 2007.

Deron, Isabel Landry. *La preuve par la Chine: La "Description" de J.-B. Du Halde, Jésuite, 1735.* Paris: Editions de l'Ecole des hautes études en sciences sociales, 2002.

Deupi, Jill Johnson. "Cultural Identity in Bourbon Naples, 1734–1799: Academies, Antiquities, and Rivalries with Rome." PhD diss., University of Virginia, 2005.

Dirlik, Arif. "Chinese History and the Question of Orientalism." *History and Theory* 35, no. 4 (1996): 96–118.

Dixon, Susan. "Forum: Women and the Academy." *Eighteenth-Century Studies* 32, no. 3 (1999): 371–90.

Dock, Terry Smiley. *Woman in the Encylopédie.* Potomac: Studia Humanitatis, 1983.

Douthwaite, Julia V. *Exotic Women: Literary Heroines and Cultural Strategies in Ancien Régime France.* Philadelphia: University of Pennsylvania Press, 1992.

Dunne, George H. *Generation of Giants: The Story of the Jesuits in China in the Last Decades of the Ming Dynasty.* Notre Dame: University of Notre Dame Press, 1962.

Durante, Sergio. "Declinazioni dell'esotismo nella rappresentazione in musica settecentesca." In Cotticelli and Maione, *Le arti della scena*, 11–22.

Eco, Umberto. "Semiotics of Theatrical Performance." *The Drama Review* 21 (1977): 107–17.

Emery, Ted. *Goldoni as Librettist: Theatrical Reform and the Drammi Giocosi per musica.* New York: Peter Lang, 1991.

———. Introduction to *Five Tales for the Theatre*, by Carlo Gozzi. Edited and translated by Albert Bermel and Ted Emery, 1–19. Chicago: University of Chicago Press, 1989.

Enciclopedia dello spettacolo. 9 vols. Rome: Le Maschere, 1954–62.

Ericani, Giuliana. "Della Cina o del Commercio dello stato. Immagini di un sogno nel declino della Serenissima." In *I linguaggi del sogno*, edited by Vittore Branca, Carlo Ossola, and Salomon Resnik, 325–39. Florence: Sansoni, 1984.

———. "L'Immagine della Cina a Venezia nel *Settecento*." In *Venezia e l'Oriente*, edited by Lionello Lanciotti, 161–88. Florence: Olschki, 1987.

———. "L'Impero della Cina sulla scene e nella festa veneziana tra '600 e '700." In *La scenografia barocca. Atti del Convegno Internazionale di Storia dell'Arte*, edited by Antoine Schapper, 95–104. Bologna: CLUEB, 1982.

Etiemble, René. *L'Europe chinoise.* 2 vols. Paris: Gallimard, 1988.

———. *Les Jesuites en Chine: La querelle des rites, 1552–1773.* Paris: Julliard, 1966.

"Exoticism." *Grove Music Online*, edited by L. Macy. http://www.grovemusic.com/.

Fairchilds, Cissie. "Women and Family." In *French Women and the Age of Enlightenment*, edited by Samia I. Spencer, 97–110. Bloomington: Indiana University Press, 1984.

Fairfax, Edmund. *The Styles of Eighteenth-Century Ballet.* Lanham, MD: Scarecrow Press, 2003.

Fauchery, Pierre. *La destinée féminine dans le roman européen du dix-huitième siècle.* Paris: A. Colin, 1972.

Feldman, Martha. "The Absent Mother in Opera Seria." In Smart, *Siren Songs*, 29–46.

———. *Opera and Sovereignty.* Chicago: University of Chicago Press, 2007.

Ferrero, Mercedes Viale. *La scenografia del '700 e i fratelli Galliari.* Turin: Fratelli Pozzo, 1963.

———. *Scenografia.* Vol. 3 of *Storia del Teatro Regio di Torino.* Turin: Cassa di Risparmio, 1980.

———. "Stage and Set." In Bianconi and Pestelli, *Opera on Stage*, 1–48.

Fido, Franco. "Giacinta nel paese degli uomini: interpretazione delle *Villeggiature* e del 'femminismo' goldoniano." Chap. in *Da Venezia all'Europa: Prospettive sull'ultimo Goldoni*, 11–58. Rome: Bulzoni, 1984.

———. "I libretti per musica scritti a Parigi." In *Goldoni and the Musical Theatre*, edited by Domenico Pietropaolo, 49–63. New York: Legas, 1995.

———. *Nuova guida a Goldoni.* Turin: Einaudi, 2000.

———. "L'Oriente sui palcoscenici veneziani del Settecento: età dell'innocenza?" Chap. in *Viaggi in Italia di don Chisciotte e Sancio e altri studi sul Settecento*, 73–92. Florence: Società Editrice Fiorentina, 2006.

———. "Il pubblico dei teatri e la questione dei generi drammatici nel *Settecento.*" *Italiana* 9 (2000): 161–72.

Findlen, Paula. "Becoming a Scientist: Gender and Knowledge in Eighteenth-Century Italy." *Science in Context* 16 (2003): 59–87.

———. "The Scientist's Body: The Nature of a Woman Philosopher in Enlightenment Italy." In *The Faces of Nature in Enlightenment Europe*, edited by Gianna Pomata and Lorraine Daston, 211–36. Berlin: Berliner Wissenschafts-Verlag, 2003.

Findlen, Paula, Wendy Wassyng Roworth, and Catherine M. Sama, eds. *Italy's Eighteenth Century: Gender and Culture in the Age of the Grand Tour.* Stanford: Stanford University Press, 2009.

Firby, Nora Kathleen. *European Travellers and Their Perceptions of Zoroastrians in the 17th and 18th Centuries.* Berlin: Dietrich Reimer, 1988.

Flauto, Vincenzo. "L'editore ai lettori." In *Opere teatrali di Giambattista Lorenzi napolitano…*, by Giambattista Lorenzi, edited by Flauto, 2:xiii-xv. Naples: Flautina, 1806–20.

Fo, Dario. *Tricks of the Trade.* Translated by Joseph Farrell. New York: Routledge, 1991.

Ford, Charles. *Così? Sexual Politics in Mozart's Operas.* Manchester: Manchester University Press, 1991.

Fort, Bernadette. "Exploring Sentiment." *Eighteenth-Century Studies* 37, no. 1 (2003): 1–89.

Foss, Theodore N. "Reflections on a Jesuit Encyclopedia: du Halde's *Description… de la Chine* (1735)." In *Actes du IIIe Colloque international de Sinologie, Chantilly, 1980*, 6: 67–77. Paris: Belles Lettres, 1983.

Foster, James R. "Sentiment from Afra Behn to Marivaux." In *The Eighteenth-Century English Novel*, edited by Harold Bloom, 43–69. Philadelphia, PA: Chelsea House, 2004.

Foster, Susan Leigh. *Reading Dancing.* Berkeley: University of California Press, 1986.

Franceschetti, Antonio. "L'Arcadia veneta." In *Dalla Controriforma alla fine della Repubblica*, edited by Girolamo Arnaldi and Manlio Pastore Stocchi. Vol. 5, pt. 1 of *Storia della Cultura Veneta*, 131–70. Vicenza: Neri Pozza, 1985.

Franko, Mark. *Dance as Text: Ideologies of the Baroque Body*. New York: Cambridge University Press, 1993.

Frazee, Charles A. *Catholics and Sultans*. Cambridge: Cambridge University Press, 1983.

Freeman, Richard. "Apostolo Zeno's Reform of the Libretto." *Journal of the American Musicological Society* 21, no. 3 (1968): 321–41.

———. "Friebert, Joseph." *Grove Music Online*, edited by L. Macy. http://www.grovemusic.com.

———. "Opera Without Drama: Currents of Change in Italian Opera, 1675–1725." PhD diss., Princeton University, 1967.

Fubini, Enrico. *Music and Culture in Eighteenth-Century Europe*. Translated by Wolfgang Freis, Lisa Gasbarrone, and Michael Louis Leone. Edited by Bonnie J. Blackburn. Chicago: University of Chicago Press, 1994.

Gallotta, Aldo, and Ugo Marazzi, eds. *La conoscenza dell'Asia e dell'Africa in Italia nei secoli XVIII e XIX*. Vol. 3, pt. 1. Naples: Istituto Universitario Orientale Collana "Matteo Ripa" VIII, 1989.

Gautier, Roger. "Le Thème de l'amour dans le théâtre de Jean-Jacques Rousseau." *Revue d'Histoire du Theatre* 38, no. 3 (1986): 281–92.

Gerbi, Antonello. *The Dispute of the New World; the History of a Polemic, 1750–1900*. Rev. and enl. ed. Translated by Jeremy Moyle. Pittsburgh: University of Pittsburgh Press, 1973.

Geyer-Kiefl, Helen. "L'italiana in Pechino. (*L'inimico delle donne*, 1771)." Introduction to *L'Inimico delle donne*, by Giovanni Bertati and Baldassare Galuppi, edited by Geyer-Kiefl, 1:ix–xxxii. Milan: Ricordi, 1986.

Ghirelli, Antonio. *Storia di Napoli*. Turin: Einaudi, 1992.

Giuli, Paola. "Noblewomen and the Crisis of Traditional Marriage." Chap. in "Enlightenment, Arcadia, and Corilla: The Inscription of Eighteenth-Century Italian Women Writers in Literary History," 50–54. PhD diss., Rutgers University, 1994.

Giuntini, Francesco. *I drammi per musica di Antonio Salvi*. Reggio Emilia: Società Editrice Il Mulino, 1994.

Glixon, Beth L., and Jonathan E. Glixon. *Inventing the Business of Opera*. Oxford: Oxford University Press, 2006.

Goehring, Edmund J. "The Sentimental Muse of Opera Buffa." In Hunter and Webster, *Opera Buffa in Mozart's Vienna*, 115–45.

Goodman, Dena. *Criticism in Action: Enlightenment Experiments in Political Writing*. Ithaca: Cornell University Press, 1989.

———. "Women and the Enlightenment." In *Becoming Visible: Women in European History*, 3rd ed., edited by Renate Bridenthal, Susan Mosher Stuard, and Merry E. Wiesner, 246–59. Boston: Houghton Mifflin, 1998.

Gottlieb, Beatrice. "The Meaning of Clandestine Marriage." In *Family and Sexuality in French History*, edited by Roberto Wheaton and Tamara K. Hareven, 49–83. Philadelphia: University of Pennsylvania Press, 1980.

Greco, Franco Carmelo, ed. *Pulcinella, maschera del mondo*. Naples: Electa, 1990.

———. *Quante storie per Pulcinella/Combien d'histoires pour Polichinelle*. Naples: Edizioni scientifiche italiane, 1988.

———. *Teatro napoletano del '700*. Naples: Libreria Tullio Pironti, 1981.

———. *La tradizione e il comico a Napoli dal XVIII secolo ad oggi*. Naples: Guida, 1982.

Greenblatt, Stephen. "Learning to Curse: Aspects of Linguistic Colonialism in the Sixteenth Century." Chap. in *Learning to Curse*, 26–32. New York: Routledge, 1990.

Groos, Arthur, and Roger Parker. "Introduction." In Groos and Parker, *Reading Opera*, 1–11.

———, eds. *Reading Opera*. Princeton: Princeton University Press, 1988.

Grossato, Lucio. *Andrea Urbani, 1711–1798, scenografo e frescante*. Padua: Antoniana, 1972.

Grout, Donald J. *A Short History of Opera*. New York: Columbia University Press, 1988.

Grove, George, and Stanley Sadie, eds. *The New Grove Dictionary of Music and Musicians*. 20 vols. Reprinted with corrections. Washington, D.C.: Macmillan, 1995.

Guerci, Luciano. *La discussione sulla donna nell'Italia del Settecento. Aspetti e problemi*. Turin: Tirrenia Stampatori, 1987.

———. *La sposa obbediente. Sposa e matrimonio nella discussione dell'Italia del Settecento*. Turin: Tirrenia Stampatori, 1988.

———. "Tra scogli e fiori: una guida alla felicità coniugale per le donne del Settecento." Chap. in *Studi di storia della civiltà letteraria francese*, 549–87. Paris: Editions Honoré Champion, 1996.

Guest, Ivor. *The Dancer's Heritage. A Short History of Ballet*. London: The Dancing Times, 1977.

Günsberg, Maggie. *Playing with Gender: The Comedies of Goldoni*. Leeds: Northern Universities Press, 2001.

Guy, Basil. *The French Image of China before and after Voltaire*. Geneva: Institut et musée Voltaire, 1963.

Hacke, Daniela. "Non lo volevo per marito in modo alcuno." In Schutte, Kuehn, and Seidel, *Time, Space*, 203–21.

———. *Women, Sex and Marriage in Early Modern Venice*. Aldershot: Ashgate, 2004.

Hanlon, Gregory. *Early Modern Italy, 1550–1800*. New York: St. Martin's Press, 2000.

Hansell, Kathleen Kusmick. "Theatrical Ballet and Italian Opera." In Bianconi and Pestelli, *Opera on Stage*, 177–308.

Hayes, Jeremy. "Gluck, Christoph Willibald Ritter von (2. 1746–61)." *Grove Music Online*, edited by L. Macy. http://www.grovemusic.com.

———. "Le cinesi." *Grove Music Online*, edited by L. Macy. http://www.grovemusic.com.

Hayes, Julie C. "A Theater of Situations: Representation of the Self in the Bourgeois Drama of La Chaussée and Diderot." In *The Many Forms of Drama*, edited by Karelisa V. Hartigan, 69–77. Lanham, MD: University Presses of America, 1985.

Hays, Michael. "Representing Empire: Class, Culture and the Popular Theatre in the Nineteenth Century." In *Imperialism and Theatre*, edited by J. Ellen Gainor, 132–147. London: Routledge, 1995.

Hazard, Paul. *The European Mind, 1680–1715*. Cleveland: World Pub. Co., 1963.

Hearder, Harry. *Italy: A Short History*. New York: Cambridge University Press, 2001.

Heartz, Daniel. "The Creation of the Buffo Finale in Italian Opera." *Proceedings of the Royal Musical Association* 104 (1977–78): 67–78.

———. "Goldoni, *Don Giovanni*, and the Dramma Giocoso." Chap. in *Mozart's Operas*, 195–205. Berkeley: University of California Press, 1990.

———. "Metastasian Serious Opera." In Sadie, *History of Opera*, 71–77.

———. "Poet as Stage Director: Metastasio, Goldoni, and Da Ponte." In *Mozart's Operas*, 88–105. Berkeley: University of California Press, 1990.

———. "Vis comica: Goldoni, Galuppi, and L'Arcadia in Brenta (Venice, 1749)." In *Venezia e il melodramma nel Settecento*, edited by Maria Teresa Muraro, 33–73. Florence: Olschki, 1978.

Hecker, Kristine. "Le donne in Goldoni ovvero: trappole da evitare. Considerazioni sul personaggio femminile nelle commedie goldoniane. Appunti per una ricerca." In Alberti and Pizzamiglio, *Carlo Goldoni, 1793–1993*, 341–56.

Helbo, André. *Theory of Performing Arts*. Amsterdam: John Benjamins, 1987.

Heller, Wendy. *Emblems of Eloquence*. Berkeley: University of California Press, 2003.

———. "Venezia in Egitto: Egyptomania and Exoticism in Seventeenth-Century Venetian Opera." In Cotticelli and Maione, *Le arti della scena*, 141–55.

Hernardi, Paul, and Adriana Popescu. "Dramatic Theory." In *The Cambridge Guide to Theatre*, edited by Martin Banham, 302–7. Cambridge: Cambridge University Press, 1995.

Hill, Bridget. *Eighteenth-Century Women: An Anthology*. London: George Allen and Unwin, 1984.

Honour, Hugh. *Chinoiserie. The Vision of Cathay*. New York: E. P. Dutton, 1961.

Hsia, Adrian. *Chinesia: The European Construction of China in the Literature of the 17th and 18th Centuries*. Tübingen: Niemeyer, 1998.

———. "'The Orphan of the House Zhao' in French, English, German, and Hong Kong Literature." In *The Vision of China in the English Literature of the Seventeenth and Eighteenth Centuries*, edited by Adrian Hsia, 383–99. Hong Kong: Chinese University Press, 1998.

———. "The Transformation of Chinesia from Jesuitical Fiction to Jesuit College Drama: A Preliminary Survey." Chap. in Hsia, *Chinesia*, 55–74.

———. "The Transplanted Chinese Orphan in England, France, Germany, Italy, and His Ripatriation to Hong Kong." Chap in Hsia, *Chinesia*, 75–98.

———, ed. *The Vision of China in the English Literature of the Seventeenth and Eighteenth Centuries*. Hong Kong: Chinese University Press, 1998.

Hucker, Charles O. *China's Imperial Past*. Stanford: Stanford University Press, 1975.

Hunter, Mary K. "The *Alla Turca* style in the Late Eighteenth Century: Race and Gender in the Symphony and the Seraglio." In Bellman, *The Exotic*, 43–73.

———. "Bourgeois values and opera buffa in 1780s Vienna." In Hunter and Webster, *Opera Buffa in Mozart's Vienna*, 165–96.

———. "Buona figliuola." *Grove Music Online*, edited by L. Macy. http://www.grovemusic.com/.

———. *The Culture of Opera Buffa in Mozart's Vienna*. Princeton: Princeton University Press, 1999.

———. "Pamela: The Offspring of Richardson's Heroine in Eighteenth-Century Opera." *Mosaic* 18 (1985): 61–76.

———. "Some Representations of Opera Seria in Opera Buffa." *Cambridge Opera Journal* 3, no. 2 (1991): 89–108.

Hunter, Mary K., and James Webster, eds. *Opera Buffa in Mozart's Vienna*. Cambridge: Cambridge University Press, 1997.

Hutcheon, Linda. "Interdisciplinary Opera Studies." *PMLA* 121, no. 3 (2006): 802–10.

Iannettone, Giovanni. *Presenze italiane lungo le vie dell'Oriente nei secoli XVIII e XIX nella documentazione diplomatico-consolare italiana*. Naples: Edizioni scientifiche italiane, 1984.

Imbruglia, Girolamo, ed. *Naples in the Eighteenth Century*. Cambridge: Cambridge University Press, 2000.

Impey, Oliver. *Chinoiserie: The Impact of Oriental Styles on Western Art and Decoration*. New York: Charles Scribner's Sons, 1977.

Jacobson, Dawn. *Chinoiserie*. London: Phaidon Press, 1993.

Jarry, Madeleine. *Chinoiserie: Chinese Influence on European Decorative Art, 17th and 18th Centuries*. Translated by Gail Mangold-Vine. New York: Vendome, 1981.

Jonard, Norbert. "L'image de la femme dans les comedies de Goldoni." *Problemi di critica goldoniana* (1996): 179–98.

Jordanova, Ludmilla. *Sexual Visions: Images of Gender in Science and Medicine between the Eighteenth and Twentieth Centuries*. Madison: University of Wisconsin Press, 1989.

Kabbani, Rana. *Imperial Fictions: Europe's Myths of Orient*. London: HarperCollins, 1994.

Kamen, Henry. *Rise of Toleration*. New York: McGraw Hill, 1967.

Kerman, Joseph. *Opera as Drama*. Rev. ed. Berkeley: University California Press, 1988.

Kertzer, David I., and Marzio Barbagli. *Family Life in Early Modern Times, 1500–1789*. New Haven: Yale University Press, 2001.

Kirstein, Lincoln. *Movement and Metaphor: Four Centuries of Ballet*. New York: Praeger, 1970.

Kivy, Peter. *Osmin's Rage: Philosophical Reflections on Opera, Drama and Text*. Princeton: Princeton University Press, 1988.

Kontje, Todd. *German Orientalisms*. Ann Arbor: University of Michigan Press, 2004.

Kovach, Claudia Marie. "Reconsidering the 'Victor Vanquished': Panoplies of Power in Voltaire's *L'Orphelin de la Chine*." *Studies in Language and Literature* 5 (1992): 59–76.

Kwok, Hui-ting. "Imperial Encounters: Giuseppe Castiglione, An Italian Painter at the Chinese Court." Master's thesis, University of Auckland, 1998.

Lach, Donald F., and Edwin J. Van Kley. *Asia in the Making of Europe*. 3 vols. Chicago: University of Chicago Press, 1965–93.

Lanciotti, Lionello, ed. *Venezia e l'Oriente*. Florence: Olschki, 1987.

Lattanzi, Alessandro, and Paologiovanni Maione, eds. *Commedia dell'Arte e spettacolo in musica tra Sei e Settecento*. Naples: Editoriale Scientifica, 2003.

Lattarico, Jean-François. "Il soggetto esotico nei melodrammi veneziani del Seicento." In Cotticelli and Maione, *Le arti della scena*, 157–73.

Laver, James. *Drama: Its Costume and Décor*. London: Studio Ltd., 1951.

Lazarevich, Gordana. "Lorenzi, Giambattista." *Grove Music Online*, edited by L. Macy. http://www.grovemusic.com.

———. "La serva padrona." *Grove Music Online*, edited by L. Macy. http://www.grovemusic.com/.

Le Corbellier, Claire. *Eighteenth-Century Italian Porcelain*. New York: Metropolitan Museum of Art, 1985.

Lee, Heidi. "Musical *Chinoiserie*: Representation of China in Western European Music of the Eighteenth and Early Nineteenth Centuries." Master's thesis, University of Washington, 2001.

Lee, Thomas H. C., ed. *China and Europe: Images and Influences in Sixteenth to Eighteenth Centuries.* Hong Kong: Chinese University Press, 1991.

Leitch, Vincent B., ed. *The Norton Anthology of Theory and Criticism.* New York: Norton, 2001.

Lenzi, Deanna, and Jadranka Bentini, eds. *I Bibiena. Una famiglia europea.* Venice: Marsilio, 2000.

Leprohon, Pierre. "Esotismo." In *Enciclopedia dello spettacolo,* 4: 1611–23. Rome: Le Maschere, 1957.

Levin, David J. *Opera Through Other Eyes.* Stanford: Stanford University Press, 1994.

Lindenberger, Herbert. "Opera/Orientalism/Otherness." Chap. in *Opera in History,* 160–90. Stanford: Stanford University Press, 1998.

Locke, Ralph P. "Constructing the Oriental 'Other': Saint-Saëns's *Samson et Dalila.*" *Cambridge Opera Journal* 3 (1991): 261–302.

———. "Cutthroats and Casbah Dancers, Muezzins and Timeless Sands: Musical Images of the Middle East." In Bellman, *The Exotic,* 104–36.

———. "Exoticism." *Grove Music Online,* edited by L. Macy. http://www.grovemusic.com/.

———. "What Are These Women Doing in Opera?" In Blackmer and Smith, *En Travesti,* 59–98.

Lombardi, Daniela. "Fidanzamenti e matrimonio dal Concilio di Trento alle riforme settecentesche." In *Storia del matrimonio,* edited by Michela De Giorgio and Christiane Klapisch-Zuber, 215–50. Rome: Laterza, 1996.

Lowe, Lisa. *Critical Terrains.* Ithaca: Cornell University Press, 1991.

Lust, John. *Western Books on China Published up to 1850 in the Library of the School of Oriental and African Studies, University of London: A Descriptive Catalogue.* London: Bamboo Publishing, 1987.

Lynham, Deryk. *The Chevalier Noverre.* London: Chameleon Press, 1972.

Macfie, Alexander Lyon, ed. *Eastern Influences on Western Philosophy: A Reader.* Edinburgh: Edinburgh University Press, 2003.

———. *Orientalism.* London: Longman, 2002.

Macnutt, Richard. "Libretto (i)." *Grove Music Online,* edited by L. Macy. http://www.grovemusic.com.

Maggi, Luciano. "L'idolo cinese." *Nautilus* May 1997. http://nautilus.tv/9705it/musica/idolo.htm.

Maggs, Barbara Widenor. *Russia and "le rêve chinois": China in Eighteenth Century Russian Literature.* Oxford: Voltaire Foundation, 1984.

Magister, Sandro. "In China, Obedience Isn't a Virtue Anymore." *www.chiesa,* January 19, 2007. http://chiesa.espresso.repubblica.it/articolo/112861?&eng=y.

Magnoni, Guido. "La moda cinese e le 'cineserie' in Europa nei secoli XVII e XVIII." *Arte tra Cina e Europa.* http://www.italiacina.org/cultura/arte/arte_cineu1.htm.

Mamczarz, Irène. *Les intermèdes comiques italiens au XVIIIe siècle en France et en Italie.* Paris: Centre national de la recherche scientifique, 1972.

Marino, John A., ed. *Early Modern Italy, 1550–1796.* Oxford: Oxford University Press, 2002.

Marrone, Romualdo, ed. *Il paese di Pulcinella.* Naples: Bellini, 1991.

Marshall, P. J., and Glyndwr Williams. *The Great Map of Mankind.* Cambridge: Harvard University Press, 1982.

Martin, Richard, and Harold Koda. *Orientalism: Visions of the East in Western Dress.* New York: Metropolitan Museum of Art, 1994.

Martini, Gabriele. "La donna veneziana del '600 tra sessualità legittima ed illegittima: Alcune riflessioni sul concubinato." *Atti dell'Istituto Veneto di Scienze, Lettere ed Arti* 145 (1986–87): 301–39.

Martino, Pierre. *L'Orient dans la littérature française au XVIIe et au XVIIIe siècle.* New York: Burt Franklin, 1971.

Martorana, Pietro. *Notizie biografiche e bibliografiche degli scrittori del dialetto napolitano.* Naples: Chiurazzi, 1894.

Mayor, A. Hyatt. *The Bibiena Family.* New York: H. Bittner, 1945.

Mayrhofer, Marina. "Ideologia ed evasione, due occasioni esotiche per Salieri: *Tarare* (Parigi 1787) e *Axur Re d'Ormus* (Vienna 1788)." In Cotticelli and Maione, *Le arti della scena,* 575–93.

Mazouer, Charles, ed. *Le Théâtre italien,* by Évariste Gherardi. Vol. 1. Paris: Société des Textes Français Modernes, 1994.

McCabe, William H. *An Introduction to the Jesuit Theater,* edited by Louis J. Oldani. St. Louis: The Institute of Jesuit Sources, 1983.

McClary, Susan. *Feminine Endings.* Minneapolis: University of Minnesota Press, 1991.

McClymonds, Marita. "Aria." *Grove Music Online,* edited by L. Macy. http://www.grovemusic.com.

———. "The Myth of 'Metastasian' Dramaturgy." Paper presented at The Inaugural Conference for the Ricasoli Collection: Patrons, Politics, Music, and Art in Italy, 1738–1859, University of Louisville, Louisville, KY, March 14–18, 1989.

———. "Opera Seria? Opera Buffa? Genre and Style as Sign." In Hunter and Webster, *Opera Buffa in Mozart's Vienna,* 197–231.

———. "Style as Sign in Some Opere Serie of Hasse and Jommelli." Paper presented at The International Musicological Symposium: Johann Adolf Hasse in Seiner Zeit, Hamburg, Germany, 1999.

McClymonds, Marita, with Daniel Heartz. "Opera seria." *Grove Music Online,* edited by L. Macy. http://www.grovemusic.com.

Melis, Giorgio, ed. *Atti del convegno internazionale su Martino Martini.* Trent: Museo Tridentino di Scienze Naturali, 1983.

———. Introduction to *Ad Lectorem Praefatio,* edited by Giorgio Melis, translated by Pietro Nicolao, 9–21. Trent: Museo Tridentino di Scienze Naturali, 1983.

Messbarger, Rebecca. *The Century of Women.* Toronto: University of Toronto Press, 2002.

Minamiki, George. *The Chinese Rites Controversy: From its Beginning to Modern Times.* Chicago: Loyola University Press, 1985.

Monaco, Vanda. *Giambattista Lorenzi e la commedia per musica.* Naples: Berisio, 1968.

Monson, Dale E. "L'inimico delle donne." *Grove Music Online,* edited by L. Macy. http://www.grovemusic.com.

Moore, John E. "Prints, Salami and Cheese: Savoring the Roman Festival of the Chinea." *Art Bulletin* 77 (1995): 584–906.

Mozillo, Atanasio. *La frontiera del Grand Tour: viaggi e viaggiatori nel Mezzogiorno borbonico.* Naples: Liguori, 1992.

Mungello, David E. *Curious Land: Jesuit Accommodation and the Origins of Sinology.* Stuttgart: Franz Steiner Verlag Wiesbaden, 1985.

———. *The Great Encounter of China and the West, 1500–1800.* Lanham, MD: Rowman & Littlefield, 1999.

Muraro, Maria Teresa, ed. *Venezia e il melodramma nel Settecento.* Florence: Olschki, 1978.

————. *Scenografie di Pietro Gonzaga, Catalogo della Mostra.* Vicenza: Neri Pozza, 1967.

Muraro, Maria Teresa, and Giovanni Morelli, eds. *Opera e libretto II.* Florence: Olschki, 1993.

Muraro, Maria Teresa, and Elena Povoledo, eds. *Disegni teatrali dei Bibiena.* Venice: Fondazione Cini, 1970.

Neville, Don. "Metastasio, Pietro." *Grove Music Online,* edited by L. Macy. http://www.grovemusic.com.

Nicoll, Allardyce. *A History of Early Eighteenth Century Drama, 1700–1750.* Cambridge: Cambridge University Press, 1929.

————. *A History of Late Eighteenth Century Drama, 1750–1800.* Cambridge: Cambridge University Press, 1929.

————. *World of Harlequin.* Cambridge: Cambridge University Press, 1963.

Nunn, Joan. *Fashion in Costume, 1200–2000.* 2nd ed. Chicago: New Amsterdam Books, 2000.

Nussbaum, Felicity, ed. *The Global Eighteenth Century.* Baltimore: Johns Hopkins University Press, 2003.

Nussbaum, Felicity, and Laura Brown, eds. *The New Eighteenth Century.* New York: Methuen, 1987.

Offen, Karen. *European Feminisms, 1700–1950.* Stanford: Stanford University Press, 2000.

Ortolani, Giuseppe. "Appunti sui melodrammi giocosi." In *Il teatro di Goldoni,* edited by Marzia Pieri, 319–28. Bologna: Il Mulino, 1993.

————. Notes to *Il medico olandese.* In Ortolani, *Tutte le opere,* 6:1244–47.

————. Notes to *La sposa persiana.* In Ortolani, *Tutte le opere,* 9:1332–38.

————, ed. *Tutte le opere,* by Carlo Goldoni. 14 vols. Milan: Mondadori, 1935–55.

Padoan, Giorgio. "L'impegno civile di Carlo Goldoni." In *Il Punto su Goldoni,* edited by Giuseppe Petronio, 146–52. 2nd ed. Rome: Laterza, 1992.

"Pagoda." *WordReference.com.* http://wordreference.com.

Pallerotti, A. *Spettacoli melodrammatici e coreografici rappresentati in Padova nei teatri Obizi, Nuovo e del Prato della Valle dal 1751 al 1892.* Padua: Proserpini, 1892.

Parker, Roger, ed. *The Oxford Illustrated History of Opera.* Oxford: Oxford University Press, 1994.

Pavis, Patrice. *Analyzing Performance.* Translated by David Williams. Ann Arbor: University of Michigan Press, 2003.

Peluso, Bernardo. *Documenti diplomatici inediti intorno alle relazioni fra la Sede Apostolica e il Regno di Napoli dal 1734 al 1818.* Naples: Officina Cronotipografica Aldina, 1917.

Petrocchi, Massimo. "Il mito della Cina in Scipione Maffei." Chap. in *Miti e suggestioni nella storia europea,* 17–28. Florence: Sansoni, 1950.

Piemontese, Angelo Michele. "Persia e persiani nel dramma per musica veneziano." In Muraro and Morelli, *Opera e libretto II,* 1–34.

Pieri, Marzia. Introduction to *La sposa persiana. Ircana in Julfa. Ircana in Ispaan,* by Carlo Goldoni, 9–85. Venice: Marsilio, 1996.

————, ed. *La sposa persiana. Ircana in Julfa. Ircana in Ispaan,* by Carlo Goldoni. Venice: Marsilio, 1996.

Pietropaolo, Domenico, ed. *Goldoni and the Musical Theatre.* New York: Legas, 1995.

Pinot, Vergile. *La Chine et la formation de l'esprit philosophique en France, 1640–1740.* Geneva: Slatkine, 1971.

Piperno, Franco. "Opera Production to 1780." In Bianconi and Pestelli, *Opera Production and Its Resources,* 1–79.

Pirotta, Nino. "Commedia dell'Arte and Opera." *Musical Quarterly* 41 (1955): 305–24.

Pirovano, Carlo, ed. *Venezia e i Turchi.* Milan: Electa, 1985.

Piva, Franco, and Jean Sgard, eds. *La Sensibilité dans la littérature française au XVIIIe siècle.* Fasano, Italy: Schena, 1998.

Poliakov, Léon. *The Aryan Myth.* Translated by Edmund Howard. Edinburgh: Sussex University Press, 1974.

Pontiggia, Giuseppe. "Immagine della Cina." In *Relazione della China,* by Lorenzo Magalotti, edited by Teresa Poggi Salani, 107–27. Milan: Adelphi, 1974.

Porter, David. *Ideographia: The Chinese Cipher in Early Modern Europe.* Stanford: Stanford University Press, 2001.

Postiglia, Alberto, ed. *Un decennio di storiografia italiana sul secolo XVIII.* Naples: Officina Tipografica, 1995.

Pratt, Mary Louise. *Imperial Eyes: Travel Writing and Transculturation.* London: Routledge, 1992.

Praz, Mario. *The Romantic Agony.* Translated by Angus Davidson. London: Oxford University Press, 1970.

Preto, Paolo. "L'Illuminismo veneto." In *Dalla Controriforma alla fine della Repubblica,* edited by Girolamo Arnaldi and Manlio Pastore Stocchi. Vol. 5, pt. 1 of *Storia della Cultura Veneta,* 1–45. Vicenza: Neri Pozza, 1985.

————. *Venezia e i turchi.* Florence: Sansoni, 1975.

Pruiksma, Rose A. "Music, Sex, and Ethnicity: Signification in Lully's Theatrical Chaconnes." In *Gender, Sexuality and Early Music,* edited by Todd M. Borgerding, 227–48. New York: Routledge, 2002.

Pucci, Suzanne. *Sites of the Spectator.* Oxford: Voltaire Foundation, 2001.

Quondam, Amedeo. "La crisi dell'Arcadia." *Palatino: Rivista Romana di Cultura* 12 (1968): 160–70.

————. *Cultura e ideologia di Gian Vincenzo Gravina.* Milan: Mursia, 1968.

————. "L'istituzione Arcadica. Sociologia e ideologia di un'accademia." *Quaderni storici* 23 (1973): 389–438.

Rabin, Ronald J. "Figaro as Misogynist: On Aria Types and Aria Rhetoric." In Hunter and Webster, *Opera Buffa in Mozart's Vienna,* 232–60.

————. "Mozart, Da Ponte, and the Dramaturgy of Opera Buffa: Italian Comic Opera in Vienna, 1783–1791." PhD diss., Cornell University, 1996.

Rao, Anna Maria. *Il Regno di Napoli nel Settecento.* Naples: Guida, 1983.

Reichwein, Adolph. *China and Europe.* New York: Barnes and Noble, 1968.

Renda, Francesco. *Bernardo Tanucci e i beni gesuiti.* Catania: Università di Catania, Facoltà di Lettere e Filosofia, 1970.

Rey, Marie-Catherine. *Les Très Riches Heures de la Cour de Chine: Chefs-d'oeuvre de la Peinture Impériale des Qing, 1662–1796: Exposition Présentée au Musée Guimet du 26 avril au 24 juillet 2006.* Paris: Musée Guimet, 2006.

Reynolds, Margaret. "Ruggiero's Deceptions, Cherubino's Distractions." In Blackmer and Smith, *En Travesti,* 132–51.

Ricaldone, Luisa, and Adriana Chemello, eds. *Geografie e genealogie letterarie. Erudite, biografe, croniste, narratrici, "épisolières," utopiste tra Settecento e Ottocento.* Padua: Il Poligrafo, 2000.

Ricci, Corrado. *I Bibiena.* Milan: Alfieri & Lacroix, 1915.

Ricuperati, Giuseppe. "La cultura italiana nel secondo Settecento europeo." In *Letteratura italiana e cultura europea tra Illuminismo e Romanticismo. Atti del Convegno Internazionale di Studi Padova-Venezia, 11–13 maggio 2000,* edited by Guido Santato, 33–64. Geneva: Droz, 2003.

———. "Illuminismo e Settecento dal dopoguerra ad oggi." In *La reinvenzione dei lumi,* edited by Giuseppe Ricuperati, 201–22. Florence: Olschki, 2000.

———. "Un lungo viaggio: il concetto di Illuminismo negli anni Ottanta." In *Un decennio di storiografia italiana sul secolo XVIII,* edited by Alberto Postiglia, 387–421. Naples: Officina Tipografica, 1995.

———, ed. *La reinvenzione dei lumi.* Florence: Olschki, 2000.

Robinson, Michael F. "Paisiello, Giovanni." *Grove Music Online,* edited by L. Macy. http://www.grovemusic.com/.

———. *Naples and Neapolitan Opera.* Oxford: Oxford University Press, 1972.

———. "Opera Buffa." In Sadie, *History of Opera,* 81–85.

Robinson, Paul. "A Deconstructive Postscript: Reading Libretti and Misreading Opera." In Groos and Parker, *Reading Opera,* 328–46.

———. "Is Aida an Orientalist Opera?" Chap. 6 in *Opera, Sex, and other Vital Matters,* 123–33. Chicago: University of Chicago Press, 2002.

Romagnoli, Sergio, ed. *Il Caffè ossia brevi e vari discorsi distribuiti in fogli periodici (dal giugno 1764 a tutto il maggio 1765).* Milan: Feltrinelli, 1960.

———. "Goldoni e gli illuministi." In Alberti and Pizzamiglio, *Carlo Goldoni, 1793–1993,* 55–78.

Ronan, Charles E., and Bonnie B. C. Oh, eds. *East Meets West: the Jesuits in China, 1582–1773.* Chicago: Loyola University Press, 1988.

Rosand, Ellen. *Opera in Seventeenth-Century Venice.* Berkeley: University of California Press, 1991.

Rousseau, G. S., and Roy Porter, eds. *Exoticism in the Enlightenment.* Manchester: Manchester University Press, 1990.

Rowbotham, Arnold H. *Missionary and Mandarin: The Jesuits at the Court of China.* New York: Russell & Russell, 1966.

Rule, Paul A. *K'ung-tzu or Confucius? The Jesuit Interpretation of Confucianism.* Sydney: Allen and Unwin, 1986.

Sadie, Stanley, ed. *History of Opera.* New York: Norton, 1990.

———, ed. *The New Grove Dictionary of Opera.* 4 vols. New York: Grove's Dictionaries of Music, 1992.

Said, Edward W. "The Empire at Work: Verdi's *Aida.*" Chap. 2 in *Culture and Imperialism,* 111–32. New York: Vintage Books, 1994.

"Said, Edward W." In *The Norton Anthology of Theory and Criticism,* edited by Vincent B. Leitch, 1986–2011. New York: Norton, 2001.

———. *Orientalism.* New York: Random House, 1978.

Sala di Felice, Elena. "Delizie e saggezza dell'antica Cina secondo Metastasio." *Accademia Clementina. Atti e memorie* 30–31 (1992): 207–21.

———. "Delizie e saggezza dell'antica Cina secondo Metastasio." In Muraro and Morelli, *Opera and Libretto II,* 85–106.

———. "Esotismo americano: seduzioni edonistiche e implicazioni etico-politiche." In Cotticelli and Maione, *Le arti della scena,* 507–30.

———. "Esotismo goldoniano." *Rivista di letteratura italiana* 25, no. 1 (2007): 115–42.

———. *Metastasio: ideologia, drammaturgia, spettacolo.* Milan: F. Angeli, 1983.

———. "Osservazioni sulla meccanica drammaturgica di Metastasio." In *Il melodramma di Pietro Metastasio,* edited by Elena Sala di Felice and Rossana M. Caira Lumetti, 127–59. Rome: Aracne, 2001.

———. "Segreti, menzogne e coatti silenzi nella Clemenza di Tito del Metastasio." In Columbro and Maione, *Pietro Metastasio,* 187–201.

Sala di Felice, Elena, and Rossana M. Caira Lumetti, eds. *Il melodramma di Pietro Metastasio.* Rome: Aracne, 2001.

Salani, Teresa Poggi. Introduction to *Relazione della Cina,* by Lorenzo Magalotti, edited by Teresa Poggi Salani, 9–32. Milan: Adelphi, 1974.

Santaolalla, Isabel, ed. *"New" Exoticisms.* Amsterdam: Rodopi, 2000.

Santato, Guido. "Introduzione" to *Letteratura italiana e cultura europea tra Illuminismo e Romanticismo. Atti del Convegno Internazionale di Studi Padova-Venezia, 11–13 maggio 2000,* edited by Guido Santato, 9–29. Geneva: Droz, 2003.

———, ed. *Letteratura italiana e cultura europea tra Illuminismo e Romanticismo. Atti del Convegno Internazionale di Studi Padova-Venezia, 11–13 maggio 2000.* Geneva: Droz, 2003.

Sartori, Claudio, ed. *I libretti italiani a stampa dalle origini al 1800: catalogo analitico con 16 indici.* 5 vols. Cuneo: Bertola & Locatelli, 1990.

Savarese, Nicola. *Teatro e spettacolo fra Oriente e Occidente.* Rome-Bari: Laterza, 1992.

Scherillo, Michele. *L'opera buffa napoletana.* Bologna: Arnaldo Forni, 1975.

Schlig, Michael. "Spain as Orient in Juan Pablo Forner's *Los Gramáticos:* Historia chinesca." *Dieciocho: Hispanic Enlightenment* 23, no. 2 (2000): 313–25.

Schutte, Anne Jacobson, Thomas Kuehn, and Silvana Seidel, eds. *Time, Space, and Women's Lives in Early Modern Europe.* Kirksville: Truman State University Press, 2001.

Schwartz, Judith L., and Christena L. Schlundt, *French Court Dance and Dance Music. A Guide to Primary Source Writings, 1643–1789.* Stuyvesant, NY: Pendragon Press, 1987.

Scognamiglio, Giuseppina. *Ritratti di donna nel teatro di Carlo Goldoni.* Naples: Edizioni Scientifiche Italiane, 2002.

Scott, Katie. *The Rococo Interior: Decoration and Social Spaces in Early Eighteenth-Century Paris.* New Haven: Yale University Press, 1995.

Scuderi, Antonio. *Dario Fo and Popular Performance.* Ottawa: Legas, 1998.

———. *Dario Fo: Stage, Text and Tradition.* Carbondale: Southern Illinois University Press, 2000.

———. "Grammelot: Dario Fo and the Art of Pretending to Speak." Paper presented at the 73rd Annual Meeting of American Association of Teachers of Italian, Nashville, TN, November 21–23, 1997.

Segalen, Victor. *Essay on Exoticism: An Aesthetics of Diversity.* Edited and translated by Yaël Rachel Schlick. Durham: Duke University Press, 2002.

Seidel, Michael. *Robinson Crusoe: Island Myths and the Novel.* Boston: Twayne, 1991.

Settembrini, Luigi. *Lezioni di letteratura italiana.* Florence: Sansoni, 1964.

Smart, Mary Ann, ed. *Siren Songs.* Princeton: Princeton University Press, 2000.

Smith, Patrick J. *The Tenth Muse: A Historical Study of the Opera Libretto.* New York: Knopf, 1970.

Solie, Ruth, ed. *Musicology and Difference.* Berkeley: University of California Press, 1993.

Sonneck, Oscar. *Catalogue of Opera Librettos Printed before 1800.* New York: Johnson, 1968.

Soykut, Mustafa. *Image of the Turk in Italy.* Berlin: Klaus Schwarz, 2001.

Spacks, Patricia Meyers. "Ambiguous Practices." In *Eighteenth-Century Genre and Culture: Serious Reflections on Occasional Forms: Essays in Honor of J. Paul Hunter,* edited by Dennis Todd and Cynthia Wall, 150–63. Newark: University of Delaware Press, 2001.

Spence, Jonathan D. *The Chan's Great Continent: China in Western Minds.* New York: Norton, 1998.

Spence, Jonathan D., and John E. Wills Jr., eds. *From Ming to Ch'ing: Conquest, Region, and Continuity in Seventeenth-Century China.* New Haven: Yale University Press, 1979.

Stafutti, Stefania. "La conoscenza della Cina nella Venezia del Settecento: un'indagine attraverso i cataloghi dei 'librai' veneziani dell'epoca." In Gallotta and Marazzi, *La Conoscenza dell'Asia,* 473–520.

St. Clair, Alexandrine N. *The Image of the Turk in Europe.* New York: Metropolitan Museum of Art, 1973.

Steele, Valerie, and John S. Major. *China Chic: East Meets West.* New Haven: Yale University Press, 1999.

Sternfeld, Frederick W. "Lieto fine." *Grove Music Online,* edited by L. Macy. http://www.grovemusic.com.

Stewart, Pamela D. "Le femmes savantes e la poetica della 'naturalezza.'" Chap. in *Goldoni fra letteratura e teatro,* 161–94. Florence: Olschki, 1989.

Stocchi, Manlio Pastore. Introduction to *La trilogia di Ircana* by Carlo Goldoni, edited by Stocchi, vii–xxxiv. Vicenza: Neri Pozza, 1993.

Stone, Lawrence. *Uncertain Unions.* Oxford: Oxford University Press, 1992.

Strohm, Reinhard. *Dramma per Musica: Italian Opera Seria of the Eighteenth Century.* New Haven: Yale University Press, 1997.

———. "Towards an Understanding of the opera seria." Chap. in *Essays on Handel and the Italian Opera,* 93–105. Cambridge: Cambridge University Press, 1985.

Strohm, Reinhard, ed. *The Eighteenth-Century Diaspora of Italian Music and Musicians.* Turnhout: Brepols, 2001.

Sun, William H. "The Orphan of Chao and China: A Comparative Study of Three Revenge Plays by Ji Junxiang, Voltaire and Shakespeare." *Text and Presentation: The Journal of the Comparative Drama Conference* 11 (1991): 107–11.

Tchen, John Kuo Wei. *New York Before Chinatown: Orientalism and the Shaping of American Culture, 1776–1882.* Baltimore: Johns Hopkins University Press, 1999.

Tessarotto, Lorella. "Promesse e inganni: seduzione e matrimonio dopo il Concilio di Trento." In *Madri pervasive e figli dominanti,* edited by Luisa Accati, 33–103. Florence: European Press Academic Publishing, 2003.

Todorov, Tzvetan. *On Human Diversity: Nationalism, Racism, and Exoticism in French Thought.* Translated by Catherine Porter. Cambridge: Harvard University Press, 1993.

Toscani, Claudio. "'Alla turca': varianti italiane di un idioma musicale europeo." In Cotticelli and Maione, *Le arti della scena,* 311–28.

Tozzi, Lorenzo. *Il balletto pantomimo del Settecento, Gaspare Angiolini.* L'Aquila: L. U. Japadre, 1972.

Traer, James F. *Marriage and the Family in Eighteenth-Century France.* Ithaca: Cornell University Press, 1980.

Trowell, Brian. "Libretto (ii)." *Grove Music Online,* edited by L. Macy. http://www.grovemusic.com.

Troy, Charles. *The Comic Intermezzo.* Ann Arbor: UMI Research Press, 1979.

———. "The Intermezzo." In Sadie, *History of Opera,* 78–81.

Trubner, Henry, ed. *Catalog: China's influence on American culture in the 18th and 19th centuries: A special Bicentennial exhibition drawn from private and museum collections, China Institute in America/China House Gallery . . . April 8 through June 13, 1976.* Seattle: Seattle Art Museum, 1976.

Tung, William L. *China and the Foreign Powers: the Impact of and Reaction to Unequal Treaties.* Dobbs Ferry, NY: Oceana Publications, 1970.

Ubersfeld, Anne. *Lire le théâtre.* Paris: Editions Sociales, 1982.

Utter, Robert Palfrey, and Gwendolyn Bridges Needham. *Pamela's Daughters.* New York: Macmillan, 1937.

Valensi, Lucette. *The Birth of the Despot: Venice and the Sublime Porte.* Translated by Arthur Denner. Ithaca: Cornell University Press, 1993.

Van Kley, Edwin J. "Europe's 'Discovery' of China and the Writing of World History." *American Historical Review* 76 (1971): 358–85.

Vaughan, Dorothy M. *Europe and the Turk.* Liverpool: Liverpool University Press, 1954.

Venturi, Franco. *Italy and the Enlightenment.* Edited by Stuart Woolf. Translated by Susan Corsi. London: Longman, 1972.

———. "Oriental despotism." In Venturi, *Italy and the Enlightenment,* 41–51.

———. *Settecento Riformatore.* Turin: Einaudi, 1969–90.

———. *Utopia e riforma dell'Illuminismo.* Turin: Einaudi, 1970.

Vila, Anne. *Enlightenment and Pathology: Sensibility in the Literature and Medicine of Eighteenth-Century France.* Baltimore: Johns Hopkins University Press, 1998.

Von Grunebaum, G. E., ed. *English and Continental Views of the Ottoman Empire, 1500–1800.* Los Angeles: Williams Andrew Clark Memorial Library, 1972.

Von Pastor, Ludwig. *The History of the Popes.* 40 vols. London: Routledge & Kegan Paul, 1936–53.

Wakeman, Frederic, Jr. "The Shun Interregnum of 1644." In Spence and Wills, *From Ming to Ch'ing,* 39–87.

Ward, Adrienne. "China in 17th and 18th Century Italy: Travel Literature, Scholarly/Reformist Writings, Theater." PhD diss., University of Wisconsin–Madison, 1998.

———. "'Imaginary Imperialism': Goldoni Stages China in 18th-Century Italy." *Theatre Journal* 54 (2002): 203–21.

———. "'New Worlds' and Theatre: Goldoni's Exotic Comedies." *Annali d'Italianistica* 11 (1993): 213–24.

Watson, Walter."Montesquieu and Voltaire on China." *Comparative Civilizations Review* 2 (1979): 38–51.

Weiss, Piero. "Goldoni, Carlo." *Grove Music Online*, edited by L. Macy. http://www.grovemusic.com.

———. "Opera buffa." *Grove Music Online*, edited by L. Macy. http://www.grovemusic.com.

Whaples, Miriam K. "Early Exoticism Revisited." In Bellman, *The Exotic*, 3–25.

———. "Exoticism in Dramatic Music, 1600–1800." PhD diss., Indiana University, 1958.

Wheelock, Gretchen, Wye Jamison Allanbrook, and Mary Hunter. "Staging Mozart's Women." In Smart, *Siren Songs*, 50–57.

Wills, John E. *Embassies and Dutch and Portuguese Envoys to K'anghsi, 1666–1687.* Cambridge: Council on East Asian Studies Harvard University, 1984.

Wolf, Eric R. "Trade and Conquest in the Orient." In *Europe and the People without History*, edited by Eric R. Wolf, 232–61. Berkeley: University of California Press, 1983.

Woloch, Isser. *Eighteenth-Century Europe: Tradition and Progress, 1715–1789.* New York: Norton, 1982.

Woolf, Stuart. "La storia politica e sociale." Translated by A. Serafini and E. Negri. In *Storia d'Italia*, 3:3–508. Turin: Einaudi, 1973.

Yonan, Michael E. "Veneers of Authority: Chinese Lacquers in Maria Theresa's Vienna." *Eighteenth-Century Studies* 37, no. 4 (2004): 653–72.

Zoli, Sergio. *La Cina e la cultura italiana del Cinquecento al Settecento.* Bologna: Pàtron, 1973.

———. *La Cina e l'età dell'Illuminismo in Italia.* Bologna: Pàtron, 1974.

———. "La Cina nella cultura italiana del 700." In *La conoscenza dell'Asia e dell'Africa in Italia nei secoli XVIII e XIX*, edited by Ugo Marazzi. Vol. 1, pt. 1, 211–57. Naples: Istituto universitario orientale, 1984.

———. *Europa libertina tra Controriforma e Illuminismo: l'Oriente dei libertini e le origini dell'Illuminismo: studi e ricerche.* Bologna: Cappelli, 1989.

———. "L'immagine dell'Oriente nella cultura italiana da Marco Polo al Settecento." In *Il Paesaggio*, edited by Cesare de Seta. Vol. 5 of *Storia d'Italia*, 4–123. Turin: Einaudi, 1982.

———. "Il mito settecentesco della Cina in Europa e la moderna storiografia." *Nuova rivista storica* 3–4 (1976): 335–66.

———. "Le Polemiche sulla Cina nella cultura storica, filosofica, letteraria italiana della prima metà del 700." *Archivio Storico Italiano* 130 (1972): 409–67.

Index